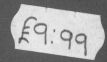

D1502411

MILLER'S

complete a-z of
collectables

Miller's Complete A–Z of Collectables
General Editor Madeleine Marsh

First published in Great Britain in 2004 by Miller's,
an imprint of Octopus Publishing Group Ltd,
2–4 Heron Quays, London E14 4JP
Miller's is a registered trademark
of Octopus Publishing Group Ltd
© 2004 Octopus Publishing Group Ltd

Senior Executive Editor Anna Sanderson
Executive Art Editor Rhonda Fisher
Senior Editor Emily Anderson
Page Design Peter Gerrish
Designer Alexa Brommer
Jacket Design Colin Goody
Indexer Sue Farr
Production Sarah Rogers
Picture Research Nick Wheldon
Photography Robin Saker, Steve Tanner

ISBN 1 84000 385 5

A CIP record for this book is available
from the British Library

Set in Frutiger and Novarese
Produced by Toppan Printing Co., (HK) Ltd.
Printed and bound in China

Front jacket (clockwise from top left):
1950s batwing-framed sunglasses; Kelly Bag
by Hermès (see p103); Clarice Cliff "Secrets"
sugar shaker, 1930s (see p37); Crosley radio,
1950s; ladies' legs corkscrew, c.1895
Back jacket (clockwise from top left): mug of
Edward VIII with modelled handle by Kent, 1936
(see p59); Guinness toucan lamp, Carltonware,
1950s (see p29); Morphy Richards toaster, 1960s;
Rolls-Royce "Spirit of Ecstasy" by Charles Sykes,
1911 (see p17); brass pull door handle, c.1890
Front flap: "Orient" vase by Crown Devon, 1920s
Half Title: "Boby" trolley by Joe Colombo, 1970
(see p148)
Full Title: felt poodle skirt, 1950s (see p79)
Contents page: Sitzendorfer figural ceramic
powder bowl, c.1920 (see p61)

The publishers would like to thank the specialists
who contributed to the following sections:

ADVERTISEMENTS & PACKAGING Mike Standen
of Ad Age Antique Advertising first appreciated
old advertising ephemera while at art college in
the 1960s. Freelance retail art director for London
advertising agencies for 30 years, Mike now enjoys
collecting "old ads" more for pleasure than profit.

AERONAUTICA AND SHIPPING Peter Boyd-Smith's
company, Cobwebs, which specializes in ocean
liner memorabilia, was established in 1975. In 2000
Cobwebs won the BACA Collectables category.
Peter is a lecturer and author and contributes
regularly to radio and television programmes.

AMUSEMENT & SLOT MACHINES Steve Hunt
publishes the only full-colour magazine covering
vintage amusement machines and runs the only
Gaming Board licensed auction house in the UK
legally able to sell slot machines.

**ARCHITECTURAL SALVAGE AND GARDEN
COLLECTABLES** Rupert van der Werff joined
Sotheby's in 1996 and worked for various
departments before joining the garden statuary
department in 1998 as an assistant cataloguer.
He is now head of this department.

**AUTOGRAPHS, CORKSCREWS, EROTICA,
NEWSPAPERS & MAGAZINES, AND TOBACCO
& SMOKING** Phil Ellis is a freelance writer
specializing in art and antiques. He has written
for several publications and spent 12 years as
assistant editor of the weekly Antiques Magazine.

AUTOMOBILIA AND BICYCLES Toby Wilson
started work at Sotheby's in 1983 and began
cataloguing automobilia soon after. In 2001 he
moved to Bonhams – world market leaders in
automobilia auctions. Toby became Head of
Department in 2003. He has been an auctioneer
since 1993 and a regular on the charity auction
circuit for many years. He has catalogued bicycles
since 1988 and is himself a keen cyclist.

BOOKS Stephen Poole, a former university
librarian, runs Biblion – a multi-dealer antiquarian
and collectable book centre in London's West End,
with a stock of around 20,000 books, from early
printed editions to hyper-modern firsts.

BOTTLES AND BREWERIANA Alan Blakeman
originally graduated as a potter from the Potteries,
Stoke-on-Trent, but is now the country's leading
dealer and collector of antique bottles and
breweriana. He is founder of the Heritage
Codswallop Bottle Museum in Barnsley, South
Yorkshire and is also director of BBR Publications,
the leading publisher, auctioneer, and show
organizer in the bottle-collecting world.

CIGARETTE CARDS Tim Davidson works for Tim
Vennett-Smith – one of the leading auctioneers
of paper-based collectables. Established in 1989, it
now runs five full public sales of cigarette cards per
annum, as well as three postal lists of individual-
type cards, and autographs, postcards, and other
ephemera. Vennett-Smith also holds bi-annual
sales of sporting memorabilia, cinema posters,
and theatre programmes.

CLOCKS Kevin Monckton has dealt in antiques
and collectbles for many years, and has owned
and managed Tickers, in Southampton since 1997.
The shop generally carries a large stock of around
300 clocks and 250 watches, and Kevin attends
most of the horological fairs in the southern UK.

COMICS & ANNUALS Malcolm Phillips founded
Comic Book Postal Auctions in 1992 from a
basement in a friend's corner shop. The quarterly
auctions now often sell out, and the website is
packed with information for comics enthusiasts.

COMMEMORATIVE WARE Andrew Hilton was
a Director of Phillips in the 1980s and established
their collectors' department, which hosted sales as
varied as Traditional River Craft and Teddy Bears,
as well as Commemoratives. On leaving in 1991
Andrew started Special Auction Services, which is
the only auction house in the world to specialize in
commemoratives, holding four auctions each year.

COMPACTS & COSMETICS Sue Wilde has worked
with film and television costume designers for the
past 20 years, providing original vintage clothing
and accessories for period productions such as
Miss Marple, Poirot, and Jeeves and Wooster.
More recently she has been researching vintage
cosmetics and accessories, and has encountered
a rich mix of innovative design and social history.

DOLLS AND TOYS & GAMES Daniel Agnew
started at Christie's in 1989 as a saleroom assistant
and joined the toy department as a junior specialist
in 1992. In 2000 he took over the running of
the teddy bear department and the following
year he became head of Christie's doll and teddy
bear department. A regular contributor to Teddy
Bear Times, Daniel has co-written Miller's Soft Toys
Collectors Guide, as well as contributing several
chapters in other books. His collection of teddy
bears and soft toys is currently on permanent
loan to the Sussex Toy and Model Museum at
Brighton railway station.

EPHEMERA Judith Grant has been well known on
the ephemera fairs circuit for over 20 years, dealing
in a very wide range of material but specializing
in items of historical and financial significance.
She is a member of the Ephemera Society.

(Continued on page 4)

MILLER'S

complete a-z of collectables

general editor **Madeleine Marsh**

(Continued from page 2)

GLASS Andy McConnell, writer, researcher, and lecturer, specializes in glassware dating from the Renaissance to the present day. He writes regularly for various magazines, has served as glass consultant to the Miller's *Price Guides* and his book, *The Decanter, An Illustrated History of Glass from 1650*, is published by the Antique Collectors' Club.

GRAMOPHONES & RECORDERS Philip Knighton, born in 1948, has been a BBC engineer, radio presenter, and music critic. For the last 23 years he has run The Gramophone Man – a business that deals with all aspects of vintage sound equipment and wireless sets. The busy workshop handles over 200 restorations a year.

LIGHTING Jennie Horrocks' love of antique lighting started approximately 20 years ago with buying and selling antique glass shades at markets and antiques fairs. Her areas of specialist interest are Arts & Crafts, Art Nouveau, and Edwardian lighting. Jennie now has a shop in Tetbury and shows at the NEC antiques fairs three times a year.

MEDALS Timothy Millett is a dealer in commemorative medals and works of art, with over 20 years' experience. He has contributed to a number of books in his field and was joint editor of *Convict Love Tokens*. This accompanied his exhibition of engraved coins, which were on display at the British Museum after touring Australian museums for a year. Timothy exhibits at many of the major London fairs.

METALWARE Vin Callcut has spent 52 years working with copper, brass, and other copper alloys. He started in research and transferred to industry and then to the Copper Development Association. Over 100 articles, books, and website articles have appeared under his name. Vin is now concentrating on domestic copperwares, specializing in late-19th and early 20th century items, and is busy preparing a new book on copper and brass collectables.

MILITARIA Roy Butler, senior partner of Wallis and Wallis Auctioneers, specialists in militaria and toys, has been with the BBC's *Antiques Roadshow* for 27 years. He is also a regular cruise lecturer.

MONEY COLLECTABLES Pam West began collecting bank notes in 1975, and established her company, British Notes, in 1990. She organizes five paper-money shows annually. She is currently the Chairperson of the London branch of the International Bank Note Society, and a life member.

PAPERWEIGHTS Anne Metcalfe runs Sweetbriar Gallery Ltd, the UK's biggest paperweight dealership, in Frodsham, Cheshire, which stocks thousands of pieces from Baccarat to abstract Chinese designs.

PHOTOGRAPHS Richard Meara, MA, MBA, MCIM, Dip M, has been a collector of photographs for 30 years and has been actively involved in dealing in 19th- and 20th-century images for the past 10 years. He is the proprietor and organizer of the London Photograph Fairs, which are the only specialist dealing events in fine and collectable photographs in the UK. Richard's shop, Jubilee Photographica, specializes in rare and collectable photographs.

POSTCARDS One of Britain's first postcard dealers, J.H.D. Smith began trading in 1966, publishing the first priced catalogue of postcards in 1975. He started the Bloomsbury Fair in 1977. Recently, J.H.D. published *The Picture Postcards of Raphael Tuck* – another priced listing. Now semi-retired, he lives in Cornwall and publishes a regular sales list.

POSTERS Charles Jeffreys started collecting posters in 1980 and amassed a large collection of traditional old posters, such as travel and general advertising. In 1998 he started his business, Charles Jeffreys Posters, specializing in post-war Modernist posters covering design, film, fashion, music, psychedelia, and Pop Art, and many other general advertising subjects.

RADIOS AND TELEVISIONS Steve Harris is a vintage technology specialist and director of On The Air. He was fascinated with wireless sets from childhood, and after working in TV broadcasting set up a museum of radio and television with an associated shop. He now supplies collectors, museums, and TV companies via the internet, and produces a magazine for enthusiasts called *Airwaves*.

RAILWAYANA Ian Wright, who founded Sheffield Railwayana Auctions in 1987, has been a collector of railwayana, and in particular locomotive nameplates, since 1971. The business has grown to be the world's foremost railwayana auction house, selling everything connected with railways except models, paintings, and rolling-stock.

ROCK & POP Dave Fowell, a specialist in The Beatles and general pop memorabilia for over 20 years, has given many interviews on the subject to the press, TV, and radio.

SCIENCE & TECHNOLOGY Charles Tomlinson has been a dealer for 30 years, specializing in scientific instruments, with particular interest in microscope slides, microscopes, sliderules, and mechanical calculating instruments.

SEWING TOOLS Elaine Gaussen has amassed a collection of more than 1,000 mostly antique thimbles, as well as other sewing tools, sewing boxes, and tables. In 1985 Elaine founded The Dorset Thimble Society for Collectors of Sewing

Tools Everywhere, of which she is Life President. She has also had numerous articles on the subject of needlework accessories published in trade magazines and newspapers.

SILVER Daniel Bexfield has been dealing in silver for 23 years, and is known to a great many collectors, enthusiasts, investors, and also to those who have seen and heard him on BBC television and radio.

SPORT Graham Budd organized Sotheby's first sales dedicated to horseracing and football memorabilia in 1998. One of his greatest finds to date was a collection of Manchester City programmes dating back to 1900, subsequently sold by Sotheby's for more than £50,000. Graham has been responsible for two books: *Horseracing Art & Memorabilia* in 1997, and *Soccer Memorabilia* in 1999. After 25 years' service Graham has recently left and established his own company, Graham Budd Auctions Ltd in association with Sotheby's, organizing sales of sporting memorabilia.

TEDDY BEARS & SOFT TOYS Sue Pearson is one of the world's leading authorities on teddy bears. A dealer and collector of antique dolls and teddy bears for many years, she also lectures around the world. Sue has a shop in Brighton, England, and also runs a doll and teddy bear hospital. She is the author of several books on teddy bears, including *Miller's Teddy Bears: A Complete Collector's Guide*, and contributes regularly to magazines.

TELEPHONES Malcolm Percival, managing director of Telephone Lines, has been specializing in telephones since 1972, bringing almost 30 years' of experience and dedication to the location, renovation, and selling of old phones.

TEXTILES Patricia Oldman began with a stall in Butter Lane Antiques Centre in Manchester (the forerunner to Affleck's Palace) before opening her first shop in Blackburn in 1981. She moved to the current premises in Todmorden in 1987.

WATCHES Nick Wiseman began specializing in wristwatches after an early background in general antiques. He has been published several times in *International WristWatch* and *QP* magazines and is also an associate dealer for Sotheby's.

WRITING ACCESSORIES Dr Jim Marshall has been buying, selling, and restoring writing equipment for over 15 years. Together with his wife, Jane, he owns The Pen & Pencil Gallery in Cumbria, is a director of The Onoto Pen Co Ltd, and consults worldwide on vintage writing antiques. He wrote *Miller's Pens and Writing Equipment Collector's Guide*, and regularly broadcasts and writes on the subject of writing accessories.

CONTENTS

6   Introduction

8   Advertisements & Packaging
11 Aeronautica
12 Amusement & Slot Machines
14 Architectural Salvage
16 Autographs
17 Automobilia
19 Bicycles
20 Books
26 Bottles
28 Breweriana
30 Buttons
31 Ceramics
53 Cigarette Cards
55 Cocktails
56 Comics & Annuals
58 Commemorative Ware
61 Compacts & Cosmetics
63 Corkscrews
64 Dolls
71 Dolls' Houses
73 Ephemera
74 Erotica
75 Fashion
82 Garden Collectables
84 Glass
100 Gramophones & Recorders
102 Handbags
104 Jewellery
111 Kitchenware
117 Lighting
120 Luggage & Travel
121 Medals
123 Metalware & Silver
133 Militaria
140 Money Collectables

142 Newspapers & Magazines
144 Photographs
147 Plastics
149 Postcards
151 Posters
155 Radios
157 Railwayana
159 Rock & Pop
166 Scent Bottles
168 Science & Technology
172 Sewing Tools
174 Shipping
176 Sport
182 Teddy Bears & Soft Toys
186 Telephones
188 Televisions
189 Textiles
193 Tobacco & Smoking
196 Toys & Games
208 Treen
209 Walking Sticks
210 Watches & Clocks
212 Writing Accessories

214 Directory of Useful Addresses
217 Index & Acknowledgments

INTRODUCTION

One question I am often asked is what makes an object collectable? There are many different factors: age, beauty, rarity, condition, fashion, but for me the most important is undoubtedly that someone wants to buy it, and the passion of that purchaser.

Over the years I have met many different collectors in every conceivable field and what else but passion could make a man acquire 250 vintage lawnmowers, a woman collect 1,500 teapots, or an enthusiast assemble a display of over 50,000 buttons? Often this love begins in childhood: the button lady began by playing with her mother's button box. My own passion for vintage fashion started with my dressing-up box, which was filled with my mother's 1950s cast-offs. Children can be the most dedicated collectors of all, swapping collectable cards and comics, and clamouring for the must-have toys of their generation, be it 1950s Dinky cars, '80s *Star Wars* toys, or '90s Beanie Babies (all of which are featured in this book). Nostalgia is a crucial factor in establishing the desirability of an object, and many adults return to the toys of their youth, buying back perfect examples of childhood favourites that broke, or were simply thrown away.

This "chuck out" factor is critical. Another question I am often asked is what is the difference between an antique and a collectable? Admittedly the distinction is often blurred, but if an antique can be described as a fine work of art, handmade by an individual craftsman for a person of some wealth or standing, then a collectable can perhaps be defined as an everyday object, mass-produced for everyday use, by ordinary people like you and me.

Many of the objects featured in this book, for example bottles, tins, and packaging, were created as purely functional items designed to be used and disposed of, hence their potential rarity and value today. The bottles shown below were literally rescued from rubbish dumps. An object doesn't have to be expensive in the first place to become collectable in the future, or to have an absorbing history. Codd bottles tell us about the invention of carbonated drinks, and the various solutions adopted to keep them fizzy until the invention of the crown cap. Behind every object, however utilitarian and humble, lies a story, and a collectable is not just a random decorative object but a little piece of 3-D history that you can hold in your hand.

Cosmetic containers (a popular collecting area) are a perfect example. An Art Deco powder compact, with its sections for rouge, lipstick, and cigarettes, reflects the fact that the new generation of crop-haired, short-skirted flappers could now wear make-up and smoke in public, and tells us as much about female liberation after World War I as the fact

Valve codd, 1893, and wooden plug bottle, c.1870; design, colour, and rarity decide value.

Clarice Cliff "Circle Tree" tea cup and saucer, 1930s; few were made so it is rare and valuable.

Willardy Lucite handbag, USA, 1950s; vintage bags are fashionable and useable collectables.

Star Wars **AT-AT, *c.*1979; the must-have toy of its day, it is sought-after by adult collectors.**

that women were at last granted the vote. It is this hands-on history that seduces many collectors. Collectables open a doorway into the past (be it distant or recent) and they are also extremely democratic. You don't need to be rich to build up a collection of buttons, and you don't have to have a university degree to become a world expert in hot water bottles or tattooing memorabilia (two more of my favourites).

History is one major attraction, another is simply shopping. As I know to my cost, what could be more enjoyable than wandering around an antiques fair, looking for bargains, never knowing what you are going to find, chatting to dealers and other enthusiasts. Whether you buy in shops, auction houses, on the internet, or at car boot (garage) sales, tracking objects down is as much part of the pleasure of collecting as owning them.

And when it comes to ownership, people collect in so many different ways. Some keep their treasures under lock-and-key as a private passion; one advertising and packaging collector I met had acquired so much and was so keen on sharing his interest that he ended up opening his own museum. Although most of the items in this book were designed to be functional, many are now too valuable or fragile to use. When I interviewed the late and great ceramic designer Susie Cooper (then in her nineties), I did end up

rather nervously drinking my tea from a hand-decorated 1920s cup and saucer. However, most collectors reserve their "Susie" and "Clarice" for the display cabinet, rather than the table. Other collectables demand to be used as they were in the past, and one of the joys of collecting vintage clothes and handbags is the pleasure of taking them out and showing them off.

Millers Complete A–Z of Collectables looks at items of every type and every value, exploring the history of objects and designers, and giving advice on what to look out for and how to collect in different fields. Many different experts have contributed to this book, which could not have been put together without the tireless efforts of antiques editor Emily Anderson. One of the questions all antiques specialists are asked is what should I collect? The standard advice is to find out as much as you can about your chosen subject before spending any serious money, and to buy the best examples in terms of quality and condition that you can possibly afford. But most important is to buy what you like. Collecting is not a necessity (though to we addicts it can sometimes feel like one), it's a pleasure. We hope you enjoy this book and that above all you enjoy your own present and future collectables.

Madeleine Marsh

ADVERTISEMENTS & PACKAGING

By the end of Queen Victoria's reign in 1901 it became obvious that in order to encourage the loyal purchase of branded items it was a good idea to decorate packaging pleasingly with a memorable design and sales slogan, or even, where room permitted, a full-colour illustration. The examples of beautiful advertising signs, counter-top displays, and often cunningly engineered containers shown here trace the development of consumerism and the rise of the "brand" over the last 120 years. From the 1880s to the 1970s the manufacturers who commissioned them to be made would have expected them to be ephemeral, having a lifespan of only a few years at most in the rough world of commerce. What would they have thought to see them here, in some cases over a century later, still being collected, preserved, cherished, and above all valued. Thanks to the huge rise in popularity in this collecting field many fine examples of early advertising art now find their way into specialist auction houses, but never neglect to explore in more prosaic locations in your quest to enlarge a collection. Old sheds, fences, allotments, and back gardens are often the final resting places for redundant enamel shop signs, and it's always worth checking out an elderly relative's store cupboard for early packaging and tin containers. Good hunting!

Freestanding diecut showcard, c.1925, with sailstrut back, for a counter point-of-sale or window display, probably at Christmas.

▼ **Huntley & Palmers library biscuit tin, 1900**

This is one of the most famous novelty biscuit tins ever made – 50,000 were produced for Christmas 1900 by the tin-box makers Huntley, Boorne and Stevens. They are beautifully detailed to represent a matching set of eight red, black, and gold blocked books bound with a brown "leather" strap, complete with metal buckle. The biscuits are obtained by lifting the entire tops of the books, which form the lid, with the aid of a movable gold pull tab, ingeniously masquerading as a bookmark (often missing in imperfect examples). The titles read *Story of Reading*, *Biscuits*, *Poetry*, *Essays*, *Travel*, *Science*, *Cakes*, and *Modern Reading*. The first and last volume are a pun on Reading – the town where both the biscuits and tin were produced! Rust-spotting on the tin plate will greatly affect value.

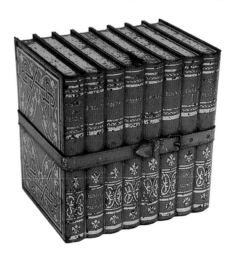

▲ **Transfer-printed white china pot lids, c.1890–1900**

Underglazed transfer-printed pot lids, mainly containing foodstuffs or cosmetic preparations, were available from as early as the 1830s. The more desirable and collectable lids, even then, were the multi-coloured Prattware examples from 1845. The lid above left is one of many designs for "Bears Grease" – the popular gentleman's hair-grooming preparation. This example, from James Atkinson of London (the largest manufacturer), shows the traditional illustration of the poor beast in chains, but also, more desirably, a price of five pence three farthings (about 2½ pence today). The other lid is for cherry toothpowder by John Connell and Co. Ltd of London. Whether young Queen Victoria actually used the product, or was consulted about her image being employed for its promotion, is unknown, but it was evidently hugely popular as numerous examples are still found today.

▼ Rowntree's coronation casket tin, 1911

Rowntree & Co Ltd were cocoa and chocolate makers to their majesties the King and Queen, which could possibly explain the high quality of this sumptuously decorated coronation souvenir chocolate box tin in the form of a jewelled casket, produced to commemorate the coronation of King George V and Queen Mary on 22nd June 1911. As the tin is pressed out to give a relief effect, some wear and scuffing to the raised edges is to be expected, although this will be reflected in the value.

▲ Fry's Chocolate "five boys" enamel sign, 1930s

One of the most famous advertising images ever made, the "five boys" first appeared in 1886 and were a brand in their own right by 1902. They were finally retired from service in 1971. This enamel metal advertising sign would have decorated the exterior wall of a sweetshop from c.1900 to the 1950s or '60s. There were three main sizes. Minor changes are found to the Royal Warrants on the signs, plus the addition of "300 Gold Medals & Diplomas" on some versions. Rare examples in red and green are known, the most desirable being the tinted faces "colour" design. Damage to the "glass" gloss enamel surface affects value.

➤ Players Tobacco pressed-tin sign, c.1920–40

John Player of Nottingham has used the image of the bearded sailor in every advertising medium for over a century. This pressed-tin sign would have been fixed to the inside wall of most of the UK's tobacconists from the 1920s, many surviving undisturbed well into the 1960s. As it is pressed out to give the "lifebelt" a lifelike 3-D effect it is very prone to damage, making mint examples rare.

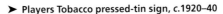

▲ Yardley's china counter-display figure, 1890s

This Dresden china figurative group represents a mother and children "up from the country", trying to sell their wares in the big city. It was modelled after one of the famous Wheatley's London Cries, "Who will buy my sweet lavender?", and was intended to stand in a chemist's window or on a counter-top next to Yardley's "Olde English" lavender soap (the same image appearing on the soap wrapper too). A scarce Royal Doulton version was produced in 1925, followed by an edition in Rubberoid (moulded rubber) in 1935.

◄ Crawford's "Fairy House" biscuit money box, 1934

The famous children's illustrator Mabel Lucie Attwell (1879–1964) illustrated and designed three biscuit money boxes for William Crawford & Sons. The first, "Bicky House", was made in 1933, this one in 1934, and the third, and most famous, "Fairy Tree", in 1935. The contents of this tin were accessed by pulling off the tightly fitting mushroom-cap lid. With most money box tins the coin slot is bent and chipped, and with repeated use the edges become worn and scuffed, with the usual reduction in value.

◄ Jacobs gipsy caravan biscuit tin, 1937
Shaped tins, especially early vehicles, often command the highest prices. W&R Jacob & Co issued this caravan with a hinged roof that opens to reveal the biscuits. This tin, with built-in "play value", must have been commissioned from a good tin toymaker as the attention to detail is superb. The steps fold up vertically and the wheels and axles are fully functioning. All these separate parts must be present and in good, unrusty, working condition with original unfaded paint finish to achieve the maximum value.

▼ Coca Cola pressed-tin serving tray, 1950
From its founding in Atlanta Georgia in 1886 to the present day, "Coke" must be the world's most heavily advertised and marketed product. Millions of promotional items have been produced, from the largest illuminated street sign to the smallest "giveaway" novelty. From the early 1900s beautifully decorated printed-tin serving trays (often with matching small oval "change" trays) were made by the company and their numerous independent bottlers throughout the USA. By the late 1950s Coca Cola had conquered the Western world – this tray was probably made in Mexico for the US market. Beware of unauthorized reproductions among the hundreds of memorabilia items produced each year.

◄ Robertson's "Golly" illuminated counter-display figure, 1963
James Robertson started marmalade production in Paisley, Yorkshire in 1864. The "Golly It's Good" image was adopted as the company's trademark in 1914. These giant golly advertising display figures were cast in plaster or Rubberoid and hand-decorated. This example from 1963 stands 71cm (28in) tall, and would have delighted children visiting the grocers with their mothers, hopefully persuading the parent into a purchase. Variations over the years include waistcoat colour, logo differences, and the position of the eyes. These early composition figures are not to be confused with the heavy resin copies made today.

➤ Homepride flour, salt, and pepper shakers, c.1969
Homepride commissioned Airfix model makers to make a plastic container for their flour, and since the launch of "Fred the Flourgrader" in 1969 over 500,000 have been produced. The removable bowler hat hides the holes that allow it to be both a shaker and a storage container. Two tokens from flour packets, plus three shillings and sixpence (17½ pence), were required to purchase your very own "Fred". Numerous other on-pack offers of Fred collectables, like the salt and pepper shakers shown here, were to follow throughout the 1970s.

AERONAUTICA

In 1903 the first heavier-than-air machine was flown at Kittyhawk in the USA. This contraption was designed and piloted by the Wright brothers – bicycle mechanics who had become fascinated by the thought of flying, and who, with very little money, designed and built the first aeroplane. In 1909 Bleriot became the first man to fly across the English Channel, and in 1919 Alcock and Brown conquered the North Atlantic pioneering transatlantic flight. The golden age of flying was the 1920s and '30s, with designers building larger and larger aircraft with more luxurious seats and even heated cabins. Pre-war aircraft was comfortable, and although the machines were not fast the flying experience would have been more civilized than today. By the 1960s more people than ever were taking planes, and airliners made the traditional ocean liner obsolete. The golden 1920s and '30s period is the most collected, with items such as china and silverplate, posters, instruments, and flying clothing much in demand. With the sad demise of Concorde, material from the first supersonic liner, launched in 1969, is avidly sought-after.

A poster commemorating Bleriot's epic flight across the English Channel in 1909, printed by Borel & Co. of Paris.

▼ Airship LZ 127 badge and a china airship by Arcadian China, c.1916
Airship memorabilia is always in demand. The Graf Zeppelin was the most successful airship ever to fly – 590 flights including world tours. At 776ft she was longer than many ocean liners, and carried up to 50 passengers in absolute luxury. This brass-and-enamel badge would have been a souvenir, probably bought by a passenger and similar to those on aircraft today. Arcadian was the trade name of Arkinstall and Sons of Stoke-on-Trent (1904–24). This china airship was one of a vast range of seaside-type souvenirs emblazoned with the crest of the local town, including ships, monuments, aircraft, and wishing wells.

▲ Watch fob, mid-19th century
The first manned balloon flight, which took place in France in 1783, was by the Montgolfier brothers. For the next 100 years balloons were used for displays, short flights, and static ascents in parks and at exhibitions. Souvenirs of these events consisted of medallions, plates, souvenir cups, and items like this swivelling intaglio watch fob.

▼ Sweet tin of the 1960s
The 1960s saw the development of package holidays and affordable flights. This tin, depicting various airlines and an airport, would have been sold in the airport shops or on board the aircraft. Pictorial tins are now in demand, but condition is paramount.

◄ World War II Luftwaffe flight jacket
Used during the winter on the Russian front and in attacks on Britain, these heavy German Air Force jackets did not offer the wearer much freedom of movement. With matching trousers, heavy sheepskin boots, and gloves the crew member would have been in one position during the flight. British and American flying crews had similar clothing, which is also now extremely collectable.

AMUSEMENT & SLOT MACHINES

Football machine, Automatic Sports Company, London, c.1896; early floor-standing machines are the most sought-after today.

Collecting slot machines didn't really establish itself in the UK until the 1970s. When decimalization happened in 1971 it coincided with the dawn of the electronic age of slot machines. Many vintage mechanical machines were too difficult to convert from the large old penny to the new one penny coin, and in any case they suddenly looked very old-fashioned sitting in the arcades and on the piers next to the latest models, which included flashing lights and colourful artwork. Thousands of the old-style machines were scrapped, burned, and thrown off the end of seaside piers. However, fortunately a few canny collectors and operators, who never threw anything away, gathered sheds full of the best machines and these have now become highly prized collectors' items. These vintage machines are great fun and always attract a lot of interest from jealous friends and fellow aficionados! As with all areas of collecting, new enthusiasts should do some home-work before buying their first machine. Very similar-looking machines to the untrained eye can have vastly different values. Don't panic-buy the first thing you see – a specialist auction sale and regular magazine will give you a good idea of availability and prices. Potential collectors should also be aware that even antique machines still come under current gambling laws. Only buy from someone registered with the Gaming Board of Great Britain, and get a receipt with the seller's licence number.

▲ **Governor, O.D. Jennings, Chicago, c.1960**
This is a classic machine and, though fairly common, is always sought-after. They got the nickname "one-arm bandit" because unscrupulous operators "fixed" them so that certain higher payouts were impossible to hit. The other common name, "fruit machine", comes from a time in the USA when gambling machines were made illegal and many machines had a gum vendor added; the reel symbols were changed to represent the flavours of the gum. Paying for a stick of gum gained you a free play on the machine.

▼ **Electra Shooter, Electra, Germany c.1898**
In the mid- to late-19th century live shooting galleries were all the rage, and could be found in virtually every town. When the permanent amusement arcade was invented just before the turn of the 20th century, shooting galleries were incorporated at first, but soon gave way to many different coin-operated versions. The Electra, patented in 1889, was one of the first and most successful, manufactured in various designs into the 1920s.

▲ **Allwin de Luxe, Jentsch & Meerz, c.1920**
There are hundreds of variations and designs of the "Allwin", which was in production from 1900 until the 1970s; recently a company has started to make it again. The name comes from the earliest models, which had a row of winning cups and no losers; you only lost if your ball missed all the cups completely. Later designs incorporated win and lose cups, and some had features like reserve balls and jackpots.

➤ **Tivoli one-arm bandit, Gunter Wulf Germany, *c.*1960**

Large quantities of these German wall-mounted one-arm bandits were imported into the UK. There was a law in Germany, established to help boost the manufacturing industry, that slot machines could only be operated for a couple of years from new, and then had to be scrapped. Some English firms bought up the redundant models and built new cases for them. However, many survive just as they were made, complete with German instructions.

▲ **Ahrens viewer, Charles Ahrens, London, *c.*1930**

Viewers were very popular from the Victorian era, when photography was invented, through into the late 1950s, by which time most people had access to televisions and the novelty had started to wear off. Some machines exhibited views of foreign lands, campaign battles, or sporting events, but it was the more risqué "What-The-Butler-Saw" verisons that really brought profits for operators, and notoriety for this kind of machine.

▼ **Space Invaders, Taito, Japan, *c.*1978**

There has been a recent surge of interest in early video games. As with the Jennings Governor, Space Invaders is one of the most common machines and also the most sought-after. When the first Space Invaders video games were released in Japan in 1978 they were so popular they caused a national coin shortage until the country's yen supply could be quadrupled. It was always destined to be a classic, but as it is a vintage electronic piece many people are put off owning one in case it breaks.

◀ **Aristocrat Nevada, Ainsworth, Australia, *c.*1975**

Ainsworth was known principally for making dentistry equipment so quite how they got into the field of slot machines is something of a mystery! These machines are ideal for beginner collectors as they are reliable, relatively easy to find, and inexpensive. There are many different designs, including this colourful Mardi Gras one, and later casino machines even came in four- or five-reel versions, as opposed to the more usual three.

ARCHITECTURAL SALVAGE

Thomas Crapper and Co produced sanitary ware for many customers, including Buckingham Palace.

Until the 1970s very little was salvaged from demolition sites and redevelopments. Sadly today some old buildings are still being demolished entirely, but more and more are having their reuseable items removed first. The term "architectural salvage" is a wide one that encompasses everything from bricks and tiles to taps and radiators. The increased interest in reusing old pieces has many reasons. Reuse fits well with growing concerns about the environment: it has been estimated that in the UK alone close to a million tons of building wood is thrown into skips every year. Much of this wood is not only better quality than what is available today, but is also cheaper than new timber. With architectural salvage it is possible to get an ecologically friendly, good-quality product with character for less than the modern alternative. Items can be found to match the period of your property or simply an attractive contrast to today's contemporary styles. As with most areas of collecting it pays to research before you buy. Be wary of reproductions and prices that seem too good.

▼ Excelsior "wash down", 1898

There were few improvements in sanitary hygiene from Roman times until patents such as J.F. Brondel's valve-type flush toilet in the 18th century. When the Prince of Wales contracted typhus fever in 1871 people's awareness of the need for higher standards of hygiene increased dramatically, and firms like Crapper and Co, Twyfords, Shanks, and Doulton produced a large number of patent designs. In keeping with the age many were highly decorative and far more appealing than today's austere pieces. If you intend to use one check that it meets current building regulations and can be fitted by a plumber.

◄ Art Deco nickel-plated mixer taps, 1930s

Taps followed the main styles of decoration that were popular throughout the late-19th and 20th centuries. Many antique taps are far more stylish than today's models and can often represent a real bargain. It is important to ensure that the taps have been well restored and that if the plumbing is of a non-standard size the seller can recommend a suitable plumber for installation. It is also worth establishing whether, if replacement parts are going to be required in the future, the supplier can provide them for a reasonable fee.

► Copper Art Nouveau finger plate and brass pull handle, *c.*1890

Door furniture has closely mirrored decorative fashions since the 18th century. A stylish pair of handles or finger plates is an easy and cheap way to create either the right introduction to a room setting or simply to improve an otherwise plain entranceway. The quality of antique pieces is very often significantly better than that of modern and reproduction items, whereas the price is usually not dissimilar.

◄ A pair of Punch and Judy door porters, 1880

Door porters have been in use for as long as doors themselves, but it wasn't until the 19th century that they took on a decorative as well as functional form. The Industrial Revolution enabled items to be made cheaply and in large quantities and the 19th-century love affair with cast iron was perfectly suited to the production of decorative door porters. Brass and copper were also used, but the cheapness of iron meant that it prevailed. Large numbers of often intricate designs were produced and it is the more unusual that are at a premium today. The most collectable, such as this pair, are being reproduced so look carefully before you buy to be sure they are original.

► An Ideal Standard cast-iron radiator, 1920–50

The history of hot-water radiators is not certain but J. Bramah undoubtedly played a major role in their development and Westminster Hospital is believed to be the first building to be fitted with them during the late-18th century. During the 19th century radiators were used mainly by large public buildings and it wasn't until the 20th century that more modest buildings began to be equipped with central heating systems. Reconditioned radiators are often better quality than modern reproductions and many are decorative enough to be considered almost as sculptural pieces in their own right.

◄ A Victorian cast-iron and tiled forward grate

Cast-iron combination grates and surrounds were made in large numbers during the 19th century when the use of coal as a domestic heating fuel became far more widespread. Cast iron became much cheaper to produce and domestic buildings were constructed in large numbers to standard plans. The use of tiles in grates, as well as being decorative, was a practical measure that added to the heat emitted by the grate; pay particular attention to these tiles as sometimes they are worth more than the grate. Many grates have been destroyed and those that have survived are still comparatively cheap, but damage is costly to repair so check for that.

► A Sofano electric fire, 1950s

The interest in 20th-century design is one of the fastest growth areas within the art and antiques world. Collectors are not bound by traditional constraints, although the form and function of an item are still paramount. This piece fits the bill well being a 1950s "classic", embodying that era's interest in spage-age styling. If you intend to use an electrical appliance make sure that the piece meets current safety standards before purchasing it, or that it can be modified; if it can't then it becomes an interesting sculptural form rather than a stylish, useable heater.

AUTOGRAPHS

Kylie Minogue has transformed from soap star to sophisticated chanteuse, and her autograph is currently highly sought-after.

In our celebrity-obsessed culture, the value of autographs has escalated. Demand is strong in every area – historical figures, filmstars, great explorers, and sporting heros, although certain names can go in and out of fashion. Medium is important to value – a signed photograph is easier to display than the inside pages of a theatre programme. The contents of a letter can enhance the value of a signature, but clipped signatures (removed at some time in the past from the original document) can also be valuable. Autographs are not difficult to fake, so buying from a reputable source is essential. Sometimes celebrity autographs were, and still are, signed by secretaries. Beatles autographs were often produced by their entourage – those signed by road manager John Aspinall are even collectable in their own right. Proof of provenance is always worth having, particularly any account of the autograph being signed in person. Some celebrities are reluctant to give autographs, so examples that do exist have a rarity value.

▲ Signed photograph of Neil Armstrong, 1970
Such was demand for autographs of the Apollo XI crew that many photographs were inscribed with autopens, which automatically reproduced their signatures. This official NASA photograph, showing Armstrong against a lunar backdrop, has an autopen signature in black but is also signed and dated by Armstrong in blue ink. It has creases to the top and bottom margins, but these do not affect the signature or, therefore, the value.

▼ Black-and-white photograph of The Beatles, 1965
Beatles autographs are the most desirable and the most faked. A combination of rarity and provenance makes this 10 x 8in (25 x 20cm) black-and-white photograph very special. Signed with jokey inscriptions from the "Fab Four", the picture was taken in the Bahamas during the filming of the 1965 film *Help*. In spite of creases and pinholes to the corners, the rarity of all four signatures on an attractive image gives it a value of £10,000 ($15,000).

▼ Charlie Chaplin clipped signature
Charlie Chaplin (1889–1977) is still revered today as the first truly great film comedian. This inscription in thick black fountain-pen ink on a piece of off-white card was sold mounted, framed, and glazed with a photograph of the star. It is common for clipped signatures to be presented in this way. The slight smudging where the paper has absorbed the ink does not detract from the value.

◄ Cheque signed by Marilyn Monroe, 1961
A cheque offered as payment by a celebrity is sometimes best left uncashed. This cheque, drawn on Marilyn Monroe Productions Inc, is made payable to Hedda Rosten and dated 15th September 1961. Signed in black ink by Monroe herself, it is worth considerably more than its face value. Sadly death and disaster will up the value of a celebrity autograph.

Motoring has been with us for over a century, and in that time it has changed our lives. This has naturally extended into the collector's market. The generic term "automobilia" applies not only to car parts and spares and accessories such as lamps, horns, dashboard instruments, clocks, badges, mascots, radiators, and mechanical spares, but also everything that either depicts or displays a motor car, relates to road transport, or was used in the petrol and motor industry in some way. It is possible to collect automobilia in every form, from toys to petrol pumps, from posters to motor-racing memorabilia. Collectors can focus on a specific marque of vehicle, such as Bugatti, Ferrari, or Rolls Royce, or a motoring era, such as Pioneer, Veteran, Vintage, Classic, or Modern. As well as collecting for display, owners of classic and vintage vehicles also buy to use. Autojumbles, swap meets, motor shows, and rallies are prime hunting grounds. There are specialist auctions for the more valuable objects, but even scrap yards can yield treasured spare parts.

1930s Gamages motor oil 5-gallon can, depicting a speedboat, a car, and a Supermarine seaplane.

➤ **The Telcote Pup mascot, 1920s**
Owners have personalized their cars since motoring began. Accessory mascots were available to suit all tastes, be it for animals, mythical creatures, nudes, or sporting figures. Among the most prized are the glass mascots by René Lalique, which, when fitted to an illuminated radiator cap, lit up at night. The mascot illustrated, inspired by "Bonzo" (the famous cartoon dog created by George Studdy) was made by A.E. Lejeune in 1923, when it cost 3 guineas. It is still being reproduced today.

▲ **Rolls-Royce "Spirit of Ecstasy" marque mascot by Charles Sykes, 1911**
In 1910 the directors of Rolls-Royce were dismayed to find the radiator caps of their fine cars decorated with assorted accessory mascots. They commissioned noted artist Charles Sykes to produce a suitably dignified mascot and on 6th February 1911 the "Spirit of Ecstasy" was born. She was first fitted to the legendary Silver Ghost range of cars, and since then has become one of the world's most instantly recognizable trademarks and a continuing symbol of the quality of "The Best Motor Car in the World".

◄ **"Monsieur Bibendum" Michelin man, c.1910**
The artist Marius Rossillon breathed life into an observation by Andre and Edouard Michelin that a stack of tyres only needed arms and legs to look like a body. "Monsieur Bibendum", named after a painting entitled *Nunc est Bibendum* ("Now is the Time to Drink"), first appeared in a poster dated 1898, and is now known across the globe. This fine plaster advertising figure is from the American market (note the spelling of the word "tires"), and is one of the earliest-known three-dimensional "Monsieur Bibendum" figures made. A whole range of Michelin man items have been produced over the years, from large advertising signs to badges and key rings.

⋏ Brooklands Automobile Racing Club badge

In 1931 Frederick Gordon-Crosby, renowned artist at *Autocar* magazine, proposed a design for a car badge for the members of the popular B.A.R.C. It was intended initially as a way for the gatemen to recognize club members, but it became a status symbol in its own right. Beautifully enamelled in seven colours on chromed brass, and individually numbered, these badges are still highly revered among collectors today. Beware of fakes, particularly the so-called "Committee" badge, which is a complete work of fiction.

➤ "Clock-face" petrol pump by Avery-Hardoll, 1950s

In the early days of motoring, petrol (gasoline) was always delivered in cans. This is despite the fact that in 1885 Sylvanus Bowser had invented the first gasoline pump, and had sold and installed it in Jake Gumper's service station in Fort Wayne, Indiana. The petrol pump was introduced to the UK in 1913. Today "petroliana" (which relates to petrol, oils, garage equipment, and advertising) is an integral part of motoring history, and has fuelled a collecting market of its own. This restored petrol pump is fitted with a post-war period glass globe. The pecten, or scallop shell, was adopted as Shell's symbol in 1904, reflecting the fact that the firm started life in 1833 as a shop selling seashells.

⋏ Bartholomew honey leather map cases, *c*.1910

Until the 1920s many places and routes were poorly signposted so the most important driver's aid of all was the map. Entire leather-cased sets, complete with compass, helped to ensure that you could choose your route with care, avoiding un-metalled roads and hazards, and would help if you became lost. Some sets even had a miniature measuring wheel that could be run over the map to calculate the mileage of the intended route. For open-topped motoring sets of maps were made in waterproof folders with plastic windows, so the map could be studied in even the foulest weather conditions.

⋏ Signed photograph of Ayrton Senna, 1993

The most recent trend to emerge from within the automobilia market is that of collecting racing memorabilia. Articles signed by an heroic racing driver always carry a premium. The late Formula 1 champion Ayrton Senna is one of the most sought-after names. The value of this photograph lies in the signature. Many fakes and forgeries of signed items exist, so most original pieces today are issued with a certificate of authenticity from the racing team to which the driver belongs.

⋏ Pressed aluminium number plate, 1973

Motor vehicle registration plates were first introduced in Paris in 1893. British drivers were initially opposed to number plates, but with 5,000 cars now on the road the government had to take control. The Motor Car Act, passed in 1904, stipulated the licensing of drivers and the registration of vehicles. Number plates have existed in many different materials, from early enamel through metals including pressed aluminium, right up to modern plastics. Most are still available for pocket-money prices, though drivers will pay a small fortune for an interesting personalized number plate, old or new.

Posts like this (1899), altered the concept of cycling as a man's sport.

Leonardo da Vinci is credited with inventing the bicycle, however no evidence exists that his design of 1490 ever left the drawing board. Other prototypes followed: de Sivrac's running machine, c.1790; Baron Von Drais' "Draisienne" (or Hobby Horse) in 1817, propelled by paddling the feet along the ground; Kirkpatrick MacMillan was the first to add foot power directly to the rear wheel through treadles in 1839; and in 1865 Ernest and Pierre Michaux added cranks and pedals to the front wheels of their velocipede (familiarly known as a bone shaker because of its rough ride). Ordinary, or "high wheel", bicycles appeared in 1870, but were superseded in the 1880s by the safety bicycle with its equal-sized wheels. The Victorian and Edwardian eras were the Golden Age of cycling, which remained the most common form of road transport until the 1920s. Today vintage bicycles themselves, as well as the objects that depict them, are highly collectable.

▲ **French carved cheroot holder, c.1900**
As cycling increased in popularity the cyclist could purchase almost any object with a design depicting a bicycle. Women are often featured, both to appeal to male purchasers and reflecting the fact that with the introduction of the safety bicycle ladies too took to the road. "The bicycle has done more for the emancipation of women than anything else in the world", claimed suffragist Susan B. Anthony in 1896.

▲ **"Hirondelle Superbe" bicycle, French, c.1890**
Made by Manufacture Française d'Armes et Cycles, this beautifully balanced bicycle represents the type of machine that appeared during the transitional period from the ordinary or high wheel bicycle (commonly known as a "penny farthing") c.1880, to the diamond-framed safety bicycles of c.1900 and later. This type has built-in suspension, which would have been needed as the machine is fitted with solid tyres; the ride would have been smoothed out by the use of the innovative C-shaped main spar.

▶ **Raleigh Chopper bicycle, 1977**
It is not just vintage bicycles that are collectable; some modern manufacturers produced limited-edition models purely for the collectors' market. Certain post-war machines are sought-after, particularly the more radical and unusual designs, such as the American Schwinn bicycles of the 1940s–'50s and the British Raleigh Chopper from the 1970s. Designed by Alan Oakley, and inspired by the customizing and "chopping" of motorbikes in the USA, the Chopper, with its motorbike seat and "ape hanger" handlebars, was the must-have bike of the decade. Its various models attract many fans today.

BOOKS

First published in the UK by Hamish Hamilton in 1951, this is now recognized as one of the seminal works of the 20th century.

Erasmus, perhaps the greatest of the scholars of the Renaissance period, once remarked that when he had money he bought books, and if he had any money over, he bought food. Most modern readers might consider this proposition laudable but unrealistic. However, there is a sense in which buying books today may well put food on the table tomorrow. At a time when confidence in the stock market is at something of a low, investors have been turning their backs on the City and have begun to invest heavily in art and antiques; a trend which, by extension, has made a significant impact on the book market, from the antiquarian through to the hyper-modern, on all subjects and for most periods. Disparaging comments have appeared deploring the "outrageous" valuations put on signed "Harry Potters" and speculating on what that kind of money could have bought if invested "sensibly" in a first edition of *Pride and Prejudice*, a *Brighton Rock*, or *The Power and the Glory*. However, Rowling, Austen, and Greene all have demonstrable investment potential, in their different ways are a wonderful read, and as objects are visually arresting, whether in a fine binding or a well-designed dust wrapper. Books exist primarily to be read. With a little care, both in making one's choice and in the subsequent handling, books can give huge pleasure over and over again to the reader and provide a handsome return for the investor. Be warned though – the value of books can go down as well.

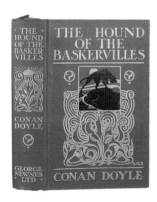
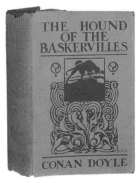

> **To the Lighthouse**, Hogarth Press, 1927
With her fourth novel Virginia Woolf established herself as a Modernist writer, unafraid of using innovative narrative techniques such as the interior monologue and stream of consciousness in her determination to get beneath the surface of things. Although the novel is still in print today, it is this Hogarth Press edition, printed by the Woolfs with a striking dustwrapper by the author's sister, Vanessa Bell, that is the one to collect. The book has become a Modernist icon, inspiring many other writers including British author Jeanette Winterson.

▲ **The Hound of the Baskervilles**, George Newnes, 1902
Arthur Conan Doyle killed off Sherlock Holmes in 1893 but public demand forced him to revive "the greatest detective of them all" in *The Hound of the Baskervilles*. This was serialized in the *Strand* magazine, August 1901 to April 1902, and published in book form that same year by George Newnes, who printed 25,000 copies at 6 shillings each. Only three first-editions of this famous novel are known to exist with dust jacket. When the example illustrated above came up for auction in 1998 it fetched a world record price for a modern first edition of £80,700.

◄ **A Farewell to Arms**, Jonathan Cape, 1929
First published in the UK in 1929, in this stunning Lee Elliott dust wrapper, *A Farewell to Arms* is one of the finest novels to come out of World War I. Turned down by the army because of poor sight, Hemingway signed up as a Red Cross ambulance driver and sailed for Europe in May 1918. In July, while distributing chocolate to Italian front-line troops, he was seriously wounded, but still helped to get other injured soldiers to a first-aid station before being evacuated to a Milan hospital, where he fell in love with his nurse. The experiences provided the inspiration for this great novel.

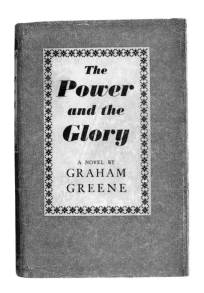

◄ *The Power and the Glory*,
William Heinemann, 1940

One of the best-known writers of his generation, Graham Greene (1904–91) is one of today's most collectable 20th-century authors. His first novel, *The Man Within* (1929) remains scarce, as does *Brighton Rock*, first published in the USA in 1938. *The Power and the Glory* won the Hawthornden Prize in 1941, a year after it was published, and is by general consent one of Graham Greene's finest works. A copy in a dustwrapper, such as this one pictured left, is very scarce and highly collectable – the presence of a dustwrapper in this case will increase the value of the book by 600 per cent, and perhaps even more if it is in perfect condition.

▲ *Four Quartets*, Faber, 1944

First published individually in pamphlet-form by Faber between 1936 and 1942, T.S. Eliot's *Four Quartets* were put together in book-form in the USA in 1943. This first US edition is now extremely rare and valuable, as most copies were destroyed because of printer errors and the few that survived were disowned by Eliot. The version illustrated above is the more common edition, published by Faber the following year. Now considered his signature work, *Four Quartets* was a major factor in the decision to award Eliot the Nobel Prize for Literature in 1948.

► *Thunderball*, Jonathan Cape, 1961
and *Casino Royale*, Pan Books, 1955

Thunderball is the ninth in the James Bond canon and familiar in its brilliant Richard Chopping dust wrapper. Chopping designed all the Bond dust wrappers with the exception of the first book, *Casino Royale*. Memorably filmed, and now hugely collectable, the original Fleming titles have been augmented by later stories written by John Gardner and Raymond Benson. First editions of the 1953 book *Casino Royale* in fine condition fetch five-figure sums, and even this Pan paperback, published two years later, is collectable.

► *Nineteen Eighty-Four*, Secker and Warburg, 1949

George Orwell's *1984* was originally intended to be published in 1948, to maximize the impact of the inverted date, but it was a year late. The story satirizes brilliantly the totalitarian state, as does *Animal Farm*, published in 1945. The considerable impact of these two books on a nervous post-war Britain has by no means faded today. Over a hundred years after Orwell's birth (25th June 1903) the horrors that dominate the two books have not diminished, they have merely metamorphosed. Incidentally, the dust wrapper of *1984* appeared in a green version and a red; preference is normally given to the copy that the book-dealer is offering for sale!

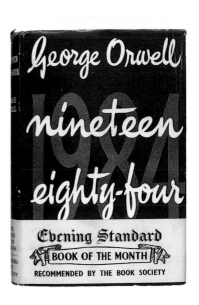

Children's Books

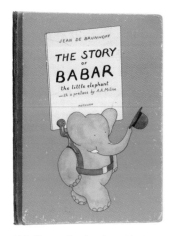

This first *Babar* book, published with an English text by Methuen in 1934, was an instant success; it is deservedly still in print today.

Today's book collector is hugely fortunate in being able to indulge in this activity at a time when the publishing of children's books is at an all-time high in terms of quality, quantity, and sheer variety. The speculative investor will be busy buying up Philip Pullman, Lemony Snicket, Philip Reeve, Eoin Colfer, G.P. Taylor, and the like. (It is already too late to collect J.K. Rowling unless you are very well-heeled). But not all collectors want to collect books written for modern children. Part of the joy of this kind of collecting is to indulge in nostalgia and to build up a collection of the books that we loved as a child and no longer have, or at least not in the condition to which a collector aspires. Timeless books such as *Alice in Wonderland*, *Winnie the Pooh*, *The Wind in the Willows*, and the Beatrix Potter and Arthur Ransome books perform well. Enid Blyton continues to exert a peculiar fascination. Other books that ought to be in decline but refuse to lie down include the *Biggles* books, *Bunter and Jennings*, and the girls' school stories of Angela Brazil, Elsie Oxenham, and Elinor Brent-Dyer. Alan Garner and Roald Dahl are tipped as pension-fund material.

▼ The Tailor of Gloucester, F. Warne & Co, 1903

The Tailor of Gloucester was the second of a long and enormously popular series of animal stories written and illustrated by Beatrix Potter. The books are still in print and have been translated into most languages (including Latin). This children's author is more popular than ever today – brought to a new audience through clever merchandising, which in turn draws attention back to the original books. The most sought-after "Tale" is that of Peter Rabbit, although many collectors have their own personal favourite.

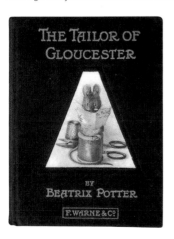

➤ Fairy Tales and Stories, Harrap, 1932

Hans Christian Andersen's *Fairy Tales and Stories* first appeared in 1835 and was added to regularly until its completion in 1872. The stories cried out for illustration, and this Harrap edition, with 12 coloured plates and many black-and-white drawings by the artist Arthur Rackham, is among the most celebrated. Rackham's idiosyncratic style continues to fascinate and has resulted in his book illustrations becoming highly sought-after and very valuable.

➤ Alice's Adventures in Wonderland, Walker Books, 1999 (left) and Elsevier Phaidon, 1975

First published by Macmillan in 1865, *Alice's Adventures in Wonderland* (and its sequel *Through the Looking-Glass*, 1872) became an instant success that was to have an enormous impact on Carroll's life as a mathematics lecturer at Oxford University. The first edition was illustrated by *Punch* cartoonist John Tenniel and since then Alice's story has inspired countless artists. Some collectors choose a favourite story and focus on the different illustrated versions produced.

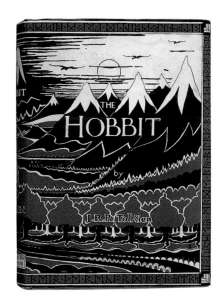

◄ *The Hobbit*, George Allen & Unwin, 1937

The Hobbit was published to immediate acclaim from critics and the reading public alike, and is still in print, having sold an estimated 35 million copies. Originally written for Tolkien's children, and some six years in the making, the book was published as a precursor to *The Lord of the Rings*. When a novel is translated onto the big screen it affects demand for first-editions. The success of the recent *Lord of the Rings* films has stimulated prices for Tolkien's works. A first-edition of *The Hobbit* auctioned in 2002 sold for a record price of just over £43,000 ($64,500). Tolkien only rarely signed books but this copy was signed and inscribed to his aunt within a fortnight of its original publication.

► *The Chalet School Reunion*,
W.R. Chambers, 1963

The Chalet School Reunion is no. 50 in a series of 58 books by E.M. Brent-Dyer. After an early life marked by privation she spent 36 years teaching in a variety of schools and ended up running her own school, which had strong echoes of the Chalet School but was nothing like as successful. She was a prolific writer on a variety of subjects and in several genres, but Brent-Dyer is best known for the *Chalet School* series, which has been in continuous print for over 70 years and is still going strong.

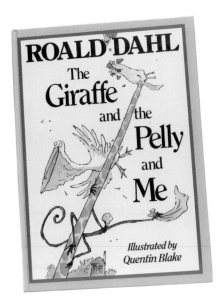

▲ *The Giraffe and the Pelly and Me*,
Jonathan Cape, 1985

Roald Dahl's *The Giraffe and the Pelly and Me* continued the highly successful collaboration with illustrator Quentin Blake that had begun in 1975. Although Dahl wrote two volumes of autobiography and some adult fiction, it is for his children's books that he will be best remembered. First editions of this story in good condition (a rarity with books for younger children) are already collectable today, and Blake's original illustrations now fetch high prices in the art market.

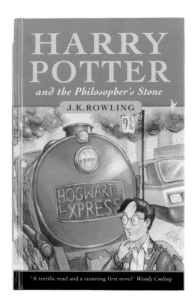

◄ *Harry Potter and the Philosopher's Stone*,
Bloomsbury, 1997

This first novel in a series about a boy wizard became a publishing phenomenon almost overnight. Written by a single mother on benefit, and finished thanks to a grant from the Scottish Arts Council, the book was rejected by several major publishers and was eventually turned out in a very small first printing, with Bloomsbury fearful of losing what little money they had invested. They need not have worried: the book was an instant success and has been reprinted in huge numbers, won numerous prizes, been turned into a major film, and made its author a millionaire. And this book was just the first of a projected series of seven! Investors might care to note that signed first printings fetch £25,000 ($37,500).

Specialist Interest Books

Away from the mad scramble for the latest *Harry Potter*, and the chase for the last reported signed copy of a novel short-listed for a major prize, are calmer regions where book collectors pursue their unhurried searches for additions to their themed collections. Subject areas that continue to attract considerable interest, and large sums of money for the most prized items, include Exploration and Topography; Sport and Pastimes; Cookery; Illustrated Books; History and Memoirs; True Crime; and Modern Art. First or early editions of older books on any of these subjects, particularly those with engraved plates or maps, tend to carry stratospheric price tags, but there is a lot of interesting late-19th and 20th-century material on all of these areas that is affordable and has investment potential in addition to its intrinsic value. The travel writing of Ernest Thesiger, Freya Stark, Robert Byron, Bruce Chatwin, Colin Thubron, and Patrick Leigh Fermor is highly readable and all attract collectors. In the cookery field, books by Elizabeth David are the ones to collect; and within the True Crime genre, those on Jack the Ripper and the Kennedy assassination.

Chatwin was drawn to Patagonia as a last outpost of humanity. The instant success of his first book (Cape, 1977) is a fitting memorial.

▼ Mrs Beeton cookery books, Ward Lock

Isabella Beeton's *Book of Household Management* made its first appearance in 1861 and remained in print for over a century. The book is a heavyweight in every sense: as well as an impressive number of recipes, it contains advice on etiquette, dinner parties, employing servants, and household management in general. The first edition was published by the author's husband, Samuel Orchard Beeton; these later editions were published by Ward Lock.

◄ Tide's Ending, Hollis & Carter, 1950

Natural History books have long generated a large and faithful following. Somewhere between the early works, with their starkly beautiful black-and-white engravings, and today's books, which overwhelm with their stunning colour photography, lies the work of Denis Watkins-Pitchford, better known as "B.B.". *Tide's Ending* is a wonderful book about wild-fowling, with its evocative text complemented by the scraperboard illustrations that begin each chapter and full-page colour reproductions of his paintings. Of the many books on the English countryside that B.B. wrote and/or illustrated, this is pehaps the most desirable.

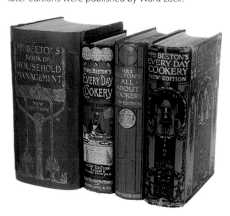

➤ The Compleat Angler, John Lane, The Bodley Head, 1897 and The Golfing Swing, Methuen & Co, 1913

Izaak Walton's *The Compleat Angler* first appeared in 1653 and is still in print. Fishing is one of the most popular sports around the world and with 350 years of continuous publication this book forms a collecting area in its own right and is probably the best-known fishing book ever written. This edition has illustrations by Edmund New. Burnham Hare's *The Golfing Swing* is a highly collectable period piece and one of the best short manuals ever written on golfing technique.

➤ *The Second World War, Vol. 1*, Cassell, 1948

First published by Cassell between 1948 and 1954, Winston Churchill's magisterial six-volume work, *The Second World War*, was an instant success on both sides of the Atlantic. After losing his position as prime minister in the post-war general election, Churchill used his new-found leisure time to produce this magnum opus. What it lacked in distance and judiciousness it gained in immediacy and passion, and as a writer on the subject Churchill is unequalled. It is the only English-language account of the War by a national wartime leader, whose reputation remains largely unsullied. It was extensively reprinted, and additionally made available through several book-club editions. Interest in the subject in today's market is undimmed; condition is as important as ever but reprints are acceptable, and cost less.

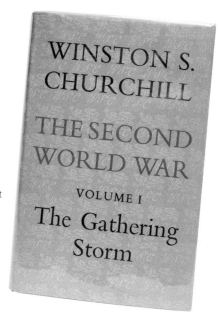

◄ *The Jack the Ripper Handbook*, Great Scot Services, 1999 and *Trial of Craig and Bentley*, William Hodge, 1954

Over a century has passed since the so-called "Ripper Murders" took place, and the flow of books on the subject shows no sign of abating. The identity of the serial murderer is still uncertain, which accounts for much of the subject's continuing fascination. Ross Strachan's *The Jack The Ripper Handbook: A Reader's Companion* is an essential bibliographical guide to the wealth of material published on the serial killer. For those whose interest is more in the legal process than the police procedures, the *Notable British Trials Series* must form a major part of any such specialist collection. *The Trial of Craig and Bentley*, edited by H. Montgomery Hyde and first published in 1954, is an important – and still controversial – addition to the series.

➤ *The Philosophy of Andy Warhol*, Harcourt Brace Jovanovich, 1975

The Philosophy of Andy Warhol (From A To B & Back Again) is very much the artist's testament. A commercial illustrator, Warhol first came to public attention with his *32 Campbell's Soup Cans*, which both parodied and celebrated our consumer society. This volume is signed by the author, which always adds value. Warhol has also included a sketch of a soup can; any doodle or drawing, particularly by an artist, will increase interest. One of the pioneers of Pop Art, Warhol's fame has lasted considerably longer than 15 minutes, and items like this are likely to remain desirable.

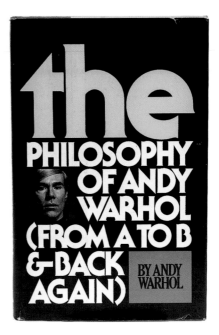

BOTTLES

Blue ribbed, "NOT TO BE TAKEN" poison bottle, c.1900; after 1863 it was required to label bottles thus.

The 19th-century Industrial Revolution created a vast consumer society in the UK, keen to try all manner of new food and drink ideas thrust upon it. Once-regional fare reached all corners of the land, ably aided by an extensive railway system and mass-production techniques in almost every industry. Now yesterday's trash has become today's collectables – empty pottery and glass bottles and jars are just a fraction of the Victorian and Edwardian products being discovered by bottle diggers in a hobby that began in the USA and Australia in the 1960s. These sturdily constructed containers, if undamaged before burial, generally withstood the rigours of up to 200 years beneath the grass. Unfortunately, the easy pickings (diggings) on the sites of the old city and town dumps have been thoroughly exhausted by keen shovel-wielding enthusiasts. But with luck, and perseverance, it is still possible to find and dig smaller village or farm sites, once permission is granted, or try car boot (garage) sales and specialist bottle fairs. You can discover some vibrant glass colours, unusual eye-catching shapes, unique designs, and many weird and wonderful patent ideas.

◄ Lord Brougham reform flask, c.1830–40
The 1832 Reform Act heralded better living-standards for most working-class English folk. Various politicians, royalty, and even music-hall stars were immortalized in these semi-figural spirit flasks made by London and Derbyshire potteries. Over 100 different designs are recorded but not all are marked; the one illustrated bears inscriptions relating to a specific public house in Sheffield. Once familiar with old salt glaze it is easy to identify reproductions, though these are not to be confused with the less collectable shiny brown Rockingham-glazed versions of the 1860s.

➤ Dark olive-green pontilled hamilton, c.1820–40
American William Hamilton is accredited with inventing the round-ended, egg-shaped "hamilton" bottle. It will not stand up, thus the cork is kept moist, and the mineral water retains its fizz. This simple but effective invention lasted over 100 years until the crown cap closure became the most popular replacement worldwide. Standard aqua (pale-green bottle glass) types are quite common; the earlier pontilled versions and the later, vividly coloured, dark-blue, green, or amber glass versions are considered rare.

▲ Marble-stoppered codd bottles, c.1880–1910
Hiram Codd's ingenious marble-stoppered bottle (patented 3rd September 1872) revolutionized the mineral-water trade worldwide. "Wallop" was the cheap beer of the day and the drink was dubbed "a load of coddswallop" – a soft option to ale. Today the word is derogatory, meaning nonsensical. Many patent variations appeared, as well as coloured-glass versions (blue, brown, green, even black), plus some with just a very striking coloured-lip section. Thousands have been dug up – testament to their phenomenal success and practicality.

▼ Ginger-beer bottles, one with a penny farthing pictorial, the other a blue-top, blue-transferred version.

Stoneware bottles helped keep ginger beer refreshingly cool, and were mass-produced in their millions in London, Bristol, Derbyshire, and Scotland, to quench an insatiable thirst in towns and villages throughout the UK, USA, South Africa, and Australasia. Most feature a tan top with black transferred lettering, but those with pictorial trade marks or brightly coloured tops are highly prized. A law suit in 1928 over the discovery of a snail shell led to the speedy demise of "stone pop".

▲ One of only five recorded G.F. Langford coffin poisons, c.1871

The somewhat gruesome coffin poison patent, with nails around the top rim, was one of many weird and wonderful designs intended to prevent accidental consumption of products for external use only. Other distinctive shapes included a submarine granted letters patent in 1906, A.W. Martin's extraordinary 1902 patent (horizontal body with U-bend in neck), J. Wilson's 1899 triangular bottle with pronounced corner serrations, the dramatic 1894 "wasp waist" (patent no. 6324), and Carlton H. Lee's American creation – "the body of which is in ... the configuration of a human skull ... and at the bottom ... crossed bones".

▼ Aqua-glass "cottage" ink bottle, c.1880–1900

In 1840 the Penny Post was first introduced. By 1842 Joseph Gillot, "pen manufacturer to Queen Victoria" was making 70 million steel nibbed pens in his Birmingham factory to keep pace with the increasing popularity of letter writing. Glass and pottery companies rose to the challenge providing consumer-appealing containers for home use. Cottage shapes are found with various roof and window designs and there are a multitude of more available, less glamorous shapes, most featuring the burst "sheared lip" to grip the cork closure tightly. Blue, brown, green, and other pretty colour variations are worth seeking out.

▲ Bungalow footwarmer and mini muffwarmer

Early-Victorian brick-shaped bedwarmers (heated in the fireside oven, then wrapped in a towel or cloth) were superseded by more attractive transfer-printed types. The Bungalow design from the 1920s–30s reflected the in-vogue housing style, while the much rarer mini "Adaptable ... for muff or pocket" warmed ladies in the back of their horsedrawn coach, landau, or new-fangled motor car! Bourne Denby manufactured a number of figural examples, such as a rabbit, penguin, and fish. By the 1950s rubber had replaced pottery, which was in turn upstaged by the innovation and increased use of central heating.

BREWERIANA

A successful manufacturer ploughs its profits back into advertising. The by-product, from the 1850s–'60s onward, of this economic shrewdness is a host of ingenious ideas and assorted paraphernalia used to promote increased sales. The drinks industry in particular has been more prudent than most in conjuring up ways of luring more custom, ever since Sir Edward Landseer's painting *Monarch of the Glen* was used to promote Dewar's whisky. Yesterday's give-away and promotional novelties – back bar, wall-hung, and table-top "disposables" – designed to promote brands and decorate pubs, are today's potentially valuable collectables. The range of material available includes framed showcards, back bar figures, lamps, counter bells, ashtrays, matchstrikers, bar top jugs, labelled bottles, vesta cases, lighters, and more. Top of the alcoholic fields of collecting (and still churned out by major drinks companies) is anything to do with whisky – the older and smaller the manufacturers, the better. Guinness material from the 1950s and '60s is not far behind in popularity, followed by beer. Given the large volumes of items made a discerning and selective approach is essential, and restricting your search to anything pre-1970 is advisable. In this, as in every other field, beware of reproductions. Guinness in particular has inspired a range of Carltonware fakes that certainly won't be "good for you".

A good-condition Mocha-ware pint ale tankard, c.1860, as used in a Victorian "spit and sawdust" pub.

▼ Shelley pub jug, Bulloch Lade Whisky, c.1920
Bar-top pub jugs, used to hold water for whisky, are easily the most popular field within breweriana, with examples from the 1970s still relatively easy to find. However, it is preferable to select older examples, especially from very small distilleries, most long-since defunct. Doulton Lambeth made huge quantities of green-topped stoneware jugs for Dewar's – classics of their type and genuine antiques. Designs often reflect period styles, such as this unusual Art Deco-influenced, Shelley-made "Bulloch Lade Scotch Whisky" example.

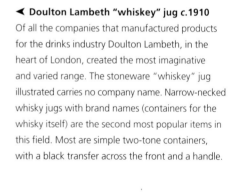

◄ Doulton Lambeth "whiskey" jug c.1910
Of all the companies that manufactured products for the drinks industry Doulton Lambeth, in the heart of London, created the most imaginative and varied range. The stoneware "whiskey" jug illustrated carries no company name. Narrow-necked whisky jugs with brand names (containers for the whisky itself) are the second most popular items in this field. Most are simple two-tone containers, with a black transfer across the front and a handle.

► A French Cognac Richarpailloud advertising fan, 1920s
The huge range of novelty products produced by the drinks companies from the Victorian period onwards is epitomized by this colourful and stylish, Moulin Rouge-influenced fan. Items that are outside the mainstream areas of whisky or beer are often less desirable, and thus more affordable for the beginner collector. Condition is of paramount importance, along with a visual appeal.

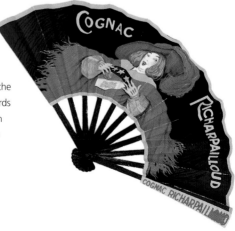

▼ Beefeater gin pourer, 1960s, and boy crown cap opener, 1950s

Novelty promotional items in the form of dispensers or openers, from the 1930s right up to the 1960s, form another field of breweriana collecting. The Beefeater pourer below is made by the Wade factory for the famous Beefeater gin brand. The turned wooden boy comes from the 1950s era, complete with top hat and moveable arms. Other variations on this theme were produced – the guardsman is another popular character. Ceramic brand-named whisky pourers have recently come into vogue – once a handful of different ones have been collected the search becomes more difficult, and more enjoyable!

▲ Promotional figures, 1950s–'60s

Often an antique product can be attributed, by a trained eye, to a particular period purely from its style. This striding Carltonware Double Diamond figure is unmistakeably from the 1950s; there are two versions, one with top hat, one without. The dapper Johnnie Walker gent, with his bright red coat and distinctive monacle, was first introduced around 1910, and is found in a multitude of sizes, from a giant 3ft (106cm) version, down to a tiny 3in (7.5cm) one, and made from various materials – wood, rubberoid, plaster compound, and plastic.

► Guinness toucan lamp, Carltonware, 1950s

Advertising agency S.H. Benson devised the "Guinness is Good for You" slogan in 1928. Artist John Gilroy produced a series of animal and zoo-keeper illustrations in the 1930s, most famously the toucan. Copywriter and crime novelist Dorothy L. Sayers provided the slogan: "How grand to be a toucan, just think what toucan do". In the 1950s and '60s Carlton Ware transformed these figures into a range of highly collectable ceramic novelties. They have inspired a wealth of reproductions, many displaying poor painting techniques – the yellow and orange are too vibrant and the gradation of colour is badly executed. Don't be duped by a Carlton Ware mark, which also appears on copies.

▲ Plastic Babycham promotional "Bambi" figure, 1960s

In the 1950s and '60s Babycham established itself as one of the major alcoholic drinks for ladies. The readily identifiable, and cute, "Bambi" figure proved an effective marketing tool, and was later utilized in television advertisements. The figure can be found in a surprisingly extensive range of items, made in pottery, plaster, brass, and plastic; the latter is the most commonly found, and was produced in a variety of sizes and different poses.

BUTTONS

From the earliest times buttons have been used for fastening and decoration – they have been found in Egyptian tombs and Henry VIII had a court costume sewn with 15,000 buttons. However, most collections begin in the 18th century, when dandies sported ornamental buttons measuring up to 4cms (1.5in) in diameter, and buttons were handmade in every medium from flax to fine porcelain. With growing mechanization in the 19th century Birmingham became centre of the industry, exporting buttons across the globe. Metal was a principal material, used for uniforms and servants' liveries. For the master and mistress there were beautiful silver and enamelled buttons – designed to be detachable for laundry purposes and often coming in handsome cases. Elaborate Victorian and Edwardian fashions stimulated demand, with special buttons for boots, gloves, and underwear, as well as decorative outerwear buttons in every style and medium. The 20th century saw the development of colourful plastic buttons, but with the introduction of zips and other new fastenings the quality and variety of buttons declined.

Silver and enamel button with Art Nouveau decoration, c.1905, popular in the 1900s when they were produced in box sets as gifts.

▲ **Mother-of-pearl button, c.1915–30**
Pearl buttons, made from mollusc shells, were mass-produced in the USA and UK from the 1880s. Pearl can be distinguished from plastic by its iridescence and heavier weight. Pearl buttons have been used for decoration by many indigenous peoples, from Native American "button blankets" to the button suits worn by London's "pearly Kings and Queens".

➤ **Cut-steel button (top) and silver lustre-glass button (bottom), 19th century**
A traditional part of court dress, cut-steel buttons made from tiny steel rivets were developed in the 18th century as a cheaper alternative to costly marcasite. However, steel is prone to rust, and from the 19th century silver lustre-glass was also used, leading to potential confusion. A magnet is the simplest way to distinguish between the two.

➤ **Victorian black-glass "French jet" button**
Queen Victoria's grief at the death of her husband, Albert, helped stimulate the fashion for mourning dress and black buttons. Very few were made from real jet, which was fragile and easily shattered. Black glass (also known as French jet) was more suitable and could be press-moulded into different patterns. Examine the back of a button – old ones tend to have metal shanks rather than holes. Usually, the heavier the shank the older the button, and brass wire also suggests an early date.

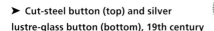

▲ **Art Deco plastic buttons, 1930s**
With the development of new materials (casein, celluloid, Bakelite) plastic buttons came into their own in the 1920s and '30s. Buttons were often large, with strong colours and geometric Art Deco shapes. Plastic also encouraged the production of children's novelty buttons. Plastic and many other vintage buttons are still very affordable.

CERAMICS

Wemyss Ware "Stuart" pot, c.1900; this Fife pottery was known for its floral and fruit designs, also used on models of pigs and cats.

1930s butterfly dish by John Beswick; delicate hand-painted wares such as this should always be checked for damage.

"Spanish Garden" by Jessie Tait for Midwinter; one of the best-selling patterns of the '60s, it is still in use in many homes today.

Ceramics are undoubtedly one of the most popular collecting areas, partly due to the huge volume of objects produced. The making of pottery is one of the earliest crafts known to man, and we have not looked back since. Who has simply one single mug or plate in their kitchen cupboards, for example? The fact that tableware is produced in sets creates a potentially limitless range of objects for collectors, to say nothing of the more purely decorative pieces, such as vases, figurines, and novelty items of all kinds, which can be found in virtually every room of every house.

The most important initial advice for any collector is to focus on a specific area. One solution is to concentrate on a particular object – for example teapots, which can provide a fantastically varied and decorative display. Trios (matching cup, saucer, and side plate) are another good way of collecting teaware and of displaying the work of different factories. Small items such as egg-cups have the dual advantage of being comparatively affordable and small enough to permit the assembling of a huge range of styles and makers.

Some collectors choose a specific designer or factory, and then refine their selection even further within these defined categories. The Clarice Cliff enthusiast, for instance, might focus on a particular named pattern or a certain shape, such as conical sugar sifters. A Cornishware collector might major in storage jars. Others collect works from a certain period, perhaps concentrating on Art Deco wall masks or 1950s Midwinter. Another option is decorative themes, such as chintz or nursery ware. Such is the choice of material that there is something available for every taste and every pocket, and the selection of ceramics in this section (which runs from the 19th century right through to the modern day) represents only the tiniest fraction of the material on offer.

Once you've chosen a subject the best route is to get a feel for it before buying. Visit antiques shops, fairs, and auctions, where you can look at and handle material. Talk to dealers and other enthusiasts, find out about collectors' clubs, read books, and surf the internet. Learn to look carefully and examine pieces, both for marks and signatures and for any signs of damage. With all ceramics condition is crucial to value. The more experience you have, the easier it is to spot traces of restoration, or to recognize the tell-tale signs of a fake.

Condition is important when it comes to displaying items too. Many plates have been ruined by being hung on the wall with metal plate hangers. Always use plastic-coated hangers, keep china out of direct sunlight to avoid fading, and clean with care – particularly hand-painted material; there are horror stories told of whole patterns being lost in the dishwasher.

Although much china is destined for the collector's cabinet, one of the joys of collecting more recent or less valuable pieces is the pleasure of actually using them – for example sitting down to an authentically dressed 1960s dinner table. Whatever you decide to collect – enjoy!

1880s–1910s

By the end of the 19th century there had been massive expansion within the ceramics industry. The Victorian building boom and concern with sanitation stimulated demand for everything from tiles, to toilets, to sewage pipes; the success of these utilitarian products funded more artistic pottery at several commercial factories. The rise of the middle-classes and the development of ever more complicated eating habits led to a huge increase in the manufacture of tableware. There were special pieces for different foods, courses, and meals, ranging from the finest bone china (pioneered by Spode) to affordable transfer-printed earthenware. Mechanization brought mass-production: C.T. Maling, manufacturer of earthenware jam jars and bottles, turned out a reputed 800,000 pots per year. Reacting against industrialization and the period taste for excessive ornament, Arts and Crafts designers pioneered a return to hand-crafted techniques and simpler decoration and by the 1900s county potteries were reviving traditional, vernacular forms. Art Nouveau in turn inspired sinuous, naturalistic designs, and art pottery flourished alongside the more commercial ceramics.

Yorkshire pottery Burmantofts (1858–1904) produced art pottery from the 1880s; this elegant vase has a rich, oriental-inspired glaze.

Art Pottery

"Have nothing in your houses that you do not know to be useful or believe to be beautiful", advised William Morris (1834–96), pioneer of the Arts and Crafts movement that emerged in the 1860s and lasted until the 1930s. Potters were at the forefront of this philosophy, which was both aesthetic and moral, promoting "truth to materials" and seeking to restore the dignity of traditional handicrafts in a mechanized age. A host of small potteries sprung up across the UK, from Bretby in Derbyshire to Brannam in Devon. Even commercial factories, such as Minton and Doulton, established art studios. Under the influence of Morris, and the art critic John Ruskin, potters looked back to the medieval past, using ancient techniques and local materials – Sir Edmund Elton (1846–1920) dug clay from his own estate to model hand-crafted pots. Oriental art was another source: William de Morgan produced tiles inspired by ancient Iznik pottery, Bernard Moore experimented with Chinese glazes, and Christopher Dresser was influenced by Japanese design. Art pottery from this period is always highly collectable.

▲ **Ault wryneck vase designed by Christopher Dresser, 1880s**
Often regarded as the UK's first truly modern designer, Dr Christopher Dresser (1834–1904) supplied pieces for Linthorpe pottery and for Ault in Derbyshire. He adapted many of his highly sought-after and unusually shaped and glazed vessels from classical, Japanese, and pre-Columbian sources.

▼ **C.H. Brannam stoneware vase, c.1900**
C.H. Brannam was founded in 1879 when Charles Herbert Brannam took over his father's pottery in Barnstaple, Devon. His art pottery was decorated with carved *sgraffito* patterns that revealed the red body of the ware; blue and green were favourite glazes. Curving forms, scrolling decoration, and often marine-inspired imagery reflected the influence of Art Nouveau. Look for a mark and date on the base.

➤ **Minton Secessionist Ware vase, 1904**
Minton was established in 1783, and in the 19th century became a leading manufacturer of high quality earthenware and porcelain. In 1900 Leon Solon was appointed art director and John W. Wadsworth became his assistant. Together they developed the Secessionist Ware range, launched in 1902. These tube-lined ornamental pieces were decorated with flowing, vibrant glazes (purple and yellow were favourite colours), and stylized naturalistic motifs inspired by Viennese Art Nouveau. Secessionist Ware has become very collectable today. Genuine pieces bear a special printed "Mintons Ltd" back stamp, and printed numbers that relate to each individual design.

▲ **Moorcroft Florian Ware vase, 1902**
William Moorcroft (1872–1945) was art director for Macintyre & Co from 1898 until 1913, before leaving to set up his own Moorcroft pottery, which still flourishes today. This early vase typifies the style that made him famous. The peacock feather was a favourite symbol of the Aesthetic movement, used by Liberty's (who sponsored Moorcroft) in its textiles. The finely controlled, tube-lined pattern covers the entire piece, the palette is subtle, and decoration provides a perfect complement to form. Moorcroft from this period commands high prices.

▲ **Bretby trompe l'oeil nut dish, 1900–1910**
Bretby (1883–1997) was founded by Henry Tooth and William Ault and was known for its adventurous art pottery earthenware design, which won several international awards. The Derbyshire company produced a huge diversity of products, including art pottery vases, umbrella stands, jardinières, wall pockets, and other domestic items. Bretby also specialized in amusing novelty pieces, such as this nut dish; the range included 3D nuts, fruit, biscuits, and even cigarettes. The pieces are marked with a sunburst motif above the name Bretby.

William de Morgan tile panel, 1890s
As the leading artist potter of his generation, de Morgan's richly coloured tiles are hugely valued.

Church floor tiles were produced in Britain in the Middle Ages but with the Dissolution of the Monasteries in the 16th century the craft disappeared. In the 17th century Delftware tiles from Holland inspired the production of English tin-glazed tiles, and the art of transfer-printing tiles was discovered in the 18th century. But it wasn't until the 1840s, another golden age of church building, that tile-making enjoyed a true renaissance. Encouraged by Gothic architect Augustus Pugin, Minton produced encaustic floor tiles inspired by medieval prototypes, and invested in the new technique of pressing powdered clay-dust between two metal die – the standard tile-making process still used today. The housing boom of the 1880s, greater concern with hygiene, and a Victorian love of decoration all fuelled demand for tiles. Shops were tiled throughout for easy cleaning, and churches and public buildings made extensive use of floor and wall tiles. Tiles appeared everywhere in the home, from the drawing room fireplace to the bathroom. Many potteries produced tiles: styles ranged from hand-painted Arts and Crafts pieces such as the panel illustrated, to mass-produced wares. Maker, subject, condition, and rarity all affect value. The back of a tile can help with identification: look out for stamps, design registration marks, and even pencilled notes, indicating where the tile was to be placed.

Tiles

Doulton

Doulton was founded in 1815 when John Doulton and John Watts took over a small factory in Lambeth, London. The firm specialized initially in salt-glazed stoneware but made their fortune in the mid-19th century by supplying drain pipes for the campaign to provide cholera-infested London with an effective sewage system. Doulton's art pottery first appeared in 1871 at an international exhibition, and in the 1880s another factory was opened in Burslem, Staffordshire. By 1900 Doulton (which became Royal Doulton in 1902) was producing every form of domestic and industrial pottery, from the finest bone china to the ceramic kitchen sink – itself a Doulton invention. Such is the range of Doulton products that there is something for every taste.

◄ Royal Doulton vase with incised scrolling decoration designed by Frank Butler, 1908
The opening of an art department at Doulton had a major influence on the development of art pottery in the UK. By 1890 there were about 350 artists working at the factory – principal (and much collected) figures include Hannah Barlow and George Tinworth. In the early 1900s Doulton was advertising "New Style" pottery in the latest Art Nouveau fashion, as typified by this vase.

► Doulton Kingsware flask, 1914
This flask commemorates a flight over Sydney harbour and was made for Dewar's whisky merchants. From its earliest years Doulton supplied jugs and bottles to the drinks industry and John Dewar, the first man to bottle his own whisky, was a major client. Whisky jugs in Kingsware, a line of richly glazed pottery developed by Charles Noke, are very popular with collectors of breweriana. The picture of an aeroplane makes this vase particularly desirable.

Bargeware

▲ Bargeware inscribed teapot, 1914
Large teapots, sometimes holding as much as half a gallon of tea, were among the most dramatic items produced in Bargeware, and must have dominated the interior of a narrowboat. This example measures over 30cm (12in) high and is inscribed and dated. The miniature teapot on the lid was a favourite addition.

Bargeware, also known as Meashamware, is the name given to treacly brown-glazed earthenware decorated with applied pieces of clay. Used by the people who worked the barges along the inland waterways, Bargeware was a popular gift, often brought back from a journey. Typical shapes include teapots, jugs, mugs, and tobacco jars. The brown glaze was covered in moulded decorations in the form of flowers, grapes, pheasants, and even lizards and newts, crudely painted in pinks, blues, and greens. Many pieces have a cartouche applied to the side, impressed with printer's block letters. Inscriptions can include a date and the name of the recipient (if the piece was a specific commission), or a more generalized phrase, such as "A Present to a Friend" or "Home Sweet Home", if it was bought off-the-shelf. Bargeware was manufactured from the second half of the 19th century until the 1920s by small potteries in the Burton-on-Trent area, the Midlands, and the Cotswolds.

Mocha Ware

Named after the mocha stone – a type of chalcedony said to have come from Mocha in Arabia – Mocha Ware was produced in large quantities from the late 18th century until the first half of the 20th century. The fern-like decoration was formed by dabbing the pot when the slip was still wet with a mixture known as "tea". This was said to contain tobacco spittle, manganese, orange or lemon juice, and somtimes even urine – every potter had his own particular recipe. The tea fanned out on the wet surface to create tree-like patterns, and further decoration was added in the form of black rings, or sometimes impressed clay badges indicating the liquid capacity of a tankard. Typical base colours include green, brown, and café au lait. Though jugs and mugs are the most commonly found pieces, Mocha was used to produce other everyday domestic ware. It can also be known as moss, tree, or fern pottery.

▲ Mocha Ware jug, *c.*1910
Mocha Ware was produced by many different factories and this Edwardian jug is by T.G. Green (makers of Cornish Ware). In the 19th century jugs and tankards were very inexpensive to buy. Although used in the home, much of this functional pottery was made for public houses – a possible reason for why it can be hard to find today, since many items were broken and discarded after use.

Torquay Pottery

Torquay Pottery is a generic name given to wares produced by a group of potteries situated in and around the Torbay area of Devon, including Aller Vale, Dartmouth, Lemon & Crute, Longpark, and Watcombe. Favourite products included decorative pottery and motto ware, aimed predominantly at visitors to the coastal resorts. The first pottery was Watcombe, established *c.*1867, which produced unglazed terracotta wares in a classical style with the local red clay. In 1881 an art pottery opened at Aller Vale, which used traditional methods and produced hand-thrown wares on a wheel. In 1901 Aller Vale and Watcombe merged and a host of other potteries sprang up in the surrounding area to meet demand for motto wares and Torquay-style pieces. The industry flourished in the inter-war years, but by the 1960s most potteries had either switched to mass-production or ceased trading.

◄ Aller Vale vase, 1910
Potters at Aller Vale looked back to a local, rural past. They were inspired by traditional country pottery, reviving ancient methods and creating forms such as tygs and udder vases. The technique of slipware had been used in the West Country since the 17th century, and in this hand-thrown vase it is given a modern twist, creating a fashionable Art Nouveau pattern on an elegant shape.

◄ Aller Vale Devon motto ware
As well as producing art pottery, Aller Vale also made motto ware. Though this advertisement dates from 1952, pieces in this style were produced from the late 19th century onward to attract the burgeoning tourist market. The red clay ware was slip-dipped and inscribed with *sgraffito* decoration and sayings, often in self-consciously vernacular language. Early examples are the most desirable as they are rarer; later pieces were manufactured in their thousands.

Decorative Ware

The development of the railways and the introduction of bank holidays in 1871 caused tourism to flourish, and everyone wanted to bring back a memento of their day out. Saucy fairings were a favourite gift, and commemorative mugs and ribbon plates were typical souvenirs. In the 1880s W.H. Goss developed a new kind of porcelain for the visitors' market: ivory-coloured miniatures, hand-painted with crests of British towns and inspired by artifacts of local interest. Portable and affordable, Goss was a huge success and a host of other companies leapt on the heraldic bandwagon, producing a stream of crested china in the form of everything from animals to newfangled inventions such as aeroplanes. Collecting crested china became a national hobby, peaking in the Edwardian period when an estimated 90 per cent of British homes contained at least one miniature, and ending with the Depression in the 1930s, when many factories either switched production or shut down altogether.

◄ W.H. Goss Norwich urn, *c.*1885–1929
Goss was aimed predominantly at the middle classes. Pieces were high in quality, sober in style, and academic in subject matter. Goss copied ancient artifacts from British museums, and a description of the original source was usually inscribed on the base or side of the Goss vessel. Many of these pots can still be purchased for under £10 ($15). Goss also produced a series of seven cottages – exact reproductions of famous British homes – which can fetch three-figure sums.

➤ Arcadian "cats on a see-saw", *c.*1925
Other crested china companies targeted a more popular market. Novelty designs reflected perennially favourite themes (such as seaside subjects), as well as contemporary events and fashions. World War I inspired a host of military miniatures, from tanks to zeppelins – much sought-after by collectors today. Post-war there was a craze for "lucky" souvenirs.

▼ Lithophane by the Royal Berlin factory, *c.*1850
Invented in France by Baron Paul de Bourgoing in 1827, a lithophane is a translucent porcelain plaque presenting an indistinct moulded design that becomes visible when held up to the light, to reveal a 3-D grisaille picture. Typical subjects include famous paintings and views. The image was carved in wax then encased in plaster to create a mould for the porcelain. Also known as "Berlin transparencies" (the Royal Berlin factory was a major producer), lithophanes were hung on windows and set in lampshades and souvenir mugs.

▲ Fairing inscribed "Going, Going, Gone", *c.*1880
Fairings are small porcelain groups, made as cheap gifts and fairground prizes. The golden age of the fairing was 1860–1900, when large fairs were in their heyday. A ceramic precursor of the comic postcard, subjects were often humorous and vaguely risqué, frequently concerning the trials of love. Although an English popular favourite, most fairings were made in Germany where the principal manufacturer was Conta & Boehme. Values are affected by subject matter, rarity, and quality. Earlier pieces tend to be better modelled than late-19th-century examples, and the clarity of caption is also important.

1920s–1930s

The years between the two World Wars were a golden age for decorative, affordable china. Catering to the needs of young newly weds (traditionally the biggest buyers of tableware), ceramic manufacturers responded to the fashionable Art Deco movement with new geometric shapes and bright, "jazzy" colours – tango orange was a favourite shade. Innovative patterns were inspired by everything from Cubist painting to textiles; wall masks and slender china figurines mirrored the look of the 1920s flapper. Fun came to the dining room, particularly at breakfast and teatime, in the form of novelty tableware: serving dishes were moulded into flowers, and teapots were created in the shape of automobiles and country cottages. Nursery designs by artists such as Mabel Lucie Attwell and Barbara Vernon (creator of "Bunnikins") flourished. Women had traditionally been employed as paintresses in the potteries, but now they came to the fore as designers and directors. While fine works by big names can command high prices, so much was produced during the period (there were over 400 potteries in Staffordshire alone) that ceramics can still be found at affordable prices.

This 1929 vase by Dutch firm Gouda displays the Samarat pattern; its bright colours and bold design are typical of Art Deco.

Leading Designers

Clarice Cliff (1899–1972) is perhaps the most collectable designer of Art Deco ceramics. She joined the firm of A.J. Wilkinson in 1916, where she caught the eye of her boss (and later husband) Colley Shorter. He set her up in her own studio, and 1928 saw the launch of the "Bizarre" range. The brilliant patterns, hand-painted by Clarice and her team of "Bizarre Girls", captured the mood of the moment, were affordably priced, and hugely successful. Susie Cooper (1902–95) was another remarkable designer and businesswoman. After working at Gray's she founded her own pottery in 1929, pioneering stylish and functional modern tableware complemented with subtle decoration that was purchased by everyone, from royalty downwards. Where Clarice fans are often seduced by pattern, those who love Susie speak of design. Form rather than decoration was key to the art of Keith Murray (1892–1981), and even in the 21st century his simple, architectural vases still look modern. Other major names of the period include Charlotte Rhead (1885–1947) and Eric Ravilious (1903–42), whose transfer-printed designs for Wedgwood are increasingly popular.

▲ Clarice Cliff "Crocus" bowl, 1930s

The "Crocus" pattern was Clarice Cliff's most successful design. "We worked in a team at a bench", recalled paintress Rene Dale. "A piece would be passed down the line, with each girl painting a different coloured crocus, but we all had to join in with green leaves because there were so many of them!" The "Crocus" pattern was produced in quantity, and in different colourways, and simpler pieces can provide an affordable introduction to collecting Clarice Cliff.

► Clarice Cliff "Secrets" sugar shaker, 1930s

Conical pieces are among the most desirable of Clarice Cliff shapes, though condition is crucial – always check the tip, holes, and base for damage. An added attraction here is the all-over "Secrets" pattern. In terms of value, the ideal combination for Cliff ceramics is a rare shape on a rare pattern, and exceptional pieces can fetch thousands of pounds.

➤ Susie Cooper Kestrel coffee pot, 1930s

"When I started there was nothing available between fine china that was very expensive and ordinary material that was very poor", remembers Susie Cooper. "I wanted to do nice things for people who had taste, but didn't have the money to satisfy it". Printed with the "Patricia Rose" pattern, this coffee pot in the Kestrel shape shows the commitment to form, function, and subtle decoration that distinguished Cooper's work, both in the 1930s and post-World War II. Transfer-printed pieces can be as collectable as earlier hand-painted designs.

▼ Charlotte Rhead "Persian Rose" vase, 1930s

Charlotte Rhead is the final figure in the triumvirate of famous female designers of this period. Born into a family of potters, she learnt many techniques from her father, Frederic Alfred Rhead, including tube-lining – a distinctive feature of her work. Charlotte worked for many different potteries, including Wardle & Co, Bursley Ltd, Elgreave Pottery, and Burgess and Leigh, and in 1931 she moved to A.G. Richardson, makers of Crown Ducal Ware. Sought-after pieces include nursery ware, chargers, and vases. This Crown Ducal vase is typical of her decorative style. The bold, textile-influenced pattern came in different colourways and on various shapes.

▼ Susie Cooper Gray's Pottery coffee cans and saucers, late 1920s

Susie Cooper made her name in the 1920s with boldly decorated pieces in strong colours, reflecting the influence of Cubism. Though she herself much preferred her more practical, later products and dismissed such early designs as "crude", they are much sought-after by collectors. Most pieces are marked with her name and those made for Gray's also include the Gray's galleon mark. 1932 saw the introduction of Cooper's famous leaping deer mark – one of the icons of 20th-century pottery design.

➤ Keith Murray vase, 1935

While many potters embraced Art Deco's jazzy patterns, Keith Murray's sculptural pots were more in the spirit of the Bauhaus. Born in New Zealand, Keith Murray moved to England and trained as an architect. He designed glass for Whitefriars and was employed by Wedgwood from 1933. His most notable ceramics are vases – clean geometric shapes, hand-thrown and decorated on an engine-turned lathe, which gives them their distinctive ridges. Glazes are muted and subtle; colours include straw, white, green, and, more rarely, blue, grey, brown, and black. His simple, modernist designs are much sought-after.

Crown Devon

Crown Devon was the trade name used by the family firm of S. Fielding and Co (1873–1982). A 1930s advertisement seduced with the words "Crown Devon – Economic prices, delightful colour schemes harmonising with modern designs …". Under the directorship of Arthur Ross Fielding, the firm produced a vast range of table and gift ware, tapping into every fashionable trend. Handsome vases were decorated with exotic gilded patterns; salad ware, modelled on leaves, echoed the designs of Carlton Ware (see p40). Successful and collectable novelties included musical mugs and jugs, and decorative teaware such as beehive honey pots. Well-modelled, Deco-style female figures were advertised as "suitable gifts for ladies", while novelty presents for men included cased smoker's sets with matching cigarette box, ashtrays, and coffee cups.

◀ **"Orient" vase, 1930s**
"Orient", introduced in the mid-1920s, is one of Crown Devon's finest patterns. The strong colours and geometric motifs, enhanced with gilding, epitomize the exotic face of Art Deco. This vase came in four sizes and should be checked inside and out for discoloration and the condition of the gilding.

Burleigh

▶ **Novelty golf jug, 1930s**
Burleigh's jugs were all hand-painted by individual decorators. The quality of design and detail affects a piece's value – a golfer in chequered plus-fours is more desirable than the same figure in plain trousers. The golfer's uniform of cap, sweater, and colourful plus-fours, was popularized in the 1920s and '30s by Edward, Prince of Wales, a keen golfer and dandy.

Burleigh Ware is the trade name used by Burgess and Leigh, established in Staffordshire 1851 and one of the few potteries still in family ownership today, under the name Burgess, Dorling and Leigh. The inter-war years were an extremely productive period. The firm employed some 500 workers and leading designers included Charlotte Rhead, Harold Bennet, Charles Wilkes, and Ernest Bailey. Products ranged from handsome Art Deco tea sets in distinctively angular shapes to cottage ware. Among the most collectable ceramics today are novelty jugs with handles in the form of birds, animals, and figures. The sporting series is particularly desirable, appealing to sports enthusiasts as well as ceramic collectors, and subjects include golf, tennis, and cricket.

Maling

Maling pottery, based in Sunderland and then Newcastle on Tyne from 1762 to 1963, made its fortune in the 19th century when Maling discovered a mechanized process for making pots for foods, medicines, and other commercial products. By 1862 nearly all jam and marmalade jars in the UK were produced by Maling. Though this business declined in the 20th century, Maling still flourished under Lucien Boullemier and his son, with pieces ranging from transfer-printed tea caddies to rich lustre ware.

◀ **"Chinese Lanterns" wall plaque, 1937**
Large chargers or wall plaques were a favourite Art Deco feature, and Maling produced a series of different designs. This example is decorated in rich enamels in a desirable colour-combination, including blue and pink. The tube-lined decoration (formed by piping liquid clay from a bag) is fragile and should be checked carefully for any damage.

Decorative Teaware

Drinking tea reached its height of popularity in the UK in the 1930s, when the population consumed an astonishing 10lbs (160oz) per head per annum – the equivalent of five cups a day for every man, woman, and child. Owning two tea sets was commonplace in many homes: earthenware for daily use, and fine china for best. For the children's tea there was cheerful nursery ware and for grown-up breakfast-in-bed the tête-à-tête, or "tea-for-two" service. Teapots were produced in an infinite variety of shapes and patterns, ranging from new patented designs, which promised greater stability and less dribbling, to comic pots in the form of nursery rhyme characters. Jam pots and cruet sets were another favourite vehicle for novelty decoration, and are popular with collectors today. Tea plates were produced in huge profusion; hand-painted examples can still be found in charity shops, and provide perhaps the cheapest way of starting a collection of Art Deco pottery.

▲ Carlton Ware cheese dish and vase, 1930s
This relief-moulded earthenware was a best-selling line for Carlton Ware in the 1930s. Colourful pieces were modelled on leaves and embossed with flowers and fruit. Some patterns, such as "Apple Blossom" (pictured above), sold in large quantities. Less successful designs, such as "Cherries", were made for a limited period only and are prized by collectors. Popular as gift ware, this china often came in presentation boxes, which are also now sought-after.

▲ Royal Winton "Hazel" Chintz ware teapot, 1934
Chintz ware – china decorated with all-over floral patterns – was made by many factories in the 1930s, but Royal Winton, owned by Grimwades, is perhaps the most famous name in the field. The first transfer-printed chintz, "Marguerite", was produced in 1928, followed by over 50 other patterns. Designs were inspired by period textiles, and according to legend the company head paid factory girls a shilling a time to copy their prettiest pinafores. Designs with a black ground, such as "Hazel", were produced in comparatively limited numbers and are therefore popular today.

▲ Cottage ware cheese dish, 1930s
The 1920s and '30s saw a vogue for Cottage ware: china modelled in the form of the archetypal English country cottage with thatched roof and roses around the door. Cottage ware was produced by many different factories, including Price, SylvaC, Carlton Ware, and Beswick; this dish is by Royal Winton. Though English in inspiration, Cottage ware was also made elsewhere, most notably in Japan for the export market. Look out for different shapes (biscuit barrels and cruet sets).

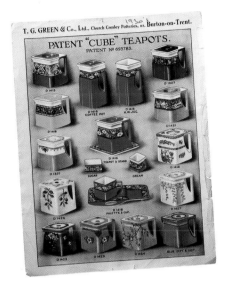

◄ Cube teapots advertisement
The cube teapot was patented in 1916 by R.C. Johnson as a safety teapot. It was used on the Cunard ship liners because it was easy to stack and did not tip over when on stormy seas. The pots were also purchased in their thousands by Lyons Corner House and other cafés. Cube teapots were produced under licence by many firms; the examples shown on this advert are from a 1930s T.G. Green catalogue.

▲ Sadler racing car teapot, c.1937
Sadler's racing car teapot, with its famous OKT42 number plate, was first made in 1937. The most common colours are green, yellow, and cream; rarer glazes include black, blue, grey, pink, and maroon. Up until 1939 all pots were finished in a platinum lustre. Post-war, chrome plating was largely abandoned in favour of a cheaper, sponged, mottled glaze, and the number plate was no longer applied. Production ceased in 1952. Values reflect the rarity of the colour.

➤ "Bunnykins" plate, Royal Doulton
Introduced in 1934, "Bunnykins" was created by Barbara Vernon, daughter of Doulton director Cuthbert Bailey, and inspired by stories he told her as a child. Barbara became a nun and her drawings of rabbit characters were submitted from the convent. By 1939 there were 66 different scenes in production and after World War II the range was expanded by various Royal Doulton designers, resulting in a hugely successful line of nursery ware and figures.

Whistling egg cup, Czech, 1930s
Novelty egg cups in lustered earthenware were made for export in Europe and Japan. Designs based on cartoon and film characters, or those with rockers or a working whistle, are very collectable.

The advantage of egg cups is that they are small, allowing the enthusiast to assemble an extensive collection with comparatively little space or expense. It was in the 19th century that eggs became a British breakfast favourite. Mrs Beeton recommended boiling an egg for 3–4 minutes for adults and 3 minutes for children and invalids. "An egg boiled very soft is not unwholesome", agreed Mr Woodhouse, father of Jane Austen's heroine Emma, and a famous hypochondriac. Egg cups were made in a wide range of materials, from porcelain to silver, but it was in the 1920s and '30s that the novelty egg cup truly came into its own. Often destined for the nursery, egg cups were modelled in the form of animals, figures, and even film stars such as Laurel and Hardy. Double egg cups could be turned over, one end used for hen's eggs and the other for larger goose eggs. Smart china egg cup sets came with miniature egg-shaped salt and pepper shakers, and a matching under plate. Values depend on design, maker, and condition. Egg cups are often unmarked because of lack of room on the base. Many novelty designs were also produced abroad and are likely to be unstamped, or simply inscribed "foreign".

Egg Cups

Novelty China

The 1920s and '30s saw a craze for novelty china, and not just on the tea table. Walls were decorated with face masks inspired by African art (an important influence on Art Deco), and modelled on movie stars and fashionable ladies. There were wall-pockets for flowers, and plaques in all shapes, from bouquets to galleons. Another classic motif was the crinoline lady who, from the 1930s to the 1950s appeared in numerous forms, from pottery teapots to embroidered tray-clothes. Shelves were decorated with figurines and animal models. Vases and posy holders came in innumerable geometric styles – the addition of a flower block compensating for the more unmanageable shapes. The growing habit of smoking (among women as well as men) also led to ceramic novelties, ranging from Bonzo-shaped tobacco jars to ashtrays decorated with playing card symbols, reflecting the period craze for bridge and other card games.

▲ Goldsheider face mask, 1930s
The Austrian firm of Goldsheider (1885–1953) was known for producing finely modelled face masks in hand-painted terracotta. These are very collectable and have been faked, so always buy from a reputable dealer. Other important manufacturers include Royal Dux, Goebel, Beswick, and J.H. Cope and Co.

▼ SylvaC Scottie dog, 1950s
SylvaC was the name first used in the 1930s by the Staffordshire firm of Shaw and Copestake (est. 1894). Its factory, the Sylvan Works, ceased trading in 1982. The company was known for fancies and novelty designs, animals in particular. Over 200 different dogs were produced, covering most breeds, but the most famous SylvaC creatures were rabbits, which came in different sizes, designs, and colours.

Shelley

▼ "Vogue" trio, 1930
Though the look of this "Vogue" trio was highly fashionable, the solid triangular handle was hard to hold and the wide bowl meant that tea cooled too quickly. "Vogue" had a short production run (1930–33) and this quintessentially Art Deco design is now very collectable. This example has the added bonus of an unusual hand-painted pattern.

▲ "Harmony" ginger jar, 1930s
The ginger jar was a favourite Art Deco shape. This example is in the "Harmony" pattern – a successful design said to have been inspired by accident when a decorator dropped some paint. Colours were dripped onto the shape as it turned on the wheel, creating a characteristic streaky design. Other colour schemes included pink, green, and blue.

Shelley (1872–1966) manufactured a wide range of high quality tableware in the 1920s and '30s. Elegant bone china tea sets were influenced by the latest geometric styles: tea plates were squared and cups from the modern "Vogue" and "Mode" ranges came with solid triangular handles. More comfortable to hold, and more successful, was the Queen Anne shape (from 1926) which had a curved, hollow handle and an octagonal panelled body. Shelley produced a huge range of patterns, from the free-style, hand-painted "Harmony" to transfer-printed chintz designs. Nursery pieces were another strong line, with decorations by well-known children's artists, including Mabel Lucie Attwell. All wares are marked; the design of the printed back stamp and the painted pattern numbers on the base provide a useful guide to dating.

Myott

Founded in Staffordshire *c*.1898, Myott, Son and Co was a family business run by two brothers, Ashley and Sydney Myott. In the 1920s and '30s, as well as producing traditional tableware, Myott developed a range of adventurous Art Deco designs. Innovative shapes, such as vases in the form of fans and pyramids, were combined with strong period colours. Orange, green, yellow, and brown were typical shades, and designs were hand-painted in a bold, free-handed style. In the inter-war years the firm collaborated with Goldsheider and The British American Glass Co and in 1976 Myott merged with Alfred Meakin. Vases and jugs are among the most popular Deco wares. Most Myott pieces are marked on the base with a crown motif.

◄ Myott Bowtie vase, 1930s
The Bowtie vase was a Myott speciality. This unusual design is much sought-after and also came in a version fitted with a handle, to form a jug. Originally this vase had a ceramic "frog", or flower block, fitted inside to hold blooms in place. With Myott products the more inventive the design the higher the value. Condition is crucial, since hand-painted pottery is prone to chipping and damage.

Radford

► Radford vase, c.1930
Vases and posy bowls were manufactured in large quantities by Radford Handcraft Pottery. The same design often appeared on different sized vessels and in different ground colours. The firm specialized in stippled backgrounds, which, like everything else, were applied by hand. They came in a range of soft colours including green, blue, pink, and fawn. This hand-thrown vase is painted with the "Broom" pattern.

Born into a family of potters, Edward Radford (1882–1969) trained at Pilkington's Tile Company. After serving with distinction during World War I, he worked for Wood & Sons who helped him set up the Radford Handcraft Pottery in Burslem, Stoke on Trent *c*.1930. The company focused on ornamental wares, using both traditional and more modern Art Deco-inspired shapes. A major selling point was that no two pieces were ever identical, since everything from throwing to painting was done by hand. Typically, vases and other objects were decorated with floral designs under a matt glaze, although bright glazes were also used. Popular patterns included "Anemone", "Clematis", "Delphinium", and "Poppy". Geometric gold and silver patterns are rarer and much sought-after by collectors today. Pieces are usually signed "Radford" and may also feature an artist's mark. Edward Radford retired in 1948 but his designs continued to be produced until the 1960s.

Cornishware

T.G. Green, established at Church Gresley, Derbyshire, in 1864, specialized in utilitarian earthenware. In 1926 it introduced a range of blue-and-white striped china called Cornish Kitchen Ware – a name suggested apparently by a salesman who claimed the colours reminded him of "the blue of the Cornish skies and the white crests of the waves". The clean, modern design became an instant classic, and the company's most famous line. A huge variety of items was produced, from plates to rolling pins. The pins were not a success since the raised stripes marked the pastry but today such rarities are highly prized. Cornish Kitchen Ware is still in production.

◄ Cornish Kitchen Ware storage jar, 1930s
Lettered storage jars were produced in profusion; the more unusual (such as Lux and Macaroni) command high prices. Green also experimented with other colourways including yellow and buff, and rare colours, such as red and black, are very sought-after. Various marks were used, including a shield-shaped mark in green and black, replaced in 1968 by a target design.

1940s–1950s

When wartime restrictions were lifted demand for ceramics boomed. "You may fashion style your table with the latest tableware just as you would buy the latest style in dress design," declared Roy Midwinter, who created some of the most innovative British tableware of the 1950s. Midwinter's inspiration came from the USA, where Eva Zeisel and Russel Wright were pioneering organic shapes and mix-and-match colours in everyday crockery. These industrial designers also influenced the Scandinavian potteries, which produced multicoloured oven-to-tableware, and stackable, affordable china to meet the needs of a new, servantless generation living in small apartments, and embracing a more informal lifestyle. Alongside this pragmatic focus on stylish mass-production there was a growing interest in craftsmanship. Small potteries such as Rye and Hornsea were established in the 1940s; major commercial factories, from Gustavsberg in Sweden to Poole in England, also ran artistic studios, producing experimental, hand-painted pieces that are very sought-after today. Post-war ceramics range from elegant, abstract designs to blatantly kitsch novelties, each in their own way reflecting a desire for the "New Look".

Designed for Beswick by Albert Hallam, these zebra-striped vases with their bright interiors and bold asymmetric shapes epitomize 1950s style.

Midwinter

Midwinter, established in 1910, is one of the most collectable names in 1950s commercial pottery. Inspired by American ceramics Roy Midwinter launched the ranges Stylecraft (1953) and Fashion (1954), which introduced organic shapes to the British table. Teapots were curved like pregnant women, and quartic dinner plates came without rims, making them easier to decorate and popularizing the American custom of shaking salt over the food, rather than piling it on the edge. These modernist forms required contemporary patterns. The firm's resident designer, the talented Jessie Tait (b. 1928), devised dozens of predominantly abstract decorations, much imitated by rival firms. Midwinter also commissioned other artists and, helpfully for collectors, certain backstamps list the name of both pattern and designer.

▼ "Riviera" coffeepot, Sir Hugh Casson, 1954
Roy Midwinter commissioned artist Hugh Casson (1910–99) to produce a series of drawings in France, having admired his sketches of the Coronation. His naturalistic watercolours provided a refreshing change from traditional country cottage views. The illustrations, entitled "Riviera", first appeared about 1954 on the Stylecraft shape. They were later used in the Fashion series, to which this curvaceous coffeepot belongs, with a new name, "Cannes", and a white background rather than a honey-coloured glaze.

◄ "Saladware" plate, Sir Terence Conran, c.1956
The young Sir Terence Conran (b. 1931) created some of Midwinter's most exciting designs, proving, in his own words, that "there could be life beyond tea roses". "Saladware" (c.1956) was inspired by a set of Piero Fornassetti ceramics decorated with vegetables. With the abandonment of rationing, and growing interest in international cuisine, food and drink became favourite decorative subjects. Conran's Midwinter designs are very sought-after.

Meakin

James Meakin founded a pottery in Hanley in 1851. His sons, James and George, took over the family film (J.&G. Meakin), and a third son, Alfred, established an independent factory in 1874. Alfred Meakin specialized in mass-produced, domestic tableware. In the 1950s the company tapped into contemporary style, not with abstract patterns and organic shapes but with cheerfully escapist illustrations. Plates were decorated with Parisian cafes, fairground scenes, and Wild West characters, reflecting the period's lust for the exotic.

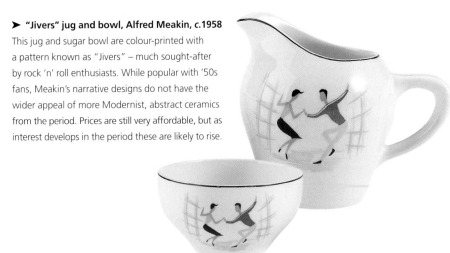

➤ **"Jivers" jug and bowl, Alfred Meakin, c.1958**
This jug and sugar bowl are colour-printed with a pattern known as "Jivers" – much sought-after by rock 'n' roll enthusiasts. While popular with '50s fans, Meakin's narrative designs do not have the wider appeal of more Modernist, abstract ceramics from the period. Prices are still very affordable, but as interest develops in the period these are likely to rise.

Russel Wright

Russel Wright (1904–76) was a leading US industrial designer. His American Modern tableware (1939) became one of the best-selling services of all time. "Good design is for everyone", insisted Wright. Working in a range of media he sought to bring quality to mass-produced household objects, pioneering a more informal domestic lifestyle. Services like American Modern, Iroquois Casual China (1946), and the 1953 melamine Residential influenced designers across the world.

◄ **American Modern ware, c.1950**
Russel Wright's American Modern tableware was produced 1939–59 by the Steubenville Pottery, Ohio, selling over 80 million pieces. Its organic shapes and mix-and-match colours set a period standard, as did Wright's marketing techniques. Rather than buying a whole service, customers could begin with an inexpensive starter set and return for more. Condition is crucial to the value of period pieces.

"Homemaker" plate, Enid Seeney, c.1955
Many "Homemaker" collectors begin with plates, produced in large numbers and still very affordable.

"Homemaker" is one of the most famous ceramic designs of the 1950s. Produced by Ridgways for Woolworth's general stores, the distinctive black-and-white china was launched in 1955. The designer was Enid Seeney (b. 1932), who, while studying at London's Royal College of Art, assembled a scrapbook of magazine pictures that inspired the "Homemaker" pattern. The design is a catalogue of contemporary household furnishing, as the kidney table, leggy plant stand, and tripod light were all period favourites; the sideboard resembles a Gordon Russel design, shown at the Festival of Britain in 1951; the armchair is based on a 1952 Robin Day recliner; and the sofa is inspired by a 1954 settee by Prince Sigvard Bernadotte. Motifs were placed on a black-and-white background, which was both fashionable and practical since the scratchy lines helped conceal imperfections in the ceramic body. "Homemaker" was an instant success, and was produced on different shapes until about 1970. Popular with collectors today, the highest prices are reserved for rarer items such as tureens, coffeepots, and teapots (made in limited numbers), and for any other non-standard products.

"Homemaker"

Poole

Poole pottery, initially called Carter and Co, was founded in Poole, Dorset in 1873. In 1921 it became known as Carter, Stabler & Adams, and from 1963 the name Poole was used. In the 1950s the company made a radical break from the floral designs of the pre-war period. Design director Alfred Burgess Read (1898–1973), and chief thrower Guy Sydenham created freeform vases decorated with abstract, textile-inspired patterns in cool, harmonious colours that epitomized contemporary taste.

◄ **Freeform bowl, 1950s**
Poole's freeform range reflected the period fashion for organic and asymmetric shapes. Hand-painted patterns by designers such as Herbert Read and Ruth Pavely complemented the swelling vessels. Subtle colours of grey, acid yellow, brick red, and turquoise were typical of the 1950s palette. These pots still suit the modern interiors of today, and handsome examples can command high prices.

Rye

In 1947 John and Walter Cole took over the Belleview Pottery in Rye, Sussex. The brothers were specialists in expensive studio pieces and ceramic historian W.B. Honey complained, "Why don't you produce something good that I can use rather than putting in a showcase?" At Rye they did just that: "We tried to bring craft and artistry to everyday pottery", said Walter. "We wanted to make decent, affordable tableware that Stoke-on-Trent couldn't produce." Rye's hand-crafted, majolica tableware sold across the world.

➤ **Lambeth squares-and-stars tankard, 1950s**
"At Rye we made traditional tin-glazed earthenware, every piece hand painted, inspired by English Delft, Lambeth and Liverpool," explained Walter Cole (1913–99). This tankard is modelled on an early piece of Lambeth pottery. Rye was exhibited at the Festival of Britain in 1951, and sold through shops such as Heals and Liberty.

Denby

Denby, founded 1809 and famous for salt-glazed stoneware, responded to changing post-war tastes, with both mass-produced tableware and studio pieces. Hungarian designer Tibor Reich designed Tigo-ware in 1956. The crisp black-and-white striped range was boldly organic in form, with harlequin-coloured interiors – everything the contemporary coffee drinker could wish for. More traditional was "Green Wheat" – a naturalistic pattern on oven-to-tableware created by Albert Colledge in the mid-'50s and exported worldwide.

◄ **Glyn Colledge tankard, early 1950s**
In 1950 Glyn Colledge (1922–2000) took over the hand-decoration department at Denby from his father, Albert. The trade name Glyn Ware was coined, and this tankard painted with scrolling leaves in autumnal colours is a typical, neo-romantic piece. Colledge also produced more abstract designs, such as the matt black Cheviot decorated with sgraffito patterns, which is a rare and sought-after piece today.

Novelties

Ceramic production was limited in the UK and decorated ware was reserved for export until 1952, when demand for novelties reasserted itself and manufacturers targeted every level of the market, beginning with children. In 1954 Wade Pottery (est. 1910) launched their famous Whimsies series. Conceived as pocket-money toys, the miniature animal models sold in sets of five. They were an instant hit, inspiring a host of other figures produced both for retail and as free promotional gifts, appearing in bags of crisps and boxes of tea across the world. Beswick (est. 1894) was another company that catered to the decorative market, making a wide range of finely modelled animal figures inspired by nature and children's literature. Once the war was over Germany continued its long-established tradition of exporting ornamental figures and other ceramic novelties aimed at the popular market, and Hummels successfully invaded many British homes.

◄ Hummel Meditation figure, 1950s
Sister Maria Innocentia Hummel (1909–46) trained as an artist before entering a convent in 1931; her drawings of winsome country children continued to be published as post-cards. The West German Goebel Porcelain Factory negotiated the rights to turn her creations into figures. Launched in 1935, they were very successful in the post-war period.

▲ PenDelphin Fairy bookends, 1954
PenDelphin was started in 1953 as a hobby by Jean Walmsley Heap and Jeannie Todd. Models included witches, fairies, elves, and later the popular rabbit family, which transformed it into a full-time business. Early pieces and rare figures can fetch large sums.

▼ Wade Dumbo figure, 1950s
In 1955 Disney's animation *Lady and the Tramp* was a huge success and Wade obtained permission to produce models from this and other films, including *Dumbo*. Lady first appears in the film as a Christmas present inside a hat box, so the figures were put in circular, stripy boxes and known as the Hat Box Series.

▲ Advertisement for Beswick Beatrix Potter figures, 1950
In 1947 Beswick obtained copyright to reproduce Beatrix Potter's characters as small-scale earthenware figures. The first model, by Arthur Greddinton, was Jemima Puddleduck – launched in 1948 along with nine other animals. The series proved so popular that by 1977 all Potter's stories had been represented.

Peynet

There was a lust for romance in the post-war period, and Paris was an endless source of decorative inspiration. One of the most famous exponents of romantic Francophile imagery was Raymond Peynet (1908–99). Born in Paris, Peynet worked as a graphic designer for perfume and advertising companies. In 1942 he created "Les Amoureux de Peynet": a romantic couple (said to have been based on him and his wife) who became an institution, appearing on books, dolls, and jewellery.

◄ Nymolle "Lovers" plate c.1955
Peynet's famous couple also found their way onto ceramics. In 1952 he was approached by German company Rosenthal (est. 1879) to produce a range of figurines, vases, and decorative tableware illustrated with his popular figures. In the mid-1950s a series of eight designs (including the example shown left) was also produced, for the Danish company Nymolle (est.1936).

Scandinavia

Pottery from Sweden, Norway, Denmark, and Finland was widely exported in the post-war period, when Scandinavian Modern design became fashionable across the world. Major factories typically produced both commercial and studio ware. "Handicrafts and industrial production go hand in hand," advised Finnish designer Timo Sarpaneva. "We need human design, sensitivity and the power of machines." At Arabia in Finland (est. 1873) art pottery was created alongside Kaj Franck's "Kilta" ware (1953) – a famous range of affordable, stackable, mix-and-match modern crockery that appeared in every Finnish kitchen. It epitomized the Scandinavian philosophy of creating "more beautiful things for everyday use". Nature and landscape were big influences, both in terms of decoration and design. At Gustavsberg (est. 1825), Sweden's leading ceramics factory, designers such as Wilhelm Kage and Stig Lindberg pioneered the soft-form, organic shapes that came to epitomize the "New Look" of the '50s.

➤ Nymolle wall plaque by Bjorn Wiinblad, 1950s
Wiinblad was born in Denmark in 1918. He became well-known for his work at Danish factory Nymolle, moved to Rorstrand in Germany from 1957 until the late 1970s, and then returned to take control of Nymolle. Wiinblad's distinctive illustrations, often inspired by folk tales and story telling, attract many collectors, especially in the USA.

◄ Marianne Westman "Picknick" jam pot, 1950s
Rorstrand (est. 1726) was another major Swedish factory that employed many important designers, including Carl-Harry Stalhane, Gunnar Nylund, and Marianne Westman (b.1925), who won awards at three Milan Triennales. The jolly, graphic pattern celebrates both colour and food – a favourite motif once rationing was over.

▲ Stig Lindberg "Lov" dish, 1950s
Stig Lindberg (1916–82) was one of Sweden's most versatile ceramicists. Working at Gustavsberg in the 1940s and '50s, he designed both mass-produced tableware and individual craft pieces, with forms and patterns inspired by leaves and nature. Look for his hand-shaped, hand-painted monogram.

Continental Kitsch

The *Oxford English Dictionary* defines kitsch as "objets d'art characterized by worthless pretentiousness". The word dates from the 1920s but it was in the '50s that kitsch design truly came into its own. New mass-production techniques developed during World War II, combined with a post-war passion for fun and decoration, resulted in a positive avalanche of frivolous objects in every medium, including ceramics. Pottery wall plaques (a fashion started in the 1930s) were produced in vast numbers, and flying ducks flapped over living room walls. Favourite ceramic animals of the period (appearing as figures or vases) included long-necked cats, long-bodied dachshunds, and the curly poodle – symbol of romantic France. As well as elegant, organic designer ware, cheap and cheerful ceramics were turned out in continental potteries, their fashionably twisted shapes and bold colours supplying a contemporary look for the popular market. Exotic figures – Nubian slaves, Spanish matadors, and ballet dancers – were turned into pottery wall decorations and lamp stands. Bad taste is in the eye of the beholder, and for many kitsch is very collectable, and certainly far from worthless.

Colourful kitsch vases, 1950s
This cat-shaped vase and organic, abstract vase are both German. Much fashionable hand-painted ware was produced for export by West German potteries.

1960s–1970s

As with so many other things, ceramics were affected by the 1960s revolution. The organic soft-forms of the 1950s were replaced by streamlined geometric shapes, just as in fashion the boyish Twiggy created a new icon of curveless female beauty. "Cylindrical and conical shapes are appearing everywhere", noted *House and Garden* magazine in 1964, and the tall can-shaped coffee pot was a period favourite. Mugs increasingly took over from cups and saucers, reflecting more informal eating habits and the popularity of tea bags and instant coffee. Decoration was inspired by a huge range of sources. Influenced by Pop Art, designers favoured strong colours and a hard-edged graphic style. Typical motifs ranged from the Mary Quant Daisy, to the Union Jack, to Victorian prints. Psychedelia expressed itself in the use of technicolour pinks, oranges, and purples. Studio pottery flourished in the 1960s, in tandem with the rise of vegetarianism and the embracing of a more alternative lifestyle, and in the 1970s even the major commercial companies sought to give mass-produced crockery a hand-crafted, country kitchen feel.

Blue jeans were the favourite unisex garment of the period, appearing on this Denim Ware cruet set by Carlton Ware, c.1978.

Portmeirion

In the late 1950s Susan Williams-Ellis began designing ceramics for her gift shop in Portmeirion, the famous holiday village in Wales created by her father, Sir Clough Williams-Ellis. Her designs proved so popular that Susan and her husband, Euan, took over Grays Pottery (1960) and Kirkham's (1961), and from 1962 traded as Portmeirion Potteries Ltd. Portmeirion became extremely fashionable. The tall, cylinder shape of cups and coffee pots captured the look of the swinging '60s, and patterns were varied and imaginative, drawing on sources from Victorian engravings to Islamic pottery. In 1972 the company launched its famous "Botanic Garden" range, inspired by antiquarian natural history books, and still in production today. 1960s Portmeirion, particularly the more Pop-Art style pieces, is sought-after by collectors.

► **"Chemist Print" mug, 1960s**
In the 19th century Kirkham's produced pot lids and containers for patent medicines. Susan Williams-Ellis discovered their original copper plates and used them on china that epitomized Pop-Art fashion and the trend for Victorian revivalism. Portmeirion produced several ranges inspired by turn-of-the-century prints and postcards; "Comfortable Corsets", inspired by Edwardian underwear advertisements, is collectable.

◄ **"Totem" coffee pot, 1960s**
The "Totem" pattern, launched in 1963, was an immediate best-seller and established Portmeirion's success. The name, and raised abstracted designs, suggested some form of primitive symbolism, and the translucent flow glaze was inspired by Victorian embossed tiles. This amber brown was a very popular colour. "Totem" was also produced in blue, green, pewter, and white (sought-after by collectors today). It was the mainstay of the company in the 1960s and many tableware shapes were added to the range.

Poole

The Poole pottery studio expanded in the 1960s under the artistic directorship of Robert Jefferson. Together with thrower Guy Sydenham, and designer Tony Morris who joined the company in 1963, Jefferson launched the Delphis range in the early 1960s. The shapes were hand-thrown, inspired by modern studio pottery and contemporary art. Textures were incised into the wet clay and works were hand-painted with abstract patterns in bright, psychedelic glazes (orange was a particular favourite).

◀ **Poole Delphis bowl by Pamela Bevens, 1960s–'70s**
The commercial Delphis range was discontinued in 1980 but developing interest in 1960s style has stimulated demand for Poole's psychedelic products. The company encouraged decorators (often from local art schools) to create their own patterns. Pots were sometimes marked with a signature or initials, which can increase value if it refers to a big-name designer.

Troika

▶ **Troika "Coffin" Vase, 1960s**
Troika fell from fashion in the 1970s and the firm closed down in 1983. However, in the 1990s it was rediscovered by antique shops and has become increasingly collectable, particularly the more abstract pieces. Troika potters saw themselves as artists/craftsmen and each pot was conceived as an individual, sculptural work of art. Look for the Troika mark, and the initials of the specific designer.

Troika was founded in St Ives in 1963 by sculptor Lesley Illsley, potter Benny Sirota, and architect Jan Thompson – hence the name, which means triumvirate. Although the local crafts establishment prophesized instant failure, the firm lasted 20 years selling innovative, hand-crafted pottery to leading stores across the world. Experimentation was combined with practicality. Clay was mixed in a second-hand bakery dough mixer, and unusual shapes were devised to pack the kiln as closely as possible. Troika was known for its distinctive, moulded forms and sculptural, abstracted style. Inspiration for design, colour, and texture came from the paintings of Paul Klee, other contemporary art, and the Cornish landscape.

Hans Coper

Hans Coper (1920–81) was one of the most important post-war potters. Born in Germany he came to England in 1939, but was arrested as an alien during World War II and sent to Canada. However, he returned and served with the British Army. Coper met fellow refugee and potter Lucie Rie in 1946 and worked with her until setting up his own studio in 1959. "Cabbage years", remembered Rie, describing their early poverty when they made pottery buttons to survive. "Cabbage for lunch and dinner." From 1963 to 1975 Coper taught at Camberwell and the Royal College of Art, where he had a huge influence on his pottery students.

◀ **Hans Coper Cycladic form, 1975**
"My concern is with extracting the essence", claimed Hans Coper. His work was poised between pottery and sculpture: surfaces were often unglazed and rubbed with oxide, giving them a natural, stone-like quality. Forms were dramatic and beautifully balanced. Coper was a perfectionist, destroying anything he felt was not up to scratch, so his work is rare and carries a premium. Look for the "HC" seal on the base.

Patterned Plates

Mass-produced crockery was decorated with a wide range of printed patterns that reflected the various fashions of the time. Kathy Winkle (b. 1932) was chief designer at James Broadhurst and Sons. Her abstract patterns (rubber stamped and then hand-coloured) provided a perfect complement to Scandinavian-style teak furniture. Contemporary art was another important influence: tableware was decorated with black-and-white Op-Art designs, and with multicoloured Pop-Art motifs. The hippy trail kindled interest in eastern styles of art, and designers also looked to the past, using Victorian and Art Nouveau patterns.

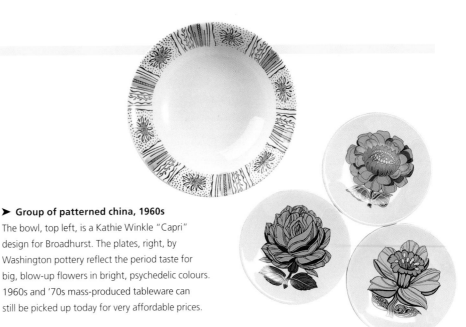

➤ **Group of patterned china, 1960s**
The bowl, top left, is a Kathie Winkle "Capri" design for Broadhurst. The plates, right, by Washington pottery reflect the period taste for big, blow-up flowers in bright, psychedelic colours. 1960s and '70s mass-produced tableware can still be picked up today for very affordable prices.

Carlton Walking Ware

In 1967 Carlton Ware Ltd was sold to Arthur Wood and Sons. With an oil crisis and industrial disputes, the early 1970s was a difficult time for many companies, but Carlton Ware flourished thanks to the introduction of a novelty line: Walking Ware. This teaware on legs was designed by husband-and-wife team Roger Michell and Danka Napiorkowska. They developed the idea at their own Lustre Pottery in 1973, before linking up with Carlton to mass-produce the design. With its Mary Jane shoes and colourful socks, Walking Ware was very successful, and the range was expanded to include "Running", "Jumping", and "Standing Still" services. A number of different designs were produced within each service.

◄ **Walking Ware plate, 1970s**
While tea cups and egg cups are fairly common in the Walking Ware ranges, rarer pieces include plates and a biscuit barrel. Teapots are also sought-after by collectors. The success of Walking Ware inspired imitators, so look out for the Carlton Ware or Lustre Pottery mark on the base to ensure the piece is genuine. Condition is also important to value, since the feet were prone to damage.

Hornsea

➤ **"Saffron" storage jars, 1970**
The "Saffron" pattern, launched by Clappison in 1970, captured the period fashion for country-style kitchenware. By the late '60s Formica counter tops and colourful lino were being replaced by wooden surfaces and terracotta tiles, and brown pottery was a top accessory. Storage jars such as these (which can still be picked up in charity shops) are also appearing on antique stalls as classic examples of '70s style.

In 1949 brothers Colin and Desmond Rawson set up a little pottery in their terraced house in the East Yorkshire town of Hornsea. In 1954 they moved to factory premises and in 1958 John Clappison became design director. Hornsea became known for contemporary, hand-decorated designs, expressing a period taste for textured patterns. By the late 1960s the firm was mass-producing tableware, although it maintained a hand-crafted appearance.

1980s to present

From the 1980s onward ceramic companies have been affected by changing eating habits, a more informal lifestyle, and cheap foreign imports. The fashion for nouvelle cuisine in the 1980s, when food was required to be decorative, stimulated demand for simple white plates. Thanks to the current vogue for minimalism and industrial-style steel kitchens these plain designs remain a favourite choice. While modern kitchens might contain all manner of gadgets, from pasta-makers to woks, they are less likely now to have a large traditional service of matching tableware. At home, as in fashion, the trend is to pick-and-mix, and potteries such as Bridgwater (est. 1985), producing pretty crockery sold as single pieces or small sets, have flourished. Teaware continues to stimulate novelty designs, and another developing area has been "limited edition" decorative ceramics, targeted at the collectors' market and ranging from fine designs to aesthetic monstrosities. Interest in studio ceramics is strong, and with potter Grayson Perry winning the Turner Prize in 2004 the division between art and craft is becoming increasingly blurred.

Emma Bridgewater teapot, 1990s; Bridgewater pottery revived traditional techniques such as sponging and stencilling.

➤ **Sally Tuffin "Double Dove" charger for Dennis China Works, 1996**

Sally Tuffin (b.1938) established herself as a fashion designer in the early 1960s when she and Marion Foale set up "Foale and Tuffin" in Carnaby Street, one of the trendiest labels in "swinging" London. The partnership was dissolved in 1972 and Tuffin turned to ceramics. She and husband Richard Dennis set up their own pottery studio in 1985 before buying a share in Moorcroft, where Tuffin was design director from 1986 to 1993. She left to establish the Dennis China Works. Inspired by traditional Arts and Crafts pottery, Tuffin's hand-thrown, hand-decorated works are very popular with collectors.

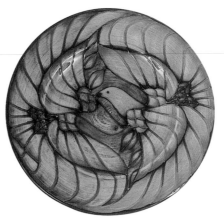

▼ **"Just for You" Royal Doulton figure**

Royal Doulton first began producing their series of figurines in 1913. Each model was given an "HN" registration mark (after chief colourist Harry Nixon) and a number, starting with HN1 for "Darling", the first model produced. It seems that, stylistically, very little has changed. "Just For You" (HN4236), modelled by John Bromley, is from the current "Pretty Ladies" range. As with most Royal Doulton figures, the design harks back to a chocolate-box vision of the past that attracts collectors worldwide.

◄ **Red Baron teapot by Carlton Ware, 1980**

Postmodernism stimulated interest in whimsical design, and manufacture of novelty teapots flourished in the 1980s. This sought-after Red Baron teapot was produced in different colourways (representing aircraft from different countries). Another well-known and very collectable Carlton Ware line from the 1980s was a range of teaware inspired by puppets from the *Spitting Image* TV series created by Roger Law and Peter Fluck. These satirical pieces include Margaret Thatcher and Ronald Regan teapots (*see* p60), and egg cups and items inspired by members of the royal family.

CIGARETTE CARDS

One of a set of 12 "Pretty Girls" cigarette cards issued by Salmon & Gluckstein, London, in 1900.

Cigarette cards, originally introduced as packet stiffeners, were a regular feature in cigarettes and some tobacco pouches from the 1880s to the outbreak of World War II. Many of the most prized examples come from the late Victorian and Edwardian periods. Since most smokers were men, the cards reflected interest in subjects such as sport, war, and female beauties. The heyday of production was in the 1920s and '30s, when women also took up smoking and cigarette card collecting became a huge craze. Some of the more common cards by Players, Gallagher, and Wills were produced in their millions and many still survive today. The value is dependent on the scarcity of the cards – many collectors look for cards with errors or variations. As with any ephemeral collectables condition is paramount. Common cards need to be in EX (excellent) or MT (mint) condition; older or rarer cards are more acceptable in lesser condition but this still affects their value.

◄ Duke's miniature novelties, 1891

This early American card is from a set of 25, each featuring a lithographic pair of small novelties of beautiful women on common household or sporting objects. The design for this issue was used earlier by a rival company, who issued them as individual, smaller die-cut designs in 1888. Such shared use of designs was commonplace under the umbrella tobacco companies of A.T.C. in the United States and B.A.T. in the UK. Both companies still dominate the tobacco industry today.

➤ Taddy "Prominent Footballers", 1907

These two cards are from an extensive set of approximately 1,400 cards issued for three seasons, listing all league players. The football market is very fan-based and there is a premium on cards from the more popular teams such as Arsenal and Manchester United. It is worth noting the variety of the backs of the cards, which is the only indication of the year of issue. The 1908 series adopted the footnotes that were lacking on the 1907 issue; the 1914 cards were issued only with the London Mixture brand, and are much scarcer and therefore worth at least double.

FELIX WEINGARTNER

NAPOLEON.

◄ Wills' variations, 1914

Both of these sets were designed and printed immediately prior to the outbreak of World War I and diplomatic sensibilities dictated that German sympathies were not reflected in any sets. The original set of 50 "Musical Celebrities" included eight German composers and singers but these were swapped for celebrities from more sympathetic nations. The other set was designed to commemorate the centenary of the battle of Waterloo in 1814. Owing to the shift in alliances, and with the outbreak of war imminent, it was judged prudent to cancel the run in case it displeased the French. Some sets of cards were printed but never issued, although they have still ended up in the hands of collectors. Both the cards shown are official reproductions of the original cards and are worth very little in comparison to the real thing. Authorized reproductions such as these can be identified by looking at the back of the cards for the name of the company (often Nostalgia Reprints or Victoria Gallery), a recent date, and a statement that this is a reproduction. Such reprints allow collectors to buy sets that would otherwise be too rare or too expensive. However, do beware of cards that have been reproduced to deceive – look carefully at the print quality as reprints are often flatter in colour.

➤ Wix Kensitas "Flowers", 1930s

This issue of woven silk panels from the early 1930s reflects the variety of cards produced. These silk cards were issued in three sizes (the one illustrated being postcard size), and were contained in cream-coloured folders with information on the two flowers in each panel. They were printed mainly in Eastern Europe, and, consequently, the occasional peculiar colour variations for these English flowers can make for some highly sought-after cards.

DOUGLAS WRIGHT
KENT

◄ Post-WWII issues – Turf (1948–56) and Doncella (1977)

Rationing during World War II and the immediate post-war period seriously curtailed the production of cigarette cards. One of the first sets to be made after the war was that for Turf cigarettes by Carreras (far left). In an effort to save paper they were printed in blue on the slider of the cigarette packet (the inner portion that pushed out, like a matchbox), as opposed to being on a separate card. The cards were often then trimmed to standard size but are worth slightly more with their original tabs. By the 1970s Players and Wills were the last of the regular issuers of cards; most from this period are larger in size and were often found in packets of their cigar brands such as Doncella, Grandee, and Embassy.

COCKTAILS

Plastic pineapple ice bucket – a favourite of the 1950s and '60s; earlier ones have glass linings.

The word "cocktail" first appeared in the USA in the early 19th century, but it was in the 1920s that cocktails truly came into their own. Prohibition resulted in the manufacture of huge amounts of illicit alcohol. To conceal its often poor taste Americans took to mixing their drinks, and the colourful cocktail became the drink of the Jazz age. Barmen wishing to escape the Depression took cocktails to Europe, and the American Harry Craddock established London's first cocktail bar in the Savoy Hotel. The drink in turn inspired new fashions and accessories. Cocktail parties (and cocktail dresses) were all the rage, and the cocktail cabinet became a favourite piece of living-room furniture, containing drinks of every type, glasses of every shape, a cocktail shaker, and related accessories. Cocktail drinking went out of fashion during World War II but came back again in the fun-loving '50s, with the addition of battery-powered shakers and pin-up motifs.

▲ "Keyhole" pin-up drinking glasses, 1950s

The term "pin-up" was coined during World War II, when servicemen pinned up pictures of glamour girls in their quarters. The 1940s and '50s saw an explosion of pin-up imagery in every form, often on objects associated with drinking. These glasses are desirable to collectors of 1950s kitsch. Look through the keyhole in the back and the lady on the front of the glass can be seen in the nude. Never put such items in the dishwasher, since you risk losing not just the girl's clothes but the whole image!

► Red Bakelite cocktail shaker, 1930s

After the repeal of prohibition in 1933 cocktail shakers were produced in vast profusion, becoming a symbol of American glamour. They were made in sterling silver and shiny chrome, came in novelty forms from penguins to Zeppelins, and in new materials such as Bakelite. The red colour makes this example particularly desirable. The silver-plated top is inscribed with the recipe for a Manhattan – a whisky-based cocktail that has been drunk, along with Cosmopolitans, by the New York heroines of the television series *Sex in the City*.

◄ Sparklets Hostmaster soda syphon, 1960s

Various patents were granted for soda syphons in the 19th century and in 1901 a US magazine advertised "A 20th century idea – a soda syphon in every home". However, it wasn't until the 1960s that soda syphons became a fashionable domestic standard; this popular model came in many colours. Vintage syphons are worth more with their original box and accessories; always check for external or internal damage.

◄ Chrome and Bakelite cocktail sticks, 1930s

Cocktail ephemera produced in the 1920s and '30s is popular with Art Deco collectors as well as drinks enthusiasts. Cocktail sticks were a favourite period accessory and often came in novelty forms; this 1930s chrome and Bakelite set is modelled as a wheelbarrow. Cocktail sticks were used both for drinks and the miniaturized cocktail food that appeared in the 1930s, when a Fortnum and Mason's catalogue proudly announced the introduction of the cocktail sausage!

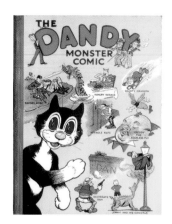

The Dandy Monster Comic no. 1, 1939, introduced the fun-packed adventures of characters such as "Korky the Cat", "Desperate Dan", and "Keyhole Kate".

Children have read comics and annuals for over a hundred and thirty years, getting their laughs from publications such as *Funny Folks* in 1874, *Magnet* and *Gem* in the 1900s, and *Adventure, Hotspur, Rover,* and *Wizard* in the 1920s. December 1937 heralded the first issue of *The Dandy Comic* and it proved so successful that it was followed just six months later by *The Beano*, which managed to keep going throughout the war – coming out every other week due to the paper shortage. The 1950s were a golden age for British comics in particular. *Eagle, Girl, Lion, Tiger, Topper,* and *TV Comic* were all born, their large, colourful pages holding youthful sway over a generation of children still using ration books to get their sweets at the corner shop. The now infamous character "Dennis The Menace" was introduced into the *Beano* in 1951, and anyone who didn't know "Desperate Dan's" favourite meal went straight to the back of the class! In 1959 American comic-books were distributed in the UK for the first time, and they were an instant hit. The super-hero genre took over and *Batman, Superman, The Amazing Spider-Man, The Incredible Hulk, The Fantastic Four,* and *The Uncanny X-Men* were soon flying off the shelves. Today their adventures are marvelled at by an even wider generation, as the movie industry cashes in on spin-offs from the original stories.

▲ **The Magnet, Amalgamated Press, 1908–1940**

It was in *The Magnet* that Charles Hamilton, alias Frank Richards, created his most famous character – "William George (Billy) Bunter" of Greyfriars School. Always in trouble, and without a redeeming feature, this mischievous boy was never further than an arm's length from pinching another pupil's food, or shy of borrowing a few pennies from the nearest gullible chum. When the long-awaited repayment failed to materialize chastisement was usually swift and heartfelt! The no. 1 issue is by far the most valuable at £100 ($150), depending on condition.

▼ **The Beano Comic no. 1, D.C. Thomson, 1938**

The Beano is perhaps the most popular UK comic of all time and is still in print today. Characters such as "Big Eggo", "Pansy Potter", "Minnie the Minx", "The Bash Street Kids", "Dennis The Menace", and his dog "Gnasher" have all become household names, endearing themselves to generations of children over the last 65 years. Only a handful of first issues have turned up in that time, and only one Whoopee Mask free gift survives. In March 2004 £12,100 ($18,150) was paid for a no. 1 issue – a world record auction price for a British comic.

Action Comics © DC Comics, Inc.

▲ **Action Comics no. 1, National Periodical Publications, December 1938**

Issue one of *Action Comics* claimed the origin and initial appearance of "Superman" – the first superhero to appear in American comics. His creators, writer Jerry Siegal and artist Joe Shuster (teenagers from Cleveland, Ohio), had tried to get him published for five years. Finally National took them on and "The Man of Steel" became one of the most successful characters of all time. Issue one is the most highly prized comic-book from the US Golden Age (1938–54), and has a book value of hundreds of thousands in near mint condition.

◄ *Detective Comics* no. 27, National Periodical Publications, May 1939
Created by Bill Finger and Bob Kane, the character "Batman" did not have the benefit of super-powers – instead he relied on his brains, his athleticism, and a sophisticated array of gadgets concealed within a menacing bat-costume that struck fear into the underworld fraternity. "Robin, the Boy Wonder" was introduced 12 issues later as Batman's sidekick and the "dynamic duo" were to defeat crime for generations to come. Copies of this particular issue sell for tens of thousands, depending on condition.

➤ *Captain America* no. 1, Timely/Marvel Comics, March 1941
Patriotism was the order of the day in the USA in the early 1940s and Joe Simon and Jack Kirby personified this perfectly with the creation of "Captain America". With a hero dressed in a stars-and-stripes costume and shield, and a cover showing a timely right hook to Hitler's jaw, there was no doubt as to the comic's contents. The Germans and the Japanese were defeated on a weekly basis by "Cap" and his gallant young ally, "Bucky". When World War II ended the title went through a weird/horror phase before Captain America went on to tackle the "communist hordes" in the 1950s.

▼ *Amazing Fantasy* no. 15, Atlas/Marvel Comics, August 1962
This issue sees the first appearance of "Spider-Man", drawn by Steve Ditko and written by Marvel editor Stan Lee. Perhaps the first comic character to suffer feelings of angst and insecurity, the teenage Peter Parker struck a chord with ordinary school kids and achieved massive popularity overnight. His own title, *The Amazing Spider-Man*, followed within six months and is still going strong today, with movie and merchandise tie-ins.

▲ *The Eagle* no. 1, Hulton Press, April 1950
The Eagle is best known for its intrepid cover character, "Dan Dare – Pilot of the Future", who, aided by his jolly sidekick, "Digby", fought his battles against the fearsome Venusians in outer space. Created and drawn by co-founder Frank Hampson, the series was extremely successful and a million copies of the comic were produced each week, at least in its early years. This first series of *The Eagle*, which also included the adventures of "PC 49" and "The Riders of the Range", lasted until 1969.

▲ *Oor Wullie* book 1, D.C. Thomson, 1940
Oor Wullie was first published in 1936 in the "Fun Section" of the Scottish *Sunday Post* newspaper. Created by legendary artist Dudley D. Watkins, the wee terror's adventures mirthfully mirrored life in working-class Glasgow, and he ended many an adventure chased and admonished by the long-suffering police constable Murdoch. The first book contains three years of early newspaper strips and there are only a handful of copies known to exist. A clean copy can fetch into the thousands at auction.

COMMEMORATIVES

The suffragette movement's demands for a vote for women was inspiration for potters (in this case Doulton) from 1907 to 1918.

The vast majority of commemoratives are to be found in ceramic form, the potter drawing inspiration from subjects as varied as royalty, politics, war, religion, exhibitions, disasters, expeditions, and sport. The earliest recorded, dated examples relate to the coronation of Charles II in 1660, although an earlier, undated plate depicting Charles I has also recently come to light. It was the invention of transfer printed decoration in 1756 by Sadler and Green of Liverpool that revolutionized decorated ceramic production and thus made available cheaply produced pottery and porcelain to a wide audience. King George III, his recovery to good health, his Golden Jubilee, and subsequent death, together with contemporary wars and political scandals, became subjects for the early commemorators. The potter has continued to record so many varied events, a recent example of which is the Golden Jubilee of HRH Queen Elizabeth II. A commemorative collector should focus on the event and also the rarity of a particular piece. While quality of manufacture is important it plays a less significant part in determining the value of commemoratives, especially those dating from before 1861 (the death of Prince Albert). Anything satirical is always favoured by the collector, especially if of political interest. The scope of material available is enormous and when starting a collection it is a good idea to identify a theme, subject, or particular monarch and concentrate on that.

➤ Tin depicting William Gladstone, 1894

Queen Victoria developed a special relationship with many of her prime ministers but nevertheless she was well known for her stubbornness. This tin pictures several of the cabinet in Gladstone's final administration of 1893–4. Commemorative tins date back to the latter part of the 19th century and continue to be produced today to mark various events. Condition, especially for the early printed ones, is all-important as they are prone to scratching and rust disfigurement.

▼ Plate showing Disraeli, late-19th century

The octagonal pottery plate, popular from 1884 to 1897, was manufactured by a variety of potters. Wallis Gimson of Fenton was the most prolific, producing a range including Victoria, the Prince of Wales, and a variety of political and other famous personages of the day. Here prime minister Disraeli is depicted inscribed with his title, Right Hon. Benjamin Disraeli, Earl of Beaconsfield KG, and his favourite flower, the primrose. The cheaper variety lacked the colour decoration and gilt rim.

◄ Staffordshire pottery pot lid, 1851

Staffordshire pots were the brainchild of Felix Edwards Pratt of Fenton and his engraver partner Jesse Austin. They first produced underglaze colour picture prints on pottery lids in the mid-1840s, and by the time of the Great Exhibition in 1851 were unsurpassed in the field. This one depicts the exhibition's famous Crystal Palace venue. Today the 400 or so different designs are highly prized by collectors of both pot lids and commemoratives.

▼ Toby jug of Marshal Foch and woven silk panel, 1914–18

Patriotism during World War I was high, and many mementos and artifacts were manufactured to raise money for the war effort. Sir Francis Caruthers Gould designed a set of 11 toby jugs, each depicting a famous Allied commander. They were manufactured by Wilkinson Ltd and sold by Soane and Smith of London. This one depicting French commander Marshal Foch is the most common, and that of the South African Louis Botha the rarest. The woven silk panel showing the Allies' flags is desirable when the colours are strong and material undamaged.

▲ Mug by Kent of Edward VIII with modelled handle, 1936

Although never crowned, Edward VIII remains one of the most popular monarchs for commemoratives. He succeeded his father, George V, on 20th January 1936, whereupon the potters went into overdrive producing commemoratives for his coronation, scheduled to take place on 12th May 1937. In abdicating on 10th December 1936 he presented the potter with a windfall, not only to overstamp existing stocks with details of his abdication, although such pieces are rare, but to produce a new range for the coronation of his younger brother George VI and Queen Elizabeth. Mugs were produced with their portraits and a GR handle.

▶ Festival of Britain powder compact, 1951

Post-war austerity in Britain lasted a number of years but the centenary of the Great Exhibition of 1851 was the perfect opportunity to help the nation back onto its feet. So it was that the Festival of Britain (a series of exhibitions and displays throughout the land) came about. The Festival's famous logo, designed by Abram Games, is depicted on the cover of this powder compact. The event was an enormous success and a wide variety of commemorative souvenirs were produced that attract specialist Festival of Britain enthusiasts.

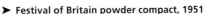

▲ Coronation mug by Eric Ravilious, 1953

Eric Ravilious (1903–42) was an accomplished designer who worked for Wedgwood, among others, and his designs for the coronation mugs of Edward VIII and George VI remain popular. This mug, marking Elizabeth II's coronation in 1953, was produced posthumously and is a variation on his Edward VIII design, with changes to the date and numerals in the monogram. It remains one of the most evocative and highly prized commemoratives of this event.

◀ Churchill biscuit tin, c.1955

Winston Churchill is upheld to this day as the greatest Britain of all time, as confirmed in a recent UK television vote. On his death in 1965 he was accorded a state funeral, a privilege previously reserved for only two other commoners, Nelson and Wellington. He was a favourite of the commemorator because however he was depicted it was obviously him, but the usual way was to show him in morning jacket, bow tie, smoking one of his famous cigars, and often sporting a Homburg hat. The huge interest in commemoratives associated with this statesman reflects his appeal to all generations.

◄ **Car bumper sticker for the Kennedy election campaign, c.1960**

The art of electioneering in the USA has been taken to new levels, from the bumper stickers of the 1960s to today's live television debates. Kennedy was a very popular president and his assassination in 1963 ensures that he remains arguably the most famous. The fact that this bumper sticker, produced in vast numbers, is of value is solely because it bears his inked signature – not that of a secretary or autopen but the genuine mark of Kennedy himself. There is a considerable market for collectables of this charismatic leader.

► **Signed photograph of the Apollo 11 astronauts, 1979**

In the hot summer of July 1969 the world watched on flickering television screens as Neil Armstrong and "Buzz" Aldrin walked out of the Apollo 11 spacecraft and onto the surface of the moon. The now legendary words "One small step for man, one giant leap for mankind", uttered by Neil Armstrong, marked this historic event. It was widely commemorated by potters, but any other associated ephemera, such as this photograph of Armstrong, Aldrin and fellow-astronaut Michael Collins, is highly prized, especially when signed by the astronauts themselves.

◄ **Luck and Flaw Regan teapot and Aynsley Thatcher plate, 1980s**

The "special relationship" that existed between Ronald Regan and Margaret Thatcher is well documented. Thatcher became the first UK woman prime minister in 1979 and was widely commemorated for her achievements, as is demonstrated with this plate by Aynsley. Few foreign politicians find favour with British commemorators and the satirical TV programme *Spitting Image*, created by Luck and Flaw, was inspiration for potters who, in 1981, made this white pottery teapot and cover (another depicting the "Iron Lady" can be paired with it). There is great demand for such commemoratives and the *Spitting Image* items remain the most collectable of all modern political pieces.

► **Signed photograph of Diana, Princess of Wales in Zimbabwe, 1993**

One of the most famous names in the world, Diana remains a very popular figure in today's collectables market. Signed photographs, cards, and letters by the Princess are especially popular. A great deal of printed material exists, as well as documents signed with an autopen, so the collector should be aware of these and strive to find unusual pictures and cards that have a genuine ink signature, with personal salutations where appropriate.

COMPACTS & COSMETICS

Biba was one of London's most famous fashion stores in the '60s and '70s; demand is high for its Art Nouveau-style packaging.

Throughout history women have enhanced their looks with cosmetics. In ancient Egypt kohl was used to emphasize the eyes and protect them from sunlight, while from the Roman period to the 18th century ladies whitened their complexions with chalk and lead. Victorians were more cautious, pinching their cheeks instead of using rouge, and restricting themselves to a dab of cold cream. Cosmetics flourished after World War I. Like the cocktail shaker and the cigarette holder, the little powder compact became a symbol of the "roaring twenties" with its Art Deco enamels and compartments for powder, lipstick, and cigarettes. Compacts became larger in the '30s, designed to be slipped into a clutch bag, and were made in every style. Production halted during World War II but resumed in the '50s, when ladies were expected to look perfect and showed no compunction about powdering their noses in public. With changing fashions, modern plastics, and disposable containers, compacts became first outdated and then collectable. Novelty designs often command the highest prices, and condition, both outside and in, is crucial. The presence of the original sifter and puff will enhance desirability and many compacts still carry traces of powder.

◄ **Boots Cold Cream jar, c.1880–1920**
Boots Cold Cream was one of the first branded toiletries to achieve great popularity in England. This type of jar was in general use until the 1920s but after this time cosmetics became much more widespread; women had been given the vote and the freedom to make the most of their physical assets, which entailed care of the skin and wearing make-up in public. The founder of Boots Cash Chemists, Jesse Boot, had great entrepreneurial skills and competed strongly in the world market, having no less than 800 retail outlets by the 1930s.

► **Sitzendorfer figural ceramic powder bowl, c.1920**
Made in Germany this is a charming example of a boudoir vanity accessory, modelled with a reclining bathing beauty holding a mirror. Such powder bowls were popular during a period when a lady and her powder puff were inseparable. China and colourful pressed glass dressing-table sets, often in classic Art Deco designs, were produced for every level of the market, and many pieces can still be found very affordably today.

◄ **"Puffs" compact by René Lalique for Coty, 1920s–'30s**
Coty's "puffs" compact, containing L'Aimant pressed powder, is possibly one of the most recognized compacts worldwide, and is now a cosmetic classic. This design of swansdown puffs on a burnt orange background was created by two renowned French artists – René Lalique, the famous glassmaker, and Leon Bask, celebrated for his innovative stage settings and costumes for the Ballets Russes. The "powder puffs" trademark has been used since 1914, and this example was available in all leading department stores and chemists' shops.

➤ Guilloche enamelled compact, 1920s–'30s

The technique of overlaying enamel on to a machined surface could be applied to precious and non-precious metals, and was employed extensively by silversmiths and craftsmen from the 1920s to '50s; perfect examples are very sought-after by collectors today. The "sunburst" design was synonymous with the spirit of the Art Deco period, representing everything that was new and modern. It was used to ornament doors and leaded light windows, public and industrial buildings, as well as small beautiful objects from radios to compacts, for over 30 years.

▼ Gwenda butterfly-wing compact, *c.*1930

The Birmingham firm of Gwenda made cosmetic containers for Coty and specialized in butterfly-wing compacts, decorated with the minute, iridescent blue feathers of the *Morpho Didius* Amazonian butterfly. The wings are extremely fragile and need to be protected from extremes of temperature. Perfect examples of these compacts, which were only produced for a short period, are rare. Cheaper foil copies were made in the 1930s and are worth less than the originals.

▲ Camera-style musical compact, 1920s–'30s

Superbly engineered, with a strong Art Deco style, this compact is decorated with mock tortoisehell enamel and brass and encompasses all the best elements of gadgetry, novelty, and innovation. It resembles a miniature pocket camera, complete with "shutter button" to activate the lid of the powder well, and a "film winder knob" attached to the lipstick, which can be removed by pulling the silk tassel. The under-side reveals a small brass winder and a release button to activate the musical movement.

◄ "Princess" compact by Strattons, 1959

This is one of a series by Strattons showing famous dancers and ballet-related subjects. A feature of this compact is the self-opening inner lid (patented as "compact in hand") – a clever mechanism designed to prevent damage to well-manicured nails! The transfer-printed portrait is of Nadia Nerina and is signed by "Baron", an established photographer in royal circles. Strattons has enjoyed amazing success in the cosmetic world since the 1930s, and continues to produce high-quality compacts today.

➤ Mary Quant novelty "wristwatch" lip gloss, c.1966

This lip gloss, produced and branded with the famous Mary Quant daisy logo, was designed with the more youthful market in mind. Quant opened her first boutique, Bazaar, in the King's Road, Chelsea, during the late 1950s and became famous as a fashion designer in the '60s, popularizing the mini skirt and skinny rib sweater, and creating a very exciting fresh look for the teenage market. She developed her cosmetic range to complement this style, concentrating on a natural, "no-makeup" look. This lip gloss, labelled "Sunsmasher", is an excellent example of her innovative style.

CORKSCREWS

A multi-tool folding bow corkscrew with eight different tools, English, *c.*1830; the more tools, the more collectable.

For most of its long history wine was stored in pottery vessels or wooden casks. When bottles first appeared in the early 17th century they were sealed with wooden pegs wrapped in waxed linen. Corks subsequently replaced pegs and were common from the mid-18th century onwards. Nobody knows who invented the corkscrew, but we do know that it was an English clergyman, the Reverend Samuel Henshall, who took out the first corkscrew patent in 1795. Countless thousands of designs have been produced since then, some of which are elaborate pieces of engineering while others are simply engaging novelties. Some collectors prefer the former, others favour the latter, but corkscrews certainly offer variety. Corkscrews today are synonymous with wine but most liquids, including perfume and medicines, were once sold in corked bottles. Therefore if you find a corkscrew that seems too delicate to open a bottle of wine, perhaps it was never intended to.

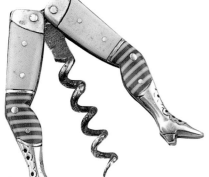

➤ **Thomason-type corkscrew, *c.*1850**
Along with Henshall, the name of Edward Thomason is one of the best-known in this field, and here we see a design patented by him in 1802. This example has an ingenious hermaphrodite screw designed to remove the cork and eject it from the corkscrew. These are among the most sought-after of corkscrews because of their design and their sheer quality; Thomason, a prolific inventor, was knighted in 1832.

▲ **Ladies' legs celluloid corkscrew, *c.*1895**
Ladies' legs corkscrews are relics of the "Naughty Nineties" (1890s) and are very popular with modern collectors. While they were clearly inspired by Parisian cancan dancers, they were made not in France but in Germany. The legs were both decorative and functional; when folded they covered the worm so the corkscrew could be safely carried in the pocket. The legs also acted as levers to help draw the cork.

◄ **Dachsund and cat figurals, *c.*1930**
The stylized nature of these charming animal figurals is suggestive of the Art Deco era to which they belong. Thousands of animal figural corkscrews were made, notably in Birmingham, for the growing souvenir and novelty market. The firm of Pearson-Page-Jewsbury produced a great many of these items, which are still readily available and make appealing additions to any collection.

◄ **Henshall-type corkscrew, c.1830**
This is an example of the Reverend Henshall's original design, patented in 1795. Henshall's innovation was a button between the shank and the worm; when the button reached the top of the cork, the cork would be turned, making extraction easier. The purpose of the brush at the top of this and many other corkscrews is often a mystery to the novice collector; it was designed simply to remove cobwebs from bottles in a dusty cellar.

DOLLS

An 1830s English wooden doll, with characteristic sloping shoulders, dressed in contemporary period costume.

The fine quality of the bisque and costume makes this Bru Jeune doll highly desirable.

A Simon & Halbig fashionable doll unusually dressed as a pedlar with her basket of wares, which include Grödnerthal dolls.

The 19th and 20th centuries saw tremendous changes in society. The Industrial Revolution sparked a period of technological innovation, which affected the way people worked, lived, and played. The increasing affluence of the period also stoked the demand for luxuries, such as playthings like toys and dolls.

Early dolls and toys were often homemade, but there were also small cottage industries producing toys and dolls for sale. To cope with increasing local and overseas demand these factories were modernized to become mass-production businesses that churned out millions of dolls. Well-crafted dolls initially were available only to the very rich, but the advent of industrialization made dolls accessible to almost every little girl of that era. From the mid-19th century to the start of World War I in 1914 was the Golden Age for doll making, and many of the valuable antique dolls on the market today date from this period.

The two World Wars in the first half of the 20th century had a tremendous impact on the trade and economics of Europe. Supplies from Germany, which had been one of the leading manufacturing countries, were halted. This led to the rise of new doll companies elsewhere, such as in the USA and Japan, and many more British firms were also now producing for the home market. The austerity of the wartime period is reflected in the materials used for dolls and toys, and the quality was also not to the same high standard as the earlier Victorian manufacturers. The next revolution in doll making was to be the advent of new materials, such as rubber, plastic, and vinyl. Trade became more global and today, with the availability of relatively cheap labour and materials, dolls generally are mass-produced in the Far East.

The sheer range of dolls available means that there is likely to be a niche to appeal to every sort of collector. While some collect out of nostalgia, others approach doll collecting from a fine-art point of view. The artistic flair and craftsmanship of many German character dolls, and the fine quality of the French *bébés*, would certainly qualify them as works of art, with a price tag to match. There are, of course, collectors who are intrigued by the social history behind dolls because they provide a fascinating glimpse of the social mores of a bygone era. The competition was very fierce among doll makers and they had to be very sensitive to the prevailing trends in fashion and taste. Changes in fashion and hairstyles in the real world were often mirrored in the dolls so it is possible to date a doll from her clothes or coiffure. Shifts in a society's ideals of beauty are also often reflected in the evolution of dolls' bodies and faces.

While high-priced dolls are often out of the reach of many collectors' pockets, there are many other fascinating dolls that are still within a reasonable budget. The difficulty is in deciding what to collect. It is useful to narrow down the focus of a collection to a particular type of doll and to collect the dolls that you will love. In this way, their future value will be secondary to the enjoyment that you will receive from your doll collection.

Wood, Wax, & Papier Mâché

Wood and wax were used in the 17th and 18th centuries to create finely crafted crèche figures. A natural progression from these figures was the manufacturing of dolls by special commission. Paintings of the era depict girls holding elaborately dressed dolls and these would most likely have been crafted especially at the request of a parent, and were therefore available only to very wealthy children. Those without rich parents would probably have had to make do with simple homemade wooden dolls, whittled by their fathers and dressed by their mothers. Wooden doll-making was firmly established as a cottage industry in England by the early 19th century. The designs became more sophisticated, and early examples are among the most expensive dolls in the world. Production continued throughout the 19th century but their quality and popularity were fast declining, especially with the import of cheaper German dolls. The German papier-mâché dolls are especially of note since they are often attractively coiffured and dressed. The more elaborate the hairstyle and the costume, the more desirable they are to today's collectors.

Early papier-mâché dolls are often prone to damage, hence an all-original 1830s doll like this would be sought-after.

◄ Grödnerthal wooden dolls, early 1800s
Germany began to mass-produce Grödnerthals to meet the high demand for cheaper dolls. They were sold without clothes and were often inexpensive, which appealed to the children of the period who could afford to buy and dress the dolls as they pleased. This family of Grödnerthals has a father in military uniform; all Grödnerthals were made as females, with a moulded yellow comb in their hair, so the original child owner is likely to have removed the comb when dressing him as a male doll.

▲ Wax-over-papier-mâché doll, c.1840
The rise of the middle-class family fanned the demand for inexpensive toys. The wax-over-composition or papier mâché technique was relatively less skilled and, therefore, less expensive than poured wax methods, which made it ideal for mass-production. This wax-over-papier-mâché doll is typical of the period, with her wig set in a slit in the crown. Later wax-over dolls are more realistically modelled than their earlier counterparts, and many still survive in good condition to this day.

► Poured wax doll, 1860s
Early wax dolls are often of solid wax, which was very expensive to use. The advent of a poured wax technique during the 19th century hailed the recovery of the English doll-making industry, following the decline of the wooden doll. The wax doll industry was dominated by a few names: among the most famous are Montanari and Pierroti. These dolls were very popular and even received patronage from the royal family. Blue-eyed dolls, like this one, were much in demand following the birth of Queen Victoria's children.

China & Bisque

In the 1840s "china" dolls were in demand. They had glazed porcelain shoulders and heads, with delicately painted features and moulded hair. The quality of finish declined toward the 1890s making earlier models more sought-after today – especially those with elaborate hairstyles, hair colours, or hair ornaments. The 1860s saw the development of bisque, an extremely versatile medium; the matt finish and colour of unglazed bisque gives it a more natural look than glossy china heads. Competition was very fierce between Germany's and France's doll industries, which resulted in the production of the some of the best dolls of the period. The compulsory inscription of the country of origin on the doll's head, introduced in the 1890s, proved to be very useful. Factories also included their names and mould numbers: bisque dolls generally are impressed on the back of the head or shoulders (often hidden under a wig) with a name or initials, and a three-digit number (or sometimes two or four) that should not be confused with the size number. Since 80 per cent of a bisque or china doll's value is in the head it is important to check it for damages or hairline cracks.

The hairstyle identifies this as an early 1860s china doll; the version with moulded morning glory hair ornaments is very rare.

▲ **Kestner all-bisque doll, 1890s**
Miniature dolls were widely produced, usually in tandem with their larger-sized counterparts. This is extremely useful as miniature dolls are often unmarked but can be identified by their similarities to larger, marked dolls. This little doll is identifiable as a Kestner from her detailed face and the style of her boots. Not only is she all-bisque, she is also a very rare swivel-waist type. Miniature dolls' size makes them easier to display in period dolls' houses and perfect for the collector with limited space.

▼ **Smiling bisque doll, French, 1870s**
The French lady doll was a natural progression from early fashion mannequins. They were available in a wide variety of poseable body types – perfect for displaying their extensive wardrobe. Dresses run the gamut from couture to factory-made, often mirroring the fashion trends of the time. Girls were encouraged to practise their sewing skills by making homemade clothes from patterns in magazines. Fine accessories (gloves, hats, jewellery, and shoes) were available in specialist shops in Paris and London.

▲ **Jumeau *bébé* doll, late 1850s**
In the latter part of the 1850s a new type of doll was introduced to the French market. The *bébé* depicts a young girl, rather than the more womanly dolls available at the time, and was a resounding success. With its charming expression and elaborate costumes, the *bébé* represented the ideal Victorian child and is one of the most beautiful and highly prized dolls. This fine example was made by Jumeau and is dressed in her original bright pink silk dress.

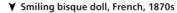

➤ Floradora doll by Armand Marseille, *c.*1910

The first dolls to be bought by a budding collector are often those by Armand Marseille. The factory began production in the 1890s and was the most prolific of its time. Generic moulds, such as AM 390 and 370 are not of high quality, but Marseille did produce a series of expensive closed-mouth dolls and googlie-eyed dolls, which are very rare. The generic doll, like this Floradora, will be most attractive to collectors when in good condition, and well dressed in a contemporary outfit.

▲ Kammer and Reinhardt series doll, *c.*1909

Among the most sought-after German dolls are the early 100 series dolls made by Kammer and Reinhardt. This fine example is a mould 114, known either as Hans or Gretchen depending on its clothing, and was said to have been modelled after Franz Reinhardt's grandchildren. The most commonly found Kammer and Reindhardt character is mould 100, the Kaiser Baby, while the most rare is mould number 108. Only one of these is known to exist, and it fetched £188,500 ($282,750) when sold at auction in 1994.

◄ Gebrüder Heubach doll, *c.*1918

The Heubach factory produced a wide range of bisque children with amazing modelling and expression, so it was easy for them to progress to character dolls. This bad-tempered child is a rare character 8548, and is even more desirable since he has glass sleeping eyes instead of the usual intaglio eyes associated with Heubach's character dolls. Small-sized character boys and babies fetch in the low hundreds, depending on their quality, but this rare doll fetched £9,000 ($13,500) at auction.

SFBJ character baby doll, 1920s

This character doll is part of the association's 200 series. It is of better finish and quality than the standard SFBJ moulds that were produced in vast quantities.

At the start of the 20th century doll manufacturers began to introduce character dolls. These were often representations of real people, modelled after children and babies. With their life-like expressions, ranging from laughing, to pouting, to crying, they were very different from the conventional dolls available at the time. Many hailed this return to realism as a "Doll Reform", but the introduction of this type of doll was not without opposition. However, the dolls began to gain popularity, and by 1910 both German and French doll makers had added character dolls to their ranges. Many were probably bought by parents who were entranced by this charming reminder of their children, as a child would have preferred a conventional doll that was more versatile for playing. The quality of German dolls was much improved at this time and due to mass-manufacturing they were also more affordable. To combat the increasing dominance of the German firms, French doll makers clubbed together and began to produce under one name: Société Française de Fabrication de Bébés et Jouets (S.F.B.J.). In order to remain competitive they too began to produce a series of good quality character dolls, under their 200 series. Character dolls are often sought-after by collectors and have numbered among the most valuable antique dolls today.

Character Dolls

Miscellaneous Dolls

Doll makers produced other types of dolls to cater to as wide a market as possible. Male child dolls were offered for sale as well as the more normal female ones, but often these were in fact standard female dolls or babies dressed in male clothes, and many would still have pierced ears! However, adult male dolls were also manufactured and these dolls are very different. They would often have moulded facial hair to distinguish them as adult male dolls. Since their production numbers were smaller, they tend to command a premium today. Doll makers also offered ethnic dolls, ranging from Oriental babies to black children, to Native American-Indian dolls. Such dolls are highly desirable, especially if they still have their original costumes and accessories. The range that was available from doll manufacturers is astounding and collectors are still discovering many new rare and wonderful dolls to this day.

This handsome man is a rare Simon and Halbig character doll, with his dashing moulded black moustache and original sailor costume.

➤ **Black cloth doll, 1920s**
Black dolls were offered as part of many factories' ranges. Initially they were simply standard dolls painted brown, but with the demand for more realism the later ones were produced with correct well-moulded facial features, and colour ranging from light coffee to the deepest brown. Black dolls were also available in various materials, including cloth and leather. This particular cloth doll is very good quality and well-made, from the stitching of his eyebrows, to the needle-sculpted nose, and to his well-fitting suit.

➤ **Oriental "Door of Hope" dolls, c.1900**
Oriental dolls were fashioned from a variety of different mediums, such as bisque, wood, and composition. "Door of Hope" dolls were named after a Shanghai sanctuary that opened to save vulnerable women and children from a life of poverty, by teaching them trade skills to support themselves. The dolls were carved by craftsmen and were then dressed in various costumes by the girls as part of their sewing training. Ones with well-carved heads and elaborate costumes, such as a bride and groom, are sought-after today.

Googlie-Eyed Dolls

In the early 20th century German bisque doll makers had a runaway success manufacturing Googlie and Kewpie dolls. Kewpies are like cupids, with pedestal feet and star-shaped hands (see p70), and were the invention of US illustrator Rose O'Neill. The all-bisque version is the most sought-after. A Googlie-eyed doll is characterized by its large, round, side-glancing eyes, surprised eyebrows, snub nose, and a smiley mouth. While inspiration for the Googlies has been attributed to US cartoon strip *The Campbell Kids* by Grace Gebbie Drayton, at the same time a designer for Dean and Farnell, Chloe Preston, also illustrated round-faced round-eyed children in her *The Peek-a-Boos* books. A range of bisque dolls closely resembling Preston's illustrations was produced, and these are rare and hard to find today. The major German firms produced their own versions of Googlie-eyed dolls, with Kestner and Kammer and Reinhardt moulds being the most sought-after, especially if they are large and well-dressed.

Gebrüder Heubach googlie-eyed doll, c.1918
The eyes are operated by string at the back of the head. Although the body is in poor condition the head is perfect, making this a valuable example.

Cloth & Composition Dolls

Traditionally dolls made from fabric were mainly homemade items with a limited lifespan, and the value of these primitive cloth dolls would depend largely on their quality, condition, and provenance. It was not until the late 19th and early 20th centuries that cloth dolls began to be produced commercially, and in great quantities. At the end of the 19th century American doll makers such as Izannah Walker and Martha Chase spearheaded the use of stockinette. Over in Europe the Steiff factory produced felt dolls, often as comical characters – sweet-looking children or militiamen. In England firms such as Chad Valley, Farnell, and Dean's Rag Book manufactured charming cloth and felt dolls, often based on characters from children books, while Norah Wellings produced soft toys from her own designs. Cloth dolls tended to get more rough use than the fragile bisque ones, perhaps because they were seen as more durable. They are prone to staining, fading, and moth damage so it is important to buy a cloth doll in the best condition possible, and to store it very carefully to avoid any further damage.

A Norah Wellings pressed-felt doll in excellent condition, with original floral printed frock and cloth label tied to her left wrist.

▼ Lenci felt doll, 1920s

Perhaps the most desirable cloth dolls today are those made by the Italian firm, Lenci. Beautifully designed and dressed in vibrant felt or organdie costumes, the dolls came in an astonishing variety, from standard dolls, to comical caricatures, to portrait dolls. Being made of felt, Lenci dolls are prone to moth damage and staining, which can be hard to repair. A prime example of an early Lenci doll in original clothes, like this little doll pictured below, can fetch in the high hundreds at auction, while rare portrait dolls, such as that of Rudolph Valentino, can fetch up to £10,000 ($15,000).

▲ Fritzl by Kathe Kruse, 1910s

In 1909, out of frustration at the prevalence of bisque dolls, which were unsuitable for very young children, Kathe Kruse started making cloth dolls for her daughters. Her designs became more sophisticated with the help of her sculptor husband and she started her own workshop, producing dolls with thoughtful expressions and realistic bodies. Kathe Kruse dolls are still produced up to the present day in celluloid and vinyl but it is the earlier cloth dolls that are very much in demand. A wonderful example like this original Doll no. 1, above, could fetch thousands at auction.

▲ Shirley Temple doll by Ideal, 1930s

Composition dolls had been manufactured for many years but gained more of a foothold in the early 20th century. Produced to cater to the lower end of the market, they tended to suffer most from damages such as crazing and flaking. The export of German dolls was stopped during World War I and this encouraged the growth of new firms in the USA. One of the most popular dolls is this Shirley Temple doll made by American firm, Ideal. She is all-original, complete with her box and badge.

Celluloid, Vinyl, & Hard Plastic

The demand for a more durable doll prompted doll makers to experiment with new materials. Celluloid was used initially, but this was superseded by the invention of hard plastic after World War II. By the 1950s vinyl dolls became more popular due to their durability and softer texture. Another plus point for using vinyl was that doll makers could root the hair into the head rather than having to produce separate wigs. The most famous vinyl success story was the Barbie® doll. Mattel bought the rights to a sultry German doll called Bild Lilli and transformed her to fit to American tastes. Like the fashionable lady dolls of the 19th century, Barbie's appeal was in her almost limitless wardrobe and accessories. Further innovations to design and merchandising concepts made Barbie into the global phenomenon that she is today. Pre-1970s Barbie dolls are highly collectable in the current market. England produced a similar teenage fashion doll in the form of Sindy; although a contemporary of Barbie, Sindy dolls and accessories are not as highly valued today.

Early Barbies, like this Suburban Shopper, are highly sought-after, and very rare Barbie dolls can fetch into the thousands.

▲ Celluloid Kewpie doll, 1930s
Many German firms produced celluloid versions of their more popular bisque dolls as a cheap alternative, often using the same mould. Kewpie dolls first appeared in the *Ladies Home Journal* in 1909, and the earliest Kewpies were manufactured by Kestner in 1913. In the 1920s and '30s firms in France and Japan were also producing original celluloid dolls. Film and book characters and novelty-type miniature celluloid dolls have massive appeal and are sought-after. This charming Kewpie doll is very similar to his bisque counterpart, but would have been much cheaper for the child who purchased it, as well as for the collector today.

▼ Roddy doll by D.G. Todd Ltd, UK, 1950s
Hard plastic dolls became a staple in the 1950s. Although heavier than celluloid, plastic is more durable and was popular with parents. One of the notable hard plastic dolls was that made by Madame Alexander in the USA. In England hard plastic dolls were produced by firms such as Pedigree and Chiltern. These are abundant today and it is important to collect only those in very good condition or that have interesting features. This Roddy doll is quite standard but it is in excellent condition and still has its original clothes, tag, and, importantly, its box.

▲ Sasha doll, 1960s
One of the more modern dolls with a cult following is the Sasha doll. They were the brainchild of Sasha Morgenther who sold them in the early 1950s, initially as one-of-a-kind portrait dolls from her Zurich workshop. She began to produce a range of vinyl dolls with matching accessories and clothes, in partnership with firms in Germany and England. The early portrait dolls with Sasha's signature on the foot, prototypes, and dolls without a philtrum (the crease between the nose and mouth) like this doll here, can command prices in the thousands.

The first recorded dolls' house was created in 1558 for Albert V, Duke of Bavaria, and was an exact copy of his princely residence. Known as "Baby Houses", the fine dolls' houses and cabinet houses produced in Germany and Holland in the 16th and 17th centuries were not so much children's toys as learning tools, designed to teach young girls the arts of housewifery. They were also intended as adult playthings, so that wealthy merchants' wives could recreate the interiors in which they lived. The passion for dolls' houses spread to Britain by the early 18th century, and to America by the late 1700s. Initially these were handmade works of art reserved for the very wealthy. However, the second half of the 19th century saw a growing middle-class interest in dolls' houses, which began to be mass-produced in Britain, Germany, and the USA. Leading makers include G&K Lines Ltd (UK), Christian Hacker and Moritz Gottshalk (Germany), and Rufus Bliss and Converse (USA). In the 20th century the commercial manufacture of dolls' houses expanded considerably. In the 1930s dolls' houses imitated the fashion for "Mock Tudor" suburban architecture. Post-war saw the introduction of plastic and the creation of houses for toy characters, from Barbie to the Sylvanian Families. Beautifully handcrafted miniatures continue to be made for the thriving adult collectors' market.

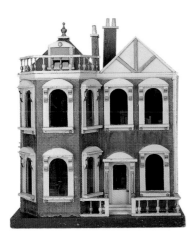

British dolls' house by G&J Lines, c.1900 reflecting period Edwardian architecture; it opens on both sides so two children can play at once.

▲ Games table, German, 1890

Until World War I interrupted trading Germany was a major international producer of toys. German dolls' houses and furniture were exported across the world, and manufacturers such as Christian Hacker (est. 1870) and Gebruder Scheegas und Sohne (est. 1845) adapted products and styles to suit the intended country. This rare German games table is made from simulated oak with a printed paper top, which slides back to reveal a storage space for the tiny chess pieces. Miniatures with moving parts are highly collectable.

➤ "Dolly Varden House", 1936

"Mock-Tudor", half-timbered homes became all the rage in the new leafy suburbs that sprung up across the UK in the inter-war years, and dolls' houses followed the prevailing trend. The "Dolly Varden House", made by Meccano Ltd, Liverpool (manufacturers of Dinky toys), was named after a coquettish character in Charles Dickens' novel *Barnaby Rudge*. The cardboard house was collapsible and came in a container that opened out to form a garden and tennis court. It was specially designed for Dinky dolls' house furniture.

◀ Dolls' house by Tudor Toys, c.1960

The fashion for stockbroker-style "Mock-Tudor" continued into the '60s. Created for small modern homes and apartments post-war dolls' houses tended to be more compact and portable than their 1930s predecessors. Leading UK makers included Amersham, Tudor Toys, Chad Valley, and Marx. Furniture was mass-produced by firms such as Dol-Toi and Tri-ang, and was imported from Hong Kong. Objects from this period are still very affordable. Look for furniture that captures the style of the period.

▲ Cardboard house, 1960s

In the 1960s there was a reaction among middle-class parents against the proliferation of television-inspired merchandise and the influence of American products. Growing awareness of the importance of nursery education inspired a revival of interest in more traditional toys, sold by new shops such as the cleverly named Early Learning Centre. Pre-printed paper dolls' houses had been manufactured since the 19th century. This 1960s example was designed by Maureen Roffey A.R.C.A., and manufactured by Robor Ltd. The ephemeral nature of this house, which combines a historical precedent with disposable pop fashion, makes this a rare collector's item.

▼ Sylvanian Families house, 1980s

In the 1980s toy production moved predominantly to the Far East, and plastic became by far the most common material. Children's toys were increasingly affected by the influence of television, and dolls' houses were no exception. Sylvanian Families was first introduced in Japan in 1985 by a company called Epoch; later that same year they were launched by Tomy in the USA and reached the UK in 1987. The families of little woodland creatures were a huge hit. They typify the '80s fashion among little girls for "cute" toys, such as Care Bears and My Little Pony, which were ruthlessly promoted across the world by colourful animated TV series. Many different Sylvanian houses were produced.

▼ Traditional-style furniture, 2002

Ever since their creation dolls' houses have appealed to adult collectors. Grown-up enthusiasts all over the world still enjoy putting together miniature houses and recreating perfect 18th- and 19th-century interiors, as well as more modern environments. Specialist dealers and fairs have sprung up to cater to their needs. Contemporary craftsmen and women are still producing dolls' house miniatures; fine examples, such as this Regency-style mahogany and silk-covered sofa created by David Booth in 2002, sell for high prices, and their appeal is likely to remain undiminished.

▲ Contemporary-style dolls' house furniture, 2001

All too often dolls' houses have a romanticized, retro-look that seems far removed from the modern world. Not so the "Kaleidoscope" house, created in 2001 by US Artist Laurie Simmons and architect Peter Wheelwright. Manufactured by Bozart toys this modernist home has sliding transparent panels in bright colours, which are pulled back to reveal rooms filled with art and furniture by leading, international contemporary designers. This drawing room set includes a sofa by Karim Rashid and a "Big Heavy" chair by Ron Arad. Nominally created for children aged 6 and upwards, "Kaleidoscope" houses are already attracting many style-conscious adult buyers and are a good bet for collectables of the future.

EPHEMERA

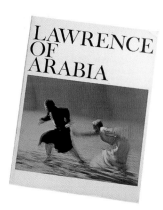

Cinema lobby programmes are a specialist spin-off from the recent surge in poster collecting.

Ephemera encompasses the whole gamut of printed and handwritten paper, and its appeal is equally diverse. Since the invention of paper, man has created documents as an inevitable part of his daily life and the surviving pieces provide an unequalled record of these lives. Ephemera can be collected for its own sake as well as any historical significance – particularly decorative items, which have benefited fully from the general rise in appreciation of Victorian art. It can also be collected as a research tool or as an adjunct to other hobbies; for example collectors of topographical postcards are increasingly adding illustrated billheads, estate plans, and advertising to supplement the scenes of their chosen locality. Indeed any collecting hobby can be enhanced by acquiring the associated catalogues or paperwork. Other popular ephemera themes are as widespread as theatre, war, breweries, exhibitions, aircraft, crime, scouting, fashion, and product advertising.

➤ **Victorian "scraps" of angels, c.1880**
A major entertainment in Victorian homes, for both children and adults, was collecting "scraps" – highly coloured, embossed, and lacquered images that were purchased by the sheet. Individual pieces were then glued into "scrap books" and duplicates could be swapped. Many collectors prefer to retrieve the scraps from the books and store them more safely in boxes. Scraps are still produced today, frequently to the original Victorian designs.

⬆ **First printed Christmas card, 1843**
The first printed Christmas card was commissioned by Sir Henry Cole, instigator of the Great Exhibition of 1851. He asked artist J.C. Horsley to design a card that he could send to friends rather than write to them in person. Cole also helped introduce the Penny Post, making this card a remarkable piece of postal history. When it came to auction it fetched a world-record price of £23,300 ($35,000).

◀ **Sheet music, c.1910**
Mass-produced sheet music with attractive covers began in the 1840s, when a sudden increase in popular music combined with the introduction of colour lithography. The joys of home musical entertainment lasted until the 1920s. Music with decorative covers by such artists as Concanen and Brandard, and other specialists, are in demand today and may be collected as part of the history of variety and music halls. This example would also appeal to a railway enthusiast, lending it added value.

◀ **Victorian punched paper and appliqué Valentine card, c.1880**
The tradition of giving gifts on St Valentine's Day, usually in the form of an anonymous keepsake, goes back to the early 19th century. By the mid-19th century these gifts were likely to consist of an embossed printed sheet on which, very often, a scrap was mounted (see above). Typically there would be a blank second page and sometimes a matching envelope; when collecting the cards it is preferable that these are present as it will increase the value.

EROTICA

1957 hot water bottle by Poynter Products, USA in the curvy form of Hollywood star Jayne Mansfield.

The history of collectable erotica is a very ancient one. Erotic artifacts have been popular with every civilization, including the Greeks, the Romans, and the Celts, and from the Far East to the Americas. There are many different fields in which to specialize, from ancient artifacts, to Japanese prints, to 1940s glamour calendars, to cigarette cases; the objects shown on this page provide an indication of the sheer diversity of this collecting field. Values can vary considerably and rarity plays an important part. For example, nude postcards of the 1920s can be difficult to find in good condition and are consequently expensive when they do appear on the market. Erotica is an important part of our social history and reflects changes in attitudes over time. Its collectable appeal also reflects these same changes: much of what was once considered risqué, titillating, or downright immoral 100 or even 50 years ago has become merely quaint by today's standards.

◄ Silvered alpaca cigarette case, 1920
Tobacco was traditionally a male pleasure and accessories were often decorated with erotic imagery. Snuff boxes opened up to reveal naughty pictures and meerschaum pipes were modelled in the form of naked beauties. Among the most expensive cigarette cases found on the market today are those decorated with risqué nudes. Germany and Austria were the main centres of production for these cases, which are still very popular with German collectors today.

◄ Pack of "Glamour Girls" playing cards, 1950s
This pack of "Glamour Girls" cards features 55 different girls. Original sets of these cards are very collectable but beware as modern technology makes it fairly easy for them to be faked. However, it is difficult to do the faking convincingly; with most fakes the images are of poorer quality and the card looks too new to be authentic.

▼ Vargas pin-up calendar, c.1944
Alberto Vargas (1896–1982) is one of the most celebrated glamour artists of all time. His famous "Vargas Girl" first appeared in *Esquire* magazine in 1939 and was introduced as a calendar in 1940. The curvaceous pin-up was just what the troops needed to boost their moral and by 1946 orders for calendars hit nearly three million. Vargas went on to produce a large volume of work for *Playboy*.

► *Playboy* "Playmate" jigsaw puzzle, 1960–70
Playboy magazine was launched by Hugh Heffner in December 1953. The first issue sold 70,000 copies, and by 1957 circulation was close on one million. Certain issues of the magazine (for example the no. 1 issue featuring a nude Marilyn Monroe) are collectable, and the *Playboy* empire, with its clubs and bunny girls, has spawned a wealth of memorabilia, from glasses to key rings. With puzzles all pieces should be complete to achieve full value.

Over the past five years collecting and wearing vintage fashion has become far more mainstream. Models and celebrities are photographed regularly in their favourite vintage frocks, and even certain leading high-street stores now sell vintage alongside their modern designs. While some enthusiasts will dress up completely in period style, others mix old and new, buying vintage to create an interesting modern look and not because they want to live in the past. Over the decades people have grown; some early clothes can be hard to wear because of their fragility and small size, and vintage shoes can be particularly hard to find in today's average fittings. Nevertheless the 20th century does offer a wealth of interesting styles from which to choose. As with modern fashion, when buying to wear the first rule is to buy what you like and what suits you. Condition is also crucial; try clothes on, check hems, and the seams underneath the arms – anywhere a garment is likely to have been strained. Big-name designer pieces and classic examples of period style can fetch high sums; however, much is still very affordable and many vintage treasures can still be picked up from charity shops and boot (garage) fairs. Vintage fashion fairs and dealers offer a wide range of garments and prices, and there are also specialist auctions. The following pages cover fashion from the 1900s through to the 1970s.

Grey top hats were for daywear, black could be worn day or night. Vintage hats in good condition and wearable size can be valuable.

◄ **Cotton and lace christening dress, c.1900**
Family christening gowns are often stored away, and many vintage examples can still be found today. Edwardian christening robes had full, long skirts (perhaps twice the length of the baby), and the bodice and hems were the principal area of decoration. Worn with a matching christening cap, dresses came in silk and fine lawn. Values depend on age, size, condition, material, and the quality of the decoration. Hand-made lace will command a premium, and any details of provenance (who originally wore the dress) can also add interest to a piece.

➤ **Boned corset, c.1910**
Modern fashion affects demand for vintage pieces, and corsets produced by designers such as Vivienne Westwood and Jean Paul Gaultier have stimulated interest in historical corsets. Not necessarily purchased to wear, they are collected rather as classic period pieces and for the information they provide on structure and technique. Labelled C.W.S. Desbeau, this unusual black example is very fine.

▲ **Edwardian motoring coat, c.1905**
The S-shaped silhouette of the 1900s, achieved by viciously controlling underwear, is a look that few modern women would choose. But the Edwardian period did offer some more wearable fashions, and coats, cloaks, and shawls can be teamed with a modern outfit. Motoring was the new craze of the wealthy, and this long coat was designed to protect a lady in an open-top car. Loose-fitting, white lace dresses are another comfortable option.

1920s

By the end of World War I women had been given the vote, and fashion reflected this new emancipation. The 1920s "flapper" shingled her hair, shortened her skirts, and cast off her corset in favour of a straight, slender, boyish silhouette that mirrored the streamlined modernism of Art Deco. "To lose weight has become an obsession", commented *Vogue* in 1928. One way of keeping slim was to party until dawn at the new night clubs. Jazz was all the rage, and loose-fitting evening dresses, sparkling with sequins and crystal beads, were perfect for dancing the Charleston or the Black Bottom. Long strings of pearls and trailing scarves adorned the neck; jewelled cigarette holders and enamelled compacts dangled from wrist straps, reflecting the fashion for smoking and wearing make-up in public. Daywear had a new sporting look: 1920s tennis star Suzanne Lenglen, dressed by Patou, created a vogue for short skirts, short sleeves, and a colourful bandeau round the head; swimsuits and beach pyjamas were the height of fashion. Gabrielle "Coco" Chanel (1883–1971) transformed jersey into outerwear, popularizing elegant, easy-to wear separates and classic suits.

Close-fitting cloche hats suited the fashionable bobbed hairstyle and were perfect for new pursuits such as motoring. Sizes are often small.

▼ Beaded flapper dresses

The beaded evening dress is possibly the most famous and collectable example of 1920s fashion. These glittering gowns still look impossibly glamorous, and their drop-waisted, shift shape (pioneered by designers such as Chanel) is easy to wear and suits the modern figure. Fine examples can fetch four-figure sums but condition is crucial to value. The weight of the decoration can cause the fine chiffon to tear, so dresses are best stored flat. Sequins and beads are also easy to snag, so carry out any repairs immediately and buy and wear with care.

◀ Lamé evening coat

Opulent evening coats and cloaks are another 1920s classic, popular with collectors and still very wearable today. Evening coats were made from embroidered silk, soft devoré velvet, and shiny, metallic lamé in exotic patterns. Silk linings could be plain or decorative, in rich, contrasting "Ballets Russes" colours. Short sleeves showed off gloves and bracelets; batwing sleeves were another favourite. High fur collars could be drawn around the face, just allowing a jewelled evening scull cap to poke out. This lamé coat is fastened with a single hip button (a typical 1920s feature) and is in perfect condition.

► Stockings and garters

"In olden days a glimpse of stocking was looked on as something shocking, now heaven knows, anything goes", sang Cole Porter. As skirts became shorter, so ladies' legs were revealed to the world, and stockings were produced in every shade from black to the new flesh tones. This pair is made from artificial silk, reflecting the fashion for coloured and patterned stockings designed to match dress styles. Stockings were rolled over the knee and held up with a ribbon garter – a favourite 1920s accessory.

1930s

The roaring 1920s were replaced by what Groucho Marx called the "threadbare '30s". *Vogue* launched make-it-yourself dress patterns; Chanel introduced cotton evening gowns and ready-to-wear sweaters. Rayon made clothes more affordable, and zip fasteners made them easier to put on. Hollywood movies provided an antidote to the Depression, and film stars became the new fashion icons, influencing trends in dress and cosmetics, from Katherine Hepburn's trousers, to Greta Garbo's plucked eyebrows, to Jean Harlow's platinum hair. More romantic, feminine styles replaced the boyish look of the 1920s. Long satin evening gowns, cut on the bias, clung to the figure and stimulated demand for silky slips and cami-knickers that would create an invisible line. Hats ranged from pancake berets to giant cartwheels, and gloves were *de rigueur*; designer Elsa Schiaparelli (1890–1973) painted black evening gloves with red-fingernails. Sheer stockings, high heels, and a clutch bag completed the ladylike look. Ocean cruises and the fashion for Riviera holidays popularized sportswear, and Schiaparelli introduced hand-knitted bathing suits with a scandalous bare back.

This bra and French knickers in artificial silk, free from bones or other shapings, created a smooth line under close-fitting '30s items.

⌄ Plus fours suit

Edward, Prince of Wales, later the Duke of Windsor, was a noted trend-setter and keen golfer who popularized plus four trousers and colourful tweeds. "I believe in bright checks for sportsmen", he declared. "The louder they are the better I like them." Colourful socks, a brightly knitted fairisle sweater, and a large, flat cap completed the golfing look. Plus fours and loose-fitting Oxford "bags" epitomized the period taste for more comfortable, informal fashions. Men began wearing leisure clothes in town. Another practical addition to male attire, pioneered by the fashion-conscious prince, was the zip fastener.

⌃ Printed dress

Printed chiffon and crêpe gowns were one of the prettiest period styles. This bias-cut crêpe dress is in a fashionable abstract pattern. The bias cut was pioneered by French designer Madeleine Vionnet (1876–1975), whose clothes were so beautifully cut that they often required no fastenings. The bias cut can be challenging to wear, requiring a flat stomach and straight posture.

⌃ Gold lamé evening dress

This dress has a romantic, floor-length skirt. It is cut on the bias with a low back, reflecting the new fashion for backless evening gowns. The matching bolero jacket has puff-sleeves – a favourite 1930s feature, which, like the little cloak on the patterned gown, gave a feminine silhouette. Shoulders were further emphasized as the decade progressed, when shoulder pads were added to suits and dresses, broadening the shoulders and slimming the waist.

1940s

During World War II women's clothes echoed the lines of the men's uniforms – tight suits with crisp lines and short skirts reflecting the need to use as little material as possible. Trousers were practical for wartime work, as were boiler suits – famously sported by Winston Churchill and called "siren" suits because they could be pulled on quickly when the air raid siren sounded. Everyone was encouraged to make do and mend – underwear was made from parachute silk and women unable to get stockings were reduced to painting their legs brown and drawing a seam down the back with an eyebrow pencil. Wartime shortages led to the creation of the Utility Scheme to provide essential clothing "of good sound construction … for sale at a reasonable price and ensuring the maximum economy of raw materials and labour". Today there is considerable interest in these emergency fashions, which are collected by World War II enthusiasts and by swing and jive fans, who like to dress up in the period style for dance events.

Utility wares were marked with the CC41 trademark – standing for Civilian Clothing 1941, the year the scheme was launched.

▲ Women's Voluntary Service overcoat
The WVS was founded by Lady Reading in 1938. This volunteer civilian force worked with other civil-defence groups during bombing raids. The only colour available for their uniform was green, rejected by other civil services because it was considered unlucky. To overcome this superstition the twill cloth was woven with green and grey wool. The badges increase the value of this coat.

▼ World War II Victory scarf
Women working in the factories had to tie up their hair, and the headscarf (knotted on top of the head) became a typical accessory. Designs could be very inventive. In 1942 Jacqmar produced a series of propaganda scarves designed by Arnold Lever and priced at two coupons apiece. Decorated with patriotic slogans (this one depicts the Allied flags), they were worn by women as head squares and by men as neck scarves. Such items are very collectable.

▲ Utility shoes
These unworn utility shoes are made of recycled material, treated to look like snakeskin. Under the Utility Scheme heels were restricted to a maximum height of 5cm (2in), and peep toes (which wasted material) were banned. In 1943 wooden soles were introduced to supplement dwindling leather supplies. These shoes, designed by Reginald Shipp, are marked on the sole with the utility mark, which was commonly referred to as "the cheeses".

➤ Boxed nylons
The first pair of nylon stockings was exhibited by Du Pont at the 1938 New York World Fair. Named after New York and London, where the company hoped to market it, nylon cost $27 million (£18 million) to develop, and as far as women were concerned it was worth every cent. British women obtained their first nylons via US servicemen, or on the black market. Boxed vintage stockings such as these, right, are collectable today.

1950s

In the UK women were still eking out their coupons when, in 1947, Christian Dior launched his famous "New Look" on the Paris catwalk. "I designed clothes for flower-like women with rounded shoulders, full feminine busts, above handspan waists, above enormous spreading skirts", he explained. Dior was sponsored by French textile manufacturer Marcel Broussac, who was worried that short-skirted austerity fashions would last into peace-time. It was a wise investment. For a world starved of feminine glamour, Dior's flowing-skirted collection was a revelation. Politicians campaigned against the scandalous waste of rationed material but women were entranced, and Dior's hourglass line launched a decade of feminine fashions, epitomized by the circle skirt, the circle stitch bra, and the stiletto heel. The USA was another crucial postwar influence, pioneering colourful casual clothes for men and affordable ready-to-wear for women. The '50s also saw the birth of the teenager, sporting denim jeans and leather jackets and dancing to the new rock 'n' roll music.

Denim moved from work-wear to fashion when sported by '50s rebel heros James Dean and Elvis Presley. This is a 1953 Levis No. 2 jacket.

◄ Dior dress

Christian Dior (1905–57) designed for the cinema during the occupation of France in World War II. The Germans promoted non-political subjects such as costume dramas, and Dior experimented with crinolines and corsets, laying the foundations of his post-war fashions. This '50s Dior dress is beautifully constructed inside. Major labels are very sought-after, although values will reflect whether it is handmade couture or a prêt-à-porter design.

► Cotton frock

There was a huge desire for colour and pattern after the war. New Look-style cotton dresses were decorated with everything, from flowers, to abstract patterns, to pictures of Paris. Frocks came in every shade and were enhanced by multicoloured net petticoats. This dress and bolero jacket is by Lo Roco. Cheerful cotton frocks and skirts were mass-produced and homemade in large numbers, and are still affordable and wearable today.

▼ Felt poodle skirt

The poodle was a classic 1950s motif, and the felt poodle skirt is one of the fashion icons of the period. Felt skirts were worn by '50s American teenagers and are sought by rock 'n' roll enthusiasts today. They came with different designs, such as musical notes, and values depend on the pattern. Condition is also crucial, since felt is prone to moth damage.

► Balenciaga suit

Born in Spain, Cristobal Balenciaga (1895–1972) was another famous Paris designer of the period. He was known for beautiful tailoring, and this suit demonstrates some of the features that he made part of the '50s look: a short, box-like jacket, weighted inside to create a perfect line; three-quarter length sleeves drawing attention to the wrist; and a cut-away collar emphasizing the length of the neck and large, elegant buttons.

1960s

In the 1950s girls dressed like their mothers; in the '60s, for the first time, mothers wanted to look like their daughters. Swinging London became the epicentre of the new teenage fashion scene. Model and actress Twiggy, aged 16 and weighing just 91lbs, established "The Look" of the decade – skinny, leggy, and breathtakingly young. Mary Quant pioneered a host of new styles, from mini-skirts to trouser suits. British pop stars such as The Beatles and The Kinks provided new, male fashion icons, and Carnaby Street, home of the peacock revolution in men's dress, became famous across the world. Look out for labels of big-name London designers and trendy boutiques. Paris too was shaken by a "youthquake". Cardin and Courrèges launched the white and silver space-age look, and Paco Rabanne experimented with metal. Described as "sculptures", his chain-mail dresses reflected a new trend in Paris fashion: the creation of provocative, fundamentally unwearable clothes, designed to publicize the designer's name and his profitable mass-market products. "Haute-Couture is dead", sniffed Balenciaga as he closed his fashion house in 1968.

Boots were a favourite '60s item and this pair is by Mary Quant, who introduced PVC to fashion. Her daisy logo appears on the heel.

▲ Paco Rabanne dress

"The only new frontier left in fashion is finding new materials", claimed the Spanish-born designer Paco Rabanne (b. 1934), who trained as an architect before becoming one of Paris' most futuristic couturiers. Paco Rabanne experimented with plastic, leather, and metal to make a series of famous chain-mail dresses and accessories. Challenging to wear, and requiring a body stocking for decency and comfort, Rabanne's dresses are collected as design classics rather than wearable fashion.

▼ Biba mini dress

Founded by Barbara Hulanicki and named after her sister, Biba began life as a small mail-order business. The first Biba boutique opened in Kensington, London, in 1964, and soon teenagers were crowding into the city's first communal dressing rooms to try on £3 dresses, such as the example shown, and to swathe themselves in feather boas. By the early 1970s Biba, then occupying the site of a huge Art Deco department store, was one of London's most famous and glamorous shops. Biba products are very sought-after by collectors.

▲ Jacket from Take 6, London

"One week he's in polka dots, the next week he's in stripes", sang The Kinks in 1966, celebrating the "dedicated followers of fashion" in Carnaby Street. Men burst into colour in the 1960s, adopting a host of different styles from collarless Beatles suits to hippie gear. This double-breasted jacket, in the 1920s Eton boating style, reflects the period taste for vintage fashions. Take 6, a successful chain of men's boutiques, was founded by Sidney Brent. Classic 1960s designs in good condition, such as this, are very sought-after.

1970s

By the early 1970s the hard-edged "mod" style of the '60s had been replaced by a more romantic, dreamy look. The maxi and the midi took over from the mini-skirt, and the Afghan coat superseded the plastic mac. Long-haired hippies (male, female, and indeterminate) sported trailing kaftans and dangling love beads. Laura Ashley dressed modern girls to look like Victorian milk maids. London designers, such as Barbara Hulanicki at Biba and Ossie Clark, looked back to the fashions of the Art Nouveau and Art Deco periods, reinterpreting vintage styles with psychedelic colour and glamour. "Glam" was another '70s feature, with shiny disco clothes, towering platform boots, and billowing flares, adopted by men as well as women. Blue jeans became the ultimate unisex garment. Reacting against the tyranny of denim and sparkly disco, the decade ended with Punk. The bondage trousers and ripped up T-shirts created by Vivienne Westwood for the kids on the street are now hotly contested in the saleroom, both by clothes collectors and rock and pop fans.

Sported by popstars from Slade to Elton John, platforms were the ultimate '70s man's shoe. Those in good condition are sought-after.

◄ **Flared blue jeans**
By the 1970s jeans had become the universal uniform of youth: flared, patched, embroidered, and customized by every cult, from hippies to skinheads. Although these jeans are collectable as an example of '70s style, the most desirable denim is "capital E" Levis from before 1971 – the year the company changed its looms and began spelling its name on the red pocket tab with a lower-case as opposed to an upper-case "e". A capital "E" on the red Levi's pocket tab could denote a valuable vintage item.

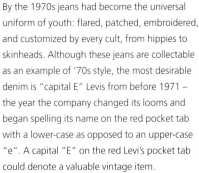

➤ **Ossie Clark dress**
"I want to dress frilly people … in colours that confuse the eye", Ossie Clark told *Vogue* in 1965. Clark (1942–96) rose from his Lancashire working-class roots, via the Royal College of Art in London, to become "King of the King's Road" in the '60s and '70s. His Quorum boutique attracted everyone from Goldie Hawn to Mick Jagger, who gyrated in his jumpsuits. Clark's great talent was cutting, and this crêpe dress, with its print designed by Clark's wife Celia Birtwell, when worn is a typically sensuous and clinging Clark creation.

▲ **Vivienne Westwood T-shirt**
Vivienne Westwood (b. 1941) is probably the UK's most famous living fashion designer. She and partner Malcolm McLaren were the pioneers of Punk, and Westwood created the classic Punk outfit of bondage trousers, mohair sweater, long-sleeved muslin shirt, and ripped up T-shirt. In the mid-'70s a T-shirt might have cost £6–8 from Sex (later called Seditionaries), her scary King's Road shop. Comparatively few of these hand-ripped shirts were made and many simply fell apart, so today rare period originals can sell for as much as £1,000 ($1,500).

GARDEN COLLECTABLES

Wooden trugs and baskets, such as this one, *c*.1920, have been in use since the earliest of times. Made by local craftsmen they are normally of utilitarian design. There are regional variations to look out for, which can add interest to a piece.

Interest in garden-related collectables is increasing all the time, reflecting our passion for gardening and the modern TV-inspired tendency to treat the garden as an outdoor room to be decorated with objects as well as plants. As the market matures certain items are becoming more valuable, while others are less desirable. Some trends are now discernable: the condition of pieces has become very important – excessive or poor restoration has a marked effect on value. A lesser piece in better condition is likely to hold or increase its value whereas a damaged piece, even if it is rare or highly regarded, is less likely to appreciate. If an object is being widely reproduced this can have a serious effect on the worth of vintage pieces. The classic example of this would be cast iron urns, where the sheer quantity of reproductions available, and their affordability, has led to a definite lowering of the originals' value. What was at one time a pair of urns worth £800 ($1,200) is probably closer to £400 ($600) in value now. Garden tools or "Gardenalia" is an area that is receiving more interest and plenty of bargains can still be found. With each year more people are recognizing the merits of antique architectural and garden ornament. However, do avoid impulse buying – think about an item's use, talk to the vendor, and try to discover as much about the piece as you can before making a purchase.

▼ Webb child's lawn mower, *c*.1955

The lawn mower was invented in England by Edwin Budding in 1830. Previously lawns were cut with a scythe and only the wealthy had large areas of grass. Thanks to the lawn mower lawns became part of the middle-class home and sports such as lawn tennis and croquet flourished. Miniature gardening tools have been made since the 19th century to encourage children's interest in gardening. Miniature lawnmowers are rare, and this example is in good working condition, which is important.

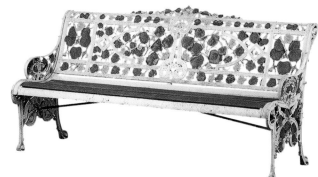

▲ Coalbrookdale "Nasturtium" seat, *c*.1870

This design was one of the most popular created by Coalbrookdale Iron Foundry, Shropshire. Many common garden plants were the inspiration for the company's famously naturalistic designs. Coalbrookdale (est. 1709) is justifiably the most sought-after foundry and, as a result, has been extensively copied. US foundry Fiske produced very closely related designs only a few years after the originals first appeared. Coalbrookdale produced its seats in four main colours, white, brown, green, and a bronze effect, of which white and green were most common.

➤ Stamped terracotta flower pot, 20th-century

The origins of the traditional flower pot shape are obscure, but it was well-established by the mid-19th century, as was an impressive array of specialized pots such as those for orchids or alpines. Generally the rarer the form or size of pot the more desirable it is. In addition a maker's stamp helps to add interest. Nurseries used enormous quantities of terracotta pots, which have now come onto the market. The tone of old terracotta makes them an inexpensive way to add interest to a garden or conservatory, as well as being very functional.

➤ Cast-iron garden roller, c.1890

Garden rollers have a long history and can be found in materials such as stone, wood, and cast iron. The dating of stone examples is difficult as form has not changed much over the years, but it is believed that some could be 18th-century, or even earlier. Owing to their weight they were necessarily constructed strongly and have consequently survived well. Although not used as much in modern gardening, rollers can make a good focal point in the garden as many of the cast-iron 19th-or early 20th-century examples were often quite decorative. There are no particular makers' names to look out for, but decorative designs by the more famous foundries tend to be the ones that command the highest prices.

▲ Compton terracotta plant pot, c.1910

The Potters Art Guild was based in Compton, a village near Guildford in England, and was a by-product of the late-19th-century Arts and Crafts movement. The guild, under the Compton name, produced famous designs such as the scroll pot (or snake pot), the best examples of which can command thousands of pounds/dollars at auction. The individual potters often initialled their work and some of these names are now well-known, which adds interest. In addition the guild made garden ornaments for Liberty's in London, using designs by Archibald Knox. Value depends on the model and its condition; a good crisp stamp also adds desirability.

◀ Undentable syringe, 1920s

Garden syringes and other related spraying devices were produced in many different designs for specific jobs during the 19th and first half of the 20th centuries, when the advent of plastics superseded the earlier metal and wooden pieces. Desirability depends on rarity and condition – a maker's stamp or plaque also helps. The plainest and most common examples are not really collectable, unlike the one pictured here. It was designed to be used for watering and for the application of fertilizers and pesticides. The term "undentable" refers to its ribbed design, which was less likely to be deformed and render the piece unusable. It was quite expensive even when it was first made, costing 35 shillings.

▲ Watering can, early 20th century

The earliest and rarest cans can command thousands at auction. This one-gallon can retains its original detachable rose, which was a push-fit as opposed to the later screw fittings. Steel examples from the 19th century were usually tinned. Many different types of can were produced, of different sizes and with specific applications, such as orchid cans, and there is a premium on the unusual varieties; copper or brass cans also tend to be more expensive than tin ones. Many interesting cans are coming on to the market from countries such as Spain, France, and Holland, giving the collector a wider choice than before.

GLASS

This 1930s centrepiece bowl by Jobling, England, resonates with the influence of René Lalique in its modelling, colour, and satin finish.

The abstract constructions of Dale Chihuly have helped to transform studio glass from a curiosity into mainstream Fine Art.

A decanter by Moser, typical of the bold, architectural Art Deco glass produced by Bohemian makers of the 1920s and '30s.

The 20th century is the fastest-growing area of interest among collectors, and of all the categories, glass is attracting greater attention than perhaps any other. It is difficult to see what could halt this trend, as objects produced relatively recently sit more comfortably in modern homes. Yet while glass has been generating increasing interest, and certain pieces can command thousands, the majority remains not only plentiful but often cheaper than equivalent brand-new, mass-produced pieces retailed in department stores, which retain little value after purchase.

Fine glassmaking, while remaining essentially craft-based, was not excluded from the technical advances that characterized the 20th century. Gas and electricity permitted the production of differing types of glass for specific uses; chemistry enabled the palette of tints and decorating techniques to be perfected and expanded, and allowed coloured glass, which had been the exception during the 18th and 19th centuries, to become the norm for even the cheapest wares. Improved transport and communications accelerated the spread of design influences.

The traditional handicap suffered by glass collectors is that few antiques are signed or maker-marked. This required each piece to be judged entirely on its own merits, such as condition and rarity, rather than as an addition to maker-orientated collections. Few glassmakers applied paper labels, let alone engraved signatures, to their work before the 1920s, with the result that identifying the work of even leading makers requires expertize. However, the practice of signing or marking glass increased dramatically during the early 20th century, largely due to American protectionist tariffs introduced between 1890 and 1919, which not only imposed duties on imports but also required that every item bear its national origin and maker's name. Most fine-quality glassmakers responded by marking their work with engraved signatures or acid-badged logos, though some, including most Bohemian and Italian workshops, opted for foil or paper labels, many of which have since been removed or washed away.

Inevitably the scenario is not entirely straightforward. Despite maker-marking, many factories continue to produce classic designs introduced decades ago. For instance, Alvar Aalto's famous vases for iittala, Finland, have remained in almost continuous production since the 1930s, while Venini's Veronese vase, dating from 1923, remains among its current best-sellers. With only early examples attracting the highest prices, collectors need to acquire the ability to differentiate between early and recent.

The following selection of items is intended as a brief introduction to 20th-century glass, its designers, and some of the companies that produced it. It spans top-of-the-range to cheap-and-cheerful, but does not attempt to be inclusive. Rather, it should be regarded as offering a flavour of the diversity of colour, form, and decoration that characterize one of the most interesting and dynamic forms of decorative collectables available today.

The UK

The British glass industry produced a large array of collectable glass between 1900 and 1980, ranging from superb quality pieces that were targeted at a sophisticated clientele when first produced, to colourful trinkets for more humble homes. The former category includes the bi-tonal, intaglio-cut effects created by Webb and Stevens & Williams in the Art Nouveau style, the textures and colours of Whitefriars, and the daringly cut contemporary pieces of the 1950s and '60s. The latter span Davidson's smokey "Cloud" range, through Bagley's home-spun pressed pieces, to Chance's jazzy "Fiesta" series. Between these extremes sat the rather cosy art pieces of Gray-Stan, Monart, Strathearn, and Nazing. Yet despite its successes the industry died because its wares failed to sell in sufficient quantities. Some designs were certainly derivative, drawn mostly from the Scandinavian repertoire, and British companies lacked confidence to back their own designers. The consequence is that most of its significant glassworks no longer exist, and pieces by British designers are now rare and highly sought-after by collectors.

The pastel tints of this Gray-Stan vase, and similar pieces by Monart, are rare examples of British 20th-century commercial studio glass.

Bagley

Bagley's Crystal Glass Co produced more colourful fancy tableglass than probably any other British maker. The works was founded in 1871 and began making crystal tableware blanks in 1911, followed by pressed glass in 1913. The company produced a huge array of styles – some original, some copies of their rivals' most successful products. The Koala Bear vase is Bagley's most desirable design by far, commanding prices of around £600 ($900) when accompanied by its original insert and stand. However, the works also made several stylish Art Deco pieces, including geometric and asymmetrical clock-mounts, vases, bowls, and plates, some designed by Royal College of Art graduate Alexander Hardie Williamson.

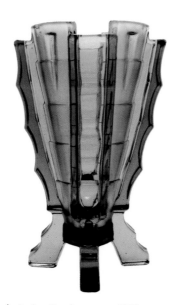

▲ Amber Bamboo vase, 1934
This vase is one of four designs produced by Alexander Hardie Williamson (1907–94) for Bagley in 1934. Williamson, a Royal College of Art graduate, was probably the most prolific 20th-century British glass designer, having produced nearly 2,000 drawings for the Sherdley and then Ravenhead divisions of industrial glassmakers United Glass.

▼ Page from Bagley brochure, c.1935
Bagley's fancy glass ranges, produced in pale pink, green, amber, and blue, sold in the tens of thousands. Some were further embellished with crudely painted flowers (which are prone to flaking), and others were set in ornate brass or chrome-plated mounts. This page from a promotional brochure illustrates some relatively common Bagley pieces alongside a lamp that is rarely found intact and is therefore more valuable.

Geoffrey Baxter

Geoffrey Baxter, recruited from London's Royal College of Art in 1954, was Whitefriars' only trained designer. Through further experience gained at St Martin's School of Art in London, and during trips to Venice and Scandinavia, he brought an entirely new look to the factory's ranges. The increasing use of cheaper, soda-based glass enabled the production of the bright, vibrant colours that distinguish much of Baxter's work, including ruby, cinnamon, indigo, willow, ocean and shadow greens, arctic and midnight blues, and, later, tangerine, kingfisher, meadow, aubergine, lilac, and sage. Baxter's work in the late 1960s focused on textured moulded forms, followed by the extensive colourless Glacier and Icicle ranges in the early '70s. Large pieces in unusual colours can now fetch £1,000 ($1,500) but standard items can still be found for just a few pounds. "Baxter-esque" pieces were produced by Davidson, Bagley, and Ravenshead but these tend to be physically lighter and lack the quality of the originals.

◀ Tangerine "Drunken Bricklayer" vase, 1967
This famous vase was designed by Geoffrey Baxter for Whitefriars and, like many of his pieces, "Drunken Bricklayers" was produced in various sizes and in several colours. Large examples in rare colours – that is, those that failed to sell at the time – are now the most sought-after, with prices varying according to colour.

Chance Brothers

Chance Brothers of Smethwick, Birmingham (1824–1981) founded its reputation in the 19th century principally as a glazing works. Pre-1945 its tableware ranges included heat-resistant Orlak, sold to Jobling in 1933, and the aptly named Spiderweb – a cheaply pressed tableglass range. Aqualux, formed from moulded sheet glass, was introduced in 1939 but abandoned at the outbreak of World War II. However, the principles behind its manufacture were resurrected for the Fiesta range – Chance Brothers' most distinctive and original range of domestic glassware, which was launched at the Ideal Home Exhibition in 1951.

▼ Handkerchief vase
This vase was inspired by superior designs by Fulvio Bianconi and Paulo Venini c.1946. Where Venini's was carefully hand-crafted, Chance Brothers' vase was made industrially by printing the design in enamels onto square, round, and oblong sheets of glass. These were then furnace-fired at 800°C (1,470°F), withdrawn as they began to sag, and then shaped by a cast-iron plunger.

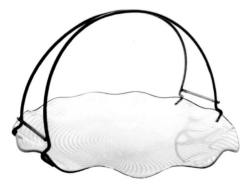

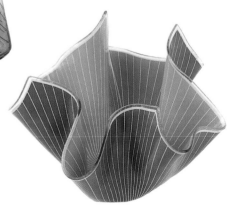

▲ Carafe, lidded pot, and tray from the "Fiesta" range, c.1955
Chance Brothers' "Fiesta" range of glass was one of Britain's most successful contemporary designs, and the popularity of the spirograph-generated, "Greco" pattern encouraged a series of others. The most stylish of these were "Swirl"(1955), a series of grey pinwheels, Margaret Casson's "Night Sky" (1957), based on the lines of an astronomical chart, and Michael Harris' eucalyptus leaf pattern "Calipto" (1959).

Davidson

George Davidson & Co of Gateshead was one of Britain's largest volume-producers of pressed tableglass between 1867 and 1987, yet its two most distinctive 20th-century ranges were designed abroad. "Chippendale" (*see* p89) was an American pattern first created in 1907, while "Jacobean" (*see* p92) belonged to the Czech glassmaker Josef Inwald. Davidson's greatest contribution was in combining "Chippendale" patterns with its own distinctive "Cloud" effects, achieved by adding molten trails of dark glass to lighter-coloured gathers. W.J.G. Fullerton was the only designer employed formally during the company's 120-year history. His best-known pieces, produced between 1939 and 1947, were his "Norman" and "Fan" vases, and the "Ripple" range, inspired by Keith Murray's pottery designs for Wedgwood.

◄ **"Cloud" vase and candlestick**
The distinctive "Cloud" range was produced in a variety of colours. Amethyst was first (1923–34), then blue (1925–34), amber/tortoiseshell (1928–57), green (1934–41), red, known as "Ora" (1929–32), orange (1933–35), and topaz, known as "Briar" (1957–61). Most of the range was formed in "Chippendale" moulds except for this vase, which was modelled on a German lager glass.

John Luxton

► **Colourless vase, c.1955–60**
This Luxton vase is characteristically decorated with deep cutting. The changing fashions and failure of British luxury glassmakers and department-store buyers to support such bold designs ultimately caused their downfall. Underlining the change in public taste, *House & Garden* magazine noted in 1964 that "it is chic to shudder at British cut-glass and set your table with uncut Scandinavian instead".

John Luxton is probably Britain's most successful and distinctive cut-glass designer. He joined Stuart Crystal in 1949, aged 29, and continues to contribute to the company's new owners, Waterford Crystal, years after retirement in 1985. A regular visitor to Scandinavian glassworks and strongly influenced by their designs, Luxton's work is characterized by deep, bold motifs – often lenses and v-groove prisms applied to colourless glass. Luxton was among several post-war British glass designers (including Irene Stevens, Geoffrey Baxter, and David Hammond) who joined various British glassworks between 1949 and 1954 as graduates from the Royal College of Art. Their natural inclination toward dynamic, Modernist forms was tempered by the factories' conservatism; their work was often applied to standard shapes, unlike the more dynamic shapes produced by Scandinavian companies.

Pre-War Whitefriars

The products of Powell's Whitefriars glasshouse are among the UK's most distinctive and collectable 20th-century decorative objects. Interest has so far centred on the designs of Geoffrey Baxter, who worked for the company 1954–80, leaving earlier work relatively cheap and available. The company remained a family affair during the 1930s, with Marriott Powell as managing director and Barnaby Powell producing most of its designs, alongside James Hogan, from 1932, and William Wilson from 1933. The Whitefriars 1930s work books illustrate thousands of designs, some of which enjoyed very limited production. Style and distinctive colours are the keys to recognizing Whitefriars pieces.

◄ **Glass by Barnaby Powell, c.1930**
This sea-green wine glass is part of Powell's M54 service – one of his best-known designs. Whitefriars' distinctive but limited range of colours, developed in its stained-glass workshop, remains the best guide to recognizing examples of the factory's pre-war output.

The USA

American glass of the 20th century is distinguished by extremes. On the one hand, crafted masterpieces by Louis C. Tiffany and Dale Chihuly can command tens if not hundreds of thousands of dollars, while on the other, the industrially produced majority of items can still be found for pennies or cents. It was with the advent of protectionist tariffs, imposed from 1824, that American glassmaking began to acquire its own identity, and profitability. The first genuinely "American" glass was formed in the press-moulds developed in New England during the 1820s, and mechanically formed glass has provided the vast majority of national production ever since. The USA's growing wealth acted as a magnet, drawing European craftsmen to its shores, including hundreds of Italian, Polish, Irish, Bohemian, and even British glassmakers. The latter included some of Stourbridge's finest talents, such as Frederick Carder, Joseph Locke, and Arthur Nash. Carder founded the Steuben works at Corning, New York, with T.G. Hawkes in 1903, Locke became famed for his complex heat-sensitive effects for Libbey's New England Glass Company from 1882, while Nash's collaboration with Louis C. Tiffany, from 1892, resulted in some of the brightest gems of Art Nouveau glass. American works, mostly situated in coal-rich Pennsylvania, Ohio, and West Virginia, produced cheap, mass-produced glassware, largely in the form of colourless pressed replicas of cut-glass. However, during the early 1920s and throughout the '30s most switched production to the patterned glassware now known as "Depression" glass. Americans were largely absent from contemporary glassmaking between Tiffany's retirement in the 1920s and the arrival in the '80s of today's unchallenged king of studio glass, Dale Chihuly, who has taken the art of glass to a new level.

A wisteria lamp by Louis C. Tiffany, *c.*1900 – an icon of American Art Nouveau. This particular example sold for over £200,000 ($300,000) in 2002.

"Carnival" Glass

"Carnival" glass is a cheap form of iridescent pressed-glass that was produced between 1907 and 1925, mostly in the USA. Its name is derived from the fact that over-production led to surplus examples being offered as prizes at fairs and carnivals. The field has become popular among glass collectors, and rare pieces can now command tens of thousands of dollars. "Carnival" pioneers included Harry Northwood who, as a teenager, had been inspired by Arthur Nash's radiant "Bronze" and "Iris" pieces, exhibited in Paris in 1878. Louis Tiffany later recruited Nash, who became the mastermind behind Tiffany's famous "Favrile" range. Where iridescent art glass was laboriously furnace-worked, carnival glass was standard pressed-glass sprayed while hot with metallic oxides, known as "dope". The resulting products poured out of the US glassmaking region priced as low as 4¢ each. As Frederick Carder, of luxury glassmakers Steuben, later lamented, "When a maid could possess iridescent glass as well as her mistress, the latter promptly lost interest in it".

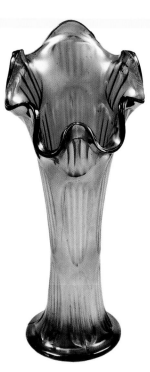

◀ Fenton "Swing" vase, *c.*1908–25
This distinctive vase derives its name from the way it was formed. Released from the mould with thick walls, a circular lip, and measuring just a few inches tall, it was then grasped and manually swung backwards and forwards to stretch it to the required height. The lip was then reheated, before being manipulated into the required shape.

Dale Chihuly

Chihuly has redefined the concept of studio glass and elevated it to a new level in the international consciousness. His flamboyant, extraordinary creations have reached an audience of millions around the world. Born in Tacoma, Washington, in 1941, Chihuly studied glassblowing under Harvey Littleton and taught at the Rhode Island School of Design until 1983. His work follows the Murano tradition, incorporating vibrant colours often assembled through complex techniques and in forms ranging in scale from table-top decorative pieces to enormous environmental installations.

◄ **"Tabac Basket", 1986**
This arrangement by Dale Chihuly is part of a continuing series of various "baskets", started in 1977. Chihuly draws from a palette of 300 colours to create asymmetrical forms, inspired by ancient traditions as diverse as American Indian textiles and Japanese flower-arranging.

"Chippendale"

► **Covered sugar bowl, 1910–40**
The "Chippendale" range extended ultimately to over 400 pieces. Most "Chippendale" is colourless, as with this sugar bowl, although some rare American examples were made in a uranium-green, and Davidson produced many of its "Chippendale" shapes in "Cloud" colours (*see* p87).

"Chippendale" is probably the most collected of all pressed-glass patterns. It was designed in 1907 by Benjamin Jacobs, manager of the Ohio Flint Glass Co of Lancaster, Ohio. The popularity of its elegant, neo-classical shapes spawned numerous imitations by rival makers, including Heisey, Duncan & Miller, Indiana and Cambridge in the USA, and Bagley in the UK (*see* p85). "Chippendale" was imported into the UK from 1913, and was manufactured by Davidson between 1930 and the early 1950s.

"Cubist" & Look-Alikes

"Cubist" is among the most stylish and popular of all "Depression" glass patterns, and provides a case-study in the difficulties of attribution for its collectors. Genuine "Cubist", also known as "Cube", was manufactured from 1929 by the Jeanette Glass Co of Pennsylvania and was produced in colourless, amber, blue, green, pink, ultramarine, and white glass. The problem for collectors is being able to recognize genuine Jeanette "Cubist" from almost exact copies produced by several US and UK glassworks, including Fostoria Glass of Moundsville, West Virginia, and the Indiana Glass Co in the USA, and James Jobling and Bagley in the UK – Bagley called its version "Honeycomb".

◄ **"Cubist" carafe, 1930–40**
The "Cubist" range was just one of thousands of "Depression" glass patterns but it remains among the most popular. It is rarer in the UK than "Chippendale" or "Jacobean" because, unlike them, it was never manufactured there. So, in the UK, copyist versions remain more common than the US originals.

"Depression" Glass

"Depression" glass is a modern term used to describe the vast quantity of cheap pressed utility glassware produced by American works during the 1930s and '40s. It was retailed at "nickel & dime" stores and given away at fairs and to cinemagoers. However, not all glass produced in the USA at that time was "Depression" glass, and not all "Depression" glass was produced during the Depression. The genre is divided into several categories, including "Depression" glass, which was retailed straight from the mould, and "Depression-Era" glass, which has finer finishes derived from firing, polishing, cutting, gilding, engraving, and acid-etching. "Depression" glass was produced by dozens of works in tens of thousands of patterns, many copied from rival designs, and in a wide range of colours and finishes.

▲ **Moulded green American pitcher, c.1930**
Manufacturers of cheap "Depression" glass used every device available to lend an air of quality to their mass-produced, injection-moulded products. The result was an extraordinary diversity of wares produced from the same moulds. The most popular techniques included bi-tonal colouring and stencilling.

▼ **Pale pink plate, c.1940**
A high proportion of "Depression" glass was decorated with fine patterns. Some of these were acid-etched – a process that requires each piece to be decorated individually. However, a majority of items were formed in moulds that were etched with the required pattern in a way that left a finish similar to acid-etching, but that was far cheaper.

Pyrex

Pyrex continues to be made by the Corning Glass Works and its many affiliates almost a century after its introduction in 1915. Driven by demands from American railroad companies for frost-proof lamp lenses, Eugene Sullivan, a Corning scientist, developed a new form of glass, based on boric oxide, with remarkable resistance to thermal shock. The resulting Pyrex range, cheap and uniquely suitable for cooking and chemistry, proved an instant global success. As the advertising stated, "It's thrifty, it's clean and it's modern!". The range was vigorously marketed and expanded rapidly into hundreds of items. As in other fields, rare forms and colours and condition determine collector values.

◀ **Advertisement for Pyrex dinner set, c.1935**
The vigorously marketed Pyrex range expanded rapidly to include hundreds of items. Until the 1940s some pieces were engraved and others were set in metal mounts, transfer-printed, or spray-painted. Later years saw the introduction of rolling pins, electric "buffet servers", coffee makers, refrigerator dishes, teapots, piggy banks, and saucepans. Vintage Pyrex survives in large numbers today.

◀ **"Gaiety" casserole dish and box, late-1950s**
This Pyrex dish is printed with a snowflake pattern and retains its original box. As in other fields of collecting, the colour of a piece and the presence of its original packaging dictates value. Brown, green, and gold dishes are considered undesirable, while white or ivory are the most common, and progressively turquoise (as seen left) and pink are more sought-after.

Bohemia

The northern and eastern strip of the Czech Republic, bordering Germany and Poland, remains known among glass aficionados by its historic title, Bohemia. The glassware made in the region since the 12th century has been of an unrivalled consistency, ingenuity, quantity, and diversity. Its makers and decorators have covered the spectra of colours, techniques, qualities, and forms. Bohemians have pioneered, reinvented, and, as elsewhere, plagiarized the entire range of glass-making and decorating techniques. Bohemian tableglass dates from around 1600 when Casper Lehmann began a fashion for Bohemian-style, or Bohème glassware, which had established its supremacy across most of Europe by 1700. The Bohemian industry suffered from war and the ascendancy of English-style cut-glass between 1770 and 1830 before a drive toward greater technical expertize led to the foundation of two important glassmaking schools in 1838 and 1870. These provided the nucleus of an industry that employed around 25,000 people by 1900; enterprises ranged from a few works with hundreds of employees to innumerable rooms or sheds housing a single decorator, or *Hausmaler*. Its traditions continued during the 20th century with Bohemian makers producing some of the world's finest, most expensive glassware, as well as some of the most forgettable, and a great deal inbetween. When in doubt about the origin of an otherwise unidentifiable piece of glassware, the chances are that the answer will be Bohemia. The problem, as ever, is in determining the specific source, as most Bohemian makers failed to sign their work, with Moser a rare exception. But with increasingly reliable literature devoted to the subject, the source of many of the most stylish pieces can now be traced – a trend that is bound to increase values.

Some of the earliest Bohemian glass was stained and enamelled for use in windows. Small, colourful Art Deco glasses remain cheap and widely available.

Chřibská

Chřibská is probably Europe's oldest productive glassworks, with documentary evidence dating its operations back to 1414 and suggestions that it began 200 years before that. Situated in northern Bohemia, near the German/Polish border, it specializes in decorative objects. Chřibská's most distinctive output remains a large series of bold, heavy vases and bowls designed by the post-war Czech painter Josef Hospodka between 1953 and 1970. The firm was nationalized by the communist regime in 1946, and with Hospodka's designs selling well in export markets, there was little incentive to introduce new models. Yet while many of the same basic designs have been produced since the 1960s, each piece is unique.

▲ **Vase or ornament by Josef Hospodka, 1953–present**
This piece is typical of the heavy but colourful designs produced by Josef Hospodka for Chřibská between 1953 and 1970. After the basic, multi-coloured shape was cased and blown into a multi-part mould it was released, manually stretched, and shaped by the blower; the items ranged widely in size, shape, and hue. Examples are commonly found today but are often attributed mistakenly to 1960s Murano or Venetian makers.

Hoffmann, Schlevogt, & Riedel

The association between Josef Riedel, Heinrich Hoffmann, and Curt Schlevogt produced some of the 20th century's most striking pressed glassware. Riedel was a seventh-generation German/Bohemian glassman and an outstanding chemist and mechanical engineer. His palette of 600 colours was used to make glassware and to sell both as a raw material and as blanks to other makers, including Hoffmann and Schlevogt. Hoffmann's best-known creations are his perfume bottles, boxes, and pin-trays. Schlevogt's reputation is based largely on his distinctive "Ingrid" range of malachite and lapis lazuli-effect vases, decanters, boxes, and scent bottles, which are still made today. Beware of reproductions that are virtually indiscernible from the originals; genuine Hoffmann pieces have an open-winged butterfly mark.

◄ Riedel vase, c.1935
Bohemian pressed-glass makers produced some of Europe's most stylish Art Deco pieces, many with strong neo-classical echoes, although the names of many of the designers remain anonymous. This large vase was made by Riedel in several colours, including this striking sky-blue.

"Jacobean"

➤ Jacobean tankard, 1920–30
This amber half-pint tankard is an exception to the general rule that the vast majority of "Jacobean" ware was made in colourless glass. Standard pieces, such as tumblers and jugs, remain so common today that they are generally cheaper than modern, industrially produced glassware, and can safely be employed for everyday use.

One of the most common pressed-glass patterns, "Jacobean" was designed and produced by Joseph Inwald AG, owners of five Bohemian glassworks. Hubert and Eric Mayers, trading as Clayton Mayers, marketed the over 400-piece "Jacobean" range in Britain. Typical of the company's innovative approach was a promotional film, A Visit to Miss Madeleine Carroll's Flat, which extolled "the beauty and utility of 'Jacobean' glassware in a modern home". Manufacture of "Jacobean" for the British market then switched to Davidson of Gateshead in 1932.

Palda

The Karel Palda glassworks, founded in Novy Bor in 1888, grew to become one of Bohemia's largest producers of table and lighting glass. By the 1930s its vast output spanned a decorative range that encompassed cutting, painted and stencilled enamelling, colouring, and engraving. Retailed originally with paper factory stickers, and never signed, much of the factory's more stylish output will be familiar to modern collectors. It included a range of distinctive Art Deco cut tableware featuring geometric transparent and black enamels. The company also produced huge numbers of perfume atomizers, vases, and lampshades in marbled and plain-coloured glass, often spray-stencilled with patterns, land and seascapes, and domestic pets.

◄ Decanter and shot glass, c.1930
The Palda works produced quality glassware of all types, including large amounts of somewhat characterless, colourless pressed glass. This fine-quality decanter and shot glass is from a set that originally included six glasses and a tray, all decorated with cutting and vitreous enamels in three colours.

France

Such was the derivative nature of its forms and decoration that it requires specialist knowledge to identify French glassware pre-1830. Political and social anarchy around 1850 caused the closure of many French glassworks, forcing leading glassmakers and decorators to emigrate. However, with the advent of Art Nouveau around 1890 French glassmaking underwent a most spectacular flowering. Art Nouveau drew on myriad influences, including the Beaux-Arts style that had flourished in France, and later the USA, from the 1870s, and led directly to the work of its greatest creative genius, Emile Gallé. One of several French art-glass makers to emerge during the 1870s, Gallé expanded the boundaries of glassmaking through the use of acids on multi-layered blanks. He inspired numerous followers, including Antonin Daum, Louis Majorelle, and Maurice Marinot, who formed part of the "new wave" of French glassmakers. The trend was to make fine-quality pieces at the lowest cost by producing them semi-industrially – typified by René Lalique who combined an amazing design sense with an understanding of moulding techniques, enabling his work to be mass-produced.

Dynamic designs and techniques developed by Emile Gallé from the 1880s inspired a generation of French glassmakers.

Baccarat

Les Cristilleries de Baccarat, founded in 1765, has produced lead crystal since 1816. The company continues today to make cut glass, *moulé en plein* moulded pieces, and various forms of coloured glass, some in designs dating from the 1820s. Russian aristocracy was a significant contributor to the company's late-19th/early 20th century success as Russian nobles embraced the extravagant custom of smashing their glassware after each meal, thus inadvertently providing employment for Baccarat's large workforce. Baccarat's most distinctive and longest-serving 20th-century designer was Georges Chevallier, who created so many pieces between 1916 and 1976 that the company is unable to quantify them.

▼ Candelabrum by Jacques Adnet, c.1935
This silvered bronze and crystal candelabrum was designed by Adnet (1900–84) for Baccarat. Adnet was one of France's leading 20th-century designers, having worked in both Art Deco and Modernist styles principally in furniture, mirrors, and lamps. In 1959 he gave up designing to become director of the École Nationale Supérieure des Arts Décoratifs.

◀ Art Deco wine glasses by Georges Chevallier, 1930s
Chevallier's early work was characterized by a painterly use of colour, but from 1925 he moved toward a more architectural and sculptural style. These glasses are among a huge number of Chevellier's cut designs, many of which extended the boundaries of the cutter's art to new limits.

Daum

➤ Green ashtray, c.1960

The output of the Daum factory at Nancy has varied greatly since its foundation in 1878. Its colourful Art Nouveau and Art Deco designs, made between the 1890s and 1930s, gradually gave way to the more sober Modernist pieces of the 1950s and '60s. All Daum pieces have been signed since 1890.

Daum is the best-known of many French glassworks that followed Gallé's lead into commercial cameo glass, and proved the most successful in adapting to Art Deco style. Cameo glass is achieved by forming a multi-layered and coloured blank, then selectively removing the layers to create the design. Early examples c.1870 required the layers to be chiselled and ground away and were expensive to make; acids made the process much faster. The presence of the Daum signature helps its popularity among today's collectors.

René Lalique

René Lalique is the world's most famous and collected glassmaker. He was apprenticed to a jeweller and enrolled at the Paris École des Arts Decoratifs in 1876 at the age of 16. He began to produce glassware in 1902 and bought his first works in 1909. He pioneered several techniques for moulding and casting glass, some derived from skills he had acquired as a jeweller, such as *cire perdu* (lost wax) casting. Most Lalique glassware was pressed and moulded using traditional methods but designed to maximize their potential. His work proved hugely influential and has been widely copied.

◄ "Thais" by René Lalique, c.1925–30

This iconic sculpture is one of a series of frosted-glass female nude figurines holding drapes. A similar version, "Suzanne", dating from the same period, is made yet more erotic by draping the material to reveal the entire upper body. Using the same moulds Lalique managed to increase his range by producing identical pieces in different colours, with opalescent highlights and the use of stains. Beware as virtually identical copies were produced at the same time in Paris by Marius Ernest Sabino (1878–1961).

Val Saint-Lambert

➤ Decanter by Joseph Simon and Charles Graffart, c.1926–29

Val Saint-Lambert produced a great deal of nondescript glass. However, its high quality ranges, in which coloured glass was enhanced by stylish cutting, rivalled the best in Europe. Many of the latter pieces resulted from collaborations between designer Joseph Simon and master-cutter Charles Graffart, as is the case with this decanter, pictured right.

Les Verreries de Val Saint-Lambert, founded near Liège in 1826, has been Belgium's leading glassmaker for nearly two centuries. By 1900 nearly half the output produced by its 6,000-strong labour force was exported to the UK and the British Empire. The works produced hundreds of services, plain and coloured, cut and acid-etched, and enjoyed associations with numerous eminent designers, including Henry van der Velde, Désiré and Henri Muller of Muller Frères, and Romain and Jeanne Gevaert. Val Saint-Lambert is also inextricably linked to Charles Graffart, who joined in 1906 at the age of 12 and was chief designer from 1942 to 1958. Others have included Nanny Still and Harvey Littleton.

Ornament of multicoloured cased glass finely cut with a mass of hexagons, by contemporary Venetian artist Lino Tagliapietra.

Venice

Venetian glass was among the glories of the Renaissance, collected by Europe's rulers and valued alongside gold, jewels, and property. Its makers were sworn to guard trade secrets and the city traded their skills as commodities in exchange for goods, favours, and concessions. However, the rise *c.*1700 of glassware engraved in the Bohemian manner (*façon de Bohème*) finally swept the Venetian style out of international fashion. By the mid-19th century the dwindling number of glassmakers on the small island of Murano had been reduced to scratching a living from making beads and tourist trinkets. A Venetian lawyer, Dr Antonio Salviati, was almost entirely responsible for Murano's revival. Salviati assembled a team of workers from leading local glass-making families and opened a new furnace in 1862; his wares, mostly reproductions of Renaissance classics, came to represent the epitome of good taste across late-19th-century Europe. By the mid-20th century Murano products had returned to the centre-stage of glassmaking, and pieces by Scarpa, Martens, and Barovier & Toso can command higher prices among today's collectors than 18th-century classics.

Ercole Barovier

The Barovier family has been making glass on Murano since at least 1295. Angelo Barovier is widely credited with perfecting *cristallo*, the brittle, soda-based glass metal used by local makers from 1450 to the present. The 20th-century story of the Barovier family is a complex one, with Giovanni, Benvenuto, Benedetto, Guiseppe, Nicolò, Ercole, and Angelo all involved in the works at various times. The most famous and creative of these was Ercole, who joined Vetreria Artistica Barovier in 1919 at the start of a 53-year career in glassmaking. A union in 1936 with rival works Ferro Toso, also of ancient island lineage, formed what became known as Barovier & Toso in 1942. Ercole produced most of the designs until he retired in 1972, when he was succeeded by son Angelo.

◄ Muranese vase, 1940
This vase by Ercole Barovier, encasing a dark blue spiral tipped with black canes and highlighted with gold leaf, typically draws from the repertoire of traditional Muranese techniques. The black canes were added to the blue core before rolling it against sheets of gold leaf. It was then twisted, before being cased within colourless glass.

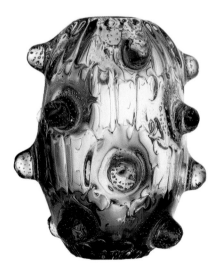

◄ Colourless vase, 1938–40
Ercole Barovier's work is generally distinguished by his vivid use of colour. However, this colourless vase with applied *bugne* nodes was designed at one of his most creative periods. It formed part of his extensive "Mugnoni" range, named after Antonio Mugnoni – a late-18th-century Venetian artist.

Venice "Tourist" Glass

Murano glassmaking exists on various levels – exclusive studios where a maestro employs a small team, or larger, prestige works, such as Venini and the Segusos, where several teams produce pieces retailed through chic boutiques and department stores in the world's leading cities. However, the majority of the island's output is made by dozens of smaller works, some open to visitors, where all kinds of decorative and colourful objects are produced for the "tourist trade", handmade by experienced craftsmen using time-honoured techniques. However, the future of the trade is increasingly threatened by copies produced in the Far East.

➤ Murano cockerel, 1960s
The reason for the popularity of ducks, chickens, and swans among glassmakers, particularly those working on Murano, remains uncertain, but examples dating as far back as the Renaissance are recorded. This large crowing cockerel, its body encased in gold leaf with a red comb, was made on the island, probably in the 1960s.

➤ Murano bowl, 1950s, and *sommerso* ashtray, 1960s
The term "tourist glass" is not necessarily pejorative because much of it demands a high degree of skill from its makers. Rather, it is applied to pieces produced at one of the hundreds of less famous Murano glassworks. Artists flow between the different works as freely as the design ideas themselves.

Venini

Venini is probably the most famous and consistent of Murano's quality glassworks. It was founded in 1921 by Milanese lawyer Paulo Venini and Venetian antique dealer Giacomo Cappellin. When this partnership collapsed in 1925 Venini continued alone, with Napoleone Martinuzzi as creative director. Martinuzzi's greatest contribution was to switch the focus from retro to Modernist through a swathe of radical designs. Over the following decades many of the world's greatest glass designers passed through Venini's doors.

A "Bolle" bottles by Tapio Wirkkala, 1966–present
Wirkkala and his compatriot Timo Sarpeneva effectively were "rented" to Venini by the Finnish government to help meet the cost of repaying a massive war debt imposed on the nation by Russia. The "Bolle" range is still produced today.

➤ "Veronese" vase by Vittorio Zecchin, 1921
This is Venini's most famous piece, which was modelled on a similar vase that featured in the background of Paolo Veronese's painting *The Annunciation* (c.1580). The shape has been adopted as the company logo but has been widely reproduced, not only by Venini but also by other makers on Murano, and even in the Far East.

Scandinavia

Orrefors' *graal* technique was adopted by several Swedish makers. This example, *c*.1950, was by Willem G. de Moor for Flygfors.

The 1920s to 1950s witnessed a transformation in Scandinavian glassmaking as designers established an entirely new look in tableglass design. The Scandinavian glass industry had an undistinguished history, with numerous small works producing derivative wares since the 16th century, mostly directed by Germans and Bohemians in their national styles. Then, in 1916–17, Johan Ekman of the Orrefors glassworks broke the impasse by hiring Simon Gate and Edward Hald. Trained artists and designers, Hald and Gate brought a radical new approach to glass design, uniting Le Corbusier and van de Rohr, neo-classicism, contemporary painting and sculpture, and more, to make a major contribution to the style that has become known as "Scandinavian Modern". Radical new ranges of tableware by Gate, Hald, and Edvin Ollers for Kosta were unveiled at the 1917 Home Exhibition in Stockholm under the motto "*vackrare vardagsvara*" ("beautiful things for everyday use"). The trend was continued at the Boda, Åfors, and Flygsfors works in Sweden, Kastrup and Holmegaard in Denmark, Hadeland in Norway, and iittala and Karhulla in Finland, and changed the look of modern glass.

Holmegaard

Holmegaard, a luxury glassmaker based on the Danish island of Zealand, was founded in 1825. It also owned the Kastrup works, run as a separate venture until 1965 when the two works merged under Holmegaard. Production from 1927 to 1998 was largely the work of two trained designers, Jacob Bang and Per Lütken. Bang, who worked for Holmegaard 1927–41 and for Kastrup 1957–65, is credited with modernizing Danish glass. Lütken spent his entire working life (1942–98) at Holmegaard – a longevity that gave the works' designs a sense of continuity through his ranges of sophisticated, free-form, coloured art glass, and functional colourless tableware.

◀ **Decanter, glass, and vase by Per Lütken, late 1950s**

The "Aristocrat" service, to which this decanter belongs, is perhaps Lütken's most distinctive design, combining simple curves, soft transparent colour tints, and a unique stopper. The drinking glass is from the "Canada" range. The base of the green tube vase is engraved "HOLMEGAARD 19PL59", which represents the date of manufacture and Lütken's monogrammed initials.

▶ **"Gul" ("Floor") vases by Otto Brauer, 1968–80**

These vases, produced in a variety of sizes and transparent and opal colours, proved to be Holmegaard's most popular product. Though often mis-attributed to the company's most famous designers, Jacob Bang and Per Lütken, they are in fact the work of Otto Brauer, master glassmaker at the company's Odense plant. The value of each vase will depend on its size and whether it is cased with a white lining or simply made of clear glass (the cased versions are at least twice as valuable in most instances).

iittala

Founded in Finland in 1881, iittala reached the major league of world glassmaking from 1932 by recruiting winners of national design competitions. Famed designer and architect Alvar Aalto, who made the classic Aalto vases, was the first winner, followed by Göran Hongell who was responsible for ranges of geometric tableglass including the Aarne service. However, iittala's most famous post-war designers have been Tapio Wirkkala and Timo Sarpaneva, whose work still forms the core of iittala's production today.

➤ **"Ultima Thule" carafe and glasses by Tapio Wirkkala, late 1960s**
This service of practical table-glass helped to establish iittala's international reputation. Originally designed in 1967 for Finnair's first transatlantic flights, the tumblers entered commercial production in 1968, the carafe in 1970, and they are still made today.

➤ **"Orkidea" ("Orchid") vase by Timo Sarpaneva, c.1957**
The "Orkidea" series of vases was first produced in 1954 and won the Grand Prix at the Milan Triennale that same year. This example is typical of the switch of emphasis away from practicality towards the sculptural organic forms that were characteristic of much post-war Scandinavian glass.

Kosta-Boda

◀ **"People" decanter by Erik Höglund, 1956**
Kosta-Boda produced two versions of this design: on the superior version the stopper was all glass, whereas the peg of that fitted to the inferior version was formed in corrugated translucent plastic. The "People" decanter was made in several colours and sizes, and collector demand is driven by quality, size, and colour.

Sweden's Kosta, founded in 1742, is one of the world's oldest glassworks. A Modernist phase began with art director Elis Bergh, who designed a series of imposing art glass in the 1930s as well as employing artists such as Sven "The X" Erixon and Tyra Lundgren to boost diversity. Kosta merged with neighbouring works Boda and Åfors in 1946 to become Kosta-Boda. Vicke Lindstrand, recruited from Orrefors in 1950, was Kosta-Boda's new art director until 1973; input from the likes of young sculptor Erik Höglund from 1953 placed a greater art-orientation on the works' products.

◀ **Vase by Vicke Lindstrand, c.1958**
This piece by Lindstrand blends a monolithic Modernist shape with a retro Venetian theme through the use of coloured canes, cased within a thick colourless body. Similar techniques were explored at the time by Kaj Franck for Nuutajärvi, Finland, and Sven Palmqvist for Orrefors, Sweden.

Paperweights

With such a diversity of styles and makers there is huge scope when collecting glass paperweights. They first appeared in the 1840s. Leading 19th-century makers include Baccarat, St Louis, and Clichy in France; high-quality paperweights were also produced in the UK, the USA, and Bohemia. In the 20th century Scotland was home to many fine makers, including Paul Ysart, Perthshire, Caithness, Peter Holmes, and John Deacons. Whitefriars has been the most important single manufacturer in England, and the USA is the centre of the modern paperweight world. Weights have been produced in many different techniques: major styles include millefiori (made from multicoloured glass canes); lampwork (in which flowers, such as those shown left, are assembled petal by petal, joined together by heating, and then overlaid with layers of clear molten gloss); sulphide weights, inset with a cameo; torchwork (painting with molten glass); and abstract (*see* below). Always check the base of a weight for an inscribed signature or number; sometimes initials or a maker's symbol appears within the weight itself on one of the canes.

"Blue Bouquet", made by the American maker Rick Ayotte, is an excellent example of lampwork.

▲ "Rooster" by Perthshire, 1977
The rooster that appears in the centre of this paperweight is actually on a lower level, and can be seen through a "hole" in the red ground. The weight is made up of many coloured rods, fixed into a template, fused, and cut into slices for the rooster cane itself. This is a paperweight of great skill and complexity. It has a P1977 cane in the base and was one of an edition of 350 weights.

▼ "Old English" paperweight, 1920
Little is known about English paperweights made in the 19th century and early 20th century. Birmingham maker Bacchus has various identifiable characteristics, as do Walsh-Walsh and Arculus from the 1920s and '30s, but there are many that cannot be identified. This weight has solid-white star canes, as used by Walsh-Walsh, but other characteristics do not match so it remains a mystery, and an interesting buy.

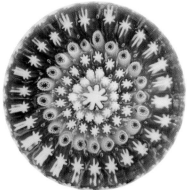
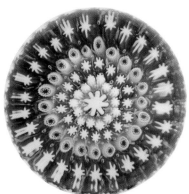

➤ "Columbine" by Daniel Salazar for Lundberg Studios, 2003
The interest of this American paperweight lies in the technique used, known as "Californian Torchwork". The plant in the middle has been painted in molten coloured glass to produce a fluid, two-dimensional effect. Brothers Daniel and David Salazar have perfected this method over the years, and Daniel is now the principal artist at Lundberg Studios in Davenport, California (est. 1975). This particular flower comes in several different colourways.

▲ "Camelot" by Caithness, 1983
This abstract paperweight, with its representation of King Arthur's legendary castle, is now regarded as a Caithness "classic" and is much sought-after, selling at a premium in most auctions. "Abstract" weights are classified as those that illustrate a personal interpretation of a subject or idea by the artist, as opposed to the realism and intricate accuracy of more traditional flower-based weights.

GRAMOPHONES & RECORDERS

His Master's Voice, model 22, 1924. The classic shape of the gramophone appeals to many; this quality product has a wooden horn, which increases its value to collectors.

Sound recording became a reality in 1877 when Thomas Edison tested his first phonograph using a tinfoil cylinder to record stylus-cut patterns, which could then be reproduced. His first recording was *Mary Had a Little Lamb*. Alexander Graham Bell and Charles Tainter improved matters by using wax cylinders, and by 1895 Edison had retaken the lead and the home entertainment market boomed. In 1888 Emile Berliner invented a second recording system, the "gramophone", which used flat discs rather than cylinders. By 1900 competition was intense and the simplicity of manufacture and duplication made records the prime source of sound and music in the home until the radio age. The introduction of wire and tape recording and the vinyl microgroove record in the late 1940s revitalized the industry, as did the cassette in 1964, leaving a rich heritage of collectables. The important factors are quality, originality, novelty, and condition, and close examination may be necessary before making a purchase as there are ever-increasing numbers of reproduction machines on the market. Always keep a look out for machines disguised as high-class furniture, or even pianos and other household items.

◄ Edison standard phonograph, 1908
This machine plays both two-minute and four-minute cylinders. Up to 1902 cylinders were individually recorded, but with introduction of the gold-moulded process, mass-production of wax cylinders at last became possible. By 1912 Edison had perfected the four-minute Blue Amberols, made of celluloid, but all production ceased in 1929. Although soon displaced by the gramophone, machines made between 1900 and 1912 survive in surprising numbers, and can still be found without too much difficulty.

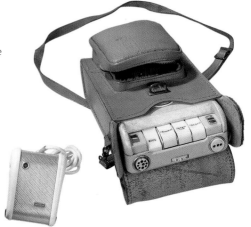

HMV model 101 portable gramophone, 1928

Music on the move became important during World War I, and by the mid-1920s portable machines were being made everywhere. HMV, Decca, and Columbia dominated the market in the UK until the mid-1930s, but from that point on the temptations of radio and the expansion of the electricity network saw sales reduce drastically. This HMV gramophone was one of the most popular and of the best quality. All parts were made by the company, and the number 4 soundbox was able to cope with the latest electrical recordings.

▲ Minifon portable wire recorder, 1953
Wire recorders never gained much popularity with the general public. By the time domestic machines became available in the late 1940s there was already competition from recorders using paper tape, and the introduction of acetate- and plastic-based recording media sealed their fate. The Minifon was the exception to the rule as it found service in many offices in the 1950s as a dictating machine, because high fidelity sound was not needed and its compact size made it convenient. All wire recorders are collectable today.

➤ Barbie record player, 1962

The golden age of the electric record player was 1955 to the late 1960s, when hundreds of models were produced. The brighter, more outrageous designs, synonymous with the rock 'n' roll era, are now in demand. Items for the children's market that linked with current fads are much rarer, as with a life expectancy of months they often did not survive. This Barbie® record player has bold period graphics that make it easy to date – essential for such items.

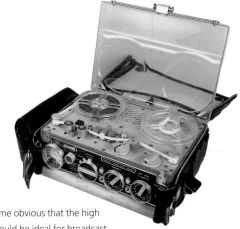

➤ Nagra III tape recorder, 1964

With the introduction of tape recording it soon became obvious that the high quality and low noise characteristics of the system would be ideal for broadcast and studio applications. By the mid-1960s Kudelski of Switzerland was producing the Nagra III, a machine of legendary quality and reliability, hand-made to exacting standards. Professional equipment is exceptionally rugged, and surviving items from any period have a ready market providing that they are unmodified and in reasonable condition.

▲ Weltron Hi Fi 2007, 1966

The novel design of the Weltron home audio system left no doubt as to the modernity of its owner. Such lifestyle products are instant collectables, but few of these were made so can be difficult to find. The advent of space travel widely influenced design, with new processes and materials available. Weltron was also known for its futuristic plastic "Space Ball".

◀ Sony Walkman, 1979

Traditionally the enjoyment of music had been a group experience, but in the 1970s society was changing and individuals were "doing their own thing". What, then, could be more sensible than a completely personal sound system? Sony saw the need and decided to produce the Walkman, which gave the cassette a new impetus through the 1980s. Millions were produced, and for collectors the earliest model is the one to go for, although few survive from the initial production of 30,000.

His Master's Voice Nipper needle tin
The many variations in design of the Nipper needle tin can form a colourful and worthwhile collection.

Nipper Tin

In 1887 Nipper the fox terrier came to artist Francis Barraud from his brother, who had recently died. A few years later his dog's rapt attention to a phonograph inspired a painting that Francis called "His Master's Voice". Initial attempts to interest phonograph companies in the picture failed and it was put to one side. However, William Owen, founder of the Gramophone Company, saw the painting and agreed to purchase it if the phonograph was replaced by his own gramophone. In 1900 he copyrighted the design that was soon to become one of the world's best-known trademarks. Nipper appeared on all kinds of advertising material for items such as speed testers, needle tins, and cleaning pads, creating a wealth of choice for today's collectors. Particularly prized are the large model dogs that adorned shop windows, but there are many reproduction terriers and careful checks should be made before buying. Nipper memorabilia is still constantly in demand.

HANDBAGS

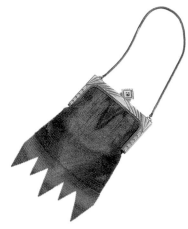

1920s Dresden mesh bag, Whiting & Davis; the coloured metal and fringe reflect the flapper fashions.

The handbag emerged in the late 18th century; previously women had worn chatelaines or loose fabric pockets taped around the waist, reached through slashes in their skirts. With the advent of neo-classical style (slimline, high-waisted dresses made of daringly diaphanous material) bulging pockets were a sartorial impossibility. Ladies adopted drawstring bags, dangled from the wrist, known as reticules. Critics dubbed them "ridicules", but the fashion stuck and the handbag became a female necessity. Handbags reflect the fashions of the day and are highly collectable. Whereas early examples can be fragile, and are often bought for display only, many vintage bags are perfectly useable. They can be teamed very successfully with modern outfits, and make a great conversation piece. Prices depend on age, shape (the more interesting the better), material, designer, and condition. Always open a handbag before buying it as the state of the lining will affect its value, and there might be something of interest inside it.

➤ 1950s Lucite bag by Willardy

An American favourite, the Lucite handbag was a by-product of wartime technology. This 1950s marbled plastic and brass bag is by Willardy. The New York company was known for its costly and curvaceous Lucite box bags inspired, claimed founder Will Hardy, by New Look fashion and Marilyn Monroe's figure. Bags came in clear and coloured Lucite, and in different sculptural shapes. Many are labelled: major manufacturers include Lewellyn, Rialto, Florida Handbags, and Patricia of Miami. When buying check for cracks and sniff for a chemical smell, which can mean plastic decay.

▲ Beaded floral reticule, c.1850

Beaded bags, woven from thousands of coloured glass or cut-steel beads, were fashionable from the Victorian to Art Deco periods. As well as being professionally produced, some were also homemade. In the 19th century beading a bag, like sewing a sampler, was a traditional female accomplishment, and some are signed and dated by their maker. Bags decorated with figural scenes often command the highest prices. Floral patterns were popular in the 19th century and bold geometric designs came in after WWI, along with colourful, celluloid clasps. Flat beaded bags were attached to metal frames; pouches had drawstrings, which on good quality bags were often threaded through ivory or tortoiseshell rings.

◄ Crocodile "Escort" bag, 1950s

Crocodile, alligator, and other skins have long been in use for handbags and travel goods. Edwardian ladies carried crocodile portmanteaux and python, lizard, and other exotic purses were clutched under-arm in the 1920s and '30s. During WWII metal fittings and many leathers were restricted due to rationing, but in the 1950s luxury returned. This American crocodile bag is labelled "Escort"; its simple shape makes it desirable today. Some period bags come decorated with the animal's head and feet, which is far less appealing to modern tastes. Condition is important since reptile skins are prone to drying out. Fine suede and leather linings denote a quality bag; watch out for imitation skins and mock-croc.

▼ The Kelly Bag by Hermès

Bags by big-name designers carry a premium, and there is a huge market for second-hand classics. In 1837 Thierry Hermès opened a harness- and saddle-making company in Paris. With the development of travel and the motor car Hermès expanded into luggage, patenting the zip fastener in France and producing a range of classic handbags from the 1930s. The Kelly Bag, modelled on a 19th-century saddlebag, is named after film icon Grace Kelly, who appeared with one on a 1956 cover of *Life* magazine. Though still in production (each bag takes a single craftsman 18 hours to hand-make), the price and waiting time for modern examples make vintage Kelly bags very sought-after. However, beware of fakes.

▲ Wicker frog bag, 1950s

Based on traditional shopping baskets, basket handbags became very popular in the 1950s, particularly in the USA. They were produced in every shape, from flower-covered box-bags to novelty designs in the form of animals and fish. This frog bag is extremely unusual and as such very desirable. Condition is also important since wicker bags can dry out and crack, and handles are vulnerable to damage and unravelling. As well as being popular with collectors, 1950s hand-bags have served as direct inspiration to contemporary handbag designers such as Lulu Guinness, whose creations are a good bet for collectables of the future.

► Silk and gilt-metal shoulder bag by Emilio Pucci, 1960s

Shoulder bags first came into general use during WWII, when women needed to carry gas masks and keep their hands free for war work. In the frivolous 1950s it was back to high heels and hand-held bags, but the "swinging sixties" saw the revival of the swinging shoulder bag. This silk and gilt-metal example is by Emilio Pucci, the Italian designer famous for his psychedelic prints. Pucci inspired many imitators, so check for the Pucci signature on the fabric. Other '60s favourites include the chain metal shoulder bag, pioneered by Spanish designer Paco Rabanne.

◄ 1970s magazine clutch bag by Mister Ernest Handbags

Popular in the 1920s, clutch bags came back into fashion in the 1970s, along with the Art Deco revival. The surrealist fashion designer Elsa Schiaparelli had experimented with newsprint handbags in the 1930s. This rigid plastic clutch, made in the 1970s by Mister Ernest Handbags in China, is in the form of a folded magazine. Many different magazine covers were used for this trompe-l'oeuil classic, which was produced by various manufacturers. Values depend on the appeal of the image and condition, since the plastic can be prone to damage and discoloration. Look out for 1970s Pop-art style handbags.

JEWELLERY

This late-Victorian pendant is made from vulcanite (a hardened rubber substitute for jet). Moulded rather than carved designs could be mass-produced.

This silver-and-paste necklace (c.1910) reflects the Edwardian fashion for delicate designs. Bows and flower baskets were popular.

This chrome choker and bracelet set with moving plastic discs is a classic example of 1960s style, and as such is very collectable.

The jewellery in this section dates from the 19th century to the 1990s and the main focus is on costume jewellery and objects made from non-precious materials. Although one tends to think of costume jewellery as a 20th-century phenomenon, in reality it has a much longer history.

The 18th century saw a fashion for paste that simulated gemstones. This was worn not only by the middle classes, who could not afford real jewels, but also by the rich – partly to confound highwaymen (the muggers of their day), but also because it was beautiful in its own right. Glass wasn't the only substitute: marcasite (iron pyrites) and cut steel, developed by the great 18th-century inventor Matthew Boulton, both provided a cheaper alternative to the sparkle of diamonds. Around 1720 London watchmaker Christopher Pinchbeck discovered an alloy of copper and zinc that looked like gold but was lighter and more hard-wearing. Pinchbeck, as it was called, proved a perfect material for typically large 19th-century brooches and bracelets.

As the following selection shows, the Victorian and Edwardian periods saw the development of affordable, mass-produced jewellery, made from a huge range of materials from Scotch pebbles to vulcanized rubber. None of the illustrated pieces is by a known maker, yet all of them are collectable and wearable today.

If costume jewellery was created initially to imitate the real thing, after World War I it became an art form in its own right. Freed from the expensive restraints of precious materials, American jewellers and European fashion designers could let their imaginations run riot. Jewellery was made in every conceivable shape, style, and colour, and with an extravagance that would have been impossible with more valuable materials. Many collectors concentrate on the big designer names, shown in this section. Other enthusiasts might focus on a particular subject or medium rather than maker – for example collecting insect brooches or designs in Bakelite. Although designers often signed their works (check necklace clasps and the backs of earrings and brooches for a stamp), many pieces will also be found unmarked. As with all jewellery condition is important, and missing stones and broken parts will affect value.

The finest costume jewellery can now fetch almost as much as the real thing. There are specialist dealers and dedicated books, and the internet has expanded the potential for buying and selling worldwide. It is possible to spend a small fortune on a big-name piece; however, you can also go out with £10 ($15) and come back with a vintage sparkling necklace – maker unknown but fabulous to wear.

Real diamonds might make you look wealthy, but costume and non-precious jewellery can make you look interesting. By collecting vintage pieces, be it Victorian jet or 1940s paste, you can combine a love of antiques with a desire to appear attractive, and perhaps just that little bit different. As in the 18th century, you are still less likely to inspire street crime than those wearing real gemstones, and what could be more fun than wearing your own collectables?

Victorian & Edwardian

In the 19th century jewellery became widely available for the first time, thanks to mass-production and cheaper materials. Improved transport was another factor. With the development of tourism cameos, and micro-mosaics were imported from Italy. Hard-stone brooches from Scotland reflected the Victorian interest in both geology and Celtic archaeology. There was a host of historic revivals, inspired by every culture from medieval England to 18th-century France. Sentimental jewellery was favoured by every level of society; popular motifs included hearts, clasped hands, and Cupid's arrows. Loving messages were spelt out in the language of flowers and with the initial letters of gemstones, for example "REGARD" (ruby, emerald, garnet, amethyst, ruby, diamond). As well as celebrating love, jewellery also commemorated death. When Prince Albert died in 1861 Queen Victoria plunged into the blackest grief, stimulating the fashion for mourning jewellery. The dark and heavy styles that complemented voluminous Victorian fashions gave way at the *fin de siecle* to lighter, more delicate jewellery and naturalistic Art Nouveau designs.

This Art Nouveau gold pendant, *c.*1900, set with blue topaz and pearls, reflects turn-of-the-century taste for delicate, pale designs.

▼ Natural jet bracelet, *c.*1875

Jet, made from fossilized wood, has been used to make jewellery since ancient times, but it became a craze in the 19th century. The combination of high mortality rates and strict social etiquette meant that Victorian women could spend years in black, and even in death they wanted to look fashionable. The jet industry in Whitby, on the Yorkshire coast, grew from two shops with 25 employees in 1832 to 200 shops and 1,500 workers in 1872. Natural jet is light in weight (making it perfect for large Victorian jewellery), and warm to the touch. Jet was usually carved and the value of a piece will reflect its decoration.

▲ Pinchbeck hair brooch, *c.*1850

Hair jewellery was worn from the 17th century and became very fashionable in the Victorian period. A few strands of hair would be set into rings and lockets, both as living love tokens and in memory of the dear departed. The Prince of Wales' feathers were a favourite pattern. Pieces often bear inscriptions, and the reverse of this swivel brooch contains a sepia photograph. Naked hair was also used for purely decorative purposes, woven and plaited into bracelets and earrings. Jewellery was both homemade and created by professional hair-workers.

◄ French jet brooch, *c.*1880

The popularity of jet spawned a host of black alternatives. French jet, made from black glass (also known as Vauxhall glass) is heavier, colder, and shatters less easily than natural jet, so was used to produce objects such as black buttons. Other substitutes included bog oak (oak wood preserved in peat and stained black), dyed horn, *bois durci* (compressed wood powder painted black), and vulcanite (or ebonite) – hardened rubber developed for tyres by Charles Goodyear in 1846. When exposed to sunlight vulcanite can fade in colour.

◀ **Scottish silver-and-agate brooch, c.1870**
Queen Victoria's love of Scotland helped stimulate the fashion for Scottish jewellery. Miniature dirks (daggers) and highland shoulder brooches were set with local agates (known as Scotch pebbles) and with Cairngorm – yellow quartz mined from the Cairngorm Mountains in Scotland that can be imitated using heat-treated Brazilian amethysts. Edinburgh was the centre of production, but as the craze for Scottish jewellery spread across Europe it was also manufactured in Birmingham. Designs were inspired by ancient Celtic prototypes and popular sentimental motifs; the anchor was a symbol of hope.

▼ **Italian mosaic brooch, 1900**
The popularity of the Italian "grand tour" stimulated demand for souvenir jewellery. *Pietra dura*, a hard stone inlay used for everything from table tops to brooches, was produced in Florence. Micro-mosaic, made from tiny pieces of coloured glass, was another Italian speciality. Detailed mosaic pictures of famous ruins and views were purchased, and then set in gold. Cheaper tourist pieces, such as this floral brooch, were sold ready mounted on brass. Cameos were another classical souvenir targeted at every level of the market, ranging from the finest carved gemstones to more affordable pieces made from shell or lava.

▲ **Silver name and gilt-metal Mizpah brooches, c.1900**
Name brooches were a popular gift and were often worn by maids and nannies to ensure that visitors knew their names. Typically the brooches are silver; sometimes letters have a gold overlay. Value depends on the current popularity of names – the resurgence of Victorian favourites such as Lily and Rose means they are in demand. Bar brooches, inscribed with sentimental motifs and mottos, set off the high Edwardian collars. "Mizpah" comes from the Old Testament and signifies: "The Lord watch between me and thee, when we are absent from one another".

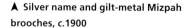

▶ **Silver-and-enamel pendant, c.1910**
In the late 19th century there was a reaction to the overblown ostentation of fine jewellery and the poor quality of cheaply manufactured products. Arts and Crafts designers cultivated simpler styles, handmade by individual craftsmen often using comparatively inexpensive materials, such as silver and semi-precious stones. These one-off, avant-garde pieces were imitated in machine-made, hand-finished jewellery by larger, more commercial firms such as Murle Bennet and Co (1814–1914) and Halifax silversmith Charles Horner. Liberty & Co in London (est. 1875) was a leading retailer of Arts and Crafts and Art Nouveau jewellery. Pendants were a period favourite, and this anonymous example is in the style of Horner.

▲ **Edwardian brass hatpin, 1900–15**
Hat pins were an essential part of an Edwardian lady's wardrobe. Large picture hats were secured on top of piled-up hair with a pair of hatpins, measuring up to (30cm) 12in in length and viciously sharp. Hat pins with uncovered ends were banned from omnibuses, and various patents were taken out for point protectors. Pins came in many different designs and materials, prominent makers including silversmith Charles Horner. Values depend on maker, medium, and style, and matching pairs are worth more than single hat pins.

Art Deco

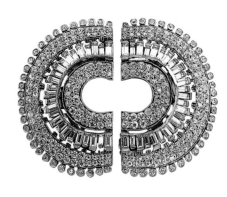

This French marcasite and paste pin (1920s) is in the "tutti-frutti" style, popularized by Cartier and inspired by "Tree of Life" designs.

After World War I a new generation of "flappers" shortened their skirts, learnt to Charleston, and embraced the latest fashions in jewellery. Dangling earrings suited the new shingled hair cuts; long necklaces and sautoirs provided a perfect complement to straight-lined, drop-waisted dresses. Bare arms were decorated with large bangles, which, thanks to new materials such as Bakelite, came in every design and colour. Costume jewellery flourished, imitating the precious creations of Cartier and Boucheron. Paste simulated the geometric Art-Deco designs and baguette-cut stones of diamond brooches. The versatile double clip, patented by Cartier in 1927, was reproduced by US costume jewellers from Coro to Trifari. Coco Chanel created fashion pieces modelled on the Romanov jewels given to her by her lover, Grand Duke Dimitri of Russia, and made the wearing of obvious fakes socially acceptable. There was a craze for the exotic; styles were taken from ancient Egypt and Africa. "Tutti- frutti" jewellery, inspired by Indian Mogul gems, provided a multicoloured contrast to classic Art Deco black-and-white.

◄ Paste double clip, 1930s

The idea for double clips came to French jeweller Louis Cartier when he saw a peasant woman hanging out her washing with clothes pegs. The two clips came in a brooch setting and could be worn together as a pin, or taken out and clipped individually to everything from lapels to shoes. Clips are worth more if, unlike this example, they retain their original brooch frame.

▲ Bakelite bracelet, 1930s

Large bangles were a period favourite and were famously sported by author Nancy Cunard, whose arms were laden with African ivory. This Bakelite hinged bracelet, probably French, was produced with matching dress clips. Bangles are perhaps the most popular of all Bakelite pieces; they were carved in different designs and came in a huge variety of colours, imitating jet, ivory amber, tortoiseshell, and, as here, jade – a very desirable colour today.

▲ Art Deco enamel cufflinks, 1930s

Derived from 17th-century jewelled sleeve buttons, cufflinks became more widely available in the Victorian period with the rise of the middle-classes, cheaper production methods, and the evolution of the modern shirt cuff. Popularized by fashion leaders such as Edward VIII, cufflinks were produced in many styles in the 1920s and '30s. Art Deco enamels were a favourite design, in both silver and base metal.

◄ Jade earrings, 1920s

Even in precious jewellery there was a fashion for combining precious stones with unusual and exotic materials. These earrings are made from diamonds, onyx, and jade. The diamond clips are set in platinum, a favourite white-on-white combination of the period. The pierced jade discs are an inch in diameter, reflecting contemporary taste for large, swinging earrings and geometric designs. 1920s earrings are immensely sought-after and command high prices.

Costume Jewellery and Silver

Over the past 20 years costume jewellery has become a well-established collectable area. The USA led the way in manufacture; from the 1920s onward jewellery companies flourished in New York and Los Angeles. Cinema was an important influence: Joseff of Hollywood provided costume jewellery for over 3,000 movies from the 1930s to the 1960s, and Joan Crawford favoured Miriam Haskell pearls. The sight of film stars bedecked in fabulous fakes, both on and off the screen, helped costume jewellery become acceptable to even the most elegant women. Diana Vreeland, editor of American *Vogue* 1962–71, formed an important costume jewellery collection, and Wallis Simpson wore real gems alongside extravagant imitations. In Europe leading couturiers such as Chanel, Schiaparelli, and Dior produced lines of jewellery to accessorize their collections and increase sales. Big-name pieces now command high prices. Thankfully for collectors makers often stamped their works, and objects should always be checked for a signature. Silver is another flourishing area of 20th-century jewellery, and demand is high for works by leading Scandinavian designers.

This 1940s fur clip by American company Eisenberg (est. 1914) is decorated with high-quality glass crystal stones by Daniel Swarovski.

➤ Lea Stein plastic brooch, 1930s–'40s

Lea Stein began producing plastic jewellery in Paris in the 1930s. Her husband was a plastics chemist and her novelty designs, often in the form of animals, were cut from a sheet composed of some 30 layers of plastic. The back is often a different colour from the front, and typically pieces are marked. Retailers were supplied with the unmounted piece, which could be attached to a tie clip, hair slide, or brooch. Similar pieces are still being made today.

▼ Trifari swordfish "Jelly Belly" brooch, 1940s

During World War II base metals were reserved for military use so manufacturers turned to silver, which they plated with gold and called "vermeil". Unable to obtain paste the New York firm Trifari (est. 1925) used clear plastic Lucite to create novelty brooches by designer Alfred Philippe, who had worked for Cartier and Van Cleef & Arpels. Known as "Jelly Bellies", these wartime designs are very collectable.

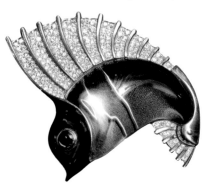

▲ Joseff bee pins, 1940s

Founded by Eugene Joseff in 1930, Joseff of Hollywood provided costume jewellery for three decades of movies, supplying everything from Shirley Temple's crown in *The Little Princess* (1939) to Elizabeth Taylor's gilded asps in *Cleopatra* (1963). Joseff also launched a retail line, c.1938, so that "every American woman could feel like a Hollywood star". Brass pieces, often modelled on his dramatic movie designs, were given a matt-gold finish – devised to minimize the glare from studio lights and create an antique look. The imperial bee was a signature motif.

◀ Corocraft hand brooch, 1944

Established in the early 1900s Coro became the USA's largest manufacturer of costume jewellery, and by 1964 was selling $33million (£22million) worth of jewellery per year. This 1940s brooch is part of a "friendship set" that includes a matching ring, designed by Adolf Katz. Inspired by Victorian hand brooches and reflecting the influence of Surrealism, this highly desirable design is made from vermeil.

➤ Miriam Haskell brooch and earrings set, 1940s–'50s

One of the most famous names in costume jewellery, Miriam Haskell opened a small shop in the elegant McAlpine Hotel, New York, in 1924, and established her own company two years later. Haskell became known for naturalistic imitation pearls, dipped up to 12 times in a solution of fish scales to give them their distinctive lustre, in a range of colours from white to brown. This set is decorated with diamante and seed pearls on "antique Russian gold" – a fusion of gold and silver on a brass and copper base.

◀ Marcel Boucher parure decorated with rhinestones, 1950s

Born in France, Marcel Boucher trained with Cartier in Paris before emigrating to the USA in the 1920s. He began his costume career with a collection of only 12 brooches, instantly snapped up by Saks Fifth Avenue, and he went on to become one of the best-known and most collectable names in the industry. Jewellery was often supplied in sets, or parures: matching necklace, earrings, brooch, and bracelet. A complete set will command a premium, and any original boxes should also be preserved to add to the value.

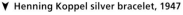

➤ Schiaparelli leaf bracelet, 1950s

Paris couturier Elsa Schiaparelli (1890–1973) was famous for her extravagant, Surrealist-inspired dress designs, reflecting the influence of artist friends such as Salvador Dali. Her costume jewellery was similarly inventive, with pieces modelled as telephones and pea pods. Made in the USA, this blue frosted-glass leaf bracelet is part of a parure, which also came in clear, brown, and red glass. It is signed "Schiaparelli" in script, but, since her designs have been faked, pieces should be checked both for authenticity and, with such fragile material, for damage.

⋏ Weiss necklace and earrings, 1950s

Albert Weiss, who worked formerly for Coro, set up his own company in 1942, specializing in high-quality rhinestone pieces. Brooches were inspired by flowers and insects, and in the 1950s Weiss revived Art Deco jewellery designs. This set is made from the famous "Aurora Borealis" stones, developed by Swarovski in the mid-1950s and named after the shimmering green lights visible in the northern skies between November and May. The effect was achieved by coating glass with a metallic sheen.

▼ Henning Koppel silver bracelet, 1947

Handsome, modernist silver jewellery was produced in Scandinavia in the post-war period. Danish designer Henning Koppel (1918–81) used his training as a sculptor to create jewellery and metalware that fused organic with abstract form. Designs are filled with vitality. "Silver demands rhythm", insisted Koppel. "I like the shape to be vigorous and alive with movement". This heavy silver bracelet was made for silver manufacturers Georg Jensen, established in Copenhagen in 1904, who became known across the world for progressive designs in metalware.

▼ Kenneth Jay Lane brooches, 1960s–'70s

"In 1963 I invented costume jewellery for the beautiful people and became one of the most splendidly beautiful of them … sitting in the back of my vintage Rolls (with matching driver) wearing my floor-length leopard coat", remembered Kenneth Jay Lane. The New York designer's flamboyant and witty creations were purchased by '60s style-makers, from Jackie Kennedy to Diana Vreeland. The leopard brooch (inspired by the big-cat pins worn by Wallis Simpson) is marked K.J.L. – a monogram used by Lane until the end of the '70s. Later, less collectable pieces are signed "Kenneth Lane" or "Kenneth Jay Lane".

▲ Christian Dior brooch, 1959

"I created clothes for flower-like women, I brought back the neglected art of pleasing", claimed Christian Dior. The French designer opened his Paris fashion house in 1947. Only a fraction of women could afford his fabulously feminine "New Look" clothes, so Dior also designed costume jewellery. Big pins were a 1950s favourite. This paste-and-pearl brooch, made by the German firm of Henkel and Grosse, is signed and dated.

▶ Butler and Wilson earrings, 1970s–'80s

The 1980s, with its taste for power dressing and glitz, saw a craze for designer jewellery. Butler and Wilson was one of the most successful firms of the period. Nicky Butler and Simon Wilson were London antique dealers who began copying vintage pieces in the early '70s, before creating their own designs. Big, bold forms, sparkling with diamante, captured the spirit of the New Romantic movement and the glam of *Dynasty* and *Dallas*. Their jewellery was worn by everyone, and is still collectable today.

▲ Chanel necklace, 1980s

Coco Chanel (1883–1971) was one of the great pioneers of costume jewellery. She based designs on her own precious gems so that, she claimed, women could look like a fortune without having to spend one, and she made faux pearls fashionable. In 1983 Karl Lagerfeld, as Chanel director, reinterpreted many classic designs, from the famous Chanel suit to the Russian-inspired gilt chains of the 1920s and '30s, accessorized with gobstopper pearls and the CC logo.

◀ Vivienne Westwood "Sex" choker and earrings, 1990s

Vivienne Westwood (b. 1941) is probably Britain's most famous fashion designer. With Malcolm McLaren she came to fame in the 1970s as the originator of Punk style. "Sex" was the name of their famous King's Road shop, the Sex Pistols was McLaren's band, and sex was the inspiration for many of Westwood's outrageous creations. Her jewellery is very fashionable and worn by celebrities.

Vintage kitchenware and appliances are collected both for their own sake and by enthusiasts decorating their house in a certain style, who perhaps want a 1950s fridge for a '50s style interior or Victorian fittings to create a traditional country cottage look. Many of us already have examples of vintage kitchenware at home – favourite family pieces that have been preserved over the years, or kitchen rejects that have ended up in the back of drawers when they are replaced by new equipment. Some of these items can now be valuable, and while Victorian and Edwardian pieces tend to command the highest prices, there is also growing interest in objects from the post-war period. The great joy of collecting kitchenware is that many of these domestic antiques can still be used, providing both practical equipment and a direct, hands-on link with the cooks of the past. Everyday kitchenware provides a fascinating insight into history: the dairy items, the elaborate jelly moulds, and the array of machines for chopping and grinding demonstrate the Victorians' love of decoration, their mechanical ingenuity, and the sheer amount of physical labour it took to provide food for the table. Up until the 1930s it was generally expected that servants would carry out these tasks. The years following World War II saw the mass-introduction of labour-saving appliances, the arrival of supermarkets, and a host of new equipment, such as woks and pasta makers, that reflected increasingly global cuisine. Another area associated with kitchenware is advertising and packaging (*see* pp8–10), as some collectors concentrate on objects associated with specific food and drink brands.

A Buttercup Dairy Co butter pot and cover, 1860s. Butter was sold from the dairy in this crock, which could be taken back for refilling.

◄ Wooden breadboard, 1897

A handmade breadboard was a popular wedding gift in the Victorian period. Borders were often inscribed with religious or moral mottos, and carved with flowers and ears of corn as a reference to the bread and a symbol of fertility. This example is dated 1897, the year of Queen Victoria's Diamond Jubilee, and is probably a commemorative piece. The value of breadboards depends on decoration and condition – avoid boards with a dry white look since these will have been immersed in water for a long period and are prone to warping. Stains can be cleaned by rubbing boards gently with an abrasive powder and then polishing with beeswax.

➤ Pewter ice-cream mould, 1868

Ice-cream originated in the Far East, arriving in Europe in the 17th century, and by the Victorian period it was a fashionable pudding. Ice-cream moulds were made from pewter, and can be distinguished from jelly moulds by the fact that they close up completely so that the mould could be thrown into the icebox. This fine example comes in three parts and has a registration mark for 11th July 1868. Lead was later banned because it was discovered to be poisonous, but although these moulds can not be used today, they are still much sought-after by collectors.

▲ Three-dimensional sycamore butter moulds, 19th century

In the 19th century many families made their own butter and cheese in the dairy adjacent to the house and surplus stock would be sold at market. When the butter had been churned, washed, worked, and patted into shape it was then stamped, both for decoration and to identify the produce of a specific dairy. Sycamore was the preferred wood because it didn't absorb smells or affect the taste of the milk. Three-dimensional butter moulds, such as these sheafs of corn, are more unusual than standard printers and therefore sought-after today.

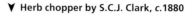

▼ Herb chopper by S.C.J. Clark, c.1880

This wooden-handled herb chopper is stamped S.C.J. Clark, and the steel blade is decorated with cut-out hearts and stars. Although much Victorian kitchen metalware was mass-produced in major industrial centres like Sheffield, herb choppers were also handmade by local craftsmen. Designs could therefore be more idiosyncratic, and today the more decorative the piece, the higher the value. Avoid pitted blades and beware replacement handles. Flat metal choppers were used on chopping boards, curved blades for wooden bowls and mortars.

◄ Wooden nutmeg grater and metal canister with pocket grater

Nutmeg became an important ingredient in food and drink with the opening up of trade routes in the Indian Ocean. Gentlemen carried pocket nutmeg graters to spice up mulled wine and hot chocolate, although Mrs Beeton advised cautious use by those of "paralytic or apoplectic habits". Dating from the mid-19th century this wooden nutmeg grater is carved from a coquilla nut; the nutmeg is kept inside the acorn, alongside the grater. Treen (small domestic objects handmade from wood) is very collectable and more valuable than the metal canister (c.1870–90), which opens up to reveal a pocket grater.

Moulds

Eating habits became increasingly elaborate in Victorian times: dinners had more courses and tables were laden with ever-expanding settings of cutlery, china, and glass. Food was required to be decorative as well as filling, and an ornamental jelly was a favourite centrepiece. Before the 1700s jellies were principally savoury, but as more sugar was imported sweet jellies also became popular. Moulds were an essential part of the 19th-century *batterie de cuisine* – at Apsley house, home of the Duke of Wellington, there were 500 – and even the most ordinary middle-class kitchen would have different examples for jellies, ice-cream, mousses, and aspic. Moulds were produced in ceramic, metalware, and, from the 1880s, pressed glass. They came in a huge variety of sizes and shapes, ranging from castellated forms to animals. *The Book of Moulds*, published in 1886 by Mrs Marshall, included over 1,000 designs. Value depends on medium, shape, and condition. They are often purchased as decorative items, since certain materials do not meet current health and safety regulations. Check for condition (beware of rust on tin moulds), and for a registration or retailer's mark that can enhance value. Whatever material the mould is made from, certainly the more elaborate the design, the higher the price.

Castellated copper mould, c.1880

Produced from 1830 copper examples, initially hand-beaten and then later machine-pressed, are among the most collectable and decorative of food moulds.

▲ Copper kettle, c.1890

Up until the mid-1700s tea was an expensive product, reserved for the wealthy, and kettles were drawing-room items made from silver. The East India Company increased imports, prices fell, and tea gradually became Britain's national drink. Annual consumption rose from 1.5lbs per head in 1800, to 6lbs in 1900, to a record high of 10lbs in 1930 – the equivalent of 5 cups a day for every adult and child. A kettle made from copper, brass, cast iron, or enamel became a feature of every kitchen. The stove model was eventually supplanted by the electric kettle, first made by Compton & Co in the UK in 1891, but with the growing popularity of range cookers traditional kettles are now collected for use as well as decoration.

▼ Wooden-handled brass smoothing iron, mid-19th century

Flat or "sad" irons (the name is a corruption of solid) were used in Europe from the 1600s. They were made in different weights and often came in pairs, so that one could be warmed at the fire while the other was in use. In the 18th century the box iron was developed, its hollow body holding a heated slug of metal; ember irons contained burning charcoal or ashes. The Victorians developed irons powered by gas and spirits, and in 1882 the electric iron was invented in France, though it only became a truly successful alternative in the 1920s, when a thermostat was added in the USA.

▲ Kenrick cast-iron coffee grinder, c.1900

Coffee was imported from Arabia in the 17th century. The first coffee house opened in Oxford in 1650, and these houses soon became centres for social and political gossip. Initially the retailer ground the beans, but the 19th century saw the proliferation of the domestic grinder. In 1815 the English firm Archibald Kenrick (est. 1791) patented a new cast-iron model; beans were put into the brass bowl, or hopper, and as the handle turned, blades ground the coffee into the drawer. Made in various sizes, the box-shaped design could be screwed to a worktop. It was produced until WWI and was copied by many manufacturers.

▼ Enamel bread bin with unusual style of lettering, 1930s

Mass-produced from the latter half of the 19th century, enamelware brought new shapes and bright colours to the kitchen. Affordable, hard to break, and easy to clean, it was used for everything from saucepans to coffeepots. Enamel bread bins such as this were popular from the 1920s to the 1950s but the shape remained virtually unchanged. Common colours include white and cream, and the green of this 1930s bin was a favourite colour of the period. Enamelware is prone to chipping (lids are particularly vulnerable), but as long as the interior is undamaged these bins, over half a century on, can still store bread.

◄ Arnold milkshake mixer with cup, 1920s

From the late-19th century until the 1960s the soda fountain was very much at the centre of small-town American life. The first soda fountain patent was granted in 1819 to serve mineral waters, but it was with the invention of the ice-cream soda in the 1870s that soda fountains (and the profession of a "soda jerk") really took off. Prohibition provided an added incentive, since sodas and milkshakes could be promoted as enjoyable temperance drinks. This Arnold milkshake mixer is dated c.1923 – its jadeite green base typical of styling of that period.

▲ Set of three French enamel canisters, 1930s

Enamelware (known as granite ware in the USA) was mass-produced from the Victorian period until World War II. Made from sheets of metal coated with powdered glass fused to the metal in a hot oven, enamel became a kitchen favourite because it was durable, affordable, easy-to-clean, and potentially colourful – although hygienic-looking white was often favoured for standard kitchen items. France specialized in bright, stencilled pieces, and sets of storage jars decorated with Art Deco-style designs, such as those above, are now highly sought-after. This set includes a canister for chicory – a coffee substitute that first became popular in France during the Napoleonic wars when, due to military blockades, coffee was hard to obtain.

▲ Goebels pottery lemon squeezer, 1930s

One way of collecting kitchenware is to focus on a specific object and to follow its development. Lemon squeezers make a perfect choice. Lemons were brought back to Europe by Crusaders from the Holy Land in the 13th century and soon became a kitchen essential, valued both for their taste and health-giving properties. From 1795 lemon, and later lime, juice was issued to British sailors to prevent scurvy, hence the expression a "limey". Lemon squeezers have been made of every material, from wood to glass, and in many designs, from mechanical juicers to the classic dome-shaped reamer, or squeezer. The 1930s saw a vogue for ceramic novelties, produced by many major potteries, which are very collectable.

▲ Spong bean slicer and mincer, 1950s

Following the Great Exhibition of 1851 a host of mechanical aids was developed for mincing, grinding, chopping, and slicing. Most items were made of cast-iron until the late 19th century, when steel and later stainless steel and aluminium became more common. However, in many instances the basic design remained virtually unchanged. This bean slicer and mincer both date from the 1950s and were made by Spong, well-known British manufacturers of catering equipment. Rarer gadgets such as vintage apple peelers and coconut graters are worth more.

➤ Juice 'O' Mat tilt-top juicer, Rival MFG Co, Kansas, USA, c.1955

After World War II and the demobilization of their menfolk, women abandoned their wartime jobs and moved back into the kitchen. More than any other room in the house the kitchen was transformed by the post-war consumer boom. The USA pioneered the concept of the "dream kitchen", filled with bright, easy-clean surfaces (Formica counter tops, vinyl flooring) and new labour-saving appliances for a servantless generation. Mixers, blenders, and juicers came in shiny chrome and candy-coloured enamel, their bold shapes reflecting the influence of auto-motive styling, combining efficiency with glamour.

▲ Cona Rex coffee percolator, 1950

The USA was not the only place to bring streamlined glamour into the post-war kitchen. This Rex coffee machine was designed for Cona in 1950 by British graphic artist Abram Games (1914–96), perhaps best remembered for his wartime posters and for the logo for the Festival of Britain in 1951, where this percolator was exhibited. The curvaceous shape of the stand and heatproof class bowls typifies the organic modernism of the 1950s. A variation of this design was manufactured by Cona from the late '50s, but to the serious collector of modern design, this original pre-mass-production model is most valuable.

◄ Sunbeam Mixmaster, 1950s

The Sunbeam Mixmaster was one of the most popular food mixers on the American and British markets. The swivelling tailfin was inscribed with settings for everything, from mixing muffins to "lower-speed less pulp juicing". The mixer could be detached from its stand for hand use and attachments included bowl-fit beaters, different sized mixing bowls, and a blender. "The Best Electrical Appliances Made", boasted the company logo. The Mixmaster also came in salmon pink, turquoise blue, primrose yellow, and chrome – rarer and more desirable than this standard white model.

The Hoover Constellation,1955

Inspired by space-age design this was arguably the first domestic vacuum cleaner to sell as a style icon; in 1956 it featured in a famous Pop Art collage.

Even the most mundane everyday objects can have a fascinating story behind them and the humble vacuum cleaner is no exception. The first vacuum cleaner, "The Puffing Billy", was invented by Englishman Cecil Booth in 1901. The huge contraption arrived at the door by horse-and-cart; suction pipes were passed through a window and operated by the white uniformed employees of Booth's British Vacuum Cleaner Company. This was such a novelty that ladies would hold "vacuum tea parties" so that guests could watch the remarkable suction process. However, it was an American who came up with the first truly portable cleaner. In 1907 James Murray Spangler, an asthmatic school janitor, cobbled together an upright cleaner with a broom handle, an old pillow case to catch the dust, and an electrical motor. He sold the idea to his relation W.H. "Boss" Hoover, a harness manufacturer and a brilliant salesman. Hoover pioneered door-to-door demonstrations and developed creative advertising campaigns. The Hoover sold across the world and became a synonym for vacuuming. "Is your cleaner a museum piece?"demanded one early Hoover advertisement accusingly. Today vintage machines can indeed be seen in museums and attract a small number of collectors interested in design technology.

The Vacuum Cleaner

◄ Morphy Richards toaster, 1960s

Toast is a traditional part of the British diet, and it was UK firm Crompton and Co that produced the first electric toaster in 1893. Although it was an improvement on the toasting fork, bread still had to be carefully watched until the invention in the USA of the Sunbeam Pop-Up Toastmaster in 1926. "Pop! Up comes the toast automatically … perfect toast every time without watching, turning or burning." This Morphy Richards toaster dates from the 1960s, its attraction lying in its Mary Quant-style daisies period decoration.

◄ Prestige Sky Line kitchen utensils, c.1960

This set of utensils is mint and packaged, which adds to its appeal for collectors. Red-and-white was a favourite combination in the 1950s and early '60s, when housewives wanted a brighter look in the kitchen. Though such items are perfectly useable today, they do require a little care. The painted wooden handles (later replaced by plastic) are prone to chipping and should certainly not be put in dishwashers or left immersed in hot water. As well as the Skyline brand, other leading names in post-war British kitchenware include Tala and Nutbrown.

▼ Crown Devon storage jars, 1960s

Storage jars from the 1960s and '70s can still be picked up in charity shops and car boot (garage) sales, although they are also beginning to appear in antiques stores. This set is by Crown Devon and the colours, the Carnaby daisy motif, and the typography are all typical of the "swinging sixties".The 1970s saw a fashion for more homespun, rustic-looking designs to match the fashionable country kitchen look. Brown storage jars by firms such as Hornsea (see p51) are also becoming popular with collectors.

▲ Tupperware storage containers, 1970s

This light, unbreakable polythene kitchenware with its patented airtight seal was invented by US plastics chemist Earl S. Tupper in 1946. It sold poorly in shops until the company introduced home demonstrations in 1948. Employee Brownie Wise came up with the idea of the Tupperware Party, and a marketing legend was born. Tupperware parties were a success across the world: for the company they offered direct access to the housewife; for women they provided not just Tupperware, but social entertainment and a job that could be combined with family life. Vintage Tupperware, particularly the more colourful items from the 1950s to the 1970s, is collected today.

When electricity was introduced at the end of the 19th century it became an exciting time for the designers of Arts and Crafts and Art Nouveau lighting. Collectable names of the period include W.A.S. Benson, the Guild of Handicrafts, C.F.A. Voysey, and F.S. Osler. When buying or collecting light fixtures be on the look out for registration numbers and maker's marks. Although nice to find, these are not always essential since many fine examples were produced without any markings at all. It is preferable when buying antique lighting to purchase a fitting that is already restored and rewired, ready to use in a modern home, as restoration can be costly and it is not always possible to meet modern electrical safety standards. To complement the light fittings it is aesthetically pleasing to use glass light shades that were produced in the same period. Some notable glass manufacturers were James Powell of Whitefriars, Walsh, and Osler. Vaseline glass was widely used for shades and looks lovely when lit, giving off warm hues. It was manufactured using uranium to give it its colour, so consequently cannot be reproduced today. Painted glass shades were also very popular and were made in the former state of Czeckoslovakia. The post-World War II period saw the emergence of plastic. Space-age imagery was an important influence and lighting expressed the most radical styles of the modern era. Classic designs and lights by major names are very collectable today.

Good-quality brass lantern in the Arts and Crafts style, with original double-etched glass; popular for use now in hallways and porches.

▲ Art Nouveau centre light fitting, c.1900
The design of this three-arm light fitting is typical of the Art Nouveau period, with the flowing curves of the metalware and glass shades. The shades are made from vaseline glass, probably by James Powell of Whitefriars. When lit vaseline glass emits lovely hues, making this type of shade extremely collectable. The fitting is suspended from the ceiling on a silk cable, and would have been essential to complete the décor of an Arts and Crafts or Art Nouveau room at the turn of the century.

◄ Brass pendant light fitting, c.1900–10
Gas lighting was first demonstrated in the 1790s and became popular in the first half of the 19th century. This pole pendant light was originally designed for use with gas but it has been sympathetically converted for electricity without losing any of its authenticity in terms of looks. The shade is made from green etched glass.

► Late-Victorian oil lamp, c.1880–90
Considerable efforts were made to improve oil lamps throughout the 19th century and with the introduction of the paraffin lamp in 1859 oil lighting became both simpler to use and more affordable. In 1865 Joseph Hinks began producing "Duplex" lamps, which had a double burner. This example has a cast-brass base and column, with an ornate foliate design. The fluted shade above the the lime-green opaque glass fount has an acid-etched design.

➤ Cast-brass desk lamp, *c.*1900–10

This good-quality desk or table lamp has a blue opaline and vaseline shade. Decorative lamps such as this were used by Edwardian ladies when doing close work for their sewing and embroidery, or when reading a book. The height of the arm is adjustable and the shade also has some movement to allow for flexibility and maximum light coverage. Taller models that stand on the floor are known as "library" lamps – these are rarer to come by and therefore more valuable.

➤ Brass banker's/professor's lamp, *c.*1920

Lamps of this kind were, as the name suggests, widely used in banks and by teachers and lecturers in schools and colleges. Alternatives to the green glass trough shade can be found in brass or tin. In all versions the inside of the trough would be white, in order to reflect the light down onto the table. The base of the lamp houses the on/off switch. Banker's/professor's lamps represent very good value for money because they are often ideal for use in a modern study, office, or library.

▼ Silver-plated crystal pendant light, *c.*1910

The shade on this pendant light fitting is made from diamond-cut crystal glass – one of a number of crystal decorations popular in the Edwardian period. The four sets of drops around the main shade are interlinked with a silver-plated chain. Unlike more common pendant lights that hang from a chain this fitting has a ceiling rose that screws straight into the ceiling, which would make it ideal for use in a room with a low ceiling.

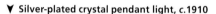

▲ Brass table lamp with painted shade, *c.*1920

The base and column of this brass table lamp has been embellished by a copper oxide finish, which gives a rich, warm glow to the lamp. Copper oxide was a common device in the early 1920s. As well as being a popular alternative to plain brass it also eliminated the need for regular cleaning, as unlike brass the copper oxide did not tarnish. The fitted painted shade, with its bronze and green urn motif, complements the colour of the lamp and would certainly have been made at the same time.

▲ Holophane pendant light, *c.*1910

One of a set of three, this light has its original brass gallery (the fitting that attaches the light to the pendant chain). Holophane lights were named after a glass-maker of the same name, who invented this prismatic white glass that does not reflect and dazzle. They were designed for use in churches, schools, and any workplace where glare-free lighting was required. When purchasing this kind of light look out for the name "Holophane" impressed on the glass around the neck of the shade, and also often imprinted on the brass gallery.

▲ "Artichoke" lamp by Poul Henningsen, 1958

Big-name designer lighting from the post-war period is currently very popular with collectors. This hanging lamp, designed by Danish architect Poul Henningsen (1894–1967), is a Modernist reinterpretation of the chandelier. It was created using overlapping steel leaves, which both reflect the light and diffuse the glare. Manufactured by well-known Danish lighting company Louis Poulsen, it illuminated fashionable interiors across the world.

◀ Matador lamp, 1950s

Kitsch lighting can be highly collectable. Large figurative lamps became popular in the USA in the 1940s and '50s. Bases were made from plaster and inspired by exotic prototypes, such as Spanish dancers or Nubian slaves. Lights often came in male/female pairs and were extremely heavy, weighing as much as 4.5–7kg (10–15lbs) a piece. Shades (also large) came in different designs and are collected in their own right. The kitsch side of the 1950s, at which the USA excelled, attracts at least as many enthusiasts as the more "serious" designer works.

◀ "Eclisse" lamp by Vico Magistrettti, 1966

Space travel was a major influence on 1960s designers in every field, and particularly in areas such as home entertainment (radios, televisions, and gramophones) and lighting. The "Eclisse" (eclipse) bedside lamp was created by Vico Magistretti in 1966 for the Italian firm Artemide. Resembling an astronaut's helmet, the light contains an inner aluminium shade that can be swivelled round to vary brightness and finally to eclipse the bulb. The "Eclisse" was produced in various different colours.

◀ Lava lamp, 1960s

The lava lamp, symbol of the psychedelic '60s, was the creation of British engineer and naturist Edward Craven Walker. He discovered the prototype, made from a cocktail shaker and a couple of tins, in an English village pub after World War II, and spent the next few years perfecting the recipe of oil and wax. He founded the Crestworth Company (later Mathmos), and in 1963 launched his new product. Initially it was unsuccessful, but as psychedelia took off sales boomed, and the lava lamp became the light of the hippy generation.

◀ "Arco" lamp by Castiglioni brothers, 1962

Italian designers created some of the most inventive lighting of the 1960s and '70s. The "Arco" lamp, made for Flos by brothers Achille and Pier Giacomo Castiglioni, is a stainless steel arc, springing like a giant flower from a rectangular marble block. It was designed to hang over a dining table or seating area, providing a flexible alternative to central lighting, as well as a piece of domestic sculpture. Regarded as a '60s classic it has been much imitated; the Castiglioni originals are very sought-after.

LUGGAGE & TRAVEL GOODS

Carrying cases for singles emerged in the 1960s; The Beatles help make this PYX bag very collectable.

As travel improved in the 19th century, with the development of the railways and shipping routes, there was an increasing need for luggage of different types. Fitted trunks, with their many compartments, served as portable wardrobes – standing as a piece of furniture in a cabin or compartment and saving their owner the labour of unpacking. Metal cases and hatboxes were a favourite with those embarking for tropical climates, providing added protection against insects. For those travelling light there was the carpet bag (developed in France), the Gladstone, and the portmanteau, all paving the way for the suitcase, which by the 1900s had become a standard portable favourite. Demand expanded further with the advent of the motorcar. Luxury manufacturers catered to the needs of wealthy tourists. In London firms such as Asprey's and Mappin & Webb supplied handsome dressing cases, with silver fixtures and fittings. On the continent Hermès (which started as saddle makers) and Gucci provided high quality luggage for an international clientele.

➤ Louis Vuitton wardrobe trunk, 1920s

Louis Vuitton is perhaps the most collectable name in vintage luggage. The company, founded in Paris in 1854, supplied travel goods to European royalty and the wealthy of the world. Vuitton developed a five-tumbler lock in 1890 that enabled each client to have an exclusive combination; 1896 saw the introduction of the famous LV monogram canvas. Introduced in the 1800s the wardrobe trunk was designed to hang clothes without crumpling them.

⋀ Leather Gladstone bag, late 19th century

The Gladstone bag, a leather portmanteau made in various sizes, derives its name from William Gladstone (1809–98) – four times Prime Minister of Britain and familiarly known as the "Grand Old Man" of British politics. A possible derivation could be Gladstone's budget bag, which was used by UK Chancellors of the Exchequer on Budget Day until the 1990s. Other Victorian politicians, including Lords Hartington and Rosebery, also had bags named after them, but only the Gladstone bag has survived. Bags in crocodile and alligator are very desirable.

➤ Brexton picnic hamper, c.1950s

The development of motoring stimulated the popularity of the picnic hamper. Edwardian examples were outfitted with the finest china and plate but the inter-war years saw the introduction of plastics, which were both light and durable. This hamper is by UK firm Brexton, one of the best-known makers of picnic sets. Other manufacturers include Glenco, Coracle, and Revelation. Values of picnic hampers depend on age, condition, materials, and the completeness of fixtures and fittings.

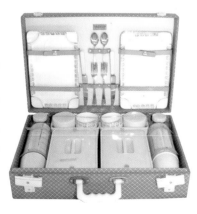

⋀ Hessian steamer trunk, c.1930

The market is currently strong for good quality designer and non-designer luggage in fine condition. This trunk is decorated with reproduction luggage labels; vintage labels are collected in their own right and can add considerably to the appeal of period luggage. Tourism flourished in the Victorian period: Thomas Cook set up his first tour in 1841; grand hotels opened across the world; and shipping lines and railways introduced luggage labels.

MEDALS

Medals have existed since ancient times, with the Romans using them to commemorate historic events. However, it was not until the 17th century that they started to appear in the UK in any great number. The events surrounding the beginnings of the English Civil War (1642–51) prompted the Royalist party and the Parliamentarians to produce medals as a form of propaganda, with a number of medals being awarded on the battlefield, which became a precursor of military rewards. Following the defeat of the Royalist cause and the execution of Charles I in 1649 the propaganda war between the Jacobites and anti-Jacobites became more intense, with the tit-for-tat issuing of medals continuing for a further century. As the 18th century progressed, more and more events became commemorated by the commissioning of medals – a high number of these being connected to royal events. By the 19th century medal production in the UK had reached its zenith with the famous Wyon family producing a vast array of commemoratives throughout the century, many for events that today seem inconsequential. As with many areas of collectables, medal collecting has followed various fashions over the past decades. With limited resources many collectors have latched on to a theme, which provides an interest without being too daunting and expensive. Examples that are very popular today include the English Civil War, the life and times of Admiral Lord Nelson and the Duke of Wellington, the Napoleonic era, anti-slavery, and British prime ministers, to name but a few.

Aberdeenshire Fetter Cairn Farmer's Club, silver prize, 1895. Agricultural prize medals became quite prolific by the mid-19th century. Many of the medals were produced by the main engravers of the day, making use of standard images that could then be adapted for use by local societies.

▲ Union of England and Scotland, silver medal by J. Croker, 1707

The Act of Union between England and Scotland, a highly political and contentious event (as it remains today), received royal assent on 6th March 1707 and came into operation on 1st May that year. There is a large number of medals that commemorate this event, several of which were produced on the Continent. This one shows the bust of Queen Anne, crowned and draped, and the British shield upon a pedestal inscribed with the double cipher of "AR", supported by a lion and unicorn.

▼ Anstruther Beggars Benison Society, oval silver-gilt ticket, 1739

The Beggars Benison Society of Anstruther, Fife, ostensibly existed to collect good stories and songs, but it was in fact "an outlet for the most exuberant and outrageous fun and jocularity of the roughest description" for eminent men, from the royal family downwards. The legends of some of their medals are of a considerably explicit nature. This ticket was a member's pass for admission to the club.

▲ Bristol Theatre Royal, silver pass, 1766

This famous theatre, situated in the heart of the Georgian section of Bristol, was originally opened in 1766, and 50 initial subscribers each put £50 toward the building. This ticket, number 26, was given to one of the original subscribers and entitled the owner and his successors entry to each play in perpetuity. This pass continues to be valid today, although the theatre does not guarantee a seat but, as the ticket implies, only a "sight of every performance". This pass is extremely rare and therefore worth into the thousands.

➤ Silver medal to celebrate the recovery of George III from an illness, 1789

By January 1789 the King's health had begun to improve after a long illness, and the *London Gazette* announced in February that no further bulletins on his health would be issued. March 14th saw the King's return to Windsor, and 23rd April 1789 was appointed by Royal Proclamation to be observed as a day of general thanksgiving. The King, the Queen, the royal family, both Houses of Parliament, and the Corporation of London attended a service at St Paul's Cathedral, where these medals were worn.

▲ First balloon flight in England by Vincent Lunardi, 1784

This white-metal mdeal shows the bust of Vincenzo Lunardi (1759–1806), secretary to the Neapolitan ambassador in England. He made the first balloon ascent from Moorfields in London on 15th September 1784. It was reported that George III, in council with his ministers, broke off the meeting by saying "we may resume our deliberations on the subject before us at pleasure, but we may never see poor Lunardi again". The King and Prime Minister Pitt followed the flight with telescopoes until the balloon was out of sight. In the same year Lunardi's balloon was exhibited at the Pantheon in Oxford Street.

▲ Battle of Trafalgar bronze-gilt medal by C.H. Kuchler, 1805

The combined French and Spanish fleets lost 20 vessels at Trafalgar while no British ships were lost, although Nelson, in HMS *Victory*, was killed in the hour of triumph. The battle left Britain in an unchallenged position of maritime supremacy and confirmed what Napoleon had already surmised – that Villeneuve, his commander who surrendered, was incapable of breaking through Nelson's fleet and giving Napoleon the mastery of the seas which he required for his successful invasion. Originally contained in Boulton brass shells, these medals are extremely rare, particularly in this metal and fine condition.

▲ Battle of Waterloo white-metal medal by T. Halliday, 1815

It was at the Battle of Waterloo in June 1815 that the combined forces of England and Prussia, under Wellington and Blucher, finally put an end to Napoleon's imperial designs, much to the relief of the rest of Europe. John Parish (1742–1829), who sponsored this medal, was born in Leith, Scotland, and was a prominent figure in Hamburg. During the Napoleonic Wars he acted as an emissary between England and Germany. This example of the medal is extremely fine and rare.

◀ Cyphering award, silver prize, c.1820

Silver engraved school prize medals became quite popular towards the end of the 18th century. The fashion continued for another 100 years or so, although later these prizes tended to be struck dies rather than engraved, many with repetitive themes of Minerva presenting a child with a laurel wreath. As well as a profusion of medals made in London and the suburbs toward the middle of the 19th century, they also became increasingly common in Scotland, many deriving from the dux system of education used north of the border.

In the late-19th century tastes moved away from the florid Victorian styles that were displayed at the Great Exhibition of 1851. The simpler designs of the Arts and Crafts, Secessionist, Jungenstil, and Shaker movements were adopted, initially by handicrafts guilds, then by a few leading stores, and later went on to influence mass-production. There were also the sweeping lines of the Art Nouveau style, followed after World War I by the geometric simplicity of Art Deco and Minimalism. There are many famous names that influenced these styles and it is rewarding to learn to recognize them, and to sort genuine originals from those that just followed the trends. Occasionally items of metalware were designed to be purely decorative, but most are essentially functional. For the domestic market they must have eye appeal, and this gives us a very wide choice from a treasury of design ideas.

Contemporary reproductions have always been made, and items continue to reappear so be aware of poor-quality imitations, which should be avoided. Whether obtained in a shop, antiques mall, or collectors' fair, the advice of a good dealer can be invaluable. Metalware can be expected to show genuine signs of having been used but will still retain its appeal. The price paid for metalware collectables is generally much less than it would now cost to make a good-quality copy using original methods. Restoration to "as new" condition is frequently possible, if wanted, although this is usually best left to the experts. Above all, successful designs for practical items ensure that they are fit for the purpose for which they were made, and manufactured to a standard that provides longevity. What looks good is good; these items are part of our heritage.

For every different type of object made in silver, of which there are hundreds, there are dedicated collectors of such pieces who are gaining great enjoyment from researching their acquisitions. Unlike any other area of antiques and collectables, silver has one great advantage – the British Hallmark – which dates back to the 16th century and is the world's oldest law for consumer protection. A good hallmark will be able to tell us the quality of silver used, the date and city where the item was assayed, as well as the silversmith's name. Collectors then will often delve into the life of a particular silversmith, looking at his place of work, who he was apprenticed to, and who he may have trained, all of which can provide a fascinating social history.

Without doubt the most collected silver item, with centuries of manufacture to the present day, is the spoon, which can be found at virtually any antiques and collectables fair, shop, or auction, and which can be bought for pocket money up to many thousands for the rarest examples. Collectable silver can be arranged in many different categories and subsequent sub-categories, such as boxes and then snuff, pill, patch, seal, and trinket, or by periods, such as early and late Georgian, Victorian and Edwardian, or by fashion and style – aesthetics, Arts and Crafts, Art Nouveau, Art Deco, and Modernism. Wherever your interests may lie, you will be able to find collectable silver to fulfil your needs.

Jardinières were made in a variety of sizes to hold plant pots securely. This small copper one, c.1910, by Benham & Co, has a classic Arts and Crafts design.

An Irish silver bright-cut cream jug on four ball feet, made in Dublin by Daniel Egan in 1808 and retailed by Clarke & West.

An Edwardian silver napkin ring with pierced thistle decoration around the centre, made in 1904 by A. Seymour of Birmingham.

Metalware

The metalware shown on these pages includes copper, brass, cast-iron, and pewter, and focuses on ordinary household objects that can still be found easily today. Metalware flourished in the 19th century thanks to improved and more affordable production methods. Manufacture of brass had developed in Britain in the 17th century, and by the Victorian period brass was being employed throughout the home for everything from plumbing to lighting. Copper was another household favourite, much used in the kitchen because of its high heat conductivity. As the 19th century progressed metals were no longer reserved for purely practical purposes. Arts and Crafts designers exploited the potential of copper and brass, producing domestic metalware that was both functional and artistic. Leading manufacturers included W.A. Benson (1854–1924), whose lighting and tableware was simply designed, well-made, and comparatively affordable, embodying the Arts and Crafts philosophy and selling through Morris & Co in Oxford Street and Samuel Bing's Maison de L'Art Nouveau in Paris. Much 19th- and 20th-century metalware is unmarked but objects can be dated by style and method of manufacture. Many period designs were reproduced in the 20th century and collectors should beware of modern replicas. Some collectors like their metal gleaming; others prefer a good patina to build up.

Brass candlestick by William Tonks & Co; finely cast with symbolic shapes it is typical of the late 19th and early 20th centuries.

➤ **Brass and copper water cans, c.1880–1920**
Cans with short spouts were used to carry hot water to bedroom washstands before piped household hot water was installed. Made of copper, brass, or galvanized iron, they came in many sizes. In the UK most were made in the Black Country (near Birmingham) by Beldray, Fearncombe, Loveridge, and Sankey. The thin sides were strengthened with ribbing or decoratively patterned. Recent lightweight reproductions are also available.

▼ **Copper tokens, 1788**
Tokens were issued by companies, traders, and individuals during times when there was a shortage of coinage. They provide a splendid way of studying social and industrial history. This example was issued in 1788 by John Wilkinson, Ironmaster of Broseley, Shropshire – the centre of the Industrial Revolution. There were other issues made around that time, and many other counterfeits and "mules" were made for collectors, both then and in later years.

◄ **"Ladybell" brass handbell, c.1930**
Collecting bells is a fascinating hobby, and "ladybells" are an interesting speciality. Handbells have been used for years, and these became a popular design in the late 19th and early 20th centuries; the crinoline dress makes an ideal shape to house the bell. Other popular handbell shapes include Dutch children and windmills. This example comes complete with its original "legs" clapper instead of the usual ball, making it even more collectable.

◄ Collection of brass "Three Wise Monkeys" items, c.1900–60
From the late 19th century onward the "Three Wise Monkeys" ("Speak no Evil", "Hear no Evil", "See no Evil") were a favourite ornamental subject, often appearing as brass paperweights. The story of the monkeys is said to have been introduced to Japan from China in the 8th century. The monkeys were associated with Vadjra – a fiercesome blue-faced god with three eyes and many hands. They appear carved over the door of the 17th-century Toshogu shrine in Nikko, Japan. According to legend there was also a fourth monkey, who signified "Do no Evil" and whose hands covered his lap!

◄ Copper tray, 1890s
Trays made of copper or brass offer a tremendous range of designs. Examples made in India, and elsewhere, during the 1920s and '30s are often engraved with folkloric patterns. The Arts and Crafts workers of the late 19th and early 20th centuries also enjoyed expressing themselves by making trays. This "Acanthus" design was made for a short time during the 1890s by Townshends of Birmingham; the company registered several design variations. Trays can be found in a range of shapes and sizes; this kidney shape made the tray easier to carry.

◄ Brass oil lamp, c.1900–20
Oil (kerosene) lamps became the mainstay of domestic lighting in the 19th century. Each lamp was composed of four main parts: the base (containing the fount or reservoir for fuel), the wick and carrier, the glass chimney, and the glass shade. Brass invariably was used to make the important burner components; it was also used for the fount supports by imaginative designers, to create lamps that looked superb independent of their decorative shades. This example was made by Joseph Hinks Ltd of Birmingham during the early 20th century. It measures about 600mm (24in) in height and is still in working order.

▲ Copper electric kettle, c.1910
There is a great variety of early electric kettles to be found, made by many different makers. Some of these were converted from ordinary stove kettles. This particular example was made by art metalworkers W.A.S. Benson of London. Adapted from one of their table kettle designs, it has a false bottom containing the electrical elements. These items are now decorative only as they do not meet modern electrical safety regulations.

► Copper saucepan, c.1920
With its high conductivity and good looks, copper has been the preferred material for cookware for centuries. Items that are damaged can still be mended and re-tinned for use today. Pans were made for many special purposes, ranging from brandy-warmers to giant fish kettles, stewpans, and water boilers. This well-used, quality saucepan was made by Jaeggi, London, and bears the maker's Swiss Cross trademark.

▼ Brass shoe mantlepiece ornament, *c.*1900

Traditionally the boot is a sign of luck, which is one of the reasons why shoes or boots were thrown at married couples. One, or a pair, of ornamental boots were often kept on the mantlepiece over the fire. Some were made commercially but collectors search out the best items that were handmade during workshop lunch hours. This "mantleback" was made expertly from an old brass pipe-flange and some boiler plate.

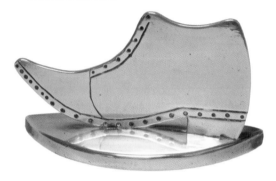

▲ Pewter tea set by Civic, *c.*1900s

Pewter was used for tableware from Roman times until the end of the 18th century, when ceramics, glass, and other metalware provided increasingly popular and affordable alternatives. In the Victorian period pewter remained in use in pubs, where drinkers required unbreakable tankards. At the turn of the 19th century there was a revival in decorative pewter, particularly among Arts and Crafts and Art Nouveau designers. This hexagonal design was used by Civic to create a number of tea sets. Pewter originally contained lead so is not suitable for food or drink. However, modern pewter is safe to use.

◄ Traditional brass candlesticks

Of the many designs of candlestick being made through the late 19th and early 20th centuries, this "Beehive and Diamonds" pattern is one of the more popular. The sticks come in a range of sizes, from 150mm (6in) up to 350mm (14in); these two are the smaller size. The candlestick on the left was made by Storrar of Chester c.1880; the one on the right is a reproduction by Peerage of Birmingham made in the late 1930s and again in the 1950s. Clues to the age of each stick are that the original has a good patina inside the base area and skilled riveting on the base and column, whereas the reproduction has a heavier and more clumsy casting.

▼ Copper table kettle, *c.*1900

Table kettles provided hot water to top up the teapot when needed. Also known as "tea kettles", "spirit kettles", and sometimes "tilting kettles", they were designed to be admired as a centrepiece. There are hundreds of variations, representing all styles. Many can be found complete, although frequently the burner needs attention. This model is made by W.M.F. of Geislingen in Würtemburg, Germany.

► Pedestal brass fruit bowl, *c.*1920

Still ideal for its original purpose after about 80 years, this compote, or fruit bowl, is made from thin brass sheet with an intricate foliate pattern. The base has two rows of decorative beading. It was made by Bradley & Co of the West Midlands under the trade name Beldray, with the logo of a diagrammatic bell over a dray (truck). Beldray has a good reputation as a brass manufacturer so a piece with its mark will be more valuable than an unmarked item. The original cut-glass liner was broken long ago and has been replaced by a modern glass dish, which retains its usefulness.

▼ Coalbrookdale cast-iron, copper-plated fruit dish, c.1850s

Cast-iron was used not just outside the house for garden furniture, but inside for beds, fire surrounds, door stoppers, and other domestic items. Coalbrookdale Iron Foundry was established in 1709 at Ironbridge, Shropshire, by Abraham Darby, and nearby, at the Ironbridge World Heritage Centre, is the first large bridge to be made of cast iron. The company exhibited its high-quality art castings at the Great Exhibition in 1851. This cast-iron fruit dish has a fine, intricate pattern of mythological characters and foliage, copper-plated to create an attractive lustre.

▲ Cast-iron trivets, original c.1960 and reproduction c.1980

Collecting these three-legged stands can be fascinating. Originally made so that kettles and pans could be kept warm by the fire, they are also now designed with shorter legs for use at the table, or to support an iron when hot. These legs make them suitable for display by wall mounting. The stand trivet on the left is by Colebrookdale Iron Co, Pottstown, Pennsylvania. The round trivet was cast in the late 20th century to commemorate the Coalbrookdale Company, England.

► Copper Benson jugs, c.1880–1914

W.A.S. Benson was a friend of William Morris, one of the founders of the Arts and Crafts movement. Based in a factory in Hammersmith, London, Benson created many superb items for use in public places. For hotels, tea-rooms, and breakfast buffets he designed and patented a range of copper jugs that enclosed an enamelled inner, with air-gap insulation. They were made in several shapes and sizes and are usually marked on the handle or base.

▲ HMS Victory brassware, 1930s and 1950s–'60s

These items are among many that celebrate affection for the world's oldest naval vessel in continuous commission. Great interest was raised during the 1905 centenary of the Battle of Trafalgar, and the production of mementos continues to this day. Shields and medallions were struck from the ship's own copper sheathing. Brass replicas of the ship were made by several Birmingham makers for use on fire irons, gongs, crumb brushes, knockers, and bells. Collecting these, or similar items with the theme, provides a fascinating historical study.

▼ Guernsey copper milk jugs, original c.1890 (left) and modern

Also called creamers or pots, these jugs were once standard for the local delivery of creamy milk from Guernsey and Jersey cows on the Channel Islands. The spherical bodies were made of eight simply formed segments, lock-seamed and soldered to the base and neck; larger jugs had strengthening fillets to the handles. Modern replicas made for the tourist market have bodies pressed from just two halves, with mock seams raised around the body.

Silver Spoons

Spoons have been used from ancient times and early silver ones tend to command the highest prices. The medieval period saw the development of the large-bowled table spoon with a decorative top, or "knop". Silver spoons were often given as presents at weddings and christenings – hence the expression "born with a silver spoon in your mouth". Apostle spoons, decorated with the figure of the child's patron saint, were a popular gift; seal-topped spoons could be pricked with the initials of the owner. During the Commonwealth spoon design became simpler, but with the restoration of the monarchy in the late 17th century fancy patterns came back in vogue and spoons were lavishly engraved. New shapes and sizes were gradually introduced: the dessert spoon, the teaspoon, and a host of specific designs for spices, condiments, and other fashionable luxuries, such as the mote spoon, caddy spoon, and marrow spoons for extracting bone marrow (a favourite delicacy). There are many slants a collector can take; types of spoon, patterns, makers, or provincial hallmarks.

Salt spoon with rope-twist handle and shell bowl, by Robert Hennell, London, 1856. Salt is corrosive to silver so check for any damage.

▲ Rococo mote spoon by James Wilks, c.1745

These teaspoon-sized spoons, with pierced bowls and pointed handles with a spike on the end, were used for removing from a cup any tea leaves that had escaped from the teapot. The spike was used to clear blockages from the teapot spout's internal strainer. They were in general use from the 1700s to 1770s and the piercing can range from simple drilled holes to elaborate scrolls, crosslets, and fleur-de-lys. This example has a shell and scroll-back design.

▼ Silver and enamel souvenir teaspoon, 1927

This souvenir teaspoon with the town crest of Bournemouth was made in Birmingham. Virtually every seaside and tourist town in the UK has at some point commissioned souvenir spoons to celebrate and promote themselves. Typically they are of teaspoon size and will have the town's coat-of-arms as the finial of the handle; sometimes the bowl is embossed with a local historical landmark or person of importance.

▲ Shell-bowled tea caddy spoon, c.1795

This tea caddy spoon has a bright-cut decorated handle and was made in London by Peter and Anne Bateman. This type of spoon was used for removing and measuring the tea leaves from the caddy (tin or box) into the teapot. Occasionally it might be used to mix a number of different teas to create a favourite blend to suit a personal taste.

▼ Sugar-sifter spoon by Alstons & Hallam, London, 1914

Sifter spoons were invented at a time when sugar was not so refined as it is today and sifting was needed to removed any unwanted impurities. The workmanship of piercing the bowl is often taken for granted, but to get a balanced pattern requires great skill. This spoon is further adorned with a finial depicting one of the 12 apostles. Apostle spoons were produced from the 15th to the 17th centuries, and the early examples can fetch thousands.

Silver Boxes

Silver boxes have been made to house all manner of substances and items over the centuries, including snuff, pins, and vestas (matches). Acquiring them is certainly not a recent pastime of the antiques hunter, as collections were compiled as long ago as the 18th century, when ladies and gentlemen from royalty downward collected snuff boxes. There is an endearing appeal to these small objects of desire, and to what they may contain. Adding to the beauty of these treasures is the endless variety of decoration, accomplished by skilled silversmiths, engravers, and enamellers who spent years as apprentices learning their trade. Boxes in daily use would have been very personal and beloved items of the owner, which is evident by the wear and tear that many have taken from being carried in a pocket or brought out and handled on a regular basis. Loving messages and tokens of esteem and friendship are occasionally engraved on the lids, which all adds to the boxes' broad appeal. They can also be found incorporating exotic materials of the time, such as a lid or base in tortoiseshell, mother of pearl, and agates, which would indicate the owner was well-travelled.

Silver patch box made by John Turner of Birmingham in 1799, with prick-dot and bright-cut decoration around the edge.

▲ Snuff box by Thomas Phipps & Edward Robinson II, 1806
This George III silver snuff box, made in London, has a prick-dot Greek key decoration and a gilded interior. Snorting ground tobacco (snuff) has been a popular habit for both men and women from the 17th century almost to the present day, and therefore these are the most common type of all boxes. The majority were designed to fit in the pocket, although there were a few larger table-sized ones. Often used every day, the quality and condition of snuff boxes can vary considerably.

▼ Toothpick box by Thomas Phipps and Edward Robinson II, 1789
Dental hygiene is not what it is today, and people's teeth would have had many cavities that would need to be cleared. One would need a box to store one's wooden, ivory, or quill picks, and they were often lined in velvet with a mirror inside the lid. This example has bright-cut decoration on all the edges and a central crest of a hound within a bright-cut cartouche.

◄ Vinaigrette by William Simpson of Birmingham, 1835
The lid of this William IV vinaigrette depicts Abbotsford – the home of the great poet Lord Byron. A vinaigrette is usually a small box with a hinged lid, which opens to reveal a pierced grill that is also hinged. Underneath the grill would be a small sponge soaked in an oily, sweet-smelling substance. Used both by men and women, generally it was carried while travelling, to give a pleasant aroma to mask that of the streets or their travelling companions. Inside, all the surfaces would be gilded to protect the silver from being stained by the oily contents.

▲ Trinket box by Nathan & Hayes, Birmingham, 1891

The trinket box is quite a generic term, usually used to describe a small box that seems to have no specific purpose, but was often served for storing jewellery, hairpins, or cufflinks. Invariably they are made of quite thin silver, and are pressed out with a highly embossed decoration on the lid and body, as with this example above, which also has crimpled edges. Do look carefully for any holes that have worn through due to excessive polishing.

▼ Heart-shaped vesta case, 1895

This Victorian vesta case was made in Birmingham by S. Blanckensee & Sons. The pocket-sized cases for carrying matches were in great use between the 1860s and 1920s. They took their name from Vesta, Roman goddess of the hearth and home. A match was known as a "vesta" up until the 20th century; it was essential to carry the vestas in a case as they were highly flammable and needed to be kept dry. The inside of the case would often be gilded to protect the silver from the vesta's sulphur head.

▲ Pill box by William Devenport & Co, 1948

The pill box is another generic term, used for any small box that does not have an obvious purpose of use. The majority of these boxes date from the late Victorian period right up to the present day. This pill box, made in Birmingham, has an Art-Deco style geometric design.

◄ Seal (skippet) box, 1770

This rare George III seal or skippet box of oval form was made by William and Aaron Lestourgeon in London. The coat-of-arms of Oxford University is finely engraved on the lid within a scrolling cartouche. A wax seal would be housed in the box, and there are slits at the top and bottom of the base to allow seal strings or ribbon to come through, thus enabling a document to be sealed. Occasionally the original wax can be still be found inside these boxes.

➤ Counter box and counters, c.1630

Counters would have been used by gentlemen when gambling or playing games. The ones pictured right are part of a group of 26 by Simon van de Passe, die-stamped with the portraits and coats-of-arms of various kings and queens. The lid of the box is pierced with the bust of Charles I, and the base is pierced with that of his queen, Henrietta Maria. It is very unusual to find one of these boxes hallmarked.

Other Silver Items

Silver primarily was used to store and demonstrate one's wealth, and if money ever needed to be raised the silver would be melted down and sold. Things have not changed much over the last five hundred years or so, except that items are not melted down anymore – they are simply sold on, as the value is now in the item itself, not necessarily the weight. There is one other difference: collectors do not always buy for the value alone; more often it is now also about the appeal of owning an item with such history, which can be dated precisely to the year of assay from the hallmark. When researching a hallmark always start by establishing the town mark, as this will give you the information necessary to decipher the date letter. The desirability of having such items of quality, as those that survive usually are, can be overwhelming for the collector and a pastime can become an obsession. Many owners of silver do not use their pieces, they simply have them on display. This is rather disappointing, as the majority of silver can and should be used, instead of just being adored from afar.

Edwardian silver pin-cushion in the form of an elephant, made by Adie and Lovekin Ltd of Birmingham in 1905.

▼ **Wine funnel by Joseph Scammell, 1795**
In the 18th and 19th centuries it was necessary to decant the sediment from wine, something that is now not often necessary with today's modern wine-making methods. The bowl of this London-made funnel is pierced in order to catch and separate the larger dregs, then the funnel could be detached in the middle to enable a piece of muslin to be added to filter the finer residue.

▲ **"Trowel" bookmark by Crisford & Norris, Birmingham, 1907**
Silver bookmarks have recently become very popular with collectors, as they can be picked up relatively cheaply and do not take up much space. There are many designs to search for. However, be aware that they are normally light in weight and are therefore prone to damage.

➤ **Manicure set by S. & M. of Birmingham, 1950**
This is a late-Art-Deco silver, black plastic, and steel manicure set. Good quality Art Deco items made in silver are relatively difficult to find as "modern" materials such as chromium and Bakelite were often favoured by designers for their innovative style. The popularity of Art Deco is growing quite considerably, as reflected by the number of related exhibitions. However, there are still bargains to be found by collectors who are willing to search the shops, markets, and auctions.

◄ Mustard pot by Thomas Goodfellow, London, 1899

Mustard as we know it today, as a paste, became popular in the late 18th century. Prior to that it was used as a dry powdered spice and was kept in casters. Most mustard pots would have a glass liner, which made them easier to clean; however, some pots were just gilded to protect the silver. This Victorian example has pierced symmetrical decoration and a Bristol-blue glass liner. Pots that are missing their liners will be reduced in value by up to 25 per cent. However, if you can find a sympathetic dealer it is possible to have the liners re-made from as little as £25 ($40) for a standard blue version.

▶ Picture frame by Walker and Hall, 1906

This Art Nouveau picture frame, made in Birmingham, depicts a woman sitting below a tree, attending her goat. Frames of this period were pressed into shape with dies, using rather thin silver sheet, which has made them prone to damage. It is quite common to see them with holes worn through on high spots of the decoration.

▼ Globe inkwell, 1924

This inkwell was made in Birmingham by The Goldsmiths & Silversmiths Company for the British Empire Exhibition of 1924. The earliest-known English silver inkstand was produced in 1630. A hundred years later Paul de Lamerie made some exquisite inkstands, one of which sold at auction in 1998 in New York for $1.25 million (£832,400). Pieces made for exhibition are often highly ingenious and consequently very collectable.

◄ Cast-silver taperstick by Ebenezer Coker, London, 1759

Generally found on a writing desk, and about 12.5cm (5in) in height, tapersticks were used to hold the small candle (taper) that melted sealing wax. Early Georgian tapersticks such as this were cast in silver, as opposed to later Victorian ones that were pressed out and joined, and then filed with pitch. They mirrored the fashions of their large counterpart, the candlestick, but unlike candlesticks they more often than not came as a single item, rather than a pair.

◄ Pierced bon-bon dish by William Evans, 1892

The term "bon-bon dish" encompasses most small dishes and baskets, normally of light weight with embossing and pierce work; earlier examples would have been referred to as "sweet-meat" dishes or baskets. This dish, decorated with flowers and swags, was made by William Evans of London and retailed by The Goldsmiths & Silversmiths Company of Regent Street.

Victorian Scottish sergeant's brass basket-hilted broadsword; they were a sign of sergeant rank as other swords had steel hilts.

The high-quality craftsmanship and potent historical interest of wartime relics and artifacts has made militaria a fascination for collectors over the years. The subject of militaria embraces a wide range of objects, from badges, head dress, and uniforms, to medals, firearms, and even ephemera such as posters and cigarette cards. You may decide to focus on a particular regiment, a certain type of object, or a period of military history, or your interest may be prompted by your own, or a member of your family's, service record. Many collectors are drawn to this field by the satisfaction of researching the historical, social, and political background to each item – discovering details of the service of the original owner, including battles fought and promotions won. This information can be gleaned from the Public Records office, books on regimental histories, and of course the infinite resources on the internet, although some kind of provenance, such as a letter or official document, will always increase the value considerably. Collecting larger-scale items such as head dress and uniforms requires a considerable amount of space; if uniforms are not on continuous display they must be stored away carefully, wrapped in airtight and moth-free bags. Similar care must be taken with head dress: heat can soften the patent leather peaks and trims so it is advisable to apply a thin coating of Vaseline to prevent this. And before purchasing antique firearms check whether a special licence is needed – in most countries you will need one if you intend to use the gun. When searching for militaria be sure to go to reputable sources, such as recommended dealers or auction houses.

▲ French 1st Empire Imperial Garde helmet
The 22 years of the Napoleonic wars (1793–1815) provided a large resource of militaria for the collector. Although French accoutrements, like this fine dragoon helmet, are more scarce in the UK, they do occasionally appear at auction. The original leopard skin on this helmet indicates it belonged to an officer – other ranks had only imitation skin.

▼ Black Watch ostrich feather bonnet, 1801
The Scottish Infantry Regiment the Black Watch is the only regiment to wear the red hackle ostrich feather. The badge on this bonnet shows the sphinx over a tablet reading "Egypt". This was to mark the victory of the Black Watch forces against Napoleon's troops in Egypt at the Battle of Alexandria in 1801. These bonnets were given in honour of that occasion.

▲ King's Own Light Infantry helmet, c.1881
The officer's spiked cloth helmet was first introduced in 1878, when regiments were still identified by number rather than name. In 1881 the Cardwell system was adopted, by which each English county gained its own individually named regiment; this one is for the Yorkshire regiment. The traditional British policeman's helmet was based on this military design.

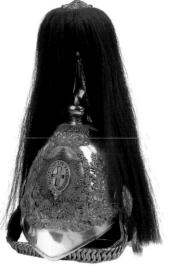

▲ Royal Horse Guards helmet, late 19th century

Prior to 1922 there were three regiments of household cavalry – the 1st and 2nd Life Guards and the Royal Horse Guards. Today there are just two – the Life Guards and the Blues and Royals (the name that replaced the Royal House Guards). It is easy to differentiate between the two regiments as the Life Guards have a distinctive white plume on their helmets while the Blues and Royals use scarlet. The plumes must be in good condition for the helmet to retain its full value.

➤ Imperial German Garde du Corps, c.1900

This regiment was the elite corps of the Kaiser's cavalry, and many photographs exist today that show the Kaiser himself wearing this type of helmet. For everyday, non-ceremonial duties the eagles would be removed and replaced with a spike finial. The grand appearance of these helmets makes them highly sought-after in today's market, and Imperial German head dress in general is very collectable in both the USA and the UK.

◀ Bearskin of the Coldstream Guards

The five regiments comprising the Brigade of Guards wear various coloured plumes, with the exception of the Scots Guards who have just plain bearskins. The bearskin was first bestowed on the Guards regiments in recognition of their success in beating Napoleon's Old Guard at Waterloo, who themselves wore very tall bearskins. This distinctive design has not altered over the years and can still be seen on Coldstream Guards today.

▲ Forage cap of Royal Scots Fusiliers, c.1900

Forage caps were designed for undress wear, that is everyday wear, and are sometimes referred to as "patrol" or "drill" caps. Every regiment had its own version, bearing its particular bullion-wire, woven cap badge. It is rare to find these badges separately as they were sewn-on to the caps rather than pinned.

◀ Lance cap of the 16th Lancers, c.1920

The British army did not have regiments of lancers until 1816. Having experienced the devastation by Napoleon's Polish lancers in the Peninsular War, it was decided to form lancer regiments of their own. Although the number of regiments has been reduced due to amalgamation, the lancers do still exist today as an armoured force. This example of a lance cap is from the reign of King George V (1910–36), identified by his royal cypher on the boss of the cap, partly hidden under the plume.

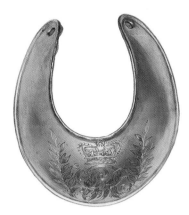

◄ Copper-gilt Gorget, *c*.1800

The Gorget was originally part of a suit of armour that covered the shoulders and protected the neck; the example illustrated, from the turn of the 19th century, would have been worn throughout the Napoleonic Wars. As firearms became more powerful less armour was worn because there was less direct contact between soldiers. Over the years copper-gilt Gorgets became smaller and smaller, until eventually they were just badges to indicate officer rank. They were finally abolished altogether in 1830.

► Officer's uniform of the 2nd Bengal Light Cavalry, *c*.1830

British Indian Army uniforms are very hard to come by; this is partly due to the hot climate endured by the soldiers, as perspiration would have destroyed the cloth. As a result full dress uniform such as this would have been worn only on special parades. Many of the regiments in India consisted of English officers and Indian troopers. Collectors wishing to display their uniforms should search tailors' shops for unwanted dressmakers' dummies, like the one used here.

► Sabretache of the South Nottinghamshire Yeomanry Cavalry, late 19th century

The sabretache was principally the equipment of the light cavalry Hussars and Lancers. Hussars wore tight clothing, hence the need to create a "tache" (pocket). Light cavalry were used as dispatch riders so the sabretache was often adopted to carry military documents or personal items. This particular regiment was part of the Yeomanry force of Britain, first formed during the Napoleonic Wars to defend the homeland in the absence of the regular cavalry, who were fighting overseas.

▼ Waterloo Medal, awarded 1816

The Waterloo Medal was the first officially awarded medal for all ranks. Previously only regimental medals were given, although officers were awarded gold crosses and gold medals. It was not until 1847 that a general service medal with clasps for various battles was given to all ranks. It was mainly as a result of service in the Napoleonic Wars, but it could not be awarded posthumously.

◄ Officer's khaki doublet, *c*.1914

Uniforms from the World War I period are quite hard to find in good condition. Apart from the hazard of annual moth, the drab khaki coats were not favourite items to preserve for posterity. Genuine collectors are always eager to buy when they do appear on the market, so prices can be pushed quite high for these rarities. The one pictured left is the uniform of the Argyll and Sutherland Highlanders.

◄ Group of King's Own Scottish Borderers Military Medals, c.1914–18
The Military Medal (pictured far left) was instituted during World War I and a total of 115,500 were awarded. However, this in no way diminishes the bravery of the action – many were given for wiping out machine-gun nests. The other three medals are nicknamed "Pip", "Squeak", and "Wilfrid", after three animals (a dog, penguin, and rabbit respectively) that appeared in a cartoon strip in the *Daily Mirror* newspaper in 1916. Medals sold in groups are worth more than when sold singly. If they also have some form of provenance, such as the original citation or documentation, the value will increase further.

◄ Hallmarked silver Glengarry badge, 1897
Collecting officers' badges, especially if they are made in hallmarked silver, is very rewarding as not only are they well made and sometimes hand-finished, but the hallmark also gives the exact year in which a badge was made. It also provides collectors with the opportunity to research the activities of the regiment at that time. This badge belongs to the Argyll and Sutherland Highlanders regiment.

▼ Silver plaid brooch of the Highland Light Infantry, c.1905
Officers and pipers of all the Scottish regiments wore a brooch such as this to fasten the plaid (swathe of tartan material) over their left shoulder. The Highland Light Infantry displayed all their battle honours in the scrolls around the edge of the badge, with probably their most famous battle, that of "Assaye" in India in September 1803, represented by the Indian elephant in the centre, just below the bugle.

► Gilt Glengarry cap badge of the 50th (Queen's Own) Regiment, late 1870s
The Glengarry cap badge was introduced in 1875, at a time when all regiments were known by number. This badge must date somewhere between then and 1881, when the Cardwell System was introduced and county names were adopted instead of numbers. Under the new system the 50th regiment became The 1st Battalion of The Royal West Kent regiment. The sphinx and the word "Egypt" refer to the victory won there against Napoleon's army in 1801.

◄ Officer's badge of the Liverpool Pals, c.1914–18
The Liverpool Pals regiment was part of the army raised in World War I by Lord Kitchener. They were just some of the men who answered Kitchener's call to arms, as displayed on the famous poster "Your Country Needs You". This badge, struck in sterling silver, bears the eagle crest and motto of the Earl of Derby; the Earl had some of his own family silver melted down to make these badges. Badges should show some evidence of their age through general wear and tear – be suspicious of those in perfect condition.

◄ Imperial German Iron Cross, 1914

The Iron Cross was instituted in 1813 and was awarded again in 1870 during the Franco Prussian War of 1870–71, and then a third and fourth time in 1914 and 1939. German decorations and badges were very prolific in the Third Reich period of the late 1930s, and they lend themselves naturally to the collectors' market due to the large variety of awards available. Many come in three "classes" – gold (gilt), silver, and bronze – depending on the category of the award given.

▲ London Irish Rifles drum, c.1960

Due to the shrinkage of many army battalions there are now a considerable number of redundant army drums that have found their way onto the collectors' market. The fact that the army have abandoned the traditional calf skin in favour of plastic drum heads is also good news for the militaria enthusiast as they too are now available to collect. However, this surplus of drums will not last forever and prices are likely to rise, making them a wise investment for the future.

➤ Tenor drum of the Royal Marines, 1940s

Drums have played an important role within armies since ancient times, rallying the men with their beats – on Nelson's ships the Royal Marine drummer would beat every quarter of an hour on action stations – and contributing to the music for all occasions. The original Royal Marines Band Service (RMBS), together with its headquarters, the Royal Naval School of Music, was founded in 1930 to provide Bands for the Royal Navy. It has now become an integral part of the Royal Marines Corps.

◄ Officer's 1912 Pattern Cavalry Sword

In 1908 a version of this pattern cavalry sword was issued to other ranks; this 1912 pattern is the final version of the officer's sword to be issued to the British Army. Three hundred years went into the development of this type of sword but by World War I they had become largely redundant as they were not practical for use in trench warfare. However, they were still used by Field Marshall Edmund Allenby during battles against the Turkish-German army in Palestine. The blades of World War I examples are made of fine tempered steel.

➤ German SS Third Reich dagger, 1933

This dagger bears an engraved inscription on the blade "Presented by Ernest Rohm", and his signature. Rohm was chief of staff for the Sturmabteilung (SA) – a paramilitary organization within the Nazi Party. When Hitler decided in 1934 that he needed civilian control of the army he ordered the SS (his personal body-guard under Heinrich Himmler) to murder all members of the SA, including Rohm. Subsequently all daggers had to have their inscriptions erased, so it is extremely rare to find an example that still bears the original wording and they can fetch well over £1,000 ($1,500) at auction. SA daggers have brown handles.

▼ **Adams five-shot double-action percussion revolver with leather holster, c.1850s**
The Adams revolver, designed by Robert Adams and patented in 1851, was very popular with officers serving in the Crimean War (1854–56) and the Indian Mutiny (1857–58). Its main rival was the Colt revolver, designed by Colonel Sam Colt in the USA and patented in 1836. A friendly contest was held between Adams and Colt to see which gun performed best, and Adams won. However, the Colt was the popular choice in the USA and Canada.

▼ **Remington army percussion revolver, c.1865**
The Remington, along with the Colt revolver (*see* left), was used by both sides in the American Civil War of 1861–65. They are popular now with collectors in the USA and the UK but condition is paramount. Other US gun manufacturers of the time included Starr and Smith & Wesson; the latter is still making guns today.

▼ **Model of a 13-pounder field gun and limber, c.1914**
An area of collecting that will be forever popular, model cannons of all periods can be found in auctions and on dealers' stands at fairs. With so many on the market it is advisable to buy only the best-crafted models. This 13-pounder is a model of the gun used by The Royal Horse Artillery King's Troop. It brings to mind "L" battery in World War I, when the rapid firing of a single gun could keep a German division at bay.

▼ **Silhouette by John Buncombe, c.1825**
Military silhouettes are another facet of collecting military memorabilia and perhaps the most famous artist in this field is John Buncombe. His work was probably quite expensive even in his own lifetime, although he would have charged a lot less than a society portrait artist. For this reason many of Buncombe's subjects are middle-ranking army officers, as portrayed here. Buncombe silhouettes are quite scarce and valuable and have been much copied, so do beware of fakes.

➤ **Watercolour by Orlando Norie, c.1860–80**
Orlando Norie was a popular military artist who flourished in the late-19th century. Many of his works were of the Crimean War and the Indian Mutiny, although pictures of regimental parades and single figures can also sometimes be found. His signed paintings are highly sought-after and command high prices at auction.

◄ **Spelter figure of an Austro-Hungarian cuirassier (heavy cavalry),** *c.*1870–90

There is great scope for those who decide to collect military figures. They come in a number of media, such as porcelain, resin, spelter (zinc, as in the case of this figure), and other metals, and varying sizes, from 7.5cm (3in) to 30cm (12in) models, such as those made by Royal Worcester. Many figures do not have a maker's mark but painted pewter figures by the artist Chas Stadden are particularly popular.

▲ **Hallmarked silver figure of a City of London Volunteer, 1903**

Silver figurines were very popular during the Boer War period (1899–1902). A great many British regiments were sent out to South Africa in those years, both cavalry and infantry, and there was a constant demand on silversmiths for presentation pieces such as this.

➤ **Cigarette cards issued by Ogdens, early 20th century**

From 1900 until the years of World War I (1914–18) many sets of cigarette cards were devoted to military subjects, such as badges, flags, military personalities, uniforms, and military vehicles. This particular set of 50 cards, produced by Ogdens, was entitled "Soldiers of the King". Manufacturers such as Wills and Players also issued many sets of military subjects.

▲ **World War I recruiting poster, 1914–18**

Posters produced during World War I, mainly for the purposes of recruiting, can often still be found in reasonably good condition but be careful as to their authenticity as the Imperial War Museum in London has made reproductions over the years. Look out for the words "Reproduced by the Imperial War Museum" along the bottom edge, and be particularly wary of posters that have had the borders trimmed off completely.

▲ **Embroidered silk postcard for the South Lancashire Volunteers, c.1916**

Cards such as this were made in large numbers during World War I, often depicting a particular regiment or to commemorate a certain battle. Cards were also produced for the Air Force and the Royal Navy to send home to their loved ones. The fragile nature of the embroidery meant that most cards were protected in envelopes, so few are found with any postal franking marks.

When metal became widely available again, following the rationing of World War II, souvenirs and mementos of the time appeared in the guise of metal brooches, each depicting a miniature Treasury note.

All of us like to collect money but money itself has spawned a wealth of collectables. Money boxes, known as money banks in the USA, have been produced since ancient times, when hoards of coins were buried in terracotta pots. Decorative boxes such as the piggy bank were produced in Europe from the 17th century – the fat pig being a traditional symbol of wealth. The 19th century saw the development of the cast-iron bank, particularly in America where "still" (non-moving) and mechanical banks of great ingenuity were produced. In the 20th century many boxes were created as advertising tools for banks and post offices, perhaps the most famous modern UK example being the NatWest Pigs by Wade Pottery. Paper money attracts "notaphilists" across the world: some focus on a specific country, or a particular period of time such as World War II. Bank notes with no face value, for example those with printing errors, can be of great worth to the collector. The Bank of England was established in 1694 and its first printed notes were almost immediately forged. Though it was, and still is, an offence to produce imitations of Bank of England notes in any format, this has not prevented the production of a plethora of bank-note decorated collectables.

◄ Enamelled cufflink white five pound note, 1920s

Enamelled versions of the £5, £10, and £20 white notes of the 1880s were often depicted on tie tacks, pins, brooches, and cufflinks in the 1920s. White notes existed from the inauguration of the Bank of England in 1694 and remained in circulation until 1960. The white £5 was superseded in 1956 by a blue bank note, which was smaller and more in keeping with the new-sized notes that were circulating at the time. It is always advisable to check the condition of enamelled items as they are prone to chipping.

▲ Cigarette case, *c.*1930

Cigarette cases made around this time could often be found with the Britannia "Series A & B" 10 shilling, £1, and £5 notes. Originally produced in colour, wear-and-tear has affected the delicate coating. As with many of the illegal reproduction products, these cases were made outside the UK.

▲ Note keyring, *c.*1991

Keyrings that depict current notes were, and still are, easy and cheap to make. Made from photographic reproductions this set has appeared from the 1970s. Similar examples, using local currencies, have been produced overseas, although in many instances these have now been replaced with Euro keyrings. Political events cause paper money both to appear and disappear, and currently sought-after by collectors are Iraqi bank notes bearing the portrait of Saddam Hussein.

▲ China money box, c.1960

The idea of saving in a money box existed long before this particular china box was made. It is designed to look like a £1 pictorial note series "C", which was first issued in 1960. Called "Bank of Toyland", the prefix of the featured note is "IOU" and "AD 1066"; the queen pictured is Queen Elizabeth I. The tiny bung hole in the base allowed banknotes to be inserted, but the box ultimately would have to be smashed to get to the money.

◄ ▲ Comic postcards, c.1915

The postcard craze of the Victorian and Edwardian eras provided great scope for the comic artists of the time. The humour can appear crude, and sometimes even offensive, by today's standards but the situations are often as pertinent now as they were then. The drawings were based on actual bank notes but in a cartoon style to match the rest of the design.

➤ First-issue one pound Treasury note, 1914

The declaration of World War I on 4th August 1914 almost caused a financial crisis; gold sovereigns were withdrawn and replaced by paper money. These first-issue one pound and ten shilling notes were printed on simple cypher watermarked paper (initially used for stamp production), as no proper bank note paper existed for values below £5. The £1 note, printed in black on white, was uniface (printed on one side only) and featured the head of George V. These emergency Treasury notes were nicknamed "Bradburys", referring to the signature of the Secretary to the Treasury, which appeared at the bottom.

▼ Lion and Key five pound note, 1957

The Lion and Key £5, designed by Stephen Gooden, superseded the White Fiver. Although only a short-lived issue it was striking in design and colour, and was the first colour £5 note issued by the Bank of England since its inception in 1694. The note's features gave a feeling of a sense of pride and strength in the economy.

▲ White Fiver, 1947

The White Fiver was first issued in its fully printed version in 1873. Small changes were introduced over the years: in 1945 a metallic thread was incorporated as a major anti-forgery device. The notes remained uniface and were finally recalled in 1961. Forgery of these white notes was rife during World War II; even the spy, Cicero, was believed to have been paid off in forged notes, as were many traitors and suppliers.

NEWSPAPERS & MAGAZINES

The Impartial Protestant Mercury from 1684; 17th-century advances in printing technology led to the birth of the newspaper industry around this time.

Newspapers began in the late 16th century, when Continental printers produced "relations" – single sheets of paper reporting a specific event. Over a week or more several sheets might be gathered into a *coranto* (newsbook); the first English newsbook was published in 1621. The Civil War (1642–46) stimulated huge demand for news, but under Cromwell and Charles II there was considerable censorship. In the 1700s the rise of the London coffee houses, where gossip was rife, fuelled the desire for journals such as T*he Tatler* (est. 1709) and T*he Spectator* (est. 1711). The 18th century was a golden age, with the launch of local and Sunday newspapers, and the founding of T*he Times* in 1785. By the 19th century the press had expanded enormously, with publications for every class and taste. For both magazines and newspapers the most important factors for collectors include content (the events reported), title, and rarity. No 1 issues are always desirable and a good cover image affects value. Condition is crucial: ironically, pre-1900 newspapers printed on linen paper, as opposed to wood pulp used in the 20th century, often survive better than their modern equivalent.

➤ *Le Petit Journal*, 1899

Crime and punishment is a fascinating subject and forms a theme for many collectors in its own right. This copy of the French publication *Le Petit Journal* has a back cover image depicting an electrocution scene in the USA. The first ever execution by electric chair had taken place just nine years earlier; this new form of capital punishment initially was hailed as scientific and humane.

➤ *Paris Match*, "Special France" edition, 1961

Paris Match, with its winning combination of news and celebrity stories, is among the best-known magazines in the world. Its reputation for quality journalism and outstanding photography ensures collector interest; issues featuring stars such as Grace Kelly are among the most popular. Also in demand are those that celebrate French icons, like the *SS France* in this issue, which provides a cross-over appeal to collectors of nautical memorabilia.

▲ *Bristol Evening Post*, "Victory Day", 1945

The *Bristol Evening Post* first appeared in 1932 and is now one of the UK's best-known regional papers. Local papers are usually of particular interest to local historians, but this issue commemorates an event of global importance: the Allied Victory in 1945. Bristol suffered major devastation during the Blitz, and this paper recalls the contribution of the city to the war effort.

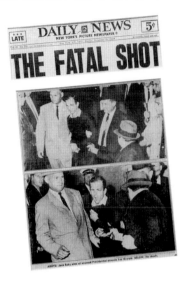

▲ Daily News, 1963

The assassination of John F. Kennedy has spawned an industry, and prompted countless conspiracy theories, so anything to do with that tragic event attracts collectors. This copy of the *Daily News* is of great historical interest, reporting the shooting of assassin Lee Harvey Oswald by Jack Ruby. By the 1960s print could not compete with television for impact (the shooting was captured live by TV cameras), but newspapers relating to the incident are certainly collectable today.

▼ Time magazine, 1966

This edition of the famous news magazine represents a piece of cultural history, for it was here that the phrase "Swinging London" was coined to sum up the vibrant atmosphere of Britain's capital in 1966. The magazine's coverage of the most significant people and places of the time gives the collector an insight into the era as viewed by contemporary commentators. This issue is sought-after by 1960s enthusiasts.

▲ Oz magazine, issues 1–48, 1967–'73

The satirical *Oz* magazine is best remembered for issue 28, the "Schoolkids Issue", which resulted in the prosecution of its editors for obscenity. That issue is certainly the most collectable and valuable of the 48 published, but any copy is interesting to collectors because of the magazine's contribution to 1960s "counter culture". This complete run of the magazine (1967–'73) can fetch four-figure sums.

➤ Vogue magazine, "Gold Issue", 2000

The famous style bible *Vogue*, established in the USA in 1892 and the UK in 1916, is always interesting to connoisseurs of fashion as a guide to what was the last word in chic at the time it was published. Collectable interest was added in 1999 and 2000 when the magazine published special "Silver" and "Gold" issues respectively – both are already collectable, and may well become even more so as time passes.

▲ Biba, introducing the new store in Kensington High Street, 1973

Biba was founded in 1964 and went on to become one of the most celebrated names in UK fashion. Great excitement surrounded the opening of its new department store in Kensington High Street, London, in 1973, but sadly it closed down just a few years later. This promotional newspaper for the new store is very collectable, as are Biba catalogues, because it provides prime source material for all dedicated followers of fashion.

PHOTOGRAPHS

Cased images is a generic term for photographs that are contained in a shallow-hinged case for safe-keeping and display. This ambrotype (a photograph on glass) is dated *c*.1860.

Photography was invented almost simultaneously in France and England in 1839 by Louis Jacques Daguerre and Fox Talbot respectively. Initially its use was restricted by patents, but by the 1850s it had become more widespread, helped both by technical developments and by being given the royal seal of approval at the Great Exhibition in London in 1851. During the second half of the 19th century photography was largely the preserve of the upper classes and of professional operators. Amateur photography as we know it began in the late 19th century with the introduction of roll film, smaller box cameras, and the Kodak slogan "You press the button, We'll do the rest". The 20th century saw the development of faster film and of the 35mm camera, and with it the ability to catch the "decisive moment". News photography and fashion photography became the defining genres of the medium. The closing years of the 20th century have seen the development of digital imaging, with its opportunities for manipulation and enhancement of the print. Photographic prints can be produced without using traditional gelatin silver papers. Photography is now routinely used as a means of expression by contemporary artists. Since it was invented, photography has been regarded as a collectable medium. The choice of what to collect is now wider than ever, as shown by the categories described on the following pages.

▲ Stereoscopic card, *c*.1865

The stereoscopic viewer was invented in 1838 by Sir Charles Wheatstone and stereoscopic images were first exhibited at the Great Exhibition of 1851. Due to interest expressed by Queen Victoria and Prince Albert they became a popular collecting pastime. Soon every middle- and upper-class Victorian home possessed a viewer and a collection of cards. Millions of cards were produced in the next 20 years, and again in a second phase of production from 1890 to 1920. The majority of cards show topographical locations from all over the world, but some show portraits, genre scenes, humorous tableaux, or still lives. Both the cards and viewers are keenly collected, especially rare early cards in good condition.

▲ *Carte de visite* of Italian peasants, 1860s

Much early portrait photography was expensive to buy, so in 1854 a French photographer Adolphe Eugene Disderi invented a camera with four lenses that could take small, visiting card-sized photographs. The vast majority of these were portraits, taken in the photographer's studio against backdrops of various kinds. Millions of *cartes de visite* were produced from the 1850s up until the early years of the 20th century, and were collected in specially fitted albums. Collectors today search out cards of royalty, famous people, actors and actresses, topographical cards, and those showing fashion of the day. In addition well-known photographers are collected, as are those who worked in specific locations.

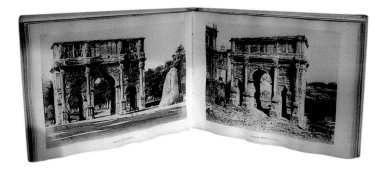

▲ Album of photographs of Rome, taken in the 1860s by Altobelli
The Victorians used albums to store and preserve their photographs, just as we use them today. They pasted larger format photographs into leather-bound albums and inserted *carte de visite* photographs into specially made albums. Sometimes travel albums show a mixture of prints from many different countries, while others will just contain prints of one country, such as Egypt, Italy, or India. As the 19th century wore on and more people learnt how to take and process their own photographs, they also used albums to keep a record of country-house living, visits from friends, theatricals, fancy dress, and games such as croquet.

▼ A view of Kashmir, northern India, 1870
The Victorians used photography to record their foreign travels, as well as tours and holidays in the UK. Most travellers bought prints from commercial photographers who had studios and shops in the countries they visited. They could be purchased in a variety of sizes and would then be stuck into albums on the traveller's return home. Sometimes specially made albums prepared by the photographer would be available. The photographs showed the common tourist sights, as well as local architecture, street scenes, and natives. Most commonly found today are albums showing Mediterranean countries, India and South East Asia, and Japan. Sometimes the prints are hand-coloured, particularly Japanese ones.

▲ A cynatype of Indian elephants, c.1875
Since its invention photography has developed a multitude of different processes, for the creation of the negative and positive (or final print). The earliest photographs were either daguerreotypes, one-of-a-kind images on silvered copper plates, or salted paper prints from waxed paper negatives. The most common combination in the Victorian period was a glass negative and a print on thin paper coated with albumen, or egg white. The latter part of the 19th century saw an explosion of different processes, including carbon and Woodbury-type prints, platinum prints, cynatypes (the same process as blueprints used for plans and maps), photogravures, bromoil, and gum-bichromate prints. All are now the subject of special-interest collections.

◄ "Having His Portrait Taken" by Lady Roscoe, 1886
A conscious attempt to argue that photographs possessed artistic qualities and could be regarded as the equivalent of paintings and prints developed in the 1860s, and was a theme in the photographic activity of the pictorialist movement during the 1870s to 1890s. Such consciously artistic photography is highly prized today, and is based inevitably on the big-name photographers of the period, such as Julia Margaret Cameron, Oscar Reijlander, Henry Peach Robinson, Peter Henry Emerson, and Frederick Evans, among others. The pictorialist movement began in the UK and was taken up strongly in the USA at the turn of the 20th century by Alfred Steiglitz and his circle.

◄ Press print, Fox Photo Agency, 1929
Press photographs taken at the end of the 19th
and through the 20th centuries are very collectable.
The majority are attributed only to the agency that
employed the photographer. Some are collected
for the famous events they show, the well-known
personalities featured, or simply because they depict
quirky or unusual episodes. Events such as the two
world wars and space exploration are particularly
collected, as are sporting celebrities, politicians,
royalty, or elements of urban and rural life that no
longer exist. This photograph shows the R101,
Britain's largest airship, at its mooring mast.

► Anonymous fashion print, 1950s
Fashion photographs are one of the strongest
collecting areas, in particular those taken during
the second half of the 20th century. Fashion
photography began in the early 1900s with Mlle
Reutlinger in Paris. Early photographers such as
Baron de Meyer, Steichen, Horst, and Man Ray
are all highly collectable and their work is now
scarce. Signed exhibition prints are also quite
rare – often produced once the photographer
was well-known and in demand. Fashion prints
are collected as much for their graphic qualities
and portraiture of famous models as they are
for showing the fashions of the day.

**▲ A vernacular photograph of two
policemen carrying prize parrots, 1935**
Interest in collecting what is called "vernacular
photography" is a relatively recent phenomenon.
"Vernacular" refers to quirky, unposed images that
have an unusual or arresting quality about them.
They can be professionally taken or amateur
snapshots, but they most often gain their appeal
from being unintentionally attractive images.
This photograph was intended simply as a record
of the bird show at Crystal Palace, but it is both
unusual and amusing to modern-day eyes. Many
amateur photographs possess this quality.

▼ A unique untitled photogram by Adam Fuss, 1990
The term "contemporary photography" is used to refer to the images that
are both made very recently and consciously attempt to make an artistic
statement. Much contemporary work has a conceptual edge to it – in other
words it is trying to convey a message through visual means. It aims to evoke
a reaction in the viewer or to make them challenge their own point of view,
and reflects the crossover between art and photography that has occurred
in the last 10 years. Photography such as this is as likely to appear in
contemporary art sales as in photography sales.

▲ Reportage shot of a Dinka Elder in Sudan, by John Goldblatt, 1972
Reportage photography has a history as long as that of photography itself.
Roger Fenton was one of the first – he went to the Crimea in 1854 to cover
the war there and the conditions of the soldiers at Balaklava. Reportage
photography is concerned with the documentation of current events, and
much of what is collected is work that dates from the second half of the
20th century, covering politics, war, natural disasters, and famine, as well as
photographers by the Magnum collective – an agency that still exists today.

PLASTICS

The word "plastic" comes from the Greek "plasma", meaning mould or form. Natural plastics such as horn, amber, and tortoiseshell, which can be softened by heat and pressed into shape, had been in use for centuries before inventors began to experiment with semi-synthetic plastics. It could be a risky business. In 1839 the American Charles Goodyear mixed India rubber with sulphur on a stove to produce Vulcanite. Though his invention made millions for others, Goodyear lost his patent and died in 1860, $200,000 in debt. English chemist Alexander Parkes developed Parkesine, using cellulose from plants but his plastics were too brittle to be used commercially and in 1868 the company folded. However, in the USA the Hyatt Brothers combined cellulose with camphor, patenting celluloid in 1869. And in 1907 Leo Baekeland, a Belgian-born chemist in the USA, came up with the first completely synthetic plastic, combining phenol (carbolic acid) with formaldehyde. In the 1920s and '30s a huge number of domestic products were made from Bakelite, and post-war technological developments led to plastic becoming increasingly important in the home. Early plastics, Bakelite, and post-war designer pieces are all popular.

Vulcanite was a popular substitute for jet mourning jewellery in the 1800s; it was also used in smoking accessories, pens, and dentures!

▲ Celluloid hair combs, 1920s

Ornate hair combs became extremely popular during the Victorian and Edwardian periods, when ladies pinned up their long tresses with large, decorative combs made from tortoiseshell and other precious materials. One of the advantages of celluloid was that it could provide a near-perfect imitation of tortoiseshell, coral, ivory, and pearl. Celluloid combs such as these were highly prized and often beautifully handcrafted. The flammability of the plastic did not put wearers off and hair combs remained in vogue until the late 1920s when short hairstyles for women were introduced.

▼ Bakelite bedwarmer by Rothermel, c.1930

Bakelite was described as "the material of 1001 uses", and thanks to its insulating properties it was much employed for electrical appliances, from radios to telephones. This Rothermel RAR electric heater (patented in 1943) came in brown and black Bakelite. To reassure those worried about using electricity in the bed, it was styled like a traditional rubber hot water bottle, although the asbestos lining should certainly deter any modern users. Manufacturers claimed a wide range of therapeutic benefits from sleeping with electricity.

◄ Plastic camera, 1938

Cameras are another example of a technology revolutionized by plastic. Celluloid film (introduced in 1889) replaced glass and metal plates, and as photography grew in popularity Bakelite was used to make cheap and sturdy mass-produced cameras, such as Kodak's 1934 "Baby Brownie", which cost $1 and sold 4 million. This Edbar International Corp VP Twin plastic novelty camera was made for Woolworth's. It came in various colours; blue is the rarest and black the most common.

▼ Beatl Urea Formaldehyde bowl, 1930s

Bakelite tended to be produced in dark colours, most notably black and brown (to imitate wood). The 1920s and '30s saw developments in urea formaldehyde, a colourless resin that, when mixed with powdered colours, created marbled effects in a range of brilliant tones. This bright plastic, promoted as being both "artistic and useful", became fashionable for kitchen and tableware in the inter-war years, even receiving the royal seal of approval when Queen Mary bought a plastic picnic set in 1931. Trade names include Bandalasta, Beatl, and Linga-Longa.

▲ Melamine tableware, 1950s

Melamine was developed in the 1930s and refined in the 1940s when the US Navy commissioned unbreakable dishes for shipboard use. In the 1950s it entered the domestic kitchen, providing colourful competition for traditional ceramics. US Designer Russel Wright (1904–76) launched his melamine "Residential" tableware in 1953 and won the Museum of Modern Art's Good Design Award. The flowing organic forms came in a range of mix-and-match colours, providing plastic tableware that was elegant enough for the dining room.

▼ "Boby" trolley by Joe Colombo, 1970

Italy produced some of the most stylish plastic furniture in the 1960s and '70s, until the oil crisis of 1973 raised prices and halted most experimentation. This "Boby" trolley, made from glossy ABS plastic, was produced in 1970 by Joe Colombo (1930–71) – one of the most influential Italian designers of the period. It was designed initially for the drawing studio, but was soon being wheeled around the kitchens and bathrooms of the fashion conscious. The trolley was first manufactured by Bieffeplast and came in various colours. Look out for Colombo's moulded signature on the bottom shelf.

▲ PVC cushion, 1960s

One of the most important plastics to emerge in the post-war period was PVC. Plastic furnishing became an important part of the 1960s look. The Milanese firm Zanotta produced the first blow-up PVC chair in 1967, which was promoted as fun furniture that could be moved from house to garden, and even used in the swimming pool. Many other companies, including Quasar Khan in France, produced inflatable furniture. This blow-up plastic cushion is by US psychedelic artist Peter Max and is collectable as a classic example of '60s ephemera, in a medium that often simply perished.

▶ Perspex ice bucket, 1970s

As well as offering limitless opportunity for bright mix-and-match colours, plastic also provided a transparent and unbreakable substitute for glass. Acrylic (clear plastic) was developed in the 1930s. During the war it was used in the aircraft industry and to create protective screens, and in peace time it entered the home. Known by popular trade names such as Perspex, Lucite, and Plexiglas, acrylic has been used for everything, from handbags to furniture. This ice bucket is by Italian firm Guzzini.

POSTCARDS

The first postcards appeared in Austria in 1869 and Britain in 1870. The plain buff card came ready printed with a halfpenny stamp (half the price of a letter). Initially the Post Office stipulated that illustrations could only appear on the message side of the card, but in 1902 Britain became the first country to divide the back of the card for address and message, leaving the front free for decoration. This led to an explosion in manufacture and the Golden Age of the postcard, which ran from 1902 to 1914 and produced the bulk of postcards collected today, most of which remain relatively inexpensive. At this time postcard collecting was a national craze. Every drawing room had its postcard album, every country in the world produced postcards, and this has left today's enthusiast with an unimaginable number to choose from. After World War I interest declined and the hobby lay relatively dormant until the postcard revival of the 1960s, which saw the publication of larger-sized modern cards, which continue to the present. Today postcard collecting is one of the most popular hobbies, with specialist dealers, fairs, and auctions.

A Victorian card, c.1897, printed by chromo-litho in Germany, showing vignettes of Swansea, Wales. Note the space left on the front for the message.

▼ Mrs Pankhurst and daugher Christabel
Picture postcards form an often neglected, yet invaluable source material for the social history of our times. They recorded strikes, disasters, accidents, shipwrecks, parades, and all kinds of special events, often being the only photographic record in existence. Below is a contemporary portrait of Mrs. Pankhurst with her daughter Christabel, taken in the 1900s. Suffragette cards are keenly sought-after, many selling at auction in excess of £100 ($150).

▲ A Dutch Love Story greeting card, c.1911
Greetings cards of all kinds were produced in huge numbers by the publishers of the time, and many of them can be obtained for a few pence. Dealers' boxes are full of the more common Birthday, Christmas, and Easter cards, as well as countless others. This is better and therefore slightly more valuable. Dutch themes were popular and this is a good example of a beautifully coloured card that can still be picked up for a very modest sum.

➤ View of Castletown, Portland, c.1900–10
Topographical cards showing bygone views of cities, towns, and villages are the most popular collecting theme in the world of postcards. The answer lies in the nostalgia we all feel for the place of our upbringing. This view of Castletown, Portland is a typical example. Note the horse-drawn transport and the absence of any motor vehicles. An important point here is that real photographic cards produced by the local photographer are generally worth much more than a mass-produced image by a national publisher. Cinemas, theatres, railway stations, children in the street, and similar local images are all highly collectable.

◄ The *Esperia*, Sitmar Line, *c*.1912
The military, railways, and shipping are all major collecting themes. In the shipping classification a vast number of cards was produced by the many shipping lines of the day, and this is a typical example. The star attraction are cards of the *Titanic*, which can fetch £100 ($150) plus. There is also a great many cards of other merchant interests, including paddle steamers, lifeboats, and the whaling industry, plus naval cards, from depictions of Nelson to the battles of World War I.

➤ Embroidered regimental badge, *c*.1914–18
Embroidered silk cards from World War I, which were usually handmade by young French girls, are a popular collecting theme. The most common kind are the greetings cards, known as "Hearts and Flowers", which the soldiers would buy to send home to their loved ones. At the other end of the scale are the cards of regimental badges, the rarest of which can sell at auction for prices well into three figures. The card illustrated is one of the better ones, showing the badge of the RND Divisional Engineers.

▲ Comic postcard by Donald McGill, *c*.1929
Comic cards were a staple of Edwardian and pre-war publishers, and are among the cards most easily found today. Unfortunately they are often incorrectly seen by the media as representing the whole postcard spectrum. Many famous artists designed for the picture postcard market, including Louis Wain, Mabel Lucie Attwell, Phil May, and John Hassall, although the great majority of comic cards can still be picked up at very reasonable prices. This example is by Donald McGill (1875–1962), perhaps the doyen of comic artists; cards dated pre-1939 are valuable but later reprints are worthless.

➤ Elvis Presley in *Jailhouse Rock*, 1957
Original cards like this, although comparatively modern, are sought-after by collectors. Postcards celebrating major stars are desirable – the more important the star, the higher the price. Contemporary photographs of Marilyn Monroe, for example, always fetch a premium. This is only one instance of the modern card, which today is a booming industry published by hundreds of publishers, both large and small.

▲ Glamour postcard *Little Lady Demure* by Philip Boileau, 1907
Glamour has always been a favourite collecting theme from the earliest years of postcards, and manufacturers catered to every taste. The American artist Philip Boileau (1864–1917) was well-known for his ladylike Edwardian beauties, very popular in Anglo-Saxon countries. French taste veered more towards ladies with their clothes off. The French authorities attempted to make models wear bodystockings, and photographs were often retouched, but still the term "French postcard" became synonymous with the naughty nude. Racy images can in certain instances command high prices.

Étoile du Nord by A.M. Cassandre, 1927; this glamorous design of the converging railtracks was typical of Cassandre's work.

Posters can be divided into the following main areas: travel, general interest, advertising, and film. Travel has long been the most recognized, due to the history of the railways and the days of pioneering air travel in the 1920s and '30s. The diverse range of film posters available makes them very popular, and in most cases, excepting certain rarities such as some Bond posters or *Breakfast at Tiffany's*, quite affordable. The Modernist poster is also developing as a collectable. From the 1950s onward designers and manufacturers used the freedom and investment of the post-war years to develop a flexibility and imagination in poster design. Cars, fashion, and music attracted powerful advertising campaigns. The 1960s proved a breeding ground for new ideas, with psychedelia hitting the scene. In the USA a similar movement was happening, with designers such as Wes Wilson drawing inspiration from artists like Beardsley and Mucha. The value of a poster is down to three things: artist, subject, and condition. Posters generally were produced in large quantities but as they were for commercial distribution, and not domestic use, few have survived. There is no other art form today that can decorate our walls with colour and nostalgia at such an affordable price, and with the knowledge that it could be appreciating in value; current posters may be thought of as collectables in 50 years.

▲ *Babylone d'Allemagne* by Henri Toulouse-Lautrec, 1894

This poster provoked a protest from the German ambassador to France and almost caused an international incident because of its exposé of the decadence of Berlin society. The spectator in the foreground is a caricature of Kaiser Wilhelm II himself. Despite the uproar Lautrec refused to stop distribution of the poster. Any work by Toulouse-Lautrec is highly collectable – this particular poster reached £16,650 ($25,000) at auction in 2003.

▼ Forth Bridge by H.G. Gawthorn, c.1928

In the 1930s nearly every station platform in the UK had a free art gallery, displaying posters designed by the foremost artists of the day. Families had time and money to spend on leisure and this was the golden age of travel. In the last 20 years there has been remarkable growth in collecting travel posters, mainly the categories of railways, airlines, and ocean liners. But potential new collectors should not be put off as there is much on offer at affordable prices.

▲ *Kleine Dada Soireé* (*Little Dada Evening*), 1923

This small-sized masterpiece is in fact a flyer that was sent out by artists Kurt Schwitters (1887–1948) and Théo van Doesburg (1883–1931) to advertise a gathering of artists and followers of the Dada movement, which was led by Hugo Ball and Marcel Duchamp. During these evenings the artists would promote and perform this progressive art form in many different ways. This image has a dual appeal to both Dada enthusiasts and poster collectors.

◀ *Mondriaan* by Steendrukkerij de Jong & Co, The Netherlands, 1972
This bold depiction of Piet Mondrian shows a powerful image of a powerful artist. The figure of Mondrian is in a medium that looks like modelling clay or even oil paint. The poster is clean and ordered, rather like Mondrian's own abstract paintings, with a refreshing Modernist feel. Few posters exist that depict the artist himself, and this is an exquisite example. It was used to advertise a Mondrian exhibition in 1972 so very few copies would have been printed, making it a rare and valuable item.

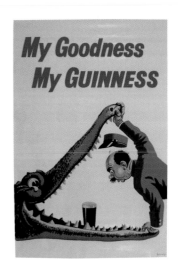

▲ Guinness advert by John Gilroy, 1938
The famous Guinness publicity campaign, based on the slogan "Guinness is good for you", began in 1928, and artist John Gilroy (1898–1985) produced a series of classic images for the campaign. This was one of a number with an animal theme, inspired by a visit to Bertram Mills' Circus, although the most famous Guinness creature is certainly the toucan. Guinness memorabilia is very popular today, but beware of fakes as the high values have encouraged unscrupulous reproductions.

➤ *A is for Apple* by The Fool, 1967
The Fool was a team of Dutch designers, painters, and musicians who were part of The Beatles' entourage. They designed the clothes the band wore for the TV broadcast of *All You Need Is Love*. They also painted, in psychedelic colours, the legendery façade of The Beatles' Apple Boutique in London, as well as John Lennon's Rolls Royce and piano, George Harrison's Mini, and bungalow, and his and Eric Clapton's guitars. This iconic poster reflects the interest in the cosmos and the somewhat hallucinogenic overtones that prevailed in both art and music in the late 1960s.

➤ Exhibition poster by Tadanoori Yokoo, Tokyo, 1968
Yokoo, who came to the world's attention in the 1960s, was the East's equivalent of Andy Warhol. He took traditional Japanese motifs, such as ladies dressed in kimonos, and majestic sweeping land-scapes, and interpreted them in Modernist, abstract ways. This poster, which was made for the 6th International Biennial Exhibition of Prints in Tokyo, is calmer in tone and content than some of Yokoo's other designs, but it still displays the influence of Pop Art on his work. Yokoo's posters are hard to come by and are popular worldwide so when they appear on the market they attract much interest.

▲ *Brillo* by Andy Warhol, 1970
This poster advertised an exhibition of work by Andy Warhol (1928–87) at the Pasadena Art Museum in California, USA. Warhol was an American artist and filmmaker, and founder of the Pop Art movement. This poster illustrates his characteristic method of screen-printing images of everyday objects. Designed at Warhol's studio, "The Factory", it was distributed by the museum in limited numbers. It provides an affordable piece of Warhol history.

➤ **Silkscreen print by Larry Smart, 1967**
This poster is one of the more understated psychedelic images of John Lennon to come out of the underground artists' studios of the late 1960s and very rarely appears on the open market. It is a silkscreen print of mammoth proportions – 127 x 100cm (50 x 40in) – and makes a considerable impact when viewed framed. This image was one of a series of five produced by Smart in 1967; the other musicians he printed were Jimi Hendrix, Bob Dylan, Frank Zappa, and Mick Jagger.

▲ *The Beatles* **by Richard Avedon, 1967**
If there is one poster that encapsulates the "psychedelic" time of The Beatles then this is it. Undertaken by Richard Avedon, using solar filters, it truly depicts what The Beatles, and other people of the era, were experiencing. The poster was made as a limited edition for the *Daily Express* newspaper and was printed by Waterlow and Sons. As with any Beatles memorabilia this poster is highly collectable, and would easily fetch around £1,500 ($2,250), if not more, at auction.

▲ *A Film About Jimi Hendrix*, **printed by W.E. Berry Ltd, England, c.1970**
This is the poster for the film of Hendrix's live performances from 1966 to 1970, and shows an absorbed Hendrix, strumming away at his guitar. The drawing is quite cartoonish in style and has some poetic licence (as is often the case with film posters) but nevertheless it stays true to Hendrix's real-life appearance. The artist is unknown but the poster is still valued in the high hundreds for its crossover interest to film, music, and general poster collectors.

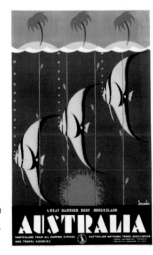

▲ *Alfa Romeo*, **Switzerland, 1960**
This slickly designed poster was printed by Sauberlin & Pfeiffer. As is common with Swiss-made items, the quality of the print is of the highest standards and it provides a powerful advertisement for one of the most stylish cars of the decade. The iconic '60s image is reminiscent of contemporary film posters such as those for *Get Carter* and *Bullitt*, particularly as the Alfa Romeo was often linked with the mafia and the criminal underworld of the time.

➤ *Australia* **by Gert Sellheim, 1930s**
Gert Sellheim is considered one of the best Art Deco-style designers to come out of Australia. This colourful tropical image was designed by Sellheim to promote the Great Barrier Reef in Queensland, Australia, to locals and tourists alike. Such is Sellheim's importance and popularity with collectors that this poster sold for 6,720 euros (£4,480) at auction in The Netherlands in 2003, even though the reserve price was just 350 euros (£525).

▲ *Batman* poster, New York, 1966
Printed by G & F Posters this is a true "comic book" poster in the style of the Marvel comic-strip cartoons, with its bold colours and graphic simplicity. There are a number of Batman posters, by various artists, in circulation but this screen-printed example is one of the best. Silk-screen printing produces a far better quality of image than litho-printing and indicates that this poster was created as a piece of commercial merchandise as opposed to temporary advertising material. Comic posters are relatively rare and therefore highly sought-after.

➤ *Fasching Munchen* by Vesseday, 1971
Printed in Germany by Pera-Druck, this is an advertisement for Fashion Week in Munich. A poster was created by a different artist every year and each poster would serve as an indication of its times. The swirls and contours of this poster indicate the influences of Victorian artist Aubrey Beardsley, whose work was popular in the early 1970s. Event-based posters such as this are always popular and the nostalgia of past fashions provides an extra pull. The strength of a poster's image is often just as important as the artist, as well as the product or event being advertised, when determining value.

◄ *Flims Graubunden-Grisons* by Eric de Coulon, 1935
Vintage travel posters with a skiing theme command a premium at auction today. Skiing posters are all about the image, the action, the artist, and the resort. Some of the best examples are those by artist Roger Broders. His travel posters used bold colours and stunning images, making him one of the foremost collectable poster artists of the Art Deco era. Eric de Coulon, who designed this graphic, movement-filled image, is another artist who was responsible for action posters in the field of skiing.

▲ *Sunbeam Talbot "90"*, Frank Wootton, 1952
Frank Wootton is largely known for his aviation art as official war artist to the RAF and Royal Canadian Air Force in World War II. When the war finished Wootton continued as an artist, moving into illustrations for car posters in the 1940s and '50s. This poster for the Sunbeam Talbot "90" depicts a typical view of a sunshine-filled time when motoring was fun and not the grind it is today. Posters of this kind are collectable because they represent a bygone era for which many people feel a fond nostalgia.

◄ 25th anniversary of the Russian space programme, Moscow, 1974
The artist of this poster is unknown, as is usual with items that were created under the communist Russian regime, but the message is strong – that Russia could challenge NASA and the USA and come out on top. In the late 1950s and early '60s the Soviet Union sent Sputnik to retrieve the first shots of the Moon, Mars, and Venus, followed by the first men and women to orbit the Earth. They lost the race to the Moon in 1969, but by the early '70s Russia had begun to build the first manned orbital space stations and was gaining power in space once again. This poster provides a fascinating insight into the political climate of the 1970s.

Burndept "Ethophone" crystal set, 1922. Crystal sets used no electrical power but needed a long aerial wire, usually suspended from a roof. They are now very collectable but originality is vital.

Radio broadcasting began in the UK in 1922, and the "wireless" became the latest craze. Crystal sets were the cheapest option as valve sets were expensive and needed large batteries, although many people built their own. Commercially made radios from the 1920s are quite rare. Originality is essential – values vary from under a hundred to several thousand pounds/dollars for the most desirable sets. By the 1930s the radio had become part of the home and hundreds of different models were available. Some were styled to look like traditional pieces of furniture while others were more modern in design, often using new materials such as Bakelite. Collectors tend to look for particular styles and often prefer Art Deco-influenced designs. After World War II radios became more standardized, and although there are some desirable items from all periods right up to the 1970s, there are many more later radios, and values tend to be lower. The transistor, invented in the 1940s, enabled miniature radios to be produced, which appealed to the newly affluent teenage market. Early transitor radios now have a following, mainly limited to unusual or rare models. Always remember that old electrical goods may be dangerous, and should only be used if restored and checked by an expert.

▲ **Marconiphone Model 42, 1932**
Wireless cabinets came in many shapes, styles, and materials. Today collectors are interested in the more unusual and decorative sets, or ones with special features. This Marconi set has a distinctive shaped and fretted walnut cabinet, distinguishing it from the plainer models that tended to appear later, as radios became more alike and were adapted to mass-production throughout the 1930s.

▼ **Console radio by RCA, 1931**
By the 1930s the radio set had become a piece of furniture, often the most expensive possession in the home. This imposing American RCA console model would have been the focal point of the living room. The British Radio Manufacturers Association did not encourage the import of radios from abroad, at first blacklisting shops that sold imported sets. Later some American companies, such as Philco, Ferguson, and Pilot got round this by assembling sets in UK factories.

▲ **AD65 circular radio by Wells Coates, 1934**
E.K. Cole Ltd commissioned cabinets from several leading designers of the 1930s for their Ekco radios. One of their best-known models was this AD65. Although it was the cheapest mains radio in the range, the unusual shape makes it popular with collectors today. The brown version shown is the most common, but it was also made in black with chrome details, and a few were made in coloured cabinets, of which only a handful has survived. Undamaged original examples of these rare coloured cabinet models can sell for several thousand pounds/dollars in today's market.

◄ Yellow Fada "Bullet" radio, 1945

Catalin was an early plastic that could be made in bright colours, and was used to make cabinets for cheap radios, mainly in the USA. They are very decorative, but the plastic can be unstable and as they were inexpensive products many were thrown away. The plastic tends to crack and distort, so perfect examples in rare colour combinations can sell for thousands of dollars. They were never sold in any quantity in the UK, but the internet has now brought them into the hands of UK collectors.

► Bush transistor TR82, 1959

Early transistor radios were no smaller than valve radios. The Bush TR82 in fact used a cabinet designed for an earlier valve set by David Ogle (designer of the Reliant Scimitar car). Now considered a classic and available new as a reproduction, there are thousands still in daily use. Due to the numbers that have survived the originals are only worth around the same as the reproductions, which also have the advantage of receiving FM transmissions.

▲ 1950s ivory Bakelite Bush DAC90A

One of the most common radios from the 1950s is this Bush model, first introduced in 1946 as the DAC90 at the "Britain Can Make It" exhibition, then revised in 1950 and made for several years after. They were very reliable, and many survived as second sets or in workshops for many years without attention. Most are brown, but the ivory Bakelite version cost £1 more when new, and is therefore less common. However, the ivory-coloured Bakelite is prone to hairline cracks, which will reduce the value of the radio to collectors.

◄ Micronic "Ruby", 1965

The transistor was the first step toward today's microelectronics. This Micronic "Ruby" radio is the size of a matchbox, the main reduction in size being due to the use of tiny alkaline batteries. Personal radios were a novelty that has never really captured the mass market, but early examples were expensive and are now collectable. Japanese "shirt pocket" sets from the 1950s are widely collected as they are attractive and easy to display, but they are also easily damaged and only perfect examples are of significant value.

Pye "Sunrise" M78F

In 1948 Pye Radio of Cambridge produced a miniature "personal" portable radio utilizing techniques developed during World War II. New, smaller valves that had been developed for clandestine communications equipment were employed in a cabinet made of coloured Perspex – a new plastic first used in aircraft. This use of coloured plastic was ahead of its time. Pye used its original trademark logo of the stylized "rising sun" on this model; it was first used in 1929 but had been dropped a few years later. Unfortunately these M78F radios were very unreliable, and following news reports of atrocities committed against British troops in Japanese hands, the logo was seen to resemble the Japanese flag and the set was withdrawn. Legend has it that the remaining stocks were burnt on a bonfire in the factory yard. The survivors that have emerged over the years have commanded increasingly high prices, but the case is very fragile and condition is paramount for it to reach its maximum value.

Art Deco sunset

The M78F came in at least two colourways, black and green with cream. The design is pure Art Deco.

A Waterford & Tramore Railway Irish cast-iron gate sign, believed to be the only surviving example. Many railway companies displayed warning signs on their gates, the ones from smaller companies inevitably being the rarest and therefore the most sought-after.

The year 2004 marks the bicentenary of the birth of steam railway locomotion. From small beginnings railways have spread from England to cover the world, and have created a vast array of memorabilia, which is known as railwayana. Items from locomotives are keenly collected, and include nameplates, makers' plates, number plates, and whistles. Stations had nameboards, lamps, clocks, and furniture. Signal boxes incorporated wooden-cased instruments for safely signalling the trains from one section of track to another. Tableware from station refreshment rooms, hotels, and railway-owned ships is avidly sought-after. Posters advertising the services and destinations of each railway company are very popular, as are cast-iron and enamel trackside signs, handlamps, uniforms, and watches used by railway staff, and coloured prints once displayed in the coaches. Photographs, postcards, timetables, tickets, buttons, medals, and paperwork of all kinds have their own devotees. All these collectables are only the tip of the iceberg as railway companies were huge businesses, usually emblazoning their possessions with company names or initials. The range is vast, from locomotive nameplates now worth many thousands of pounds to simple sheets of toilet-paper.

▲ Block instrument, 1880s

In the 19th century there were several thousand signal boxes, operated by well over 100 railway companies. Each of these signal boxes contained an array of wooden-cased instruments and bells operated by telegraph to signal the safe passage of trains from one signal box to its adjacent boxes. They were precision instruments, often with brass fittings, and are regarded as attractive items by many railway collectors, not just signalling enthusiasts. This one was owned by the London, Brighton & South Coast Railway and is among the most sought-after.

▼ Blue transfer-printed mug, 1850s

When the earliest railways were being built in the 1830s and '40s commemorative china was produced to celebrate line and station openings, and to depict the trains operated by each particular railway company. Most popular are the transfer-printed mugs, especially in blue and white, but there were also jugs, bowls, and plates produced. Many different scenes were used, incorporating a large variety of locomotives, so these mugs can form the basis of a considerable collection.

➤ Nestle chocolate machine, c.1900

Many railway stations displayed vending machines that enabled the travelling, and waiting, public to buy items for the journey quickly and easily. These items included postcards, cigarettes, and chocolate. Most popular among collectors are the chocolate vending machines, which can still be used for the purpose for which they were originally intended. Some were wall fitting, others, as illustrated above, had their own free-standing base. Few survive today so they can command prices into the thousands at auction.

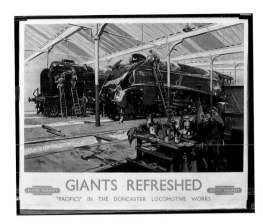

▲ *Giants Refreshed* poster by Terence Cuneo, 1947

From the late 19th century railway companies realized the value of poster advertising. Many displayed posters on their stations to advertise the company's services, and to show the travelling public the delightful places that could be reached via the company's trains. Usually lithographed in full colour, and often painted by famous artists of the time, few survive today because the majority were pasted on boards and therefore lost to collectors. Terence Cuneo is considered to be one of the best of the poster artists, painting for railway companies from the late 1940s into the 1990s. *Giants Refreshed* was painted for the London & North Eastern Railway and is a very popular design.

➤ Station lamp, *c.*1900

Every railway station was equipped with gas or paraffin lamps for the convenience of passengers. Some are more ornate than others, but the most ornate are the lamps from the Great Eastern Railway's royal station at Wolferton, Norfolk, used frequently by the royal family when in residence at Sandringham. Uniquely these lamps display a crown and the royal crest. Very few have been retrieved from the station so they are considered to be the most desirable of all station lamps to collect.

▲ "Boat of Garten" and "Stocksfield" totems, 1950s

From the early 1950s British Railways equipped its stations with a new style of sign, called "totems". Enamelled on steel, they were usually fixed to lamp posts or screwed to station building walls. Each region had its own colour – tangerine for the North Eastern Region, light blue for the Scottish Region, dark blue for the Eastern Region, chocolate and cream for the Western Region, green for the Southern Region, and maroon for the Midland Region. Those most keenly collected are from London termini, famous places like Kyle of Lochalsh and Penzance, and small halts where there may have been only one or two totems on the station. Prices range from a few hundred pounds to several thousand.

▲ Group of worksplates

Most locomotives carried two brass plates that identified the manufacturer. Many of the larger railway companies had their own workshops to build locomotives, but the smaller companies had to go to private locomotive builders for their needs. Worksplates come in all shapes and sizes and are keenly collected, especially if they are from early locomotives (known examples survive from the 1860s), or if the private builder built only a few engines. The ten examples illustrated above are all plates that were attached to locomotives when they were rebuilt in more recent years.

▲ "Dunraven Castle" nameplate and numberplate set, 1920s

Nameplates are the most collectable, and valuable, of all railway antiques. Many railway companies gave kudos to their best express locomotives by giving them names, one displayed on each side. Prominent in this practice was the Great Western Railway, which named all its passenger locomotives. It had a class of locomotive called the Castle class, built from the 1920s to the early 1950s, and each named after castles on its system. These nameplates were brass on steel and were fitted over the middle driving wheel. Each locomotive also carried a brass numberplate on either side of the cab. A set like this is worth tens of thousands.

The Explosive Little Richard UK
LP, issued on the Columbia label
in 1967; the title says it all!

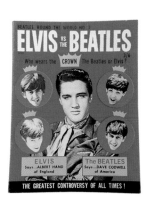

A fun American magazine issued
in 1965, but a serious question
for collectors: who wears the
crown – The Beatles or Elvis?

A Worcester Ware 1960s tray;
this is a great display item and
originals have a "Made in Gt
Britain" imprint to identify them.

This area of collecting can involve many emotions, not least because it has at its core the enjoyment of music. Music can both polarize and alienate, but it can also still bring people together. The music collector, through a choice of specific artists, styles, genres, or eras, can choose either to ignore the latest fads of the music industry or embrace current artists' material. Rock and Pop encompass more than just those two genres. The Beatles, The Rolling Stones, Elvis Presley, Jimi Hendrix, and Madonna may get the publicity, but there are many lesser-known acts and styles of music with an avid collectors' following. Performers including Bob Marley, Sonny Boy Williamson, Miles Davis, and The Action, to name just a few, have a strong fanbase. There is a huge underground interest in genres of music such as Jazz, Blues, Rockabilly, Northern Soul, Reggae, Punk, and various forms of dance music. Music does not have to be old to be collectable, and many collectors concentrate on records and merchandise relating to new, or relatively new, performers and music.

Nostalgia is often the main factor in collecting rock and pop memorabilia, providing tangible evidence of past experiences of, for example, The Beatles at The Cavern Club, the Soul club all-nighters, the Isle of Wight Festival, or David Bowie as Ziggy at the local "Top Rank"! Younger collectors discover these same musicians because of their vast influence upon contemporary artists. A classic example of this is The Beatles, who gained masses of young fans after their endorsement by Oasis. Other examples are James Brown's influence on Hip-Hop and Rap, The Small Faces on successive generations of mods and groups, The Velvet Underground, who have had almost 40 years of influence on popular music and culture, and Kraftwerk – the enigmatic godfathers of electronic Dance music.

Lifestyle is another important consideration for some collectors; the 1950s fans may turn up at a jukebox fair in a classic car, wearing vintage clothing, to buy original records for their jukebox, and also leave with an original Buddy Holly tour handbill and Elvis Presley film poster. On the other hand, young retro-mods wearing the right combination of clothes and accessories, a vintage Lambretta scooter in their garages, attend record fairs looking for elusive psychedelic posters or '60s club membership cards. Many of yesterday's punks now have a completely different lifestyle, with a disposable income to match. They regard the Sex Pistols as their generation's "Beatles", and have the spare cash to snap up rare 'Pistols memorabilia.

Not all Rock and Pop collectables are expensive, and there are modestly priced items to be found in all categories. Mass-produced items such as magazines, music papers, and postcards can be bought at low prices but are still evocative of their time. A magazine devoted to The Beatles has a lot more content than most Beatles concert programmes, and at a much lower price; a slightly later version of the Sex Pistols' "God save the Queen" single on the Virgin label comes with a great picture sleeve but will cost a fraction of the price of an original issue on the "A&M" label. However, for those with the money and inclination there are many tempting rarities on the market, including personal effects, hand-written lyrics, and concert ephemera.

Records and CDs

Collecting records, arguably the most established area of Rock and Pop, offers a wealth of interest and enjoyment. As early as the late 1950s and 1960s vinyl records were collectable. Deletions and obscure imports increased in value and were often only available from specialist mail-order dealers, who supplied collectors of Rock 'n' Roll, Soul, and Reggae. In the late 1970s record collecting was firmly established in the UK with the opening of specialist collectors' record shops, and the advent of weekly record fairs. This coincided with the explosion of Punk and New Wave music, which injected much-needed excitement into the music industry, and enticed a new generation of collectors with limited-edition picture-cover singles, coloured vinyl, and special packaging. All of this was sold alongside vintage records from the '50s, '60s and '70s. Record collecting was consolidated in the 1980s and '90s, despite the CD format taking over from vinyl for the majority of contemporary issues. Some CDs, such as limited-edition box sets and promotional CDs, are now much sought-after, and have taken their place alongside vinyl rarities.

Maybe Tomorrow UK EP, 1959; this is a rare item by Britain's well-loved and much-missed pop icon Billy Fury.

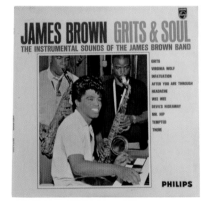

◄ James Brown *Grits & Soul* LP, 1965
This UK album of instrumental tracks was issued on the Phillips label and featured James Brown on keyboards. Although renowned for his relentless vocals, James Brown had total control over the instrumentation of his backing bands. He invented Funk in the mid-1960s, with tracks such as *Papa's Got A Brand New Bag*, long before Funk was popularized in the '70s. He has had an enormous effect upon both black and white culture, and influenced early mod groups such as The Who and, later, US Rap acts.

▲ The Beatles *Love Me Do* UK Demo, 1963
Love Me Do/P.S. I Love You was The Beatles' first UK single for the Parlophone company; first issued on the red label and later on a black label, both are fairly collectable. However, this demo issue was produced in small quantities for review purposes and radio airplay, making it one of the most sought-after of all Beatles records. A signed copy would rank among the most desirable of signed Beatles items available to collectors.

◄ The Artwoods *Jazz in Jeans* EP, 1966
Issued on UK label Decca by mod favourites The Artwoods, this is one of the most collectable UK EPs. Led by Ronnie Wood's brother, Art Wood, the band had a huge following in London's R&B clubs but little success with their recorded material. They issued a further seven singles and one LP between 1964 and 1966, which are all now very collectable. Other members included Jon Lord, who later had success with Deep Purple. As with all EPs, the value is significantly reduced without the cover.

▲ The Best of Martin Denny LP, mid-1960s

Martin Denny was classically trained as a pianist but he used Hawaiian, Oriental, and Latin influences and birdsong impersonations to create his innovative sound. Trained in New York he performed in South America and later Hawaii with a small group of musicians, using unusual percussive instruments. His first album *Exotica*, issued in the UK as a 10" LP, created a genre of the same name, which is very collectable. A favourite of Brian Wilson of The Beach Boys, Denny influenced their *Pet Sounds* LP.

◄ Thunderbirds Are Go UK LP, 1967

This rare and sought-after album combines music from both the *Thunderbirds* film and TV series, performed by the Barry Gray Orchestra. Unlike most of *Thunderbirds* creator Gerry Anderson's spin-off records, which were issued on the Century 21 label, this LP came out on the United Artists label. Most of the Century 21 records were issued on the EP format with superb picture covers, and also featured shows such as *Fireball XL5*, *Stingray*, and *Captain Scarlet*.

▼ Curtis Mayfield Back to the World LP, 1973

This record, combining politics, social comment, and progressive musicianship, was one of a number of Curtis Mayfield's classic 1970s LPs. A talent whose music ranks alongside that of James Brown, Marvin Gaye, and Stevie Wonder, Mayfield also wrote many hit songs for other artists. In the 1960s he led gospel-influenced Soul group The Impressions, who were an influence upon Jamaican music and were "mod" favourites. He also wrote the musical score to the film *Superfly*, which was issued as a soundtrack LP in 1972.

▲ The Sex Pistols God Save the Queen UK single, 1977

Not to be confused with the re-issue on the Virgin label, this A&M release is the pinnacle for collectors of Sex Pistols' vinyl. A few copies survived after its release was cancelled by A&M Records, who severed their contract with the 'Pistols and melted down around 25,000 copies. The Sex Pistols got to keep £75,000 ($112,500) in compensation and soon afterwards were voted Young Businessmen Of The Year by a financial journal.

▲ U2 Melon CD, 1995

This nine-track album of re-mixed tracks was a limited fan-club issue of 20,000. With post-Punk roots and a career spanning 25 years, U2 have many collectable vinyl issues in their catalogue. However, *Melon* is an example of how limited CD issues by bands of their stature can also be sought-after, because of the exclusive nature of material unavailable elsewhere, often with unique packaging.

Paper Items

Often described as "ephemera", paper items are both important and popular in the field of Rock and Pop. This area encompasses concert memorabilia, music papers and magazines, sheet music, and photographs, as well as fan club material, and bubble gum cards. Concert memorabilia is particularly popular as it provides a visual record of specific live appearances by collectable artists, and comes in a variety of sizes. Tickets, handbills, flyers, and programmes are compact enough to be stored in a small space, whereas larger concert posters, when framed, make excellent wall-display pieces. The combination of written word, photographs, and advertisements, makes magazines and newspapers attractive items to collect, as well as invaluable sources for reference. They are less valuable when they have missing pages, cuttings, and tears. Sheet music is also attractive to collectors, providing interesting visual companion pieces to records and songs. The sheets often feature unique photographs and graphics, which makes them ideal for display purposes.

The Beatles *Black Light* poster, US, 1967. A psychedelic 3D effect is achieved when the poster is illuminated by an ultra-violet light.

▼ **The Beatles UK tour programme, 1965**
Although not one of the rarest Beatles concert programmes, this is significant as it was their last British tour. The tour lasted ten days, from Monday 3rd December to Sunday 12th December 1965. The cover, shown below, features an image of all four Beatles taken from an American cartoon series; the programme originally came with a small poster, which is often missing from surviving examples. It was during this tour that The Beatles decided that their live appearances would have to end.

◄ **The Rolling Stones UK concert poster, 1965**
The ABC Theatre in Stockton-on-Tees was one of North-East England's most popular venues, attracting many major pop artists in the 1950s and '60s. This visually stunning poster for The Rolling Stones' appearance there in 1965 is highly collectable. The Stones were playing on the same stage as Buddy Holly and the Crickets, who performed there in 1958 and recorded the original version of the Stones' hit *Not Fade Away*.

➤ **Elvis Presley *Tickle Me* cinema poster, 1965**
This is a British 30 x 40in poster for the American Allied Artists Picture Corporation film release, and has a kitsch visual quality typical of Elvis' 1960s film posters. Most of Elvis' Hollywood films are shunned by Rock 'n' Roll purists, but they were a great influence on Indian "Bollywood" cinema. These posters are sought-after both by Elvis fans and by collectors of 1960s kitsch, making excellent display pieces for shops, homes, and museums.

Bob Dylan signed poster, c.1965

Bob Dylan, like The Rolling Stones, has been recording and touring for four decades. He still plays sell-out concerts in huge arenas to fans both young and old. Although not as collectable as The Beatles or The Rolling Stones, he has a strong fan base and a solid collectors' following. His 1960s memorabilia is particularly collectable and his signatures on posters, photographs, and programmes are much sought-after. Despite his continuous touring Dylan rarely signs photographs or other items today.

➤ **The Small Faces signed promo photo, 1966**

This signed Decca record company promotional card also has details of The Small Faces' record releases on the reverse. One of the most influential yet under-rated groups of the 1960s, The Small Faces offered a combination of powerful music and mod/psychedelic style that has made them popular with generations of fans and musicians. In addition to Ian McClagan and Kenney Jones, this card also bears the signatures of the band's chief songwriters, vocalist and guitarist Steve Marriott and co-vocalist and bass player Ronnie "Plonk" Lane.

▼ **Jimi Hendrix Saville Theatre poster, 1967**

One of a series of four posters commissioned for Brian Epstein's Saville Theatre concerts, this was designed by Nigel Weymouth and Michael English, known collectively as "Hapshash And The Coloured Coat". Although all "Hapshash" posters are collectable the presence of Jimi Hendrix makes this one a very desirable item. Produced by Osiris Visions, this is a classic example of psychedelic artwork.

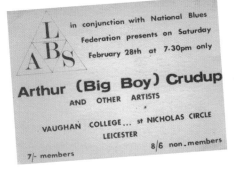

◄ **Arthur "Big Boy" Crudup signed UK concert ticket, c. 1966**

The signature on the reverse of this ticket enhances an already important concert souvenir of this legendary black Blues musician. He was a big favourite of Elvis Presley who recorded *That's All Right*, composed by Crudup and originally released in the USA on a 78 record, c.1948. Few of Crudup's records were issued in the UK, but in 1969 he recorded an LP, *Mean Ole 'Frisco*, for the collectable British label Blue Horizon. There is a strong demand for original concert memorabilia featuring US Blues artists.

➤ **The Sex Pistols' contract for a 1976 concert**

Handwritten by their manager, Malcolm McLaren, this is a contract for one of The Sex Pistols' legendary appearances at The 100 Club, Oxford Street, London, in September 1976. The fact that it is handwritten and signed by McLaren adds extra importance to what is already a one-off piece of 'Pistols memorabilia. The importance of The 100 Club in The Sex Pistols' history was recognized when they held a press conference there, in March 1996, to announce their reunion and forthcoming *Filthy Lucre* tour.

3-D Memorabilia

Encompassing both tacky and upmarket merchandise, 3-D memorabilia offers a varied and fun arena for Rock and Pop collectors, from mass-produced spin-offs and cash-ins to one-off pieces, such as clothing and musical instruments. Mass-merchandising in pop music began in the USA with Elvis Presley in the 1950s, when a huge variety of material was produced and licensed to capitalize on his popularity. The Beatles received the same treatment in the USA in the mid-'60s. The UK and other countries offered fewer items, as they were less geared-up for mass-production and licensing, although eventually a fair amount of Beatles memorabilia was made in the UK. Not all pop acts were suitable for this form of exploitation, and Elvis Presley, The Beatles, The Monkees, and Abba fare better than Jimi Hendrix, The Who, or The Sex Pistols. An artist's personal property is often in short supply but, because of its close connection to a specific performer, always generates a lot of interest. Stage-worn clothing and celebrity-owned musical instruments and furniture can fetch vast sums of money, more often than not ending up on display in restaurants or museums.

An ABBA soap, made in the 1970s by J. Grossmith of Cheshire, England; the name is a humorous reference to *ABBA The Movie*.

▼ Gretsch "Anniversary" guitar, USA, 1959
Gretsch electric guitars have been associated with popular music from the mid-'50s to the present day. Numerous great players have been attracted by their twangy, jangly sound, including Eddie Cochran, George Harrison, Johnny Marr of The Smiths, and The Stone Roses' guitarist, John Squire. The "Anniversary" range was introduced in 1958 to commemorate Gretsch's 75th anniversary, and was available in sunburst and two-tone smoke green finishes.

▲ Beatles Subbuteo figures, *c.*1964
Better-known for the manufacture of "flick to kick" miniature football sets, Subbuteo diversified into the world of Pop with these hand-painted 5cm (2in) high figures. The Beatles were the only set to be produced in a projected series of pop stars. Unlike their sporting counterparts, which came on a semi-spherical base enabling them to wobble, the Beatles figures were set in flat bases. However, this was compensated for by the inclusion of finely detailed instruments. The box trebles their value.

◄ Tin of Beatles talcum powder, *c.*1965
Manufactured by Margo of Mayfair, London, this tin has two different grey-and-white pictures of The Beatles on either side. At the time of manufacture it was a somewhat "upmarket" item, with high-quality printing and construction. Part of the lettering is in red, although on some examples this has faded to pink. Rust is another problem as the tins were often stored in bathrooms. A very popular collectors' item, clean, rust-free examples that still contain the original powder are the most sought-after.

➤ **Beatles blanket, *c.*1964**

Measuring a generous 158 x 203cm (62 x 80in),
this blanket is a good display item for those
collectors with plenty of space. It is more valuable
if the makers' tag, Witney of Oxford, is still present.
Many examples have faded due to over-washing,
or have suffered from wear and tear. Unfortunately,
some blankets that have survived in pristine
condition are then damaged by inappropriate
laundering. Other officially licensed Beatles soft
furnishings produced at the time included rugs,
curtain material, tablecloths, and tea towels.

▼ ***Ready Steady Goes Live!* material
swatches, 1966**

Ready Steady Go! was a revolutionary UK Pop and
youth culture television show that ran from 1963
to 1966. Early shows featured both mimed and
live performances by UK and US acts and soon
attracted an audience of genuine "mods", whose
style and dancing prowess influenced viewers
and left other shows, such as *Top of The Pops*,
in the shade. In spring 1966 the show adopted
an "all live" policy. This promotional material was
produced by Cepea Fabrics Ltd in four colourways.

◄ **The Monkees jigsaw puzzle, 1967**

The Monkees were "manufactured" in the USA
to star in their own television show. A total of 28
shows were produced and broadcast by NBC in
the USA, and by the BBC in the UK. Davy, Peter,
Mickey, and Mike soon had a massive following.
The merchandising opportunity was phenomenal,
with a range of products in the USA to rival those
of The Beatles. This is one of a set of four Monkees
puzzles made in the UK; they come in a kitsch box
and measure 28 x 43cm (11 x 17in) when assembled.

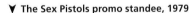

▼ **The Sex Pistols promo standee, 1979**

This 84cm (33in) wide cardboard "cut-out" was used in cinemas and record
shops to promote the soundtrack of the film *The Great Rock and Roll Swindle*.
It features a rogues' gallery of Sex Pistols members, their manager Malcolm
McLaren, and infamous train robber Ronnie Biggs (who also starred in the film).
The movie was released after the break-up of the 'Pistols and used the slogan,
"The film that incriminates its audience", on the original UK cinema posters.

➤ **Madonna signed Gaultier bustier, 1987**

A union of two great icons of popular culture
makes this a very special item indeed. The fact that
it is also signed by Madonna in gold felt tip is the
icing on the cake, adding extra value to an already
very expensive piece. Jean Paul Gaultier designed
this and other stage-worn outfits for Madonna's
Who's That Girl tour. The innovative ideas of both
designer and singer have produced startling work
that continues to thrill their fans to this day.

SCENT BOTTLES

This Baccarat scent bottle is dated *c*.1880. The design of the engraved glass stopper mirrors that of the bottle, a factor that should always be checked when buying.

The collecting of scent bottles has grown in popularity in recent years with the development of collectors' clubs, specialist dealers, and dedicated auctions. Up until the late 19th century ladies and gentlemen would decant oils and flower waters, which were either purchased from a perfumer or homemade, into their own personal bottles. These came in every size, from large dressing-table flaçons to small portable flasks that could be slipped into a handbag, or even worn suspended from chatelaines or finger rings. The 20th century saw the development of the commercial industry as we know it today, with branded perfumes sold in specifically designed bottles and boxes – a complete "presentation" created to market a named fragrance. "Chanel No 5", launched in 1921, was the first scent to bear the name of a designer, and bottles became ever more inventive as the fashion industry competed with long-established traditional perfume makers such as Guerlain. Both non-commercial and commercial bottles have their collectors, and in each field condition is crucial to value. Check for chips and other damage and ensure that stoppers are original. With commercial perfume bottles the more complete the presentation the better. Bottles still with their original boxes will command a premium, and any remaining perfume should not be decanted.

▼ Double-ended bottle, 1880s

In the 19th century there was a fashion for double-ended scent bottles. Tightly corseted Victorian ladies were prone to fainting fits. The double-ended bottle (made by welding two flasks together) held perfume in one end and in the other smelling salts, or a small sponge soaked in aromatic vinegar. These portable bottles, designed to be used in public, were often extremely decorative. This example is made from faceted blue glass with silver fittings.

◄ Lalique bottle, 1912

Bottles by major glass manufacturers such as Lalique and Baccarat command a premium. As well as producing commercial perfume bottles for French perfumer Francois Coty, René Lalique created designs for his own retail catalogue. This dressing-table flask is known as "Fougeres" (ferns), after the stylized fronds covering the bottle. It is decorated with two frosted glass medallions, lined with gold leaf and featuring different women. This rare and valuable bottle is signed "R. Lalique" and numbered 486.

► "Chanel No 5", 1920s

When Marilyn Monroe was asked what she wore in bed she replied simply, "Chanel No 5". Coco Chanel (1883–1971) was the first couturier to lend her name to a scent. Created in 1921, "No 5" was a revolutionary combination of floral and synthetic notes. According to legend, perfumer Ernest Beaux offered Chanel several mixtures, she chose the fifth sample and five was her lucky number. This sophisticated perfume needed suitably modern packaging, and the famous presentation epitomizes the classic simplicity that made Coco Chanel famous.

◄ "Evening in Paris" by Bourgeois, 1930s

One of the most successful perfumes of the inter-war years, particularly in the USA, was "Evening in Paris", launched by Bourgeois in 1928. The small blue bottle with a silver label was designed by French artist Jean Helleu, who also named the perfume. The bottle could be bought inside a variety of blue Bakelite boxes, each one depicting a night-time theme, such as the owl and the grandfather clock shown here.

► Schiaparelli "Shocking", 1950s

Elsa Schiaparelli (1890–1973) was one of Paris' inventive couturiers. Like her fashion her perfume presentations drew on surrealist motifs. "Shocking" was launched in 1936. Conceived with the artist Eleanor Fini the bottle was in the form of a dressmaker's dummy, inspired by the generous figure of Mae West (a Schiaparelli client), topped with glass flowers. For the packaging Schiaparelli came up with a new colour, "Shocking Pink", which became her trademark.

► "It's You" by Elizabeth Arden, 1939

Elizabeth Arden (1878–1966) is one of the greatest names in 20th-century cosmetics. The creator of countless beauty products, she owned over 100 beauty salons. She invariably dressed in pink and insisted that her strings of horses be treated with Arden creams rather than liniment. Inspired by a Victorian posy vase, this hand-shaped bottle for "It's You" perfume was created by Baccarat. The flask came in different colours; this combination of pink, blue, clear, and frosted glass is rare and desirable.

► Mitsouko miniature by Guerlain, 1976

Many collectors focus on miniature perfumes. Known as *echantillons* in France, miniatures were devised as free samples but are also produced for retail, often coming in boxed sets containing several fragrances. Value reflects not size, but rarity: this Guerlain bottle contains only 1ml of perfume. The pagoda-shaped plastic stopper was unpopular, and this miniature (also used for other Guerlain perfumes) was quickly withdrawn, making it rare and collectable.

Novelty Avon bottles, 1960s

Mass-produced designs such as these are very affordable. Mint, boxed items are sought-after, and rarer examples command higher prices.

In 1880s America David H. McConnell, an enterprising young businessman, was selling books door-to-door. To encourage customers he gave away a free bottle of cologne with every purchase. He soon realized that the scent was more popular than the books, and in 1886 he and his wife founded the California Perfume Company in Manhattan. Understanding the importance of direct sales he recruited women to sell his perfumes door-to-door, and promised that any dissatisfied customers would be refunded (a new and radical policy at the time). Business boomed in the 20th century, and in 1939 the company was renamed Avon Products, apparently because their laboratory in Suffern, New York, reminded the McConnell family of the landscape of Stratford-on-Avon, England. In the 1950s Avon, with its short and catchy name, was launched across the globe, and the company also adopted their famous "Avon Calling" advertising campaign. Cheap and cheerful, Avon perfumes came in a wide range of novelty bottles. Many of these can still be picked up very affordably today from boot (garage) fairs and flea markets.

Avon

ollectors of scientific instruments have a wide variety of periods and categories on which to focus their interest. The instruments available today date mainly from the late 18th, 19th, and 20th centuries; it is still possible to buy items from the second half of the 18th century for very reasonable prices, compared to many other collectable areas. The range of categories covers instruments for the measurement of time, distance, weight, and volume, optical instruments allowing man to see distant objects and to magnify very small ones, early frictional electric machines, instruments for navigation, surveying, astronomy, drawing, calculating and many more. Collecting scientific instruments gives the collector the chance to own works of superb craftsmanship and ingenuity, as well as examples of the steps in progress, small and large, along the path to the world we know today. These pieces are in a different category from many other collectables as, despite their beauty, their function is of more importance than their looks, as they were made not merely for decorative purposes but to be used. In the 21st century complex technology plays an important role in our daily lives, but the major part of this process of advancement in technology has been achieved in just over three hundred years, and the inventors and makers of scientific instruments have made a very significant contribution to this achievement.

Anemometer (airmeter), Negretti & Zambra, c.1890, used to measure the velocity of air wherever ventilation was important.

▲ Early-18th-century telescope
This instrument has three draws made from pasteboard, covered with dyed vellum with polished-horn lens mounts. These early telescopes are sometimes found with ornate tooled decoration and silver mounts. This type of construction does not stand up to the kind of harsh conditions in which they were often used, making them rarer than the more robust telescopes of the late-18th and 19th centuries. The lenses on these and later models are often found to be damaged and are difficult to replace.

▲ Six-draw pocket telescope, c.1850
By 1800 the techniques for the manufacture of brass tubing had improved, allowing more compact telescopes with the use of much shorter lengths of tube that fitted and telescoped into each other. The main body tube usually was covered with leather, but sometimes a painted finish or wood veneer was used; naval telescopes often used plaited rope. This model is by Mills, late Tully, of London.

➤ Binocular microscope, c.1890
This large oxidized and lacquered brass-compound microscope, with its separate Bullseye Light Condensor, is by J.H. Steward, London. The significant advance in binocular microscope design came in 1861 when Francis Wenham of London invented a new beam-splitting prism, which left one tube straight and the other inclined. This invention set the pattern for British binocular microscopes for the remainder of the 19th century. Always check the prism is in place and undamaged.

◄ Large compound monocular microscope by Charles Baker, _c._1855
This microscope, made in London, has retained almost all its original lacquered finish. The compound microscope has two or more lenses, which have to be held at a fair distance from each other by being mounted in a rigid tube, usually made of brass. In the 19th century, when serious design changes were applied to the optical system of the microscope, the lens elements became more complex. The multiple objective lenses of 19th-century microscopes should not be dismounted for examination except by a specialist.

▼ Direct vision spectroscope, London, _c._1880
The spectroscope is one of the most important instruments invented during the 19th century; in its various forms it has contributed more to modern science than any other instrument. It is an optical instrument used for chemical analysis and for analysing the nature and composition of the stars. Spectroscopes from the late-19th and early-20th centuries do turn up for sale. This one is by Adam Hilger, one of two early makers with John Browning.

◄ Mahogany boxed drum microscope, _c._1840
Benjamin Martin introduced his microscope design in 1738 while living in Chichester. He later set up shop in Fleet Street, London, where he produced instruments made, at first, of pasteboard covered with dyed vellum or rayskin, with turned wood and gilt brass fittings; these later became all brass. Martin's design was widely copied in the UK and France, and was still being offered for sale in the 1870s. Original signed Martin microscopes fetch considerably higher prices than the later attractive, but not uncommon, Martin-type microscopes.

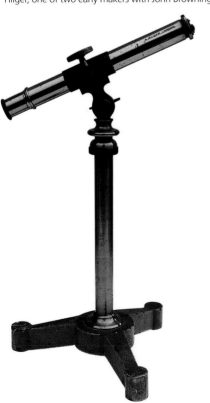

➤ Fullers cylindrical sliderule, _c._1950
In May 1878 Professor George E. Fuller of Belfast was granted Patent Number 1044, headed "Spiral Slide Rule for Working Arithmetical Calculations". Over the next 90 years Stanley of London manufactured and sold, in various forms, many thousands of this very successful sliderule. The Fullers sliderule consists principally of a calculating scale, 1,270cm (500in) in length, spiralling around the cylinder. The sliderules bought both by firms and individuals were highly valued and consequently many have survived. Collectors of calculating instruments now appreciate them as an important step in the development of calculating.

⌃ Pantograph in ebony and ivory, c.1830

The pantograph is an instrument devised originally in the early 17th century to speed up and make easier the task of changing scale, a function often required by draughtsmen. The building of the railways and the expansion of ship-building in the 19th century assured the continued demand for this instrument. This pantograph is unusual in being made of ebony and ivory as they are more commonly found in brass. Produced by William Harris & Co of London and Hamburg, it is of continental design and will have been manufactured in the German factory and imported to the UK.

◄ Customs officer's ivory sliderule, 1700

In 1683 Thomas Everard described a sliderule for use by gaugers (customs officers) when assessing duty on wines and spirits. The Everard sliderule was rectangular in section, with slides on two sides, and came in various lengths up to 90cm (36in). This example is in ivory, is 30cm (12in) long, and is inscribed "Made for Mr Daniel Elwell by T. Tuttell at Charing X Mathematical Instrument Maker to the Kings Most Excellent Majesty ano 1700". Thomas Tuttell was a maker of instruments of the finest quality who sadly drowned in the River Thames in 1702 when just a young man.

⌃ 19th-century brass sextant

This instrument measures angles on the celestial sphere and has been a favourite of sailors for many years. In 1731 John Hadley invented the reflecting octant, which consisted of a sector of 45°. The later nautical sextant, as shown above, consists of a 60° arc, the periphery of which is calibrated. Captain Cook was greatly aided in his Pacific surveys, 1769–70, by the use of the sextant; he circumnavigated New Zealand and charted 2,400 miles of coastline in only six months. The sextant is still in use today.

▼ A cased brass camera lucida, c.1830

William Wollaston invented this optical Instrument in 1806. It uses a lens, or prism, to allow the simultaneous viewing of an artist's subject and his drawing paper, which means the artist effectively is able to trace the subject onto his paper. Later, more sophisticated instruments were made with sets of lenses with varying degrees of magnification, which could be used for increasing the size of the subject to be drawn. They were also adapted for use with the microscope, to aid in the drawing of microscopic subjects.

◀ **Curta calculator, 1960s**

The Curta is a precision instrument that performs calculations mechanically. It was invented by Curt Herztark of Austria while a prisoner at Buchenwald concentration camp in Germany during World War II. Following his liberation he began producing Curtas in April 1947. There were two models – the Curta I and the Curta II with its larger numeric capacity. Between the years 1949 and 1970 approximately 80,000 Curta I models and 60,000 of the type II were produced. Production ended in 1970 when the Curta was made obsolete by the invention of the electronic calculator.

◀ **Augsburg equinoctial sundial compass, c.1830**

Augsburg was famous for its instrument makers, who produced these compass dials throughout the 17th, 18th, and 19th centuries. They are characterized by their octagonal dial plates, containing a compass with a hinged latitude arm on one side and hinged hour ring engraved in Roman numerals. The sundial gnomon (pin) is a narrow pointed rod, and latitudes for various European cities are engraved on the base. The sundials came in a shaped case, usually made of leather-covered card. The one illustrated is engraved "Abraham Liverpool", and will have been imported by Abrahams from Augsburg into the UK.

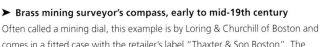

▶ **Brass mining surveyor's compass, early to mid-19th century**

Often called a mining dial, this example is by Loring & Churchill of Boston and comes in a fitted case with the retailer's label "Thaxter & Son Boston". The sights are hinged to fold down when out of use and it has twin bubble levels. The compass is gimballed (levelled) so that sights may be taken on inclined ground. A typical example of the use of a mining compass would be for charting mineshafts and mineral deposits, by taking bearings above and below ground.

Scmalcalder's prismatic compass, c.1830
This design brought a much greater accuracy to an important item of surveying equipment.

Charles Augustus Scmalcalder, mathematical instrument maker in the Strand, London, invented and patented the prismatic compass in 1812. A right-angled prism is fitted into the back-sight, which is positioned over the rim of the compass card; the degrees can then be read at the same time as sighting the point of observation. The card is divided into 360°, with the figures printed in reverse as they are read in reflection. When the patent expired many other makers produced the design and it became established as an indispensable piece of equipment for the military, explorers, mountaineers, and hill walkers; it has undoubtedly saved many lives over the years. However, Scmalcalder suffered the same fate as many of his contemporaries: due to the toxicity of the materials and processes used in production, together with poor working conditions, inventors often developed failing eyesight and health and were unable to earn a living. Scmalcalder died in poverty in the workhouse in 1843.

Prismatic Compass

SEWING TOOLS

Age, condition, and the degree of ingenuity and craftsmanship used to make sewing tools are all factors that excite collectors, together with the social history of the time – who may have used the items and the needlework they helped create. Tools have been made for use by men and women throughout society at varying times in history. Dating the century or period in which a tool was made is frequently all that can be determined as many makers are anonymous. The most exquisite examples are carved ivory tools, particularly those identified as "Dieppe-work" and "Palais Royal" – distinctive tools of mother-of-pearl with gold, silver-gilt, or silver, made around the Palace of Versailles, Paris, in the 18th and 19th centuries. Research has only really been taken seriously since the late 19th century, but sewing tools have been required for making and repairing garments since clothes were first fashioned. Until medieval times the tools were primitive in style and construction, and made of bone or flint, and later iron; bronze examples date back at least as far as the 9th–12th centuries AD. While collecting frequently extends to include examples of needlework and tools for allied crafts, such as knitting and lace-making, this selection concentrates on the main categories found in a good, basic sewing tools collection.

Brass hemming bird clamp with pincushion and emery, USA, c.1860; the beak grasps one end of a hem to hold it steady.

▼ Silver "Atlantic cable" thimble, c.1860 and American Simons scenic gold thimble, c. 1900
Although exhibits are sometimes labelled "Roman", in fact the oldest metal thimbles found date from the 9th to the 12th centuries AD. Dutchman John Lofting introduced the commercial production of brass thimbles to Britain in 1693. A proliferation of shapes and materials incapable of being used are sold as "for collectors" in souvenir shops worldwide, but for a thimble to be truly collectable it must be capable of being used for the purpose it was intended.

A Tunbridge stickware pin-wheel, c. 1840
Initially used to secure two pieces of skin or fabric together, pins were also used as loose change by the Romans and could be objects of considerable expense – hence the term "pin money". They were frequently also employed as love tokens, purchased by gentlemen for their ladies. Pincushions were smaller in the 18th century than they are now, as they tended to be used by ladies when travelling with their needlework. Pin-wheels – two flat discs joined together, allowing pins to be inserted between them – were often decorated, covered with printed paper (such as Scottish tartan ware), or with a mosaic veneer, as illustrated here.

➤ American celluloid thimble holder in the form of a Geisha, 1920s
Until industrialization brought mass-production and lowered costs, thimbles were expensive to buy, particularly those of more intricate design, and were made from precious metals. Cases to protect them became the norm, some homemade from felt, others more robustly made of wood or metal. With the arrival of material such as celluloid (1871) and ivorine (1897), along came decorative, frivolous examples, more for show than function. Beware that celluloid gives off a destructive gas and should never be stored with metal.

◄ **Two Victorian glass needlecases, overlaid with beadwork decoration, 1850–70**

Beadwork had many decorative uses, but only the Victorians could think of putting multicoloured glass beads over a thin, delicate base of glass to make needlecases. Today the cases often have chips, or beads missing, but it is amazing that any have survived at all. Once beads start coming off the condition is bound to deteriorate. Purchase is ill-advised unless the tool is in really good condition, despite what you may be told to the contrary.

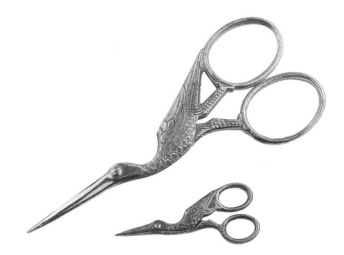

▲ **English embroidery and miniature stork scissors, 1910–30**

Until the 10th century AD scissors resembled the sheep shears used today. Gradually the design developed into the shape we recognize, and from the mid-1400s refinement and decoration was incorporated. Initially scissors were housed in sheaths for safety, and later for the protection of their ornate decoration. This is another sewing tool that was often a much-appreciated gift from a husband to his wife or a parent to a daughter.

▼ **French mother-of-pearl and gilded-brass etui, 1860–80**

The etui illustrated was meant for display, perhaps as a gift for a young French girl who had attained an excellent standard in needlework. However, many etuis were compact, useable, and often taken on journeys. The shell is mother-of-pearl and the metalwork is gilded brass; if it had been intended for nobility the metal would have been silver-gilt or gold. Etuis commonly contained a thimble, scissors, a bodkin, a stiletto, and often a scent bottle.

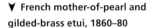

◄ **"Stanhope peep" needlecase with tape measure, c.1865**

Needlecases and tape measures were often made as souvenirs of places visited, of events (both historical and personal), or as tokens of love. In 1859 French businessman René Dagron combined the microscopic lens invented by Lord Charles Stanhope with his own microfilm process in order to miniaturize photographic images for inclusion in souvenir ware. Today delicate "Stanhope peeps", as they are known, are often damaged or missing from the tools.

► **English needlework box, 1876**

Many needlework boxes, from George III through to the end of Victoria's reign, came complete with elaborate interiors and matching sewing tools and accessories. Some had secret compartments and included either toiletries and hair brushes or writing materials, or both. They were often presented as gifts of appreciation by employers, maybe to mark a marriage or retirement. It is comparatively rare to find even a Victorian example in original or very good condition so are they are valuable pieces.

SHIPPING

For centuries items associated with the sea, and ships in particular, have been avidly collected. Ships' wheels, bells, navigational instruments, lamps, and paintings have always been popular, but during the last 30 years there has been a growing trend toward collecting items associated with the great ocean liners. These tourist vessels developed in the 19th century. In 1838 the *Great Western*, designed by Isambard Kingdom Brunel, crossed the Atlantic in 14.5 days, and immediately announced a regular service from Bristol to New York at 31 pounds and ten shillings. Brunel was responsible for the *Great Britain*, launched 1843, the first large iron ship to be screw-driven, and the *Great Eastern* (1858), the biggest vessel built for the next 40 years. She rolled in heavy seas, was unpopular with passengers, and commercially unsuccessful. By the end of the 19th century the Atlantic route to the USA was dominated by the White Star Line, Cunard Line, and the ships of the French and German companies. By the time the new Cunard ships, the Lusitania and the Mauretania, were launched in 1906–7, first-class passengers enjoyed luxurious cabins, restaurants, and lounges, and emigrants had the benefits of electric light, heating, and hot water for washing within their third-class accommodation.

Royal Yachts **by C.M. Gavin, 1932. Limited edition of 1,000 books including all the yachts until 1932. Illustrated with prints and photos.**

▲ *Titanic* **tissue printed in 1912**

There were four different designs printed to mark the sinking of the *Titanic* on 15th April 1912. They were sold by street vendors to raise funds for the families and survivors of the disaster. The *Titanic* collided with an iceberg in the North Atlantic on the night of 14th April 1912 and sank at 2.20am on the 15th, with the loss of 1,500 people. There were just 705 survivors. Later, tissues were made depicting the sinking of the *Lusitania* and the crash of the airship R101. When found their condition is usually very fragile, and they are best framed and kept out of direct sunlight to prevent fading.

➤ *Arundel Castle* **silver-plated inkpot, 1920–50**

The *Arundel Castle* was a Union Castle Line four-funnelled steamer that ran between Southampton and Capetown, South Africa. Built and launched by Harland and Wolff in 1922, she was scrapped in 1959. Plated items similar to this were usually manufactured in the Midlands, and sold in shops on board as souvenirs. The ship's shop also sold china and other souvenirs of the voyage.

▲ *Queen Mary* **cardboard model, 1936**

The *Queen Mary* was the UK's showpiece of engineering in the 1930s. Her magnificent interiors ensured her popularity with the rich and famous from 1936 until the 1960s. This model, made by the toy company Chad Valley in 1936, comes apart deck-by-deck and has a paper key. Every room can be identified. It was for sale not only aboard ship, but in shops on shore as well.

▼ Bensons' sweet tin, *c.*1955

This tin, depicting *RMS Queen Mary* on the lid, was one of a series of tins illustrated with ships. Others included the *Queen Elizabeth*, *United States*, *France*, *Empress of Britain*, and the *Royal Yacht Britannia*. They date from the 1950s and '60s and, providing they are in good condition, make a colourful and interesting collection.

◄ Wooden lifebuoy frame, *c.*1900

These frames were common souvenirs for the Victorian and Edwardian sailor – usually they had a portrait of the ship in the centre, although sometimes they contained the portrait of the sailor himself, or a port that he had visited. Although these types of frame had lost their appeal by the 1930s, the Goan crew of the P&O liners were still making them for passengers between the 1950s and 1980s.

▼ White Star Line bowl, 1910–20

This first-class bowl is based on an Indian design and was used on ships in service between 1902 and 1934. The bowls were supplied by Stoniers, a Liverpool merchants that was contracted to supply White Star Line with most of its china between the 1890s and 1934. Each piece is stamped with the shipping company's name and/or cipher.

▲ A *Lusitania* watchcase, *c.*1915

This was salvaged from the shipwreck of the *Lusitania* in 1982. The Cunarder *Lusitania* was one of the largest ships in the world when she was torpedoed in the Irish Sea during World War I on 7th May 1915, with the loss of 1,198 lives. This silver watchcase was made by the Philadelphia Watch Company in the USA and was part of the cargo on her last voyage. The watch movements were shipped in a separate consignment for reassembly in England to avoid tax.

➤ Brass name plate from the *Royal Yacht Britannia*, 1960s

The "Royal Brow" was the part of the deck on the *Royal Yacht Britannia* where the Queen and members of her family had a quiet area to themselves. The nameplate was removed during a 1980s refit of the yacht. *Britannia* was launched on 16th April 1953 in Scotland, and decommissioned in 1997. She is now open to the public at Leith Docks in Edinburgh, Scotland.

SPORT

A ceramic inkwell with equestrian motifs and a jockey's cap for the cover, 1880–90; similar items appear in silver and metalware.

A Mecca cigarettes baseball card featuring Johnny Evers of the Chicago Nationals, 1911; one of many affordable cards to collect.

A tin of Dunlop tennis balls, USA, c.1960, with a pop-off lid. Examples from the early 20th century were completely sealed.

Sporting memorabilia is now firmly established as a leading field in the world of collectables. The market is supported by all the major auction houses, as well as many independent auctioneers who provide a speciality in this niche market. In addition there are many dealers operating in the field, a calendar of fairs, and the establishment of collectors' clubs and magazines. For new and seasoned collectors alike there has never been a better time to be involved in the scene.

In the UK the first specialized sporting auctions began taking place in the early 1980s and were particularly focused on traditional sports such as golf and cricket. During the 1990s the football memorabilia market began to boom, and has proved to be the fastest-growing sporting sub-market in recent years. Today virtually every sport enjoys some form of representation in sporting catalogues but the main areas for collecting are golf, cricket, tennis, horse-racing, the Olympic Games, boxing, and indoor sports, covered by billiards and snooker. In the USA too, sporting memorabilia is a huge market that caters especially to American sports – none more so than baseball, where prices for top-of-the-range items can dwarf those commanded in the UK.

The memorabilia market is underpinned by the incredible worldwide interest in sport that occupies a place in the centre of popular culture, and plays such an important part in people's everyday lives. Collecting as a hobby is an extension of this interest beyond the sports field, and a reflection of an individual's passion for sporting pursuits. It is also an accessible and inclusive area of collecting that does not necessarily demand any advanced technical or academic knowledge to understand and participate in the subject, as can be the case in mainstream art and antiques markets. The main qualification is simply to be a sports fan, and to have an appreciation of our remarkable sporting heritage. The pages of the history book can come to life in a real and tangible form through the collecting of sporting artifacts.

The vast majority of collectors primarily are active for the love of the sport and the hobby. However, a significant number of individuals have entered the scene as investors and speculators – perhaps as an alternative strategy to traditional investments that have been performing poorly in difficult and volatile market conditions in recent years. This has helped fuel prices that continue to climb in many areas, and currently provides a very exciting and vibrant sporting memorabilia market.

It is hoped that the following pages will help stimulate an interest in this fascinating field of collecting and provide a brief overview of the sports that are particularly popular and the types of things that can be collected. Sporting memorabilia is fun and does not necessarily require a very deep pocket to collect, and you will find that there is a wealth of further information and advice available to you from professionals within the business. Happy collecting!

Football & Rugby

Football as we know it today first emerged in the 19th century. The Football Association (ruling body for English soccer) was founded in 1863 and the Football League established in 1888. Britain was largely responsible for exporting the game around the world and the international body FIFA was founded in 1904. Today the collectables market in this area is thriving, and prices improve year-on-year. Glamorous items include players' medals, trophies, awards, and the shirts and boots they have worn on famous occasions in their careers. Contemporary celebrities, such as David Beckham, can often match the prices commanded by the sport's all-time greats. Paper collecting is particularly popular: football programmes, match tickets, autographs, and other general ephemera is collected with great gusto. Age and rarity are the main factors: in 2003 a world record auction price of £14,400 ($21,600) was set for a 1901 football programme; 1960 is considered the landmark between the old and modern eras. England's historic triumph in the Rugby World Cup in November 2003 triggered a surge of interest in rugby collectables, so expect a rise in prices too.

A painted spelter figure of a rugby player by Raphanel, *c.*1900; many figures are anonymous, one signed by the sculptor is worth more.

▼ A spelter figure of a football player, French, *c.*1930

This boldly modelled player is striking a powerful right-footed volley. Football is a game with historical working-class roots and the potential audience for decorative items was therefore somewhat limited. Spelter was a cheap and easy metal to work in and proved ideal in this market. The appearance of the surface could also be altered to produce a bronze-like patina or a verdigris effect, as with this figure.

▲ A 15ct gold FA Cup winner's medal, 1910

The reverse of this medal is engraved "English Cup, won by NUFC, P McWilliam, 1910", and it is displayed in its original fitted case. The romance of the FA Cup, the oldest knockout football competition in the world, translates into the prices fetched for FA Cup memorabilia. A winner's medal often represents the pinnacle of a player's career. Newcastle United won the competition in 1910, defeating Barnsley 2-0 in a replay.

▼ FA Cup Final programme Manchester City v. Portsmouth, 1934

The content of many football auctions can be dominated by football programmes. They are hugely popular, and high prices are paid for early or scarce examples. FA Cup Finals are often an essential backbone of collections, so expect to pay a premium on these particular football match programmes. This fine example bears artwork that is typical of the 1930s. It is preserved in fine condition and involves two teams who enjoyed much success at the time.

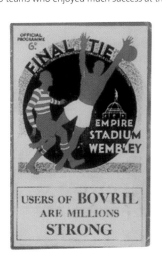

▲ A ticket for the Red Star Belgrade v Manchester United European Cup match, 5th February 1958

This emotive item is an entrance ticket from the last match played by the ill-fated Manchester United "Busby Babes" team of 1958, many of whom perished in the Munich Air Disaster after a refuelling stop during the return journey. Both the programme and the ticket for this game are scarce. This factor, added to the significance of the occasion, produces high prices at auction.

▼ Northern Ireland international cap, 1962–63

Right from the outset of international football, players from the UK and Ireland have received caps from their Football Associations in honour of their appearances for their countries. The tradition of the cap comes from the early uniform of footballers, when the colours of the team were defined by the caps, as opposed to their shirts, and the skills of heading a ball were not a large part of the repertoire. The Northern Ireland FA presented caps each season.

▼ Beckham No 7 England international jersey

When buying a modern jersey always enquire with the auctioneer or seller as to the item's provenance. This particular David Beckham jersey, signed by him and the rest of the England squad, was sold with a signed letter of provenance from Les Reed, the Football Association's National Coach and Director of Technical Dvelopment, who confirmed that it was one of the shirts issued to England's iconic player for the historic last ever match at Wembley Stadium, against Germany, in 2000.

◄ A 1966 World Cup superintendant's lapel badge in gilt-metal and enamel

Interest in the 1966 World Cup remains undiminished in the UK today and all things associated with the most famous moment in English football history are eagerly sought-after. This attractive collectable, enamelled with the official insignia of the competition against a Union Jack background, was worn by an official at Wembley stadium during the tournament.

➤ Butter dish shaped like a rugby ball, 1930s

This highly unusual item has a ceramic body modelled in upper and lower halves. The exterior has then been covered with leather to provide a realistic simulation of a miniature rugby ball. It is complete with lacing – a device that helps lift the cover of the butter dish. It is an interesting example of how sporting design has been applied to everyday household items.

Golf

Golf has been played for hundreds of years, and the world's first society of golfers was founded in Blackheath, London in 1608. Golf clubs have been manufactured with a wide variety of design concepts over the years, and the diversity this offers to collectors is clear to see. For the time-being the market centres on hickory-shafted clubs, and ignores the steel-shafted examples that began to take over during the 1930s. Golf balls can be categorized into three eras, the feather ball being the earliest and scarcest. In Victorian times "featheries" made way for the less expensive gutta percha or "gutty" ball, which in turn was superseded around the end of the 19th century by the rubber core ball. Away from equipment, a wide range of other golfing memorabilia is available to collectors, including decorative and commemorative objects, autographs, pictures, and prints. Golf collecting is particularly popular in the USA, making it a dollar-strong market, although there is plenty of competition from collectors in the UK, Europe, and many other parts of the world, in keeping with the sport's global status.

H.L. Curtis scared-head putter, c.1905. To tell the age of a wooden-headed club examine its attachment to the shaft.

⋀ A gutta percha golf ball, c.1860
The earliest form of golf ball was the "featherie". These were handmade by highly skilled craftsmen and were very expensive to buy. The discovery and appliance of gutta percha (a rubber-like substance) by the Victorians revolutionized the game, as golf balls could be produced in larger numbers. This had a direct effect on the number of players who took up golf. This example is not in great condition.

➤ A J.S. Caird wry-necked putter, c.1900
This putter has two strip arms and a wide blade; the hickory shaft bears the maker's stamp. The highest prices for golf clubs are usually reserved for the most popular examples from the game's history. However, there is also a good deal of interest in the rather unorthodox designs that have been tried with varying degrees of success over the years. The point of Caird's putter is that the golfer can see the whole ball in the gap between the two arms. The hosel points in front of the ball, rather than at the centre or striking spot.

◄ Silver-mounted pottery match striker, 1909
From the late 19th century, when the popularity of golf spread rapidly among the wealthy, many golf-related ceramics and other decorative items were produced. This smoker's accessory doubles up as a match holder (inside the hollowed ball) and a striker – the simulated markings of the ball presenting the right roughened conditions for ignition.

◄ A Johnny Walker Ryder Cup water jug, 1995
The worlds of golf collecting and drinks memorabilia combine in this fun modern collectable. For many years the Ryder Cup (est. 1927), a bi-annual contest between golfers in the USA and Europe, resulted in an almost routine victory for the Americans. However, in recent years the competition has been far more even, and some exciting and close-fought matches have taken place. This has led to a surge of interest in Ryder Cup memorabilia, such as this golf-bag water jug.

Other Sports

Portrait frontispiece from Don Bradman's *Farewell To Cricket*, first edition, 1950; Bradman is the greatest cricketer of all time.

Traditional sports such as cricket and tennis have a loyal and knowledgeable group of followers. Cricket sales can often be dominated by books; the celebrated annual *Wisden's Cricketers' Almanack*, first published in 1864, remains the most popular. With England and Australia the key markets, Ashes memorabilia can command high prices. There is also a very strong emphasis on "golden age" items, and Don Bradman is unchallenged as the sport's most important historical figure. There are many collectors of tennis racquets and related equipment. Recent tennis sales have highlighted competition for the finest quality decorative works-of-art. Other racquet sports, such as real tennis and ping pong, also have their enthusiasts. Angling auctions are the preserve of the country saleroom; early and fine equipment can command high prices and UK maker Hardy remains the magic name. Fishing books are another significant element, while the highly skilled art of fish taxidermy shares the limelight. Of other activities horse racing, boxing (popular in the USA), and the Olympics feature strongly at auction. High-quality billiards and snooker equipment represent indoor sports.

▼ Hardy brass multiplying reel, c.1890s
William Hardy established himself in 1872 as a gunsmith in Alnwick, Northumberland; the following year he was joined by his brothers and the Hardy Brothers partnership came into operation. Hardy fishing equipment is deemed to be of the highest quality and the firm boasted an impressive client list, including royalty. This reputation is reflected in the price achieved for vintage Hardy equipment.

▲ An Amhurst tennis racquet, c.1900
A good tip for deciding the age of a tennis racquet is an examination of the wedge – the piece of timber between the base of the head frame and the top of the handle. On early racquets, such as this Amhurst, the wedge is convex. The later fashion during the 20th century was a concave wedge that follows the shape and line of the frame, forming a proper oval. Various different racquet designs were trialled; other early examples include a long, grooved handle in the shape of a fish tail, supposed to prevent the hand from getting sweaty, and a waisted, fan-tail handle, curved like an Edwardian lady.

◄ A stuffed and mounted rudd fish, 1908
Fishing is one of the most popular sports across the world and cased fish are always in demand at auction, regularly attracting many buyers and commanding impressive prices. The rarest examples are those that encase multiple fish. They are often signed by the taxidermist (in this instance W.F. Homer), and the name to look out for in particular is that of J. Cooper – considered the master of his trade his cased fish command a premium at auction.

◄ A bronze model of a kangaroo with a cricket bat, 1938
This is a souvenir commemorating the Ashes tour of the 19th Australians to England in 1938. As was the case in the previous tours of 1930 and 1934, the performances of the legendary Don Bradman dominated the test series, and his batting average was over 100. However, England managed to emerge with a 1-1 series draw against their formidable Australian opponents thanks to an innings win in the Oval test, when Engalnd posted an incredible score of 903 for 7 declared.

▲ A St Amand pottery plate, 1920s
During the 1920s the St Amand factory in France produced a whole series of sporting plates with a variety of printed, cartoon-style decorations. Typically they portray a slapstick incident, usually resulting in a sportsman being injured or embarrassed, as is the case in this humorous tennis scene.

▲ Henry Downes Miles' *Pugilistica* in three volumes, 1880
This impressive work provides readers with a detailed history of the ancient sport of boxing in Britain, from 1718 to 1862. The brutal aspects of the bare knuckle pugilist and his "noble art" are relayed in a vivid way. The market for boxing memorabilia is today stronger in the USA than the UK as boxing has become rather a marginalized sport in Britain with the advent of pay-per-view television, instead of showing boxing matches on terrestrial channels as was the case in the 1970s and '80s.

▲ W. Stephens & Son mahogany combined snooker and life pool scoreboard, c.1900
This attractive piece of furniture was designed to accommodate the scoring of two billiard table games, snooker and life pool. The rules and practice of the latter are now virtually defunct. It is designed with various slides and revolving drums in order to meet its complicated purpose. Another famous maker to look out for within billiards antiques is Burroughes & Watts.

▲ Three Olympic Games official programmes
Olympics collecting is a popular sub-market of sporting memorabilia. These programmes, for the years 1908, 1920, and 1928, all have attractive chromolithographic colour wrappers – quite rare for sporting programmes of this period. The Olympic Games programmes were usually produced on a daily basis for the events being held on that particular day – focusing generally on the activities in the main Olympic stadium.

TEDDY BEARS & SOFT TOYS

The toy bear was pioneered by the German company Steiff. It gained its popular name after President Theodore "Teddy" Roosevelt refused to shoot a small bear that had been tethered to a tree on a Mississipi bear hunt. The bear became Roosevelt's mascot and the teddy got its name. Teddy bears have been produced by many companies during the 20th century and the biggest problem facing collectors is trying to identify them. Often labels and paper tags have been removed but it is usually possible to date bears by certain characteristics, such as the long arms and black button eyes that denote an early example, and also the fabric, which if synthetic will be post-World War II. While bears are the most established collecting area, there is also growing interest in soft toys, which were also produced from the late-19th century. Some collectors focus on a particular animal, others on characters inspired by literature, film, and, increasingly, television. Pristine and mint-condition items may be more valuable but old and battered bears and toys do have a special appeal, and many collectors actually prefer them this way. Provenance, for example a photo of the original owner with the toy, increases desirability. Values also depend on age, maker, condition, and charm.

This Bing bear, c.1910, has a silver button under the arm; the mohair is a rare white colour and the eyes are black buttons.

▲ Steiff "Rod" bears, 1904–05

One of the earliest Steiff designs to have survived is the "rod" bear, so-called because of the metal rods that passed through the body connecting the limbs. "Rod" bears were made only between 1904 and 1905, and they vary in design from the later Steiff bears. The noses are made from sealing wax and a horizontal seam runs between the ears. They have a Steiff elephant button in the ear and, as can be seen above, these bears have long tapering paws that allow them to stand. These bears were very hard-stuffed, which meant they were not particularly cuddly.

▼ "Felix the Cat", 1920s

"Felix the Cat", America's most famous cartoon character before "Mickey Mouse", first appeared in the film *Feline Follies* in 1919. "Felix" inspired a wealth of soft toys, both in the USA and Europe. This 1920s English "Felix" is made of mohair. He is distinctively skinny, with wide-spaced teeth. His tail served as a tripod so the cat could stand with his "hands behind him", as described in his famous signature tune. Many are in poor condition and so are relatively inexpensive.

➤ "Bonzo" dog by Chad Valley, 1920s

"Bonzo" was a cartoon character created by George Studdy in the 1920s. Chad Valley was given the UK and world rights, and the company produced a variety of designs during the '20s and '30s. This "Bonzo" is particularly desirable because of his pristine condition and his original paper label; he also retains his Chad Valley button and leather collar. "Bonzo" is very sought-after by collectors but condition is important, as they were made in velvet and many are dirty and worn.

⋀ Schuco miniature powder compact, late 1920s

The German company of Schuco made novelty and miniature bears from the 1920s through to the 1970s. They are very collectable, especially the novelty items, which came in a wide variety of bright colours and designs. This pink powder-compact bear is unfaded, which adds to its value. When the head is removed the body opens to reveal a small powder compact, complete with powder puff, mirror, and lipstick. These bears were not intended as children's toys but rather as a fashion accessory for ladies to carry in their handbags.

⋀ Chad Valley bear, c.1935

Chad Valley is one of the most famous English toy manufacturers. Its first teddy bear was made around 1914, and the company was granted the Royal Warrant in 1938. It finally closed in the 1970s. This bear, from the 1930s, has a celluloid button in the ear, and the typical Chad Valley shaved muzzle and large, flat ears. The paw pads are made of tan felt, and he still has his original red-and-white foot label.

⋀ Large Dean's bear, c.1938

Dean's Rag Book Co is the oldest surviving toy manufacturer, and its toys are much-loved, especially the early ones that date before World War II. This bear is one such item. The style of label on his foot was used until 1955, and is usually found on the right foot. His mohair is gold and his head is large and triangular, with cupped ears set on the corners. The arms are short and chubby and he has felt paw pads; the eyes are black-and-amber glass. After 1947 plastic eyes were often used.

⋀ Steiff "Mickey Mouse", 1930s

Walt Disney characters are very popular with soft toy collectors. "Mickey Mouse" first appeared in the cartoon talkie *Steamboat Willie* in 1928 and became an instant star. He was made by various American companies, along with Dean's Rag Book Co and Steiff in the UK, throughout the 1930s. This "Mickey" is rare because of his large size and excellent condition – he still retains his tail. His large cardboard-lined feet enable him to stand, and a typical "Mickey" feature is the large, stuck-on cherry-pie eyes. The fabric used is felt and velveteen.

◄ **Farnell "Alpha" bear, 1930s**

J.K. Farnell is possibly the oldest English teddy bear manufacturer, and its bears are highly prized by collectors. Early designs were unmarked; a paper label was attached to the bear's chest in 1925, and from 1926 a blue-and-white embroidered foot label appeared with the words "Alpha Toys". This bear is a typical example from the 1930s: the pads are rexine with four claws sewn across the edges, the large bulbous nose is stitched in light-coloured silk, and he is made in luxurious white mohair.

▲ **Chiltern "Hugmee" bears, late-1940s**

Chiltern, established in 1908, is a famous English manufacturer and collectors love the "Hugmee" bears. They first appeared in 1923 and were still being made when the company was taken over by Chad Valley in 1967. "Hugmee" bears are quite easy to find and because Chiltern used high-quality material many of them have survived in good condition. These two 1940s toys show how bear design altered after World War II: their flatter faces, shorter limbs, and rexine pads are typical of English bears of this period.

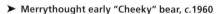

➤ **Merrythought early "Cheeky" bear, c.1960**

"Cheeky" bears have very distinctive features – a domed head and large flat ears set low on the side of the head, with bells sewn in. The muzzle is rather pointed and made of velvet and the mouth is stitched in a wide smile. This early example of a "Cheeky" from the 1960s is made from art silk. Unfortunately he has lost his Merrythought foot label. "Cheeky" bears were made in a variety of fabrics and they are still in production today.

➤ **Pedigree bear, mid-1950s**

Pedigree bears are quite often found with their labels intact; some say "Made in England", which dates them from before 1955 as after that production moved to Northern Ireland. They invariably are made from high-quality gold mohair and typically have velvet paw pads with no claw stitching. The eyes are glass; plastic eyes were also used on some bears, as were plastic stuck-on noses. Pedigree ceased trading in the 1980s, making its bears very collectable today.

▲ **"Sooty" and "Sweep" by Chad Valley, 1960s**

"Sooty" was born in 1946 when amateur magician Harry Corbet purchased a teddy bear glove puppet in Blackpool and incorporated him into his act. Harry and "Sooty" were given their own TV series in 1955. "Sweep" joined the team in 1957, followed in 1964 by "Soo the Panda", "Sooty's" girlfriend, although the BBC forbade the pair to touch on screen. Much mayhem was created with hammers and water pistols. Puppets fetch a higher price as a pair.

➤ Chad Valley golly, *c.*1960

The golly first appeared in *The Adventures of Two Dutch Dolls and a Golliwogg* (1895) by Florence and Bertha Upton, and remained a favourite nursery toy until political awareness in the 1960s caused their decline. Chad Valley gollies are quite easy to find, and were produced in various sizes, but because they are difficult to restore condition is very important. This golly is quite rare and valuable because of his mint condition and original label. His clothing is typical of Chad Valley, especially the sewn-on red-and-white striped cotton trousers.

▼ "Paddington Bear" toy and puppet, 1980s

"Paddington Bear" was created by author Michael Bond and appeared first in the book *A Bear called Paddington* in 1958. From then a new "Paddington" book was published every year, up until 1981. British toy designer Gabrielle Clarkson of Gabrielle Designs created the first soft-toy version in 1972. This example, *c.*1980, is by Eden Toys – an American company who have produced "Paddington" since 1975. Unlike the Gabrielle Designs version he is not wearing Wellington boots. The rare small glove puppet, *c.*1985, is by Gabrielle Designs, and still retains its original label.

▼ "Miss Piggy" beanbag by Dakin, *c.*1980

"Miss Piggy" is the superstar pig from the television series *The Muppets*, created by US film maker Jim Henson (1936–90) following the success of *Sesame Street*. "Miss Piggy", reputedly inspired by American actress Loretta Swift, became famous for her diva-like ways and fearsome, karate-chopping temper. Muppet toys from the 1970s and '80s are collected by enthusiasts, but values for toys such as this are still relatively low.

➤ "The End" Beanie Baby by Ty, 1999

"We want to be the Coke of collectables", claimed US toy manufacturer Ty Warner. Named after their bean (PVC pellet) stuffing, Beanie Babies were launched in 1993. Early Beanies have a white, sewn on "tush tag" and a hang tag shaped like a single heart, subsequently replaced by a double heart. The design of tags and fabric labels is vital for dating. Beanies became a worldwide craze among adults and children. Ty fuelled demand by selling only to small gift stores, by producing certain examples for specific markets, and by retiring models. In 1999 it announced the potential retirement of all Beanie Babies with this black bear, "The End". Ty allowed enthusiasts to vote for the survival of the toys, and of course they did. Beanies are still popular but there is no guarantee that retired models will hold value.

TELEPHONES

A lexander Graham Bell patented the speaking telephone in 1876. This selection of telephones demonstrates the evolution of telephony from the early 1900s. The early "Candlestick" telephone used a separate mouth and earpiece for clarity; the invention of Bakelite enabled the development of a phone with a composite handset in the late 1920s. The pyramid phone, in particular, is an Art Deco icon. These phones were rented out by the GPO (the equivalent of BT) and theoretically destroyed on rental termination, so fewer phones of this era exist in the UK than in other countries. Bakelite gave way to plastic, and the standard American phone was mirrored, with small design differences, worldwide. The "Ericofon" is always known as the first designer phone, where the miniaturization of components permitted radical design advances. This was also the first "one piece" telephone. British and Italian ripostes were the "Trimphone" and "Grillo", neither of which were great financial successes at the time, but these poor sales, equating to fewer being currently available, have now enhanced their value. The "Mickey Mouse" phone was the advent of a plethora of character and fun phones from the 1970s onward. Phonecards represent a modern, burgeoning area of telephone collectables.

The "Candlestick" phone is the epitome of speakeasy joints and Al Capone in the 1920s.

➤ Phonecards, 1990s

Phonecards were first issued in Italy in 1975 for the practical purpose of reducing thefts of money from public payphones. However, they are now thought of as decorative and collectable items. The range is vast and there are many factors to consider, such as the number produced and the reason or occasion it was produced for. The current world highest price for an individual card is £28,000 ($42,000), but many can still be bought for less than £1.

▼ "Cheese Dish" phone, 1950s

Ericsson, probably the foremost name in telephony development, introduced this phone in 1931. It had an integral bell and a good solid feel to it. The GPO took it up in 1937 and it was produced to a similar specification by several manufacturers. Phones show their date and manufacturer on the base and embossed on the handset. The valuable Bakelite phones are the coloured ones, especially if enhanced with a nice plaited cord, the original chrome dial, and a pull-out drawer, as here.

▲ Bakelite "Neophone", 1920–30

Supplied from 1929, this "pyramid" phone represented a return to the consolidated handset. It utilized a separate bellset, now rarer than the phones themselves, which either sat underneath or more commonly was put on the wall. Black is the standard colour but white, red, and green fetch the rarity premiums, with green being the rarest and most sought-after.

▼ **Standard American 500 dial phone, 1950s**

This model was used widely in the 1960s and '70s, with similar designs produced by several companies. The one pictured was designed by Henry Dreyfus for the Bell Telephone Company. The same phone appeared in the UK too. After the predominantly black phones of the past the GPO's range ran to eight different colours, the rarest perversely now being black. This was the last standard phone offered in quantity. They can still be found cheaply.

◄ **The "Ericofon" by Ericsson, c.1954**

Brought to the worldwide marketplace by Ericsson this was a quantum leap in design technology. The dial is under the phone with the on/off switch in the middle of it, and it is activated by lifting and replacing the phone on the table. The dial version eventually was superseded by a push-button version in a slightly more angular case. It came in about 14 different colours, with some colours being specific to specific countries. Pink and orange are the rarest and most collectable. The British version had no internal bell and foreign versions produced a rather faint rattle.

➤ **"Grillo" phone, mid-1960s**

This Italian dial phone was designed in 1965 by Marco Zanuso and Richard Sapper for the Italian PTT (national telephone service). The name "Grillo" means "cricket" in Italian. The ringer was incorporated into the phone plug. A later push-button version was made by Telcer of Milan. Sold primarily in Italy, and not a great seller at the time, it is now hard to come across and can therefore be fairly expensive.

▲ **"Trimphone", 1970s**

The dial version of the "Trimphone", in three two-tone standard colours (blue, green, and white) was soon superseded by this push-button pulse-dialling version, and later by a tone-dialling version. Finally there was the Snowdon Phoenix range, designed by Earl Snowdon, which consisted of refurbished phones with replacement cases in more outlandish colours. These are the most collectable. Trimphones introduced the British public to the much-imitated electronic warble.

◄ **"Mickey Mouse" novelty phone, 1970s**

First produced in the USA and sold by ATT in the late '70s under licence from Disney, this phone started off in a dial version and later was followed by push-button versions. The GPO in the UK was quick to market both "Mickey" and "Snoopy", but did not take up "Kermit" or "Winnie-the-Pooh" of the same series. There are a myriad of character and fun phones now available, including "sound trax" versions, such as a guitar-playing and singing Elvis, and a locomotive with four different sounds. When production of a model ceases it almost immediately acquires a premium, and then a steady rise in value.

TELEVISIONS

The BBC started its first official television service in the UK in 1936 but it was limited to the London area and to just half-an-hour's viewing in the evening, so a television set at very high cost had little appeal. Few sets were sold before the onset of World War II so they are now very rare, and highly prized by collectors. Television re-started in 1946 but it was well into the '50s before some areas could receive a picture. The Queen's Coronation in 1953 caused a doubling of the number of sets in use, so pre-1953 sets are again more desirable than later models, many of which are still surprisingly low in value as the transmission frequency is no longer in use. The tendency toward larger screens ruled the design of televisions right through the 1950s and '60s, but when colour was introduced in the late '60s the cost of a bigger tube was high and so smaller screens became popular again. A whole new market started for portable sets, including miniature personal models, and stylish cabinets were built around fixed models to suit the modern interiors.

Cossor 5in screen model 54, 1938; one of the least expensive sets made before the war, it was still a luxury few people could afford.

➤ Bush TV22, 1950s

The Bush TV22 was a best-selling model of the early 1950s, with a 9in screen and an attractive Bakelite cabinet. Manufacturers still thought of television as a luxury purchase, and tended to favour expensive veneered cabinets. This model used a cheaper Bakelite moulding but it did not compromise on the electronic design. It is now collected by both TV enthusiasts and collectors of Bakelite objects, and its appealing style has even been reproduced in a modern version.

▲ "Baird Townsman", 1949

Although John Logie Baird was the inventor of the first practical television system, his ideas were not utilized for the final standard adopted by the BBC. His company got into difficulties and he sold the name to another firm, eventually dying prematurely before seeing television reach maturity; this model, carrying his name, was made after his death. It had an internal aerial supposedly to suit flat-dwellers.

▼ Sinclair "Micro TV", c.1977

British inventor Clive Sinclair had already marketed a tiny radio, the "Sinclair Micro 6". His next step was to develop a miniature portable television. The first models used a conventional tube, but the final and smallest version of the "Micro TV" used a specially developed tube that was almost flat. Like some of his other products, it was ingenious but never succeeded commercially, as the demand for pocket-sized TVs has never been strong, and the LCD screen was already in development.

➤ JVC "Videosphere", 1970s

The space age brought a new visual style into the home, and this black-and-white portable TV by JVC embodied the trend. It was made in coloured plastic and could either be mounted on a stand or hung from a chain. Like the similar-looking, but much larger, "Keracolor", it was too extreme for the mainstream market and never sold in large numbers, so has now become something of a rarity. It is one of the icons of the 1970s, bought both by interior designers and TV collectors.

TEXTILES

Textiles have been at the heart of family life right throughout history, providing both warmth and comfort. Before the Industrial Revolution and the invention of the sewing machine in the 19th century, all weaving and sewing of cloth was done by hand and before the 20th century all materials were natural rather than synthetic. Textiles fall into three basic categories: decorative items, those for personal adornment, and household items. People have always sewn, either out of necessity or for pleasure, thus creating lots of possibilities for the collector, from very fine early pieces including samplers, embroideries, and lace, to household and larger items such as table covers, curtains, and bedspreads. A lot of the very early pieces from the 17th and 18th centuries can command extremely high prices and are very collectable, but in collecting textiles there is plenty of scope for all budgets and tastes. Bargains are definitely to be had for those who are in the know. As with all genres in the collectables world, condition is very important. In general, for a piece to command top price it has to be in very good condition, but if you can tolerate minor faults then items can be picked up relatively cheaply and there are new areas of interest coming into the market all the time. For example, textiles from the latter half of the 20th century are currently very popular at textiles sales and auctions.

Samplers are a highly specialized area; some very early ones are worth a lot of money but there is scope for collectors on a budget.

⋀ Sampler by Charlotte Woods, 1845
The earliest samplers, dating from at least the 17th century, were worked by professional embroiderers and the stitching is often exceptionally fine. In the 18th century they were taken up by children to practise their stitches. These samplers often featured pictures of birds, people, trees, flowers, and buildings, all two-dimensional and out-of-proportion with no perspective. By the 19th century samplers had become much simpler, with only cross-stitch being used: neatness was all-important. Most come glazed and framed to protect the stitching.

➤ Woven wool paisley shawl, c.1860
Despite its name, the paisley shawl originated in Kashmir, India, in the late 17th century and was made from Pashmina wool – the finest goats' hair. It was first introduced to Europe at the end of the 18th century and became an essential part of a lady's wardrobe throughout the 19th century, changing in shape and style to suit the fashions of the day. There were several centres of manufacture in the UK, including Edinburgh and Paisley (hence the name) in Scotland, and Norwich, England, and two main centres in France – Paris and Nîmes.

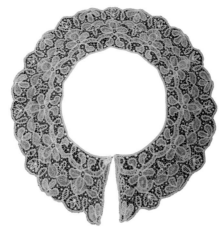

◄ Edwardian handmade lace collar
Lace is a decorative open-work fabric, but for a purist a true lace is one in which the pattern and any ground that links it are built up gradually by the interweaving of free threads. This excludes textiles such as embroidered nets, in which decoration is added to a pre-made fabric. The major techniques of lace-making are needlepoint and bobbin. Needlepoint laces are made with a needle and thread; bobbin laces are made with a multitude of threads, each carried by a bobbin, usually made of bone or wood decorated with beads.

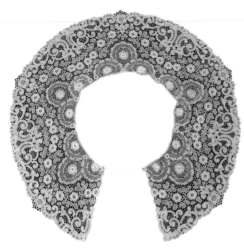

◄ Edwardian chemical-lace collar

Chemical lace is a man-made lace that was developed during the 1880s. It is made by embroidering onto a fine cotton backing, which is then chemically dissolved away to leave just the lace, hence the name. Chemical laces can be made to imitate many handmade ones, including *guipure* (netted lace with an embossed pattern) and embroidered nets. It can be difficult to tell the difference between handmade and machine-made lace, but one clue is that machine laces tend to have fuzzier threads.

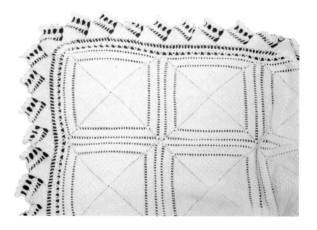

► Victorian knitted-lace bedspread

Knitting is a type of lace made with knitting needles and a single continuous thread. Knitted laces were used to edge household linens but they were also used to make bedspreads by knitting separate squares and then joining them together, often with a decorative edging of either shells or points. These bedspreads are very heavy, and although they were useful on a Victorian iron bed over sheets, they are not suitable for use with a duvet; however, they do make very attractive throws.

◄ Durham hand-stitched quilt, *c.*1900

A true Durham quilt should have a central medallion representing the circular window of Durham Cathedral, although other designs have now been put under this umbrella name. During times of extreme hardship quilts were often made by miner's wives, mining being a vital part of Durham's north-east community. The women would join together in quilting clubs, with sometimes as many as 15 working on one quilt at a time. These clubs were socially motivated as well as a practical necessity. Quilts were also made in the same way in Wales – another principal area for mining.

► Crocheted tablecloth, *c.*1920

Crochet is a type of lace made with a crochet hook and a single continuous thread. It was at the height of popularity in the latter half of the 19th century and the first half of the 20th century, when it was used to edge all manner of household linens from the smallest doilies to large bed covers. The centres of the cloths were made from either linen or cotton, but it is the linen ones that are stronger and more durable, thus making them more interesting to collectors.

▲ Victorian beaded pot stand
Beads were widely used in Victorian times to make
almost everything, from fringing, braid, and bags,
to fire screens, footstools, and cushions. For bead
embroidery the beads were either sewn by hand
or they were "tamboured", which involved holding
the fabric taut in a frame and using a fine hook,
rather like a crochet hook, to work the stitches.
For beadwork on canvas the beads were sewn
on with either tent stitch or half cross-stitch,
working from charts similar to those used
to create Berlin wool work.

▲ Petit point picture, late 19th century
Petit point is a very fine form of Berlin work, normally carried out in silk.
It is usually French in origin and was often made into bags and purses.
Today it is extremely rare and a petit point picture is considered a true work
of art. Popular themes are depictions of floral sprays in very rich colours,
as shown above in this basket of roses and foliage on a floral background.
The frame is made of moulded plaster, painted with a design aimed to
complement the petit point picture.

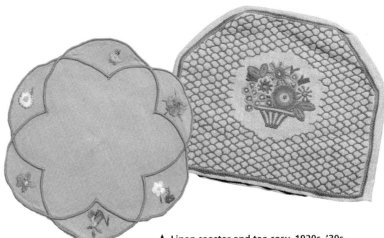

▲ Silkwork picture of a garden scene, 1920s
Most women could embroider in the 1920s but it was usually ladies
of leisure who could devote the time necessary to produce intricate
beautiful embroidery such as this cottage garden scene. Cottage gardens
were a very popular theme for embroideries at the time, as were baskets
of flowers and crinoline ladies. Most silkwork embroidery was carried out
on a fine linen ground.

▲ Linen coaster and tea cosy, 1920s–'30s
Up until the 1920s most embroidery was white-work,
but during the '20s and '30s coloured embroidery
on a coloured ground became more fashionable.
Transfers that came free with magazines could be
used for embroidering onto linen or cotton. People
had used tea cosies since tea was first imported by
the East India Company and as tea was expensive
during the 19th century the cosies were often
rather grand affairs – embroidered or painted
velvets, patchwork velvets, or beadwork tapestry,
highly padded and highly decorative. During the
20th century tea became more widespread and so
did the cosies. A linen one could be washed easily.

▲ Fabric by Lucienne Day for Heals, 1954

1950s textiles were often heavily influenced by contemporary art. Designer Lucienne Day is credited with introducing abstract furnishing materials into post-war British homes, and in "Herb Anthony" the flower is transformed into a spindly skeleton flecked with bright colours, echoing the painting style of Klee and Miró. Leading textiles designers of the period, particularly Day, are now commanding strong prices. Check the selvage of the fabric for the names of the designer, retailer, and pattern.

➤ Black cat satin underwear case, 1930s

Nightdress or underwear cases traditionally have made ideal gifts because of their practicality, as well as their attractiveness. Victorian nightdress cases were nearly always made of white-work embroidery, and they adapt well to make cushions to scatter on Victorian cast-iron beds. Throughout the earlier part of the 20th century underwear cases would be made of silk or satin, often embroidered or appliquéd. Cats, often thought to bring good luck, are collectable in many forms, and a black cat underwear case would be considered very desirable.

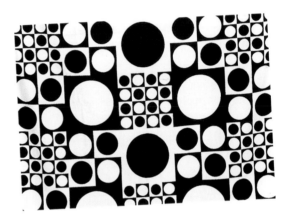

▲ "Geometri I" by Verner Panton, 1960s

The 1960s was an exciting time for design. Pop and Op Art influenced domestic furnishing as well as paintings, as demonstrated in this fabric by Danish designer Verner Panton (1926–98). The aim of Op Art was to disrupt and fragment the vision and, rather to the dismay of its fine-art originators, dizzying black-and-white patterns were applied to everything, from curtains to mini-dresses.

▲ Bathroom curtain, 1950s

As well as producing abstract patterns, 1950s textile designers also celebrated the everyday products that were now available after years of wartime rationing. Kitchen curtains were often decorated with food and drink; this bathroom material is covered with cosmetic accessories. These cheerful designs, though not as valuable as big-name abstract fabrics such as the Lucienne Day example above, are popular with '50s enthusiasts.

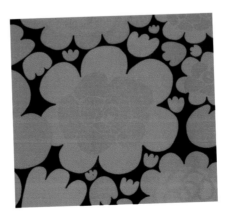

◄ Curtain fabric, 1970s

Much textile design in the 1970s was psychedelic, reflecting the popular culture of the time. Fabrics were characterized by swirling abstract patterns, often very brightly coloured. Big blow-up flowers were a favourite motif. These fabrics can still be picked up relatively cheaply, making them accessible to younger collectors with more limited budgets. However, textiles by significant designers and from major stylish retailers, such as Heals, will command a premium.

TOBACCO & SMOKING

Most people are aware that the habit of smoking tobacco was introduced to Europe by early explorers of the New World, who copied it from the Native Americans. Reports of pipe-smoking sailors in the ports of northern England and Scotland date from as early as the 1520s, and tobacco became very popular, in spite of condemnation by King James I. Although he was against tobacco, James nevertheless granted a charter to the pipemakers of Westminster. These early pipes were of clay and were fragile, but also cheap. Nobody collected them, with the possible exception of special models made for the trade guilds. The wealth of tobacco- and smoking-related collectables came about through changes and developments in smoking habits. The 19th century was a particularly productive period as the cigar, and later the cigarette, became popular, and from the 1850s the use of briarwood brought a greater versatility to pipe-making. With these developments came accessories such as pipe cases, cigar and cigarette cases and boxes, tampers, cigar cutters, and vesta cases. In the 20th century the cigarette lighter joined the older tinder box to add more possibilities for the collector. The design of tobacco and smoking accessories often reflects the period – Art Deco lighters and cigarette cases are a good example and are very popular with collectors.

A typically English leather cigar case with plain silver mounts, hallmarked 1876; Continental cases are often highly decorated.

▲ German tobacco box, c.1720–50

This brass tobacco box was made in Iserlohn, western Germany, which was a major centre of brass production in the 18th century – its products were exported all over Europe. The embossed decoration is typical of 18th-century German boxes; it depicts the military victories of Frederick the Great, King of Prussia. Battle scenes with round medallion portraits at either end are often representative of German boxes of this period.

▼ Victorian shell snuff boxes

Shell collecting became a popular pastime in the Victorian era, and shells were easily turned into snuffboxes like those seen here. The simple addition of metal mounts could transform them into useful and decorative objects. The mounts would be made of silver, silver-gilt, brass, or pinchbeck (a gold-coloured alloy). They are both affordable and collectable, but watch out for examples with dented mounts and/or chipped shells – such damage should be reflected in the price.

◄ Elaborate novelty pipe, c.1800

Staffordshire potteries of the late 18th and early 19th centuries produced many novelty pipes, which were for display only and were not meant to be smoked. This type, known as a "puzzle" pipe, was made by coiling a long tube of unfired clay, with a bowl at one end and a mouthpiece at the other. Decoration was sometimes in the form of snake markings, typically in blue, green, orange, yellow, and purple. They are hard to find in good condition and can fetch a high price.

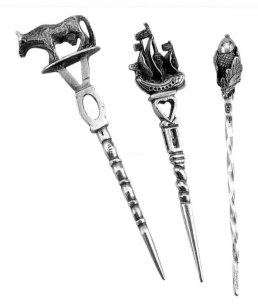

◄ Dutch silver cigar piercers, *c.*1890

Cigar piercers, like cutters, were often made of steel for added durability, but some fine examples were made in gold or silver and these are particularly rare today. Most were relatively plain but others were more decorative, sporting elaborate terminals, as shown in the picture. They would have been expensive originally, and would probably have been housed in a leather case. They were made in the Netherlands – one of the major centres of the tobacco trade.

▲ Cigar holder, *c.*1895

Cigar holders were among many new accessories prompted by the fashion for cigar smoking from the early 19th century onwards. Toward the end of that century Austrian, German, and French manufacturers excelled in the manufacture of elaborately carved meerschaum (magnesium silicate) cigar holders, such as this. They generally follow the style of meerschaum pipes, but with a small detachable bowl for holding the cigar at the end. Like most examples this one has an amber mouthpiece, but there are rare examples that use tortoiseshell instead.

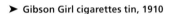

➤ Gibson Girl cigarettes tin, 1910

The "Gibson Girl" was created by American illustrator Charles Dana Gibson in the 1890s as an embodiment of the emancipated female. The German company Manoli registered "Gibson Girl" as a trademark in the early 20th century, using it as the name of a brand of cigarettes. Their version of the character is based on actress Camille Clifford, who played a "Gibson Girl" on stage, and the artwork is by the celebrated Berlin-based German designer Lucien Bernhard.

➤ Gold-plate cigarette case, 1920s

As it became socially acceptable for women to smoke during the early part of the 20th century, so manufacturers of smoking accessories began to make products designed with female customers in mind. This elegant case is made in the style of a purse or evening bag. Such quality items sometimes came with elegant silk or beaded carrying cases. Women's cigarette cases were often smaller than those made for male smokers.

◄ Molassine vesta case, 1905

Vesta cases, which are known as "matchsafes" in the USA, were made for carrying wax vesta matches, which were made from thick cotton threads dipped in paraffin wax with phosphorous heads. They caught fire quite easily and therefore had to be housed in a non-combustible container. The containers were often highly decorative – miniature works-of-art, portraying everything from soldiers to nude women. This example advertises Molassine, a London-based animal feed company.

➤ Bryant & May matchboxes, 1930s

The first friction matches were produced as early as 1826. As their inventor, John Walker, failed to patent his invention match factories soon sprang up all over Europe. Bryant & May became the best-known British firm, and the colourful designs of its matchboxes soon attracted the interest of collectors. The garden flowers series, shown here, dates from the 1930s. Matchboxes are generally more desirable if they still have their original contents.

◄ Japanese microphone lighter, c.1945

After World War II the American occupiers of Japan saw the production of novelty consumer items as a good way to get the country back to economic health. This lighter, in the form of a microphone, is a good example of early post-war production. Such lighters were originally inexpensive to buy, but they are well made, and increasingly collectable. Examples from 1945 to 1952 are usually stamped "Made in Occupied Japan", although many were assembled and sold in the USA.

◄ Festival of Britain ashtray, 1951

The 1951 Festival of Britain was a hugely successful event, attracting millions of visitors. It was a forward-looking occasion as the country tried to rebuild after the devastation of World War II. Souvenirs, such as this brass ashtray, were produced in large numbers so these mementos are readily available and affordable, but they are nevertheless of interest to collectors. Festival of Britain memorabilia represents something of a niche market.

▼ Wills's Woodbines sign, 1950s

Wills's Woodbines were introduced in the 1880s and went on to become one of the most famous of British cigarette brands. This advertising sign, in plastic and metal, is extremely collectable. The fame of the brand it is advertising helps increase its desirability, as does the pub scene illustrated, which is well-executed and evocative of the period. Collecting advertising signs is a field in its own right and is strongly driven by nostalgia.

➤ Cantrell & Cochrane ashtray, c.1960

Cantrell & Cochrane is a major soft drinks company based in Belfast. It was founded by the apothecary and surgeon Dr Thomas Cantrell in the 1850s. This ashtray advertises the company's range of mixers. It would have been made in large numbers and examples can be found for little expense. This item is of interest to collectors of breweriana and pub-related collectables, as well as those interested in smoking accessories.

TOYS & GAMES

A lithographed tinplate "penny toy" sailing boat by Meier, Germany, c.1905; these cheap toys were often sold by street vendors.

A lithographed tinplate Hudson Scott and Son *Peter Pan* motor car biscuit tin, 1920s; it has crossover appeal to other collecting areas.

Pelham puppet of Steve Zodiac from UK television programme *Fireball ZL5*, 1960s; the original box increases the puppet's value.

Nostalgia has a big influence when it comes to collecting toys of all types. Most collectors start by discovering an old toy in the attic that had belonged either to their parents or themselves, or finding one at an antiques fair or boot (garage) sale. Most collectors wish to learn more about who manufactured the toy and why, and what else that company might have made. Once they start they are usually hooked.

Toys before the 19th century were generally homemade, or manufactured by hand by a small-scale cottage industry. There were a few manufacturers making items for the very wealthy but these toys generally were intended for the adult amusement market and are extremely scarce in today's market. A collector would certainly need very deep pockets to collect that type of toy.

It was the Industrial Revolution of the mid- to late-19th century that enabled mass-market production to begin, and eventually made toys affordable to most people. However, toys were still considered precious things, and, even as late as the 1950s, most children only received a small number of toys each year. From the 1960s to the current day mass-produced Far Eastern imports have made a lot of children very happy on a more regular basis.

Germany was the most prolific manufacturer of toys during the 19th and early 20th century – Märklin, Bing, and Lehmann are perhaps the best-known – but the country was of course affected by world events. The two World Wars saw consumers revert to purchasing items from their own countries. Major British companies, such as Meccano, Hornby, and Britains, grew in this period, but, sadly, in the latter part of the 20th century cheap Far Eastern production drove a lot of the smaller manufacturers out of business.

Toys have been manufactured using many different materials, from early wooden and composition toys, which are generally hand-crafted, to machine-stamped tinplate toys, with lithographed (printed) or painted finishes but a percentage of the process still done by hand. Later in the 20th century toys produced from one-cast moulds and spray-painted en masse dominated the market, such as those manufactured by Dinky Toys, and today we have complex plastic moulded toys.

Although a few far-sighted people began to collect toys earlier, this area of collectables really only began to expand from the 1950s, and the most significant growth didn't start until the 1970s, when it escalated rapidly to the level it is today. Collectors should always try to buy the best quality toy they can. Concentrate on a few select areas or types, and look for good condition, quality, and original boxes. Avoid, where possible, restored, repainted, or heavily play-worn toys. As in any collecting subject, when an item becomes desirable and valuable, there is always someone who will try to make a dishonest profit, so watch out for fakes and reproductions. A question often asked is what will be the most collectable toys of the future? This is hard to predict, as items become collected almost as soon as they are manufactured in today's market. Whether it will be computer games, McDonald's merchandise, or toys promoting the latest sci-fi series, only time will tell.

Early Toys & Games

German composition, wood, and printed paper tumbling toy, c.1870; this illustrates the late-Victorian interest in all things Oriental.

Various forms of toys and games have been played with by children for hundreds of years, and before the mid-19th century wood was the main material used to handcraft the items. Many small companies made all kinds of wonderfully detailed toys; not much is known about these cottage industries but they are recognizable from their style of construction. Germany was the first country to show a growth in manufactured, mass-produced toys. Through the 19th and early 20th centuries Noah's arks, farms, villages, horses, and soldiers were made in great numbers, and are now highly collectable. Paper games and jigsaws, representing historic events from around the world such as coronations, wars, political events, and the discovery of new countries, were often produced by book printers rather than toy makers, and these are sought-after as well. The collecting of all types of toys and games is very specialized and it is perhaps advisable to start a collection by focusing on one particular style, make, or period, and building from there.

⋀ Wooden Noah's ark and pairs of wooden animals, c.1880
One of the most popular toys ever made is the Noah's Ark, and it is also one of few that children were allowed to play with on a Sunday. Arks were produced from the 18th century, but the most common ones found today date from the late-19th century. They can be painted, covered with printed paper, made of plain wood, or of straw-work, and they are either flat-based or with a modelled bow. An ark's value depends largely on the number of animals that accompany it; there can be up to 200 or 300 of all kinds of strange creatures, plus, of course, Noah and his family. The range of animals can be amazing, occasionally including moles, spiders, ladybirds, and moths, and many animals appear to be imaginary and fantastical rather than based on reality.

⋀ Wooden carousel, c.1900
This carousel comes from the Erzegebirge area of Saxony in Germany, which was famous for making hand-carved and painted wooden toys in the late-19th century. There were many manufacturers in the area but most, sadly, are now unidentifiable. Their ranges were extensive and included toy soldiers and forts, shops, spinning tops, and novelty toys. The condition and quality of these pieces are very important, and vary greatly.

▲ Carved wooden rocking horse by G. & J. Lines, c.1910

Rocking horses have been made since the 17th century, and have a crossover appeal to collectors as they are often bought and sold by furniture dealers too. The earliest and most sought-after are those on bow rockers, as shown above. Their carving is also of a finer quality – look out for the head that turns slightly to one side, defined muscles in the neck, and flared nostrils. By the late-19th century the bow rocker often was replaced by swing "safety" stands. The original finish is important: a repainted or restored horse, or one lacking paint, is worth 10–20 per cent of those in original condition.

▲ Kings and Queens of England wooden puzzle, Edward Wallis, c.1840

Dissected jigsaw puzzles were manufactured originally as educational games, often representing maps or monarchs, with facts and figures printed with the picture. They then began to develop into a more recreational pastime. Early 19th-century puzzles are the most valuable, but condition and the presence of original boxes are very important. A missing piece makes a large difference to value. Twentieth-century wooden puzzles are becoming popular, and, like games, they are collected by theme. Cardboard jigsaws are not widely sought-after.

▼ Elephant and Castle game, c.1822

Games played with counters and die were often printed on paper and then mounted on linen. The earliest and most valuable date from the mid-18th century, but they continued throughout the 1800s. Original condition and a protective case add to value. Typically the games represented current affairs, and are therefore historically very interesting. Board games from the 20th century are also desirable, generally collected according to themes, such as "Mickey Mouse" or transport.

▼ German wooden building blocks, c.1910

Building blocks are one of the oldest toys to be made. Sadly, most are of very low value today as they are robust toys and therefore have survived in large numbers – this German set is worth just £10–15 ($15–22.50). Usually made of wood or a composition stone-like material, they came in wooden boxes with sliding lids. Later, in the post-World War II period, more complex plastic sets were made by companies such as Lott's Bricks of Watford, England. Although very inventive, these later sets still have limited appeal.

◄ **Neptune theatre by T. Pollock, *c*.1880**
The best-known manufacturer of toy theatres is
Thomas Pollock. These theatres could be bought
made-up, or you could buy the printed sheets and
assemble it yourself. They were very popular toys,
representing all the famous plays and pantomimes
of the day. Early theatres have been found from
the mid-19th century, and the more elaborate and
larger the theatre, the more valuable. There was
also a trend for shadow theatres, where cut-out
black shapes were moved behind a back-lit scr

► **American clockwork doll, 1867–68**
This composition and metal clockwork toy of a lady
pushing a three-wheeled pram is typical of early
American toys and was made by W.M.F. Goodwin.
American toys had a distinctive style of their own,
often heavier than their European counterparts,
and they were very inventive and were some of the
earliest to be produced. Sometimes very simply
made, they are collected today mainly in the USA.
One of the most expensive toys ever sold was a US
"Charles" hose reel (a painted tinplate handcart
holding a fireman's hose) by George Brown from the
late 1800s, which fetched $231,000 (£154,000).

▲ **Cast-iron mechanical money bank, *c*.1886**
Among the most prized American toys are the late-
19th-century money banks, often sold by real
banks as an incentive for children to start saving.
They come in all sorts of wonderful forms, including
sportsmen, animals, and historical characters. Some
of them can fetch tens of thousands of pounds/
dollars: the price for one in "perfect" condition
is far greater in proportion than one in simply
"excellent" condition. Well-known makers include
Shephard Hardward Co and Kyser and Rex.

"Humpty Dumpty" circus figures, *c*.1910
This set of figures includes a Chinese acrobat, six
clowns, two bears, an elephant, and two mules.

One of the most successful wooden toy manufacturers of the 20th century was
Schönhut. Founded by Albert Schönhut in Philadelphia, USA, in 1872, it was
not until 1903, when Albert bought the rights from another inventor for the
now famous range of "Humpty Dumpty" circus figures and animals, that the
company became known worldwide. All the toys were jointed and poseable;
they also had slots in their hands and feet so they could be joined together.
Good original paint finish is very important with these toys, as is the presence
of original clothing. Some of the more unusual animals are highly sought-after,
such as gorillas, kangaroos, and giraffes. The clowns, acrobats, and ringmasters
generally have composition heads, but more collectable are the rarer bisque-
headed versions. The larger and earlier carved-headed dolls with glass eyes
are far more sought-after than the steam-pressed heads that were brought
out in 1923. The Schönhut range also included toy pianos, roly-poly toys,
vehicles, dolls' houses, and some very beautiful carved wooden-headed
dolls. Sometimes collectors will find a manufacturer that they like, such as
Schönhut, and try purchasing everything it ever made.

Schönhut

Transport

The Industrial Revolution of the 19th century in Britain heralded the steam age. Large steam engines were used to power and drive all sorts of machinery, which in turn led to steam trains and steam-powered cars. These advancements in technology made travel more accessible to all. Both children and adults began to desire these modern machines in the form of toys, and steam power caused the biggest ever growth in one particular field of toys. All forms of transport were represented, from horseless carriages, steam rollers, steam liners, battleships, and locomotives to stations, goods sheds, passengers, and an array of accessories. As each new invention came along the toy companies were quick to pick up on it, often producing the toys to coincide with the launch of the real vehicles. German makers again dominated this market, but they exported worldwide and produced toy replicas specific to each country by changing a livery to suit national colours, or adding a railway company's logo. The majority of transport toys were made of tinplate, painted or lithographed. They suffered from heavier play than static toys so condition is paramount.

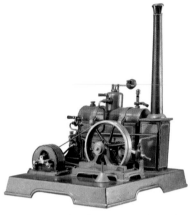

New technology was replicated in various spirit-fired stationary steam engines; this example, 1930, is by Märklin of Germany.

◄ **Tinplate steam toy, 1910**
This wonderful painted tinplate fairground wheel, made by Doll & Co of Germany, is typical of a wide range of toys that were manufactured to work with the steam stationary engines, as illustrated above left. The life-sized version of this ride would also have been steam-powered. Various accessories were produced to go with these toys, all driven by a pulley linked to the engine. They included different types of workshops and machines, such as knife grinders, saw mills, and sausage-making machines. Most German tinplate toy manufacturers made these new and exciting toys, which were also educational as they taught children the basics of how machinery and engineering worked.

▼ **Early painted floor train by Bing, 1895**
The first locomotive was invented by George Stephenson in the early 1800s, and his first passenger locomotive ran on the Stockton to Darlington Railway in 1825. The toy train began to appear in the 1870s, and ever since then toy manufacturers all around the world have represented the latest trains and their livery. This tinplate goods train is an early example; these first toy trains are very primitive in style, and very toy-like. Later they became more realistic, and more to scale.

▲ Leipzig station by Märklin, 1925

Considered by many collectors as the king of toy manufacturers, Märklin (est. in Germany 1859) has made some of the most valuable tinplate toys in the world. This is their very elaborate Gauge I Leipzig station, which also came with extra walls, sheds, and platforms. (The gauge system determines the distance between a pair of rails, and correspondingly between the wheels on the train.) Märklin made all types of trains and had a very strong export market. Consequently, they are collected all over the world and the company is still going strong today. Recently a Gauge V train, originally made for an American family, sold for £113,750 ($170,625).

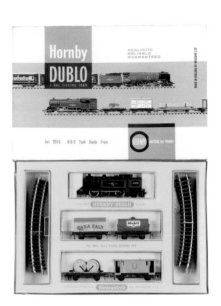

▲ Hornby-Dublo tank goods train, 1962

In response to Märklin's "Trix 00" gauge system, Hornby created their "Dublo" range in 1938. These very well-detailed diecast locomotives were available in electric and clockwork. Although production stopped during World War II it came back post-war, and quickly became the most popular system. Many children were given basic starter sets of either goods or passenger trains and, generally, if you went on to add more to your collection you would start to find the rare items. Hornby/Meccano was taken over by Triang in 1964.

▲ Hornby electric LMS tank locomotive, 1935

In 1901 Frank Hornby invented the Meccano range, and by the end of World War I he had started to make a simple railway system. This proved to be an instant success. At first, the trains were powered by clockwork, but in 1925 he introduced electric motors. This LMS tank locomotive has an electric front light. It was available in all four British liveries – LNER, GWR, and Southern being the rarest. Hornby's most expensive locomotive, selling for 105 shillings at the time, was the LMS *Princess Elizabeth*, created in 1937, which came in its own fitted wooden case.

▲ Hornby "Harry Potter" train, c.2000

The Hornby brand name is still in use today, although under different owners, and in China too. The J.K. Rowling *Harry Potter* stories and subsequent films provide a perfect opportunity to appeal to the mass-market audience with this licenced merchandise. Powered by the standard Hornby train controller and transformer, the set includes a "Hogsmead" station halt, platform, and other accessories. A toy such as this has dual appeal, to both model-train enthusiasts and fans of Harry Potter.

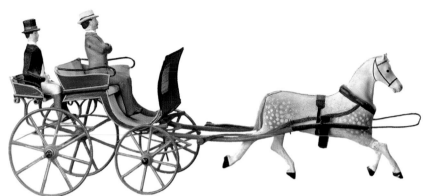

◄ **Horse-drawn carriage by Lutz, *c*.1890**
Before motorized transport the world depended on
the horse. Many early toy companies represented
various horse-drawn carriages. This fine example
of a Viennese caleche is made by the early German
toy company, Lutz. It has a carved wooden dappled
horse and a composition passenger. Often horse-
drawn vehicles were made of wood, or cast-iron
in the USA. Toys of this period rarely survive,
particularly in such excellent condition.

➤ **Clockwork "Coupe Automobile" by Bing, 1909**
Bing, founded in 1879, was one of the biggest makers of tinplate cars in the
early 20th century. Like many tinplate toy companies, Bing made all conceivable
kinds of vehicle, and when cars began to take over the streets Bing was quick
to start manufacturing toy versions. Märklin already had the top end of the
market sewn up so Bing concentrated on toys for lower budgets. It produced
cheap-quality cars for less wealthy children, but also mid-range toys for the
middle classes. This was proof that the world was getting richer, and more
parents could afford to buy manufactured toys. After World War I Meccano
and other British toy manufacturers also began to produce tinplate vehicles.

▼ **British-outline military combination
by Masudaya, mid-1930s**
The first toy motorcycle was manufactured in 1910,
probably by Günthermann in Germany. Many early
models looked simply like pedal bicycles with motors
strapped on, and were often chain-driven. This
military motorcycle, in lithographed tinplate, is a
Japanese copy of an original Tipp & Co toy, mirroring
the trend in Japan in the 1930s for copying early
German toys. There are many collectors of tinplate
toy motorcycles and the earlier models are the
scarcest. Beware of modern reproductions.

▲ **Record car by Betal, *c*.1935**
As the motor car became increasingly popular the record for land speed
became an obsession for the wealthy few. The British were pioneers in this
field, with Malcolm Campbell's Bluebird in the 1930s smashing the record,
and the Raylton Record car in the 1940s, driven by John Cobb (although sadly
he failed to break the attempted 400mph barrier on Bonneville Salt Flats,
Utah). These two cars were soon manufactured by a number of toy companies,
including Britains in the UK and Günthermann of Germany, among others.
These cars really captured small boys' imaginations and sense of adventure,
and the drivers of the real-life cars became national heroes.

◄ Meccano clockwork No. 1 constructor car, 1934

This company, which came under the Hornby umbrella, was by far the biggest manufacturer of toys in the UK in the early 20th century. Not only did Frank Hornby have huge success with his construction sets and Hornby trains, he also made a wide range of other products under the Meccano label, including tinplate cars, boats, and aeroplanes. These were available as construction and non-construction toys, the latter being the more collectable. The motor car constructor set pictured left has its original box, into which each individual piece would have been strung. Later Hornby went on to develop the highly successful Dinky Toy range. Perhaps one of his most unusual toys was a tinplate clockwork duck, which was often lost on boating ponds and so is rare today.

► Military vehicle by Hausser, 1935

During the two World Wars many toy factories were converted to manufacturing items essential for the war effort. However, during the build up to hostilities many new ranges with a military flavour were added and even once war started a few manufacturers were allowed to continue making propaganda toys. These include the toy soldier companies Elastolin and Lineol, who even produced little toy Hitlers. Immediately after the war the buying public turned their back on military toys, and demand was high for more peaceful playthings.

◄ Elektro-construction fire engine by Schuco, c.1958

The German company Schreyer & Co was founded by Heinrich Müller and Heinrich Schreyer in 1912 in Nuremberg, and originally was best-known for its novelty teddy bears and little clockwork figures. After World War I Schreyer left the company but Müller found a new partner in Adolf Kahn and they relaunched the company in 1921 under the new name Schuco. During the 1950 and '60s Schuco's clockwork toy vehicles came into their own. They are often very good-quality tinplate toys, with an ingenious mechanism. Patented designs such as whistle control, or a mechanism to stop the car from falling off the tabletop, made them unique.

► Märklin hot-air picket launch, c.1929

Some of the most costly toys have been early tinplate boats. All the large manufacturers produced them, but the most sought-after were those by Märklin. The great passenger liners of the first half of the 20th century were very popular, but many types of battleships, river craft, and pleasure boats were also created. Initially they were all hand painted, but later the manufacturers began to use lithographed tinplate. Most tinplate boats, and also aircraft, were clockwork toys. The most commonly found of the aircraft toys is the zeppelin, which was made by many different Germany companies.

Novelty

Every conceivable animal, human, and fantasy character has at sometime entertained small children in the form of a novelty toy. Zoos, circuses, and fairgrounds provided inspiration for early toymakers, and in later years toys were also influenced by characters that children would have read about in books and comics, heard on the radio, and seen on film and TV. In the post-war period space and sci-fi were a major impetus for novelty toys. Among the most collectable examples today are robots. The word "robot" derives from the Czech word *robota*, meaning forced labour, and was first used to describe the mechanical creatures that appeared in Karel Capek's 1921 play R.U.R. (*Rossum's Universal Robots*). Robots and space toys really took off in the 1950s and '60s, many made in Japan for the Western market. Japan and the Far East continue to be major producers of toys and the principal instigators of more recent novelty crazes, from Beyblades, to Pokemon Cards, to Hello Kitty products. Toys like these are produced in their millions (between 1998 and 1999 12 million Furbies – cuddly, interactive robotic creatures – sold around the globe); they are unlikely to gain value.

This Japanese celluloid circus elephant, heralding the arrival of the big top, was made by Kuramochi in the 1930s.

> **Transformers "Deception Thrust" robot, 1985**
Launched by Hasbro, USA, in 1984, Transformers were one of the "must-have" toys of the decade. They could be converted from robots into vehicles, providing two toys in one. An animated TV series and a Marvel comic book were launched at the same time to boost demand. Such aggressive marketing tactics worked, as the toys were a huge success and are now collected by the adults who originally played with them as children, many of whom attend the Transformers conventions in the UK and USA.

▲ **"Lo & Li" by Lehmann, c.1924**
Founded in 1881, and still going strong today, this German company was soon hailed as one of the greatest lithographed tinplate novelty toy makers. "Lo & Li" is one of the rarest and most complex toys produced by Lehmann; it features a dancing gent dressed in top hat and tails, accompanied by a clown playing an accordion – all brightly lithographed and with its original colour-illustrated box. This toy in excellent condition, and with its box, can make up to £5,000 ($7,500) at auction.

◄ **"Robot Lilliput" by K.T., Japan, 1930s**
One of the most collectable range of toys from the post-war era is robots and space toys, generally manufactured in Japan. They took inspiration from the space race: the first Sputnik orbited the world in 1957; the moon-landing also captivated many children; and Hollywood films started to feature robots and space travel, such as *The Forbidden Planet*, which featured Robbie the Robot. This "Robot Lilliput" was an early predecessor of those toys by a forward-thinking manufacturer, known only as K.T.. It is now worth around £1,000 ($1,500).

Model Figures & Diecast

The two best-known manufacturers in these fields are both British: Dinky for its diecast toys and Britains for its lead soldiers. Although toy soldiers had been around for much longer, in 1893 William Britain revolutionized the toy soldier industry by making hollow-cast soldiers. Rather than the more expensive solid-cast lead soldiers, he discovered that if you spun a small amount of lead in a mould it would stick to the edges. This meant he could manufacture the figures much cheaper, and toy soldiers became affordable for all. They quickly took off, and are still being made to this day. Every single regiment, from all nationalities, was manufactured. The world record price for a single Britains figure is £3,080 ($4,620). Diecast vehicles were cheap to produce as they used just one mould, as opposed to the many parts required to produce a tin toy. Dinky Toys was the leader in this field: established in 1931 to run alongside Hornby's famous "O" gauge train series, Dinky soon became popular in its own right and dominated the world of toys for the next 50 years. Other popular names include Corgi (est. 1956), famous for its film and tv-related toys, and Matchbox, which provided more affordable toys that can still be collectable in today's market .

Figure of King George VI by Britains, to commemorate his visit to South Africa in 1947. Very rare (only two are known to exist), one sold for £1,880 ($2,820) in 1989.

▲ German solid-cast lead soldiers, c.1900
The earliest toy soldiers were made of solid lead and started life as two-dimensional small figures known as "flats". Companies such as Heyde in the late-19th century had the most success with them. The bodies were generally one casting, and the arms, head, and accessories were soldered on later. Not only did they represent all nationalities, they also represented historical and ethnic figures. The larger, more exotic, and complete the set of figures, the higher the value will be. As with all lead items, collectors do not like soldiers with "lead rot" – a white powdery oxidization that can form on the surface.

▼ Model farm by Britains, 1930s
Manufacturers of toy soldiers have always looked for ways to expand their production to appeal to a wide range of tastes. After World War I Britains introduced a lot of non-military figures. Its "Home Farm" series was perhaps the most popular, but it also issued a zoo series, a circus, and a miniature garden where individual plants could be slotted into flower beds. The company also produced most English football teams, racing horses with jockeys in famous colours, and, later, famous characters such as "Mickey Mouse" and his friends. Other small UK and German manufacturers made similar figures.

◄ Pre-war Dinky "Manchester Guardian" van, 1934–35

The popularity of Hornby trains encouraged the company to create all kinds of accessories, including six miniature vehicles called "Modelled Miniatures" in 1934. These proved so popular that Hornby produced more varieties and the Dinky toy was born. The most popular Dinky toys of the pre-war years in today's market are the 28 and 280 "Delivery Van" series. One van, advertising the suburban London department store Bentalls, currently holds the world record for the most expensive at £12,650 ($18,975). The very earliest vehicles were made of lead but most pre-war diecast vehicles suffer from metal fatigue, where small cracks and pits develop in the metal. This can seriously affect value. This van is the rarest first-type model, with a tinplate radiator, two-piece lead body, and coloured solid wheel.

➤ Dinky 234 Ferrari racing car, c.1954–60

The post-war years were a boom time for Dinky. Its diecasts were far more affordable than the larger tinplate toys and the range grew rapidly – at one stage a new model came out every week. After 1953 all were issued with individual boxes. Dinky toys of this period need to be in very good, boxed condition in order to get a high price today. But what collectors are really looking for is colour variations. Most vehicles came in two or three standard colours, but for various reasons a different colour was used on a particular day, and such a toy can often be worth 4 to 10 times as much. For instance an excellent condition 153 Standard Vanguard from the late 1950s is worth £100–150 ($150–225) in mid blue or fawn, but in maroon it would be worth £800 ($1,200). Dinky produced 14 different racing cars in this period including Alfa-Romeos, Vanwalls, and Lotus.

▼ Lesney Matchbox set of cars, 1968

Lesney was the parent company responsible for making Matchbox and Models of Yesterday (M.O.Y.). The M.O.Y range was introduced in 1956; they are models of old-fashioned vintage vehicles, often collected by adults as well as children so they have a high survival rate in mint boxed condition. The Matchbox range was much more successful and affordable and compares with those of Dinky and Corgi. This Matchbox G-4 "Race'n Rally" gift set was a clever marketing idea to sell more vehicles.

▲ James Bond Aston Martin by Corgi, 1965

The Mettoy company invented the Corgi Toy in the 1950s, in direct competition to Dinky. They came into their own by offering a number of unique features, such as plastic windows (Dinky had open ones), opening doors, spring suspension, and "jewelled" headlights. This focus on moving parts made Corgi the obvious choice to produce James Bond's gadget-packed Aston Martin D.B.5, which won "Toy of the Year" in 1965. This is the rarest version, in silver with vac-formed bubble packaging and a rotating number plate.

TV & Film-Related Toys

Film and TV have had an increasingly important influence on children's toys. Charlie Chaplin and Felix the cat were among the first great movie stars to be turned into merchandise, and the advent of Mickey Mouse in 1928 saw the launch of the Disney phenomenon. Television entered the family home after World War II, bringing children's programmes and the first generation of TV toys, ranging from Muffin the Mule puppets to Davy Crocket's furry hat. Space and sci-fi subjects, popularized by comics, were a favourite on both sides of the Atlantic in the 1960s, and children's programmes from Dr Who, to Thunderbirds, to Batman all launched successful ranges of toys, which are avidly collected today. The Star Wars trilogy, launched in 1977, has sold 300 million toys around the world, and is now perhaps the most popular sci-fi category, with adult enthusiasts. The market changed in the 1980s: programmes traditionally had inspired products but now the merchandise inspired programmes. Most of the major toy crazes since the 1980s – Transformers, My Little Pony, Power Rangers, Pokemon – have been inseparably linked with and promoted by television.

This Disney tinplate bucket is an early example of the mass-market merchandising of film characters now used by so many toy makers.

◄ **Talking Dalek by Palitoy, 1970s**
Several toy versions of Dr Who's arch enemy have been made, including this Palitoy one, which speaks several appropriate phrases. In this field, more perhaps than any other, the condition of the box or packaging can be as crucial to value as the condition of the toy itself. Boxes can have a value in their own right and have been known to be faked, since the presence of a box can double the value of a toy. Modern blister packs have to be torn apart to get at the toy inside so pieces that are mint and packaged in this medium command a premium.

▲ *Star Wars* **"Luke Skywalker" figure, c.1980**
The phenomenon that is the *Star Wars* franchise is perhaps one of the most collected range of toys made by a recent manufacturer. Millions were made and there are thousands of collectors all over the world. Generally, if the toys are in unboxed, played-with condition they make only a few pounds, but some American mint boxed Kenner examples have sold for up to £1,000 ($1,500) each. A grandmother who bought two sets of 20 *Star Wars* figures in 1977 and kept the spares in case any got lost or broken has now auctioned her set for £10,100 ($15,150)!

► *Thunderbirds* **"Lady Penelope" car, c.1971**
The most collectable range of toys to be linked to a television series are those inspired by Gerry Anderson's *Thunderbirds*. This cult programme from the 1960s keeps on coming back to appeal to new audiences. Dinky made a range of *Thunderbirds* vehicles. This luminous pink version of Lady Penelope's car, FAB 1, is much rarer than the standard matt-pink one. Other Gerry Anderson shows included *Captain Scarlet* and *Space 1999*, both of which had famous vehicles that were made into toys. A whole new range was made when *Thunderbirds* was re-released in the 1990s, but this didn't damage the value of the original '60s toys.

TREEN

Lignum vitae, from the tropics, is one of the hardest and heaviest of woods, impenetrable to liquids; its name, "wood of life", derives from supposed medicinal qualities.

Treen, meaning literally "of the tree", is the name given to small domestic articles made from wood. Size matters, and larger pieces such as furniture are excluded from this category. Typical examples of treen include objects associated with food and drink (such as mugs, bowls, and butter moulds), smoking paraphernalia (snuff boxes and carved pipes) and textile-related treen, from bobbins to knitting sheaths. While much treen is practical some is purely decorative: another popular collecting area is wooden love tokens, such as Welsh love spoons. Decoration varies from simple turning, which allows the tactile beauty of the wood to shine through, to elaborate carving. Typically treen is handmade, often by anonymous country craftsmen. The development of transport in the 19th century also stimulated the production of mass-produced wooden items for the burgeoning tourist market, such as Tunbridge ware, with its mosaic patterns, and Mauchline ware decorated with transfer-prints.

▼ Mahogany bookholder, c.1900

While most treen is made entirely out of wood, some items make use of other materials, while still being considered as treen. This mahogany bookholder has been embellished with brass and ivory and is a good example of how the decorative appeal of items can be enhanced. It combines a practical function with aesthetic appeal.

▼ Carved wooden flying fish from Pitcairn Island, c.1930

Pitcairn Island is famous for being inhabited by descendants of the mutineers from *HMS Bounty* who captured the ship in 1789. Carvings from the local hardwoods, which are still made today, were first produced in the 1820s, but this example of a flying fish dates from the 1930s. The '30s was a profitable time for the island, as ocean liners had begun to call regularly at Pitcairn on the run from New Zealand to the Americas.

▲ Tunbridge ware match box, c.1900

Tunbridge ware is a form of mosaic decoration made from sticks of different coloured woods, stuck together in a block with a pattern running through – rather like a stick of rock. This was then sliced into sheets of veneer, one block producing several identical images. Produced by craftsmen from Tunbridge Wells in Kent (and other areas), Tunbridge ware was a popular tourist purchase, resulting in a large number of boxes and other items.

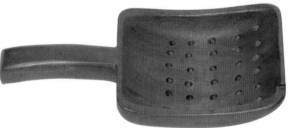

▲ Cream skimmer, c.1900

This cream skimmer is a good example of functional, domestic treen. Skimmers were often made from metal, but wood was a favourite material for use in the dairy. Woods used in the kitchen and for dairying had to be non-absorbent and free from smells. Sycamore and boxwood were favourite choices for butter moulds; elm was often used for ladles and skimmers.

WALKING STICKS

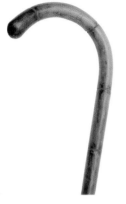

Bamboo-effect walking stick, c.1941; this normally inexpensive stick is worth thousands as it was owned by author Virginia Woolf.

Today walking sticks are perceived predominately as practical aids, but in the Victorian and Edwardian periods they were an essential male fashion accessory. A gentleman needed a minimum of three sticks: a Malacca cane for daytime, an ebonized model for evening, and a stout wooden stick for country walking. Many owned a good deal more, since canes were a popular gift and can often be found with engraved silver presentation plaques. Handles came in innumerable shapes and there were dual-purpose sticks to meet every need: for smokers there were sticks holding lighters or pipes, for drinker's canes with a hidden spirit flask. Cities could be dangerous places; men carried defence sticks concealing swords and even pistols, while doctors' sticks opened up to reveal medical instruments. In 1900 there were some 60 cane shops in the London area alone, but the golden age of the stick came to an end with World War I. Values depend on material, quality, condition, and novelty.

◄ Air cane in original oak case by E.M. Reilly, c.1900
The air cane was a useful walking stick that doubled as an air rifle, and was produced by several manufacturers. This one has a simulated wood finish and detachable horn handle, with air pump and fitting. This is a fine example and comes with its original green baize-lined oak case, which increases its value. Defence sticks tended to be very plain and undecorated, so as not to attract attention.

➤ Bulldog's head ivory stick handle, 19th century
Animals were favourite subjects for decorating walking sticks and dogs made an obvious choice for those going "walkies". Ivory, along with silver, was a popular choice of decorative material and could readily be carved into shape; the more elaborate carvings are miniature works-of-art. Glass eyes were often used in animal heads, though they are missing from this bulldog. Nevertheless, it still has great intrinsic and aesthetic value.

▲ Malacca cane, c.1910
Malacca is a natural cane taken from a species of rattan palm (*Calamus ascipionum*) that grows long, slim, tall stems and is believed to have been imported to Europe from the Far East as far back as the 15th century. It is ideally suited to the manufacture of walking sticks, although it is difficult to carve. This Malacca cane from the early-20th century has a shagreen crook handle with a gilt collar and horn ferrule.

▲ Folk-art walking stick, 19th century
This folk art walking stick is carved as a snake eating a frog, entwined around a thorny branch. While some of the more refined sticks may bear a maker's name, folk-art sticks are generally anonymous. However, this doesn't detract from their aesthetic appeal or collector interest, especially if they are as interesting as this piece, as the anonymity of the maker has no bearing on the quality of the carving.

WATCHES & CLOCKS

Classic elegant 18ct Longines dress watch, c.1958; the 1950s are arguably Longines' most creative and respected period.

The wristwatch evolved naturally from the pocketwatch somewhere around the start of the 20th century. It is difficult to establish the exact date as many makers claim its initial conception; however, it is generally agreed that the wristwatch as we know it today evolved during World War I. Like all other decorative and practical objects the wristwatch has followed all the fashion trends of the 20th century, but it has also relied heavily on technical and mechanical advances. When collecting wristwatches condition, rarity, and brand of manufacturer should remain of utmost importance, as should the quality of the movement. The collecting of clocks (horology) is a vast subject but it can be relatively cheap if you buy predominately from boot (garage) sales and fairs as opposed to dealers and auction houses. The best place to start is the period from 1850 to the 1930s, as at this time there was a boom in clock-making and many different styles emerged, to suit all pockets. Consider the different types of clock and their origins – mantle, wall, French, English, American; some were made to meet a specific need, such as the dial clocks used for precise timekeeping in railway stations. Quality will vary so always buy the best you can afford.

◄ World War I officer's watch, c.1915

This early example of a silver half-hunter manual-wind officer's watch was first used in the trenches of western France. These watches were produced quickly to help the war effort and often the name of the maker is unknown. With obvious aesthetic similarities to pocket watches of the day, this one has a quick release pusher at 7 o'clock to disengage the half-hunter, or shrapnel, cover. Its practicality was soon transferred to watches for other ranks.

◄ Benrus watch, c.1930

Watch designs generally mirror their period, and this rare 14ct gold American Benrus illustrates the transition between Art Nouveau and Art Deco styling, with the organic design on the shoulders and the square, geometric case. Around the late 1920s and early '30s US manufacturers came into their own and produced some very underrated pieces. At that stage design and concept overshadowed movement and mechanical innovation, as these advances were not yet economically achievable, so manufacturers relied heavily on aesthetic beauty.

➤ Eterna Kontiki automatic, c.1950

The technical advantages of a self-winding automatic watch soon became apparent and their practicality quickly found an adventurous outlet. This 1950s Eterna Super Kontiki diver's watch was worn by the explorer Thor Heyerdal when he travelled across the Pacific Ocean as it was capable of enduring extreme temperatures. With its rotating diver's bezel and quick-set date it has become a platform for the modern sports watch. This model is not an original because it has a gold commerative plaque showing the Kontiki craft on the case back, but it is still of interest.

➤ "Spaceman", c.1974

The design extremes of the 1970s are popular today and are often imitated with cheap quartz movements; certain models from the original era are so undervalued that they can be found cheaper than the modern versions. The "Spaceman", created by André Le Marquand and inspired by the helmets of the early astronauts, sold nearly 150,000 in various versions, but it is unclear how many were produced of each model. This bracelet model is certainly a future collectable.

◄ Weight-driven regulator, c.1860

The weight-driven regulator is also often known as a Vienna regulator. This example is a single-weight version and a timepiece only, but it is possible to find two-weight versions that strike, and three-weight versions that strike and chime (a *grand sonnier*). Weight-driven regulators are one of the most sought-after types of clock as they keep very good time in most cases; the prices vary greatly but generally the thinner the case the higher the price.

▲ American mantle clock, c.1850

This example by Ansonia Clock Co is typical of the mantle clocks manufactured in the USA in the 1850s. They are mostly timepieces or strikers – chimers are very rare. The movements in these clocks were mass-produced and shared by different companies, who simply added their own names and logos. They were often known as "gingerbread clocks" because of their shape. The level of decoration on the glass panel or "tablet" determines the value of the clock.

➤ American wall regulator, late 19th century

Made by the British United Clock Co in the USA, this is a drop-dial version of a wall regulator. The glass at the bottom of the clock usually has the word "regulator" on it, but this one has been altered at some time. Wall regulators were made from the 1860s through to the 1900s. Businesses would often put their names or some kind of advertising onto the clock face, which, depending on the "ad" in question, tends to increase the value.

▲ Dial clock, 1950s

This type of clock is known as a dial, schoolroom, or station clock. There are two main movements to consider: the less expensive deadbeat, or the more desirable fusee. A premium is paid by collectors if the clock is from a railway or any other government establishment, such as the military. In all cases a written provenance for the clock will pay a much higher dividend.

▲ "Napoleon hat" clock, 1930s

Commonly known as the "Napoleon hat" clock, this is possibly the easiest style to come by and the cheapest to start with. It is the type of clock that most people remember from their grandparents' house as a child, and seems to be the first clock in most collections. It comes in three different types: timepiece (one key hole); striker (two holes); and chimer (three holes); the higher the number of holes the higher the value of the clock. Most of these clocks are by either English or German manufacturers.

WRITING ACCESSORIES

Writing became the people's practice in the 19th century when mass-production brought the price of writing accessories to within their reach. Writing demanded time to prepare and assemble items before beginning, and the variety of quills, nibs, holders, ink, paper, seals, wax, tapers, rulers, pencils, and blotters has created a rich area for collectors. By the 1850s the invention of steel nibs, patented mechanical pencils, the "Penny Post", green glass for small inkbottles, blotting paper, and cheap cedar pencils had made makers such as Mordan, Mitchell, Gillott, Stephens, and Perry household names. The 20th century was the century of the fountain pen, pencil, and ball pen. New materials, technology, and mass-marketing all influenced the wonderful designs of the "golden age", from 1925 to '35, and fountain pens from that time, such as "Patricians", "Big Reds", "Dorics", "Vacumatics", and "Namikis", are still the most desirable today. In the 1940s British brands such as Conway Stewart, Swan, Wyvern, and Burnham were very popular, but by the mid '50s the "inexpensive" ball-pointed pen had signalled their demise. The mystique of writing a journal, or diary, with all the necessary paraphernalia had ended, but the accessories are a wonderful reminder to today's society of the era before "emails" and "texting".

Ink often dried leaving a thick deposit, which clogged steel nibs. From c.1830, decorative cleaning brush wipes such as this elephant were popular desk items.

◄ Seal by Mordan, c.1865

There was little legal or commercial heritage attached to the majority of Victorian seals. Most were personal and used as an affectation when sending a letter. Older notary seals often have crude wooden handles, but usually exquisite carved matrices. Hatched seals were used for stickers that sealed documents. Mineral handles, such as citrine, porcelain, and carved ivory, particularly in the form of clasped hands, are most desirable. Small seals, like the one illustrated, were probably originally part of a set with a pen, pencil, and paper slitter.

► Dip pens and pen rack, 1870–1930

Dip pens were the most common writing tool from about 1840 to 1950. Most pupils learned to write with a wooden dip pen, blue-steel ferrule, and steel nib, whereas the wealthier upper classes used elaborate dip pens in gold, silver, and ivory. Quills traditionally had been "parked" in inkwell holes but this damaged steel nibs, so as these nibs gained popularity the pen rack was devised. "Stand alone" cast iron was the most common kind, but they were also often combined with inkwells or pen wipes.

▲ Square glass inkwell, 1900

Inkwells, like all desk furniture, were made in a wide range of designs and materials. This type of glass cube was often a component of a desk stand or writing box, as opposed to being a stand-alone item. The most simple wells were the pot school inkwells; the most ornate were works-of-art, usually made in silver or ceramic. The styles normally reflect the period in which they were made. Mechanical and portable inkwells have their own niche collecting area.

▼ Selection of metal pencils

Graphite was superseded at the end of the 18th century by wood-encased "lead" pencils, called cedars. Mechanical pencils were only practical after small-diameter leads of sufficient strength were invented by Conte in 1790. From top to bottom: the round-barrelled Yard-O-Led "Aristocrat" was made in the late 1940s; the silver porte crayon with a perpetual calendar, made by John Betteridge in 1817, held a solid graphite stick; the silver cedar holder by Mordan, c.1840, contained a whole pencil.

▲ Sheaffer "Radite" and "Abalone" pens, 1920s–'30s

Sheaffer, together with Parker and Waterman, was one of the three major US pen makers of the 20th century. These two shapes illustrate perfectly the transition from the 1920s flat-top era (see the "Radite" above bottom) to the 1930s streamlined style (as shown in the "Abalone" above top). Radite was the first cellulose material ever used for fountain pens. The later 1930s cigar-shaped pen, in black plastic with bits of abalone, is a piston-fill pen.

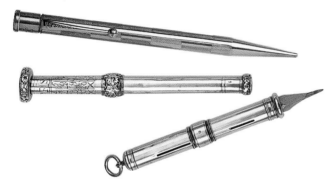

➤ Parker "51" pen, 1953

First introduced in 1941, the Parker "51" is one of the most successful pens ever made – over 40 million were produced before it was discontinued in 1972. The early models used the "vacumatic" filling system; this was changed in 1947 to the more popular streamlined shape with an "aerometric" filler. The most common colours are grey, black, burgundy, and blue, with stainless steel caps. The rarer and more valuable colours are Nassau green, cocoa, and mustard, and the rare caps are smooth silver, gold, and the Empire State pattern.

▲ Novelty Beatles ball pens, German, 1963

Cheap souvenirs of a place (such as Blackpool Tower), an event (the 1953 Coronation), or a current interest, like The Beatles in the '60s, are normally of little value. However, this complete merchandising pack would appeal to collectors of both Beatles memorabilia and ball pens. Examples of early novelty pens from the 1940s can be quite valuable, even though they have long ceased to function. Modern versions are made by the million.

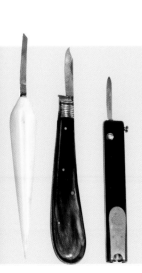

Quill knives/cutters

Speciality pen knives were prized possessions of scribes and clerks; the razor-sharp blade was used solely for cutting or sharpening quills.

Quills have been used for the last 1,400 years at least, but, perhaps surprisingly, pre-cut quills were still on regular sale in the 20th century. However, the majority of quills available to collectors are those used in the 19th century, which were self-cut using specially made quill knives. Single-edged non-folding blades were normally carried in a morocco case for safety. The blade shape was short and narrow, compared to the larger, broader blades of utility desk knives. Most 19th-century shafts were made of hardwood or ivory, with a spigot shape as illustrated left. Folding knives for cutting quills had precise, small blades, often with large handles and horn scales. The quill machine, c.1830, even cut the nib shape and slit with a "cigar-cutter-like action". These quill cutters are in great demand today by calligraphers, as well as those collecting general writing accessories.

The Scribes' Tools

Directory of Useful Addresses

Auction Houses

Bertoia Auctions
2141 DeMarco Drive
Vineland, NJ 08360
USA
Tel: +1 856 692 1881
www.bertoiaauctions.com
(Toys and games)

Bonhams
101 New Bond Street
London W1S 1SR
UK
Tel: +44 (0)20 7629 6602
www.bonhams.com

Bonhams & Butterfields
220 San Bruno Avenue
San Francisco, CA 94103
USA
Tel: +1 415 861 7500
www.butterfields.com

Christie's New York
20 Rockefeller Plaza
New York, NY 10020
USA
Tel: +1 212 636 2000
www.christies.com

Christie's South Kensington
85 Old Brompton Road
South Kensington
London SW7 3LD
UK
Tel: +44 (0)20 7930 6074
www.christies.com

Graham Budd Auctions Ltd
PO Box 47519
London N14 6XD
UK
Tel: +44 (0)20 8366 2525
Email gb@grahambuddauctions.co.uk
(Specializing in sports memorabilia)

James D. Julia Auctioneers Inc
Route 201, Skowhegan Road
PO Box 830
Fairfield, ME 04937
Tel: +1 207 453 7125
www.juliaauctions.com
(Specialized auctions of toys and doll items)

Onslows
The Coach House
Manor Road
Stourpaine
Dorset DT11 8TQ
UK
Tel: +44 (0)1258 488 838
www.onslows.co.uk
(Posters, ephemera, maritime, and travel)

Sheffield Railwayana Auctions
43 Little Norton Lane
Sheffield S8 8GA
UK
Tel: +44 (0)114 274 5085
www.sheffieldrailwayana.co.uk

Skinner Inc
357 Main Street
Bolton, MA 01740
USA
Tel: +1 978 779 6241
www.skinnerinc.com

Sotheby's
34–35 New Bond Street
London W1A 2AA
UK
Tel: +44 (0)20 7293 5283
www.sothebys.com

Sotheby's New York
1334 York Avenue
New York, NY 10021
USA
Tel: +1 541 312 5682
www.sothebys.com

Sotheby's Sussex
Summers Place
Billingshurst
West Sussex RH14 9AD
UK
Tel: +44 (0)1379 650 306
www.sothebys.com
(Gardening and architectural deptartments)

Van Sabben Poster Auctions
PO Box 2065
1620 EB Hoorn
The Netherlands
Tel: +31 (0)229 268 203
www.vsabbenposterauctions.nl

T. Vennett-Smith
11 Nottingham Road
Gotham
Nottinghamshire NG11 0HE
UK
Tel: +44 (0)1159 830 541
www.vennett-smith.com
(Postcards, cigarette and trade cards, autographs and ephemera, and sporting memorabilia)

Wallis and Wallis
West Street Auction Galleries
Lewes
Sussex BN7 2NJ
UK
Tel: +44 (0)1273 480 208
www.wallisandwallis.co.uk
(Militaria and toys)

Antiques Markets

Alfie's Antique Market
13–25 Church Street
Marylebone
London NW8 8DT
UK
Tel: +44 (0)20 7723 6066
www.alfiesantiques.com

Camden Market
Chalk Farm Road
London NW1 8AH
UK
Tel: +44 (0)20 7485 5511
www.camdenlock.net

The Coffman's Antiques Markets
Jenifer House Commons
Stockbridge Road, Route 7
PO Box 592
Great Barrington, MA 01230
USA
Tel: +1 413 528 9282
www.coffmansantiques.com

Covent Garden Antiques Market
Jubilee Market Hall
Covent Garden
London WC2
UK
Tel: +44 (0)20 7240 7405

Grays Antique Markets
58 Davies Street
Mayfair
London W1K 5LP
UK
Tel: +44 (0)20 7629 7034
www.graysantiques.com

Portobello Market
Portobello Road
London W11
UK
Tel: +44 (0)20 7229 8354
www.portobelloroad.co.uk

Dealers

Advertisements and Packaging
Mike Standen
Ad Age Antique Advertising
UK
Tel: +44 (0)1622 670 595

Aeronautics and Shipping
Peter Boyd-Smith
Cobwebs
78 Old Northam Road
Southampton SO14 0PB
UK
Tel: +44 (0)23 8022 7458
www.cobwebs.uk.com

Amusement and Slot Machines
Steve Hunt
Antique Amusement Co
Mill Lane
Swaffham Bulbeck, Cambridge CB5 0NF
UK
Tel: +44 (0)1223 813 041
www.aamag.co.uk

Books
Stephen Poole
Biblion Mayfair
1–7 Davies Mews
London W1K 5AB
UK
Tel: +44 (0)20 7629 1374
www.biblionmayfair.co.uk

Bottles and Breweriana
Alan Blakeman
BBR
Elsecar Heritage Centre
Nr Barnsley
South Yorkshire S74 8AA
UK
Tel: +44 (0)1226 745 156
www.bbrauctions.co.uk

Clocks
Kevin Monckton
Tickers
37 Old Northam Road
Northam, Southampton SO14 0PD
UK
Tel: +44 (0)23 8023 4431

Comics and Annuals
Malcolm Phillips
Comic Book Postal Auctions
40–42 Osnaburgh Street
London NW1 3ND
UK
Tel: +44 (0)20 7424 0007
www.compalcomics.com

Commemorative Ware
Andrew Hilton
Special Auction Services
Kennetholme
Midgham
Reading, Berkshire RG7 5UX
UK
Tel: +44 (0)1189 712 949
email: commemorative@aol.com

Gramophones and Recorders
Philip Knighton
The Gramophone Man
17b South Street
Wellington, Somerset TA21 8NR
UK
Tel: +44 (0)1823 661 618
email: gramman@msn.com
(Specialist repairs to wireless, gramophones,
and all valve equipment)

Lighting
Jennie Horrocks
Top Banana Antiques Mall
1 New Church Street
Tetbury
Gloucestershire GL8 8DS
UK
Tel: +44 (0)8712 881 102
www.artnouveaulighting.co.uk
(Specialist in Arts and Crafts, Art Nouveau,
and Edwardian lighting)

DIRECTORY OF USEFUL ADDRESSES

Medals
Timothy Millett
PO Box 20851
London SE22 0YN
UK
Tel: +44 (0)20 8693 1111
email: tim@timothymillett.demon.co.uk

Metalware (see also Silver)
Vin Callcut
www.oldcopper.org

Money Collectables
Pam West
British Notes
PO Box 257
Sutton, Surrey SM3 9WW
UK
Tel/Fax: +44 (0)20 8641 3224
www.britishnotes.co.uk

Paperweights
Anne Metcalfe
Sweetbriar Gallery Paperweights Ltd
3 Collinson Court
Frodsham, Cheshire WA6 6PN
UK
Tel: +44 (0)1928 730 064
www.sweetbriar.co.uk

Photographs
Richard Meara
Jubilee Photographica
10 Pierrepont Arcade, Camden Passage
Islington, London N1 8EF
UK
Tel: +44 (0)7860 793 707
email: meara@btconnect.com

Postcards
JHD Smith
International Postcard Market (IPM)
27 High Street
Delabole, Cornwall PL33 9AA
UK
Tel: +44 (0)1840 212 025
www.picturepostcards.co.uk

Vintage Postcards
312 Feather Tree Drive
Clearwater, FL 33765
USA
Tel: +1 727 467 0555
www.vintagepostcards.com

Posters
Alain Bourgouin
Studio 10, The Village
101 Amies Street
London SW11 2JW
UK
Tel: +44 (0)20 7924 2905
email: alain.bourgouin@btconnect.com
(Poster restoration and linen backing, by appt only)

Charles Jeffreys Posters & Graphics
4 Vardens Road
London SW11 1RH
UK
Tel: +44 (0)20 7978 7976
www.cjposters.com
(Original rare Modernist posters)

Radios and Televisions
Steve Harris
On the Air Ltd
The Vintage Technology Centre
The Highway, Hawarden
Nr Chester, Deeside CH5 3DN
UK
Tel: +44 (0)1244 530 300
www.vintageradio.co.uk
(Call for opening times – closed most weekends)

Rock and Pop
Dave Fowell
Collectors Corner
PO Box 8, Congleton
Cheshire CW12 4GD
UK
Tel: +44 (0)1260 270 429
(Dave Fowell is keen to purchase interesting items
of Beatles and pop memorabilia.)

Science and Technology
Charles Tomlinson
UK
Tel: +44 (0)1244 318 395
email: charlestomlinson@tiscali.co.uk

Silver
Daniel Bexfield
26 Burlington Arcade
Mayfair
London W1J 0PU
UK
Tel: +44 (0)20 7491 1720
www.bexfield.co.uk

Telephones
Malcolm Percival
Telephone Lines
304 High Street
Cheltenham
Gloucestershire GL50 3JF
UK
Tel: +44 (0)1242 583 699
www.telephonelines.net

Textiles
Pat Oldman
Echoes
650A Halifax Road
Eastwood
Todmorden, Yorkshire OL14 6DW
UK
Tel: +44 (0)1706 817 505

Toys and Games
Sue Pearson
18 Brighton Square
The Lanes
Brighton BN1 1HD
UK
Tel: +44 (0)1273 329 247
www.sue-pearson.co.uk
(Teddy bears and soft toys)

Dottie Ayers
The Calico Teddy
USA
Tel: +1 410 433 9202
www.calicoteddy.com

Watches
Nick Wiseman
Harpers
2/6 Minster Gates
York YO1 7HL
UK
Tel: +44 (0)1904 632 634
www.vintage-watches.co.uk

Writing Accessories
Jim Marshall
The Pen & Pencil Gallery
Church House
Skelton
Penrith, Cumbria CA11 9TE
UK
Tel: +44 (0)1768 484 300
www.penpencilgallery.com

INDEX

A

Action Comics 56
Adie & Lovekin Ltd *131*
Adnet, Jacques *93*
advertising & packaging **8–10**
advertisements *14, 41, 47, 90, 152, 154*
    figures *9, 10, 17, 29*
    novelty items 8, *10, 29*
    promotional items 28, *29, 143, 165, 195*
    signs 8, *9, 195*
    tins *11, 101*
aeronautica **11**
Ahrens, Charles *13*
Ainsworth *13*
Airfix *10*
Aller Vale pottery *35*
Allwin de Luxe machine *12*
Alstons & Hallam *128*
Altobelli *145*
Amazing Fantasy 57
American Modern tableware *45*
amusement & slot machines **12–13**
Andersen, Hans Christian *22*
anemometers *168*
Ansonia Clock Co. *211*
Arcadian ware *11, 36*
architectural salvage **14–15**
"Arco" lamp *119*
Arden, Elizabeth *167*
Aristocrat Nevada machine *13*
Art Deco
    buttons *30*
    ceramics *28, 37, 38, 39, 42, 42, 43*
    compacts 6, *62*
    corkscrews *63*
    glass *84,* 85, *91, 92, 93*
    jewellery *107, 109*
    metalware *14,* 123, *131*
    posters *153*
Art Nouveau
    buttons *30*
    ceramics 32, 33, *34, 35*
    glass *88, 93*
    jewellery *105*
    lighting *117*
    metalware *14,* 123, *132*
    watches *210*
art pottery 32–3, 34, *35,* 48
Artemide *119*
"Artichoke" lamp *119*
Arts & Crafts movement 32, 33, 83, *117,* 123,
    125, 127

The Artwoods *160*
Arundel Castle 174
ashtrays *94, 96, 195*
Atkinson, James *8*
Attwell, Mabel Lucie *9,* 37, 42
Ault pottery *32*
autographs **16,** *18, 60*
Automatic Sports Company *12*
automobilia **17–18,** *41, 60, 153*
Avedon, Richard *153*
Avery-Hardoll *18*
Avon *167*
Aynsley factory *60*
Ayotte, Rick *99*

B

"Babycham" figure *29*
Baccarat *93, 166*
badges *11, 18, 178*
Bagley's Crystal Glass Co *85,* 89
Baird TVs *188*
Bakelite *55, 107, 147,* 155, *156,*
    167, 186
Baker, Charles *169*
Balenciaga, Christobal *79*
"Bamboo" vase *85*
banknotes *141*
Barbie collectables *70, 101*
bargeware *34*
Barovier, Ercole *95*
baskets & basketware *82, 89, 103*
Bateman, Peter & Anne *128*
Baxter, Geoffrey *86,* 87
beadwork *76, 102, 173, 191*
Beanie Babies *185*
bearskin *134*
The Beano 56
The Beatles collectables *16, 153, 159, 160, 162,*
    164, 165, 213
Beeton, Mrs Isabella *24*
bells *124, 127*
Benham & Co *123*
Benrus watches *210*
Benson, W.A.S. *125, 127*
Berlin transparencies *36*
Berry (W.E.) Ltd *153*
Beswick factory *31,* 40, 42, *44,* 47
Betteridge, John *213*
Bevens, Pamela *50*
Biba *61, 80, 143*
bicycles **19**
Bing *182, 200, 202*

biscuit tins *196*
Blake, Quentin *23*
Blanckensee (S.) & Sons *130*
"Boby" trolley *148*
Boileau, Philip *150*
"Bolle" glassware *96*
Bond, James *21*
"Bonzo" dog *182*
bookends & bookholders *47, 208*
bookmarks *131*
books **20–5,** 56–7, *174, 181*
Boots the Chemist *61*
Borel & Co *11*
bottles & bottle openers 6, **26–7,**
    29, 96
Boucher, Marcel *109*
Bourgeois *167*
bowls
    ceramic *37, 45, 46, 50, 61, 174*
    glass *84, 96*
    metalware *126*
    plastic *148*
    treen *208*
"Bowtie" vases *43*
boxes *129–30, 193, 194*
Bozart Toys *72*
Brannam pottery *32*
Brauer, Otto *97*
breadboards & bins *111, 113*
Brent-Dyer, Elinor *22, 23*
Bretby pottery *32, 33*
breweriana **28–9,** 34, *195*
Brexton *120*
Bristol Evening Post 142
Britains *205*
British United Clock Co *211*
Broadhurst (James) & Sons *51*
Bromley, John *52*
Brown, James *160*
Bru Jeune et Cie *64*
Bryant & May *195*
building blocks *198*
Bungalow footwarmers *27*
"Bunnykins" range *37, 41*
Burleigh Ware *39*
Burmantofts pottery *32*
Burndept crystal set *155*
Bush TVs & radios *156, 188*
Butler, Frank *34*
Butler & Wilson *110*
buttons **30**

C

Caithness Glass 99
calculators *171*
calendars *74*
cameras *62, 147*
cameras lucida *170*
candelabra/candlesticks *87, 93, 124, 126, 132*
caps *134*
Captain America 57
car bumper stickers *60*
Carlton Ware *29, 40, 51, 52*
"Carnival" glass *88*
Carroll, Lewis *22*
Caspari, Van der Wal, Sauberlin & Pfeiffer *153*
Cassandre, A.M. *151*
Casson, Sir Hugh *44*
Castiglioni Brothers *119*
ceramics **31–52** *see also* individual items
Chad Valley *69, 174, 182, 183, 184, 185*
Chance Brothers *86*
Chanel *110, 166*
Chatwin, Bruce *24*
Chevallier, Georges *93*
Chihuly, Dale *84,* 88, *89*
children's books *22–3*
Chiltern 70, *184*
chintz ware *40*
"Chippendale" pattern *87, 89*
Chopper bikes *19*
choppers & slicers *112, 113*
Chopping, Richard *21*
Chřibská factory *91*
Churchill, Winston *25, 59*
cigar & cheroot holders *19, 194*
cigar piercers *194*
cigarette & cigar cases *74, 140, 193, 194*
cigarette cards **53–4,** *139, 176*
Civic *126*
clamps *172*
Clark, Ossie *81*
Clark, S.C.J. *112*
Cliff, Clarice *6, 37*
clothes *see* fashion & clothing
"Cloud" vase *87*
Coalbrookdale Iron Foundry *82, 127*
cocktail collectables **55**
codd bottles *6, 26*
coffee makers *115*
coffee pots & cups *31, 38, 44, 49*
"Coffin" vases *50*
Coker, Ebenezer *132*
Colledge, Glyn *46*

Colombo, Joe *148*
combs *147*
comics & annuals **56–7,** *154*
commemorative items *9,* 52, **58–60,** *121, 122, 127, 132, 149*
compacts & cosmetics *6, 8, 59,* **61–2,** *164, 183*
compasses *171*
Compton Potters Art Guild *83*
Cona percolators *115*
Connell (John) & Co. Ltd *8*
Conran, Sir Terence *44*
cookery books *24*
Cooper, Susie *7, 37, 38*
Coper, Hans *50*
Corgi Toys *206*
corkscrews **63**
Cornishware *43*
Corocraft *108*
Cossor TVs *188*
costume jewellery *104, 107, 108–10*
Cottage ware *40*
Coty *61, 62*
counter-top displays *8, 9, 10*
Crapper & Co. *14*
crested china *11, 36l, 174*
Crisford & Norris *131*
crochetwork *190*
Croker, J. *121*
Crown Devon ware *39, 116*
Crown Ducal ware *38*
"Cubist" pattern *89*
Cuneo, Terence *158*
"Cycladic" form *50*

D

Dadaism *151*
Dahl, Roald 22, *23*
Daily News 143
dairy items *111, 127, 178, 208*
The Dandy 56
dalek toy *207*
Daum factory 93, *94*
Davidson (George) & Co *87,* 89, *92*
Day, Lucienne *192*
de Brunhoff, Jean *22*
de Morgan, William 32, *33*
Dean's Rag Book Co 69, *183*
decanters & carafes *84, 89, 92, 94, 97, 98*
Denby factory 27, *46*
Dennis China Works *52*
Denny, Martin *161*
"Depression" glass *88, 89, 90*
desk sets *125, 212*

Detective Comics 57
Devenport (William) & Co *130*
Dinky Toys 71, *203, 205, 206, 207*
Dior, Christian *79, 110*
dishes
 ceramic *31, 33, 40, 48, 178*
 cheese & butter *40, 178*
 metalware *127, 132*
Disney collectables *47, 183, 187, 207*
Doll & Co. *200*
dolls **64–70,** *199*
dolls' houses & furniture **71–2**
"Dolly Varden House" *71*
door furniture *14*
"Door of Hope" dolls *68*
door porters *15*
Doulton factory *28, 33, 34, 52*
Doyle, Sir Arthur Conan *20*
Dresser, Dr Christopher *32*
Dreyfus, Henry *187*
drinking glasses *55, 87, 91, 92, 93, 97, 98*
"Drunken Bricklayer" vase *86*
Duke & Sons *53*
dust wrappers *20, 21*

E

Eagle 56, *57*
"Eclisse" lamp *119*
Edbar International Corp. *147*
Edison phonographs *100*
Egan, Daniel *123*
egg cups 31, *41, 52*
Eisenberg *108*
Electra *12*
electric fires *15*
Eliot, T.S. *21*
Elliott, Lee *20*
ephemera **73,** *149, 159, 162–3, 174, 177–8, 181*
Ericsson *186, 187*
erotica *55,* **74**
"Escort" bag *102*
Eterna watches *210*
etuis *173*
Evans, William *132*
Excelsior "wash down" toilet *14*

F

fabrics *192*
Fada radios *156*
fairings *36*
fans *28*

Farnell Company 69, *184*
fashion & clothing 11, **75–81**, *154, 165, 178,*
    189, 190
"Felix the Cat" *182*, 207
Fenton Art Glass Co *88*
"Fiesta" range *86*
figures & figurals
    advertising *9, 10, 17, 29*
    animals *36, 42, 47, 48, 63, 96, 181*
    ceramic *9, 36, 42, 47, 48, 52, 58, 59*
    commemoratives *58, 59*
    political *26, 58, 60*
    rock & pop *164*
    sporting themes *177, 181*
fishing collectables *180*
flasks *26, 34*
Fleming, Ian *21*
Florian Ware *33*
flower pots *82, 83*
"Flowers" cigarette cards *54*
food mixers *115*
The Fool *152*
football & rugby collectables *12, 53, 176,*
    177–8
Franck, Kaj *48*
funnels *131*
Fury, Billy *160*
Fuss, Adam *146*

G

G & F Posters *154*
Gallé, Emile *93*
garden collectables **82–3**
garden seats *82*
garden syringes *83*
Gavin, C.M. *174*
Gawthorn, H.G. *151*
Gebrüder Heubach *67, 68*
ginger beer bottles *27*
ginger jars *42*
glamour collectables *53, 55, 74, 150, 194*
glass *30,* **84–99,** *117*
    American *84, 87, 88–90*
    Bohemian *84, 87, 91–2, 117*
    English *84, 85–7*
    French *93–4*
    Scandinavian *84, 97–8*
    vaseline *117*
    Venetian *84, 86, 95–6*
Glyn Ware *46*
Goldblatt, John *146*
Goldsheider factory *42, 43*
golf collectables *24, 39, 179*

Goodfellow, Thomas *132*
gorget *135*
Goss crested china *36*
Governor machine *12*
Graffart, Charles *94*
gramophones & recorders **100–1**
grates *15*
Gray-Stan *85*
Gray wares 37, *38*
Green (T.G.) & Co Ltd *35, 41, 43*
Greene, Graham *21*
greetings cards *73, 149*
Gretsch guitar *164*
"Grillo" phone 186, *187*
grinders *112, 113*
Grödnerthal dolls *64, 65*
Guerlain *167*
Guinness collectables 28, *29, 152*
"Gul" vases *97*
Gunter Wulf *13*
Gustavsberg factory 44, *48*
Gwenda *62*

H

Hallam, Arthur *44*
Halliday, T. *122*
handbags *7,* **102–3**
Hardy Brothers *180*
Hare, Burnham *24*
Harris (William) & Co *170*
Harry Potter trainset *201*
Haskell, Miriam *109*
hat pins *106*
hats & caps *75, 76, 178*
helmets *133–34*
Hemingway, Ernest *20*
Hennell, Robert *128*
Henningsen, Poul *119*
Henshall, Rev Samuel *63*
Hermès *103*
Hilger, Adam *169*
Hinks, James *117*
Hinks (Joseph) Ltd *125*
"Hirondelle Superbe" bicycle *19*
HMV gramophones *100,* 101
Hoffmann, Heinrich *92*
Höglund, Erik *98*
Holmegaard factory *97*
"Homemaker" range *45*
Homepride "Fred" figures *10*
Hoover Constellation *115*
Hornby trains *201,* 203, 206
Horner, Charles 106

Hornsea pottery 44, *51*
Hospodka, Josef *91*
hot water bottles *74*
Hudson Scott & Son *196*
Hummel *47*
"Humpty Dumpty" circus figures *199*
Huntley, Boorne & Stevens *8*

I

ice buckets *55, 148*
Ideal *69*
iittala factory 84, *97, 98*
The Impartial Protestant Mercury 142
ink bottles *27*
inkwells *132, 174, 176, 212*
irons *113*

J

"Jacobean" pattern 87, 89, *92*
Jaeggi *125*
jam pots *48*
jardinières *123*
jars *42, 43, 51, 61*
Jennings, O.D. *12*
Jentsch & Meerz *12*
jewellery **104–10,** *140, 147*
jigsaw puzzles *74, 165, 198*
Jobling, James *84,* 89
Joseff of Hollywood *108*
jugs
    ceramic *28, 34, 35, 39, 43, 45,*
        59, 179
    glass *90*
    metalware *123, 124, 127*
    toby *59*
juicers & squeezers *114, 115*
Jumeau, Pierre *66*
JVC TVs *188*

K

"Kaleidoscope" houses *72*
Kämmer & Reinhardt *67, 68*
    The Kelly Bag *103*
Kenrick, Archibald *113*
Kestner, J.D. *66,* 68
kettles *113, 125, 126*
keyrings *140*
kitchen tools *116*
kitchenware *10, 43, 51, 90,* **111–16,** *125, 126, 208*
kitsch *48, 55, 119*
Koppel, Henning *109*

INDEX

Kosta-Boda factory 98
Kruse, Käthe 69
K.T. toys 204
Kuchler, C.H. 122
Kuramochi 204

L

lace 189, 190
Lalique, René 17, 61, 93, 94, 166
lamps 29, 88, 117, 118, 119, 125, 158
Lane, Kenneth Jay 110
Langford, G.F. 27
lanterns 117
lawn mowers & rollers 82, 83
Le Marquand, André 211
Le Petit Journal 142
Lehmann 204
Lenci dolls 69
Lennon, John 153
Lestourgeon, William & Aaron 130
lighters 195
lighting 29, 88, **117–19**, 125, 158
Lindberg, Stig 48
Lindstrand, Vicke 98
Lines Brothers 71, 198
Linthorpe pottery 32
lithophanes 36
Little Richard 159
"Lo & Li" toy 204
Longines watches 210
Loring & Churchill 171
luggage & travel goods **120**
Lundberg Studios 99
Lusitania 175
Lütken, Per 97
Lutz 202
Luxton, John 87

M

Magistretti, Vico 119
Magnet 56
Maling pottery 32, 39
manicure sets 131
Manufacture Française d'Armes et Cycles 19
map cases 18
Marconiphone radios 155
Märklin 200, 201, 203
Marseille, Armand 67
mascots 17, 101
masks 42
match & vesta containers 130, 194, 195, 208
Matchbox range 206

Mathmos Lights 119
Mayfield, Curtis 161
McGill, Donald 150
Meakin factory 43, 45
Meccano Ltd 71, 203
medals **121–2**, 177, 135–7
Meier 196
memoirs 24, 25
Merrythought 184
metalware **123–8**
"Michelin man" figure 17
"Mickey Mouse" collectables 183, 187, 207
Micronic radios 156
microscopes 168, 169
Midwinter factory 31, 44
Miles, Henry Downes 181
militaria **133–9**
    badges 136
    bonnets 133
    brooches 136
    daggers 137
    drums 137
    watercolour paintings 138
    silhouettes 138
    uniforms 133, 135
milkshake mixers 114
mincers 114
Minifon recorders 100
Minton factory 32, 33
"Miss Piggy" 185
Mister Ernest Handbags 103
Mocha Ware 28, 35
Modernism 151, 152, 153
money collectables 9, 16, **140–1**, 199
moneyboxes 9, 141, 199
Monsieur Bibendum (Michelin) 17
Moorcroft, William 33
Mordan (S.) & Co 212, 213
Morphy Richards 116
Moser Glass 84, 91
motoring collectables **17–18**
motto ware 35
moulds 111, 112
mugs 49, 59, 157
Murray, Keith 37, 38
mustard pots 132
Myott, Son & Co 43

N

Nagra III recorders 101
name plates 158, 175
napkin rings 123
"Nasturtium" seat 82

Nathan & Hayes 130
needlecases 173
needlework see sewing tools; textiles
needlework boxes 173
Negretti & Zambra 168
newspapers & magazines **142–3**, 159
Noah's Arks 197
novelty items
    advertising & promotional 8, 10, 29
    bottles 26, 27
    cameras 62, 147
    ceramics 39, 41, 42, 47, 52, 60, 114
    compacts & cosmetics 62, 183
    corkscrews 63
    handbags 103
    jewellery 108
    scent bottles 167
    smoking-related 19, 193
    teapots 41, 52, 60
    telephones 187
    tins 8, 10
    toys 204
number plates 18, 158
nursery ware 40, 41, 42
Nymolle factory 47, 48

O

oil cans 17
"Old English" paperweights 99
"one-arm bandits" 12, 13
Oor Wullie 57
Op Art 49, 51, 192
"Orkidea" vase 98
Orrefors factory 97
Orwell, George 21
Osiris Visions 163
Oxenbury, Helen 22
Oz magazine 143

P

"Paddington Bear" 185
Paisley shawls 189
Palda, Karel 92
pantographs 170
Panton, Verner 192
paperweights 99, 125
Paris Match 142
Parker pens 213
Pedigree 70, 184
Pelham puppets 196
pencils 213
PenDelphin 47

pens & penwipers *212, 213*
"People" decanter *98*
Perthshire Paperweights *99*
petrol pumps *18*
Peynet, Raymond *47*
Philadelphia Watch Company *175*
Phipps, Thomas *129*
phonecards *186*
photographs *16, 18, 60,* **144–6***, 149, 150, 163, 180*
picnic hampers *120*
pictures & picture frames *132, 174, 191*
pin-cushions/wheels *131, 172*
Pingo, L. *122*
pipes *193*
plastics *7, 30, 70, 102, 104, 108,* **147–9***, 156*
    see also Bakelite
plates
    ceramic *44, 45, 47, 51, 52, 58, 60, 181*
    glass *90*
playing cards *74*
poison bottles *26, 27*
political collectables *26, 52, 58, 59, 60*
Pollock, Thomas *199*
pontilled hamilton bottles *26*
Poole pottery *44, 46, 50*
Pop Art *49, 51, 103, 152*
Portmeirion Potteries Ltd *49*
postcards *73, 74, 139, 141,* **149–50**
posters *11, 19, 73, 139,* **151–4***, 158, 162, 163*
pot lids *8, 58*
Potter, Beatrix *22, 47*
pourers *29*
Powell, Barnaby *87*
Powell, James of Whitefriars *117*
Poynter Products *74*
Prestige Sky Line utensils *116*
"Princess" compact *62*
programmes *73, 162, 177, 181*
psychedelia *49, 50, 103, 152, 153, 162, 163*
Pucci, Emilio *103*
"Puffs" compact *61*
puppets *184, 196*
PVC *148*
Pye radios *156*
Pyrex *90*

Q

Quant, Mary *62, 80*
Queen Mary 174, 175
quill knives/cutters *212*
quilts *190*

R

Rabanne, Paco *80*
Rackham, Arthur *22*
Radford Handcraft Pottery *43*
radiators *15*
radios **155–6**
railwayana *151,* **157–8**
Raleigh cycles *19*
Ramsdell, F.W. *19*
Ravilious, Eric *37, 59*
RCA radios *155*
records & CDs *159, 160–1*
Reilly, E.M. *209*
revolvers *138*
Rhead, Charlotte *37, 38, 39*
Ridgways factory *45*
Riedel, Josef *92*
Rival MFG Co *115*
Robertson's "Golly" figure *10*
Robinson, Edward *129*
Robor Ltd *72*
"Robot Lilliput" *204*
rock & pop collectables *151, 152, 153,* **159–65**
rocking horses *198*
Roddy dolls *70*
Rorstrand factory *48*
Rossillon, Marius *17*
Rothermel *147*
Rowling, J.K. *20, 22, 23*
Royal Berlin factory *36*
Royal Doulton factory *52*
Royal Winton factory *40*
Royal Yacht Britannia 175
Royal Yachts (Gavin) *174*
royalty collectables *58, 59, 60, 175*
Rye pottery *44, 46*

S

Sadler (J.) & Sons Ltd *41*
St Amand factory *181*
Salazar, Daniel *99*
Salinger, J.D. *20*
Salmon & Gluckstein *53*
samplers *189*
Sarpaneva, Timo *96, 98*
Sasha dolls *70*
saucepans *125*
Scammell, Joseph *131*
Scandinavian ceramics *44, 48*
scent bottles **166–7**
Schiaparelli, Elsa *109, 167*
Schlevogt, Curt *92*

Schönhut *199*
Schuco *183, 203*
science & technology collectables **168–71**
scissors *173*
Scmalcalder, Charles Augustus *171*
seals & seal boxes *130, 212*
Secessionist Ware *33*
Seeney, Enid *45*
Sellheim, Gert *153*
sewing tools *131,* **172–3**
The Sex Pistols *161*
sextants *170*
Seymour, A. *123*
S.F.B.J. dolls *67*
Sheaffer pens *213*
Shelley factory *28, 42*
Shipp, Reginald *78*
shipping-related collectables *142, 150,* **174–5**
shoes *78, 80, 81*
shooting machines *12*
signal box instruments *157*
signs *8, 9, 157*
silver *30, 104, 106, 109, 123,* **128–32***, 139*
Simon, Joseph *94*
Simon & Halbig *64, 68*
Simpson, William *129*
Sinclair "Micro TVs" *188*
Sitzendorfer factory *61*
sliderules *169, 170*
soda syphons *55*
Sony Walkmans *101*
"Sooty" and "Sweep" *184*
souvenir ware *9, 11, 36, 128, 173, 174, 175, 195*
Space Invaders games *13*
space travel *154*
Sparklets soda syphons *55*
spectroscopes *169*
spelter figures *139, 177*
"Spirit of Ecstasy" (Rolls-Royce) *17*
Spitting Image teaware *52, 60*
spoons *128*
sporting collectables *24, 39, 53, 154,* **176–81**
Staffordshire pottery *58*
"Star Wars" collectables *7, 207*
Steendrukkerij de Jong & Co *152*
Steiff *182, 183*
Stein, Lea *108*
Stephens (W.) & Son *181*
stereoscopic cards *144*
Steuberville Pottery *45*
Steward, J.H. *168*
stoneware *26, 27, 32, 46*
Stoniers of Liverpool *175*
storage jars & containers *43, 51, 114, 116*

Strachan, Ross 25
Strattons 62
suffragette collectables 58, 149
sugar bowls & shakers 37, 89
Sunbeam Mixmaster 115
Swarovski, Daniel 108, 109
"Swing" vase 88
swords 133, 137
Sykes, Charles 17
SylvaC factory 40, 42
Sylvanian Families house 72

T

"Tabac Basket" 89
Taddy & Co 53
Tagliapietra, Lino 95
Tait, Jessie 31, 44
Taito 13
Take 6 80
tankards 28, 46, 92
taps 14
tea cosies 191
teapots & teaware 6, 34, 40–1, 45, 52, 60, 126
teddy bears & soft toys **182–5**
Telcote Pup mascot 17
telephones **186–7**
telescopes 168
televisions **188**
tennis balls & rackets 176, 180
textiles 54, 59, 150, 165, **189–92**
thimbles & thimbleholders 172
Thomason, Edward 63
"Three Wise Monkeys" 125
"Thunderbirds" collectables 161, 207
tickets 163, 178
Tiffany, Louis C. 88
tiles 15, 33
Time magazine 143
tins 58, 101, 176
    biscuit 8, 9, 10, 59, 196
    sweet 11, 175
Tipp & Co 202, 207
Titanic collectables 174
toasters 116
tobacco & smoking-related collectables 9, 19, 74, 94, 96, 129, 140, 179, **193–5**
tokens 124
Tolkien, J.R.R. 23
Tonks (William) & Co 124
Torquay Pottery 35
totems 158
Toulouse-Lautrec, Henri 151
Townshends 125

toy soldiers 205
toy theatres 199
toys & games **196–207**
    cardboard 72, 174
    clockwork 199, 202
    diecast 205, 206
    lawn mowers 82
    novelty 204
    tinplate 10, 196, 200, 201, 204, 207
    transport 196, 200–3, 206, 207
    wooden 197–8, 199
    see also dolls; dolls' houses; teddy bears
        & soft toys
Transformers toy 204
travel books 24
travel-related collectables 17–18, 41, 60, 142, 150, 151, 157–8, 174–5
trays 10, 125, 159
treen 172, **208**
Trifari 108
"Trimphone" 186, 187
trios 31, 42
trivets 127
Troika pottery 50
true crime books 24, 25
Tudor Toys 71
Tuffin, Sally 52
Tunbridge ware 172, 208
Tupperware 116
Turner, John 129
Tuttell, Thomas 170
TV & film-related collectables 7, 47, 60, 151, 161, 182, 183, 187, 207
Ty 185

U

U2 161
underwear & cases 75, 76, 77, 192

V

vacuum cleaners 115
Val Saint-Lambert factory 94
van de Passe, Simon 130
Vargas, Alberto 74
vases
    ceramic 32–3, 34, 35, 38–9, 40, 43, 44, 48, 50
    glass 85, 86–7, 88, 92, 93, 95, 96–7, 98
vending machines 157
Venini factory 84, 86, 96
Vernon, Barbara 37, 41
Vesseday 154
video games 13

viewers 13
visiting cards 144
Vogue magazine 143
Vuitton, Louis 120

W

Wade Pottery 29, 47
Walker, Edward Craven 119
Walker & Hall 132
walking sticks **209**
"Walking Ware" 51
wall plaques 39, 48, 48
Wallis, Edward 198
Walton, Izaak 24
Warhol, Andy 25, 153
warming devices 27, 74, 147
watch cases & fobs 11, 175
watches & clocks **210–11**
watering cans 83
Webb 82
Weiss, Albert 109
Wellings, Norah 69
Wells Coates radio 155
Weltron audio system 101
Wemyss Ware 31
Westman, Marianne 48
Westwood, Vivienne 81, 110
"What-The-Butler-Saw" viewers 13
whisky collectables 28, 29, 34, 179
White Star Line china 174
Whitefriars factory 86, 87, 117
Whiting & Davis 102
Wiinblad, Bjorn 48
Wilkinson Ltd 59
Wilks, James 128
Willardy 7, 102
Winkle, Kathy 51
Wirkkala, Tapio 96, 98
Witney blankets 165
Woolf, Virginia 20
Worcester Ware 159
worksplates 158
World War collectables 59, 78, 150
Wright, Russel 44, 45, 148
writing accessories 27, 132, **212–13**

Y

Yokoo, Tadanoori 153

Z

Zecchin, Vittorio 96

ACKNOWLEDGMENTS

The publishers would like to thank the following people for their kind permission to reproduce the photographs in the book:

Key

t top; **b** bottom; **c** centre; **l** left; **r** right; **AAC** Antique Amusement Co; **AMcC** Andy McConnell; **B** Bonhams; **C** Christie's Images; **CJ** Charles Jeffreys Posters; **DH** David Huxtable; **OTA** On the Air; **OPG** Octopus Publishing Group Ltd; **PO** Patrick Onslows Auctions; **RS** Robin Saker; **S** Skinner, Auctioneers and Appraisers of Antiques and Fine Art, Boston, MA; **So** Sotheby's; **SRA** Sheffield Railwayana Auctions; **ST** Steve Tanner; **TR** Tim Ridley; **VS** Van Sabben Auctions; **WW** Wallis & Wallis Auctioneers

1 OPG/TR/Boom; **3** OPG/TR/Sparkle Moore; **5** OPG/Bath Antiques Online; **6l** OPG/ST/Alan Blakeman; **6r** OPG/TR/B& B Adams; **6c** OPG/ST/Alan Blakeman; **7l** OPG/ST/J.Rothman; **7r** OPG/Childhood Memories; **8r** OPG/ST/Alan Blakeman; **8t** OPG/M.Pearson/F.Miller; **8cr** BBR; **8b** OPG/Warboys Antiques; **9l** OPG/DH; **9r** OPG/ST/Alan Blakeman; **9tl** OPG/Warboys Antiques; **9tr** Alan Blakeman; **9b** OPG/DH; **10t** OPG/DH; **10c** OPG/Alan Blakeman; **10bl** OPG/TR; **10br** OPG/ST/Flying Duck; **11l** OPG/Malcolm Welch Antiques; **11r** OPG; **11t** OPG/Cobwebs; **11b l** OPG; **11br** OPG; **12l** OPG/AAC; **12r** OPG/AAC; **12t** AAC/AAC; **12b** OPG/AAC; **13tl** OPG/AAC; **13tr** OPG/Saffron Walden Auctions; **13bl** OPG/AAC; **13br** OPG/Williams Amusements Ltd; **14t** OPG/J.R&S.J.Symes; **14c** OPG/Walcot Reclamations; **14bl** OPG/Olliff's Architectural Antiques; **14br** OPG; **15l** OPG/Walcot Reclamations; **15r** OPG/Oliff's Arcitectural Antiques; **15t** OPG; **15b** OPG/Zoom; **16** Fraser's Autographs; **17l** OPG/Robert Brooks; **17r** OPG/Robert Brooks; **17t** OPG/Junktion; **17b** OPG/Robert Brooks; **18tl** OPG/Robert Brooks; **18tr** OPG; **18c** OPG/Robert Brooks; **18bl** OPG/So; **18br** OPG/Malcolm Wells; **19l** B; **19r** OPG/Auto Suggestion; **19t** OPG/Robert Brooks; **19b** B; **20l** OPG/So; **20r** OPG/(c)1927 Harcourt Inc, renewed 1974 by Sonia Orwell, (c)1961 The Estate of Vanessa Bell, courtesy of Henrietta Garnett; **20t** OPG/RS/Biblion; **20b** OPG/RS/Biblion; **21tl** OPG/K.Adlard; **21tr** OPG/RS/Biblion; **21ct** OPG/Woolley & Wallis; **21cb** OPG/I Booth; **21b** OPG/K.Adlard; **22l** OPG/Dominic Winter Book Auctions; **22r** OPG/K. Adlard; **22t** OPG/RS/Biblion; **22b** OPG/RS/Biblion; **23l** OPG/RS/Biblion; **23r** OPG/The Old Children's Bookshelf; **23t** OPG/So; **23b** OPG/Adrian Harrington; **24l** OPG/RS/Biblion; **24r** OPG/RS/Biblion; **24b** OPG/K.Adlard; **24br** OPG/K.Adlard; **25l** OPG/RS/Biblion; **25t** OPG/RS/Biblion; **25cl** OPG/RS/Biblion; **25b** The Andy Warhol Foundation for The Visual Arts Inc; **26l** OPG/ST/Alan Blakeman; **26t** OPG/Quiet Woman Antiques Co; **26cl** OPG/ST/Alan Blakeman; **26cr** OPG/Bounty Antiques Co; **26b** OPG/ST/Alan Blakeman; **27** OPG/ST/Alan Blakeman; **28t** OPG/Wenderton Antiques; **28c** OPG/BBR; **28bl** OPG; **28br** OPG/DH; **29tl** OPG/ST/C.Sykes Antiques; **29cl** OPG/ST/C.Sykes

Antiques; **29tcr** OPG/ST/Alan Blakeman; **29tr** OPG/DH; **29bl** OPG/Medway Auctions; **29br** OPG/ST/Alan Blakeman; **30l** OPG/M.Evans; **30t** OPG/Tender Buttons; **30tr** OPG/M.Evans; **30b** OPG/M.Evans; **30bl** OPG; **30br** OPG; **31t** OPG/Rogers De Rin; **31cl** OPG/TR; **31b** OPG/ST/S.Jenkins; **32t** OPG/B; **32c** OPG/Huntercombe Manor Barn; **32br** OPG/Ambrose; **33tl** Richard Dennis Publications; **33tr** C; **33c** Private Collection; **33b** OPG/So; **34r** OPG/BBR; **34t** OPG; **34b** OPG/J.Bland; **35t** OPG/W.Carmichael; **35bl** OPG/J.Smalley/Hanley Reference Library; **35br** OPG/J.Smalley/Private Collection; **36r** OPG/ST/L.Pine; **36t** OPG/ST/L.Pine; **36bl** OPG/Special Auction Services; **36br** OPG/B; **37t** OPG/P.Oosthuizen; **37c** OPG/Gorringes Auction Galleries; **37b** OPG/TR/Beverley & Beth Adams; **38r** OPG/Rowley Fine Art; **38t** OPG/TR/Beverley & Beth Adams; **38bl** OPG/TR/Beverley & Beth Adams; **38br** OPG/TR/Beverley & Beth Adams; **38t** OPG/TR/Beverley & Beth Adams; **39** OPG/TR/Beverley & Beth Adams; **40l** OPG/TR/Beverley & Beth Adams; **40t** OPG/TR/Beverley & Beth Adams; **40b** OPG/Jezebel; **41tl** Richard Dennis Publications; **41tr** OPG; **41c** OPG/I.Booth/Newhaven Flea Market; **41b** OPG/Beverley; **42** OPG/TR/Beverley & Beth Adams; **43t** OPG/TR/Beverley & Beth Adams; **43c** OPG/Beverley; **43b** OPG/Cedar Antiques; **44** OPG/TR; **45t** OPG/ST; **45c** OPG/TR; **45b** OPG/TR; **46t** OPG/TR; **46c** OPG/ST; **46b** OPG/ST; **47l** PenDelphin; **47r** Royal Doulton UK Ltd; **47t** OPG/Apple Tree House; **47c** OPG/Private Collection; **47b** OPG/ST/Steven Jenkins; **48l** OPG/ST/Steven Jenkins; **48r** OPG/I.Booth; **48t** OPG/I.Booth; **48bl** OPG/I.Booth; **48br** OPG/ST/Steven Jenkins; **49t** OPG/I.Booth/StClere; **49c** Portmeirion Potteries Ltd.; **49b** OPG/ST/Steven Jenkins; **50t** OPG/Hardy's Collectables; **50c** OPG/ST; **50b** C; **51t** OPG/Malcolm Law Collectables; **51tr** OPG/T. Ridley/N.Lynes; **51c** OPG/I.Booth/St Clere Antiques; **51b** OPG/ST/K.Higgins; **52t** OPG/R.Durka/Bridgewater; **52c** OPG/Neville Pundole Gallery; **52bl** Carlton Ware/Private Collection; **52br** Royal Doulton UK Ltd; **53–54** Vennett-Smith Auctioneers; **55tl** OPG/TR/Flying Duck Enterprises; **55cl** OPG/TR/Sparkle Moore; **55cb** OPG/Zoom; **55cr** OPG/Beverley; **55bl** OPG/Beverley; **56tl** Comic Postal Book Auctions; **56l** Comic Postal Book Auctions; **56c** Comic Postal Book Auctions; **57cl** Comic Postal Book Auctions; **57cr** Comic Postal Book Auctions; **58t** OPG/ST/BBR Auctions; **58c** OPG/Special Auction Services; **58bl** B; **58br** OPG/Book Shop; **59tl** Special Auction Services; **59tc** Special Auction Services; **59tr** OPG/Ian Booth/Hope & Glory, London; **59cl** OPG/ST/Steven Jenkins; **59cr** OPG/DH; **59b** OPG/DH; **60tl** OPG/Cloud Cuckooland; **60cl** Special Auction Services; **60c** OPG/DH; **60cr** OPG/Frasers; **60b** OPG/Argyll Etkin Ltd; **61r** OPG/Bath Antiques Online; **61tl** OPG; **61cl** OPG/ST/BBR Auctions; **61b** OPG/A.J.Photographics/Juliette Edwards; **62t** OPG/A.J.Photographics/Juliette Edwards; **62cl** OPG/A.J.Photographics/Juliette Edwards; **62cb** OPG/A.J.Photographics/Juliette Edwards; **62cr** OPG/A.J.Photographics/Juliette

Edwards; **62b** OPG/TR/Target Gallery; **63** OPG/ST/Christopher Sykes Antiques, Woburn, Bedfordshire; **64–67** C; **68tl** C; **68cl** OPG/D. Agnew/Strutt; **68c** C; **68br** C; **69** C; **70tl** C; **70cl** OPG/D. Agnew/Strutt; **70cr** OPG/D. Agnew/Strutt; **70bc** OPG/D. Agnew/Strutt; **71tl** OPG/ST; **71cl** OPG/Ian Booth; **71cr** OPG/ST; **71bc** OPG/ST; **72tl** OPG/TR/Target Gallery; **72tr** OPG/ST; **72bl** OPG/ST/Madeleine Marsh; **72br** OPG/Caroline Nevill Miniatures; **73l** OPG/Henry Aldridge & Son; **73r** OPG/Stage Door Prints; **73t** OPG/ST/S; **73b** OPG/J.R.&S.J.Symes; **73br** OPG/SRA; **74l** OPG/Pieces of Time; **74r** OPG/Sparkle Moore; **74t** OPG/I.Booth; **74b l** OPG/Cobwebs; **74br** OPG/B; **75tl** OPG/Cobwebs; **75bl** OPG/Echoes; **75bc** OPG; **75br** OPG/ST; **76tl** OPG/Lucia Collectables; **76c** OPG/ST; **76bl** OPG/Echoes; **76bcl** OPG/Tin Tin Collectables; **76bcr** OPG/ST; **76br** OPG/ST; **77r** OPG/ST; **77tl** OPG/ST; **77cl** OPG/ST; **77b** OPG/Tin Tin Collectables; **77bc** OPG/TR/So; **78tl** OPG; **78tr** OPG/I.Booth/C; **78cl** OPG/ST; **78c** OPG/Paul & Karen Rennie; **78br** Sparkle Moore, The Girl Can't Help It!, Alfie's Antique Market; **79tl** OPG/Ian Booth/Rokit; **79tr** OPG/TR/Madeleine Marsh; **79cl** OPG/Ian Booth/Linda Bee; **79bl** OPG/TR/Sparkle Moore; **79br** OPG/TR/Steinbeck & Tolkien; **80r** OPG/TR/Radio Days; **80tl** OPG/TR/Nikki Lynes; **80bl** OPG/Ian Booth/C; **80bc** OPG/TR/Nikki Lynes; **81r** Madeleine Marsh/courtesy of Stephen at Rellik; **81tl** OPG/Old Hat; **81cl** OPG/ST.Clive Parks; **81bc** OPG/TR/Steinberg & Tolkein; **82tl** OPG/Skip & Janie Smithson Antiques; **82tr** So, Sussex; **82bl** OPG/Glynn Clarkson/Alastair Morris; **82br** OPG/Glynn Clarkson/Alastair Morris; **83** So; **84t** OPG/TR; **84c** Chihuly Studio/Scott M Leen; **84b** AMcC; **85t** OPG/Premier Photography; **85c** AMcC; **85br** Pontefract Museum; **86l** AMcC; **86t** The Country Seat; **86c** OPG/ST; **86br** OPG/TR; **87t** AMcC; **87c** AMcC/John Luxton; **87b** AMcC; **88t** AMcC/So; **88b** OPG/A.Sedgewick; **89t** Chihuly Studio/Scott M. Leen; **89c** AMcC; **89b** AMcC; **90t** OPG/A.J.Photographics/R.Notley; **90tr** AMcC; **90bl** AMcC; **90br** AMcC; **91** AMcC; **92t** AMcC; **92c** AMcC; **92b** Mark J West; **93r** OPG/TR; **93t** AMcC/So; **93b** AMcC/Musee de Baccarat; **94** AMcC; **95** Galleria Marina Barovier; **96tl** OPG/ST; **96tc** OPG/TR/Boom!; **96tr** AMcC; **96bl** Venini Glass; **96br** Venini Glass; **97t** OPG/ST; **97cl** OPG/ST; **97cr** AMcC; **97b** OPG/TR/Planet Bazaar; **98tl** OPG/ST; **98tr** OPG/I.Booth/C; **98bl** OPG/ST; **98br** OPG/I.Booth/C; **99** Sweetbriar Gallery; **100r** Jon Bird; **100tl** OPG/Chris Baker Gramophones, All Our Yesterdays; **100cl** OPG/Philip Knighton; **100bc** OPG/Chris Baker Gramophones, All Our Yesterdays; **101tl** OPG/TR/Planet Bazaar; **101tc** OPG/Toys & Dolls; **101tr** Jon Bird; **101c** Sony United Kingdom Limited; **101bl** Robert Opie; **102r** OPG/ST/Joel Rothman; **102tl** OPG/ST/Steinberg & Tolkein; **102cl** OPG/ST/Joel Rothman; **102bc** OPG/ST/Steinberg & Tolkien; **103tl** Hermès; **103tr** OPG/Cristobal; **103bl** OPG/ST/Steinberg & Tolkien; **103br** OPG/Steinberg & Tolkien; **104t** OPG/Linda Bee; **104c** OPG/ST/Steinberg&Tolkien; **104b** OPG/TR/Target Gallery; **105r** OPG/A.Massey;

ACKNOWLEDGMENTS

105t OPG/A.Caswell; 105cl OPG/ST/Steinberg & Tolkien; 105b OPG/A.Massey; 106l OPG/ST/J.Rothman; 106tl OPG/Bow Well Antiques; 106tr OPG/Spectrum; 106cr OPG/Spectrum; 106b OPG/Pro-Photo; 106br OPG/Variety Box; 107r OPG/ST/J.Rothman; 107t OPG/Cristobal; 107cl OPG/ST/Steinberg&Tolkien; 107bl OPG/Sparkle Moore; 107br OPG; 108l OPG/ST/Cristobal; 108r OPG/Cristobal; 108t OPG/ST/Steinberg&Tolkien; 108c OPG/Heather's Treasures; 108b OPG/ST/Steinberg&Tolkien; 109l OPG/ST/Cristobal; 109tl OPG/ST/Cristobal; 109tr OPG/ST/William Wain; 109b OPG/I.Booth; 109bl OPG/ST/Cristobal; 110tl OPG/ST/Steinberg&Tolkien; 110tc OPG/ST/Cristobal; 110tr OPG/ST/Cristobal; 110b OPG/Identity; 110bl OPG/ST/Steinberg & Tolkien; 110br OPG/Twentieth Century Style; 111tl OPG/Manor Farm Barn Antiques; 111c OPG/Skip & Janie Smithson; 111br OPG/Martin Norris/Christina Bishop; 112tl OPG/Martin Norris/Annie Marchant; 112tr OPG/Skip & Janie Smithson; 112cl OPG/Martin Norris/Annie Marchant; 112c OPG/Martin Norris/Annie Marchant; 112br OPG/Wenderton Antiques; 113tl OPG/Ann Lingard, Ropewalk Antiques; 113tr OPG/Mark Seabrook Antiques; 113bl OPG/Skip & Janie Smithson; 113br OPG/Martin Norris/Christina Bishop; 114tl OPG/Ekkehart, USA; 114tr OPG/Bread & Roses; 114cl OPG/Beverley; 114bl Richard Meara; 114bc OPG/Martin Norris/Christina Bishop; 114br OPG/Martin Norris/Christina Bishop; 115tl Target Gallery; 115tr OPG/Robin Saker/Ginnels; 115c OPG/Robin Saker/Sunbeam Corporation; 115b OPG/Robin Saker/Design Goes Pop; 116tl OPG/TR/Nikki Lynes; 116cl OPG/Mr Moore; 116cr OPG/High Street Antiques; 116br OPG/TR/Zambesi; 117–118 Jennie Horrocks; 119tl OPG/Ian Booth/B; 119tr OPG/TR/Deco Inspired; 119c OPG/TR/Twenty Twenty One; 119bl OPG/TR/Boom!; 119br Flos; 120tl OPG/Collector's Corner; 120cl OPG/ST/Steinberg & Tolkien; 120cr OPG/Robert Brooks Auctioneers; 120bl OPG/Period Picnic Hampers; 120br OPG/Houghton Antiques; 121–122 Timothy Millett; 123t Vin Calcutt; 123c Daniel Bexfield; 123b Daniel Bexfield; 124–127 Vin Calcutt; 128–132 Daniel Bexfield; 133–134 WW; 135r WW; 135t WW; 135c OPG/WW; 135bl WW; 135b r WW; 136 WW; 137tl WW; 137tr WW; 137c WW; 137bl OPG/WW; 137br WW; 138r WW; 138tl OPG/Gorringes; 138tr WW; 138bl WW; 138br WW; 139tl WW; 139tr WW; 139c WW; 139bl OPG/Gabrian Antiques; 139br WW; 140 OPG/ST/P.West; 141r Pam West; 141tl OPG/ST/P.West; 141tr OPG/ST/P.West; 141bl Pam West; 141br Pam West; 142tl OPG/Mr A Harris; 142cr OPG/Cloud Cuckooland; 142bl OPG/JR & SJ Symes of Bristol; 142br OPG/Cobwebs; 143tl OPG/Cloud Cuckooland; 143tr OPG/Andrew Sclanders; 143c OPG/Andrew Sclanders; 143bl OPG/Collector's Corner; 143br OPG/Private Collection; 144–145 Richard Meara; 146tl Richard Meara; 146tr Richard Meara; 146c Richard Meara; 146bl Richard Meara/Goldblatt; 146br Richard Meara/Fuss; 147l OPG/Le Boudoir Collectables; 147r OPG/Junktion;

147tl OPG/Forget-Me-Knot Antiques; 147b OPG/Stuart Heggie; 148tl OPG/Decodence; 148tr OPG/I.Booth; 148c OPG/TR/Delta of Venus; 148bl OPG/TR/Boom; 148br OPG/Twinkled; 149l OPG/Vennett-Smith; 149r OPG/S&D Postcards; 149t OPG/J&M Collectables; 149b OPG/Dalkeith Auctions Ltd; 150t OPG/S&D Postcards; 150tr OPG/J&M Collectables; 150c OPG/Specialised Postcard Auctions; 150bl OPG/S&D Postcards; 150br OPG/Collectors Corner; 151l VS; 151t VS; 151b PO; 151br VS; 152tl CJ; 152tr PO; 152c CJ; 152bl CJ; 152br CJ; 153l CJ; 153r CJ; 153tl CJ; 153tr CJ; 153br VS; 154l PO; 154r PO; 154tl CJ; 154tr CJ; 154b CJ; 155l OTA; 155r OTA; 155t OPG/P.Knighton; 155b OTA; 156l OTA; 156tl OPG/Ekkehart; 156tr OTA; 156c OPG/I.Booth/OTA; 156b OTA; 157–158 SRA; 159t OPG/ST/Columbia/EMI Archive; 159c OPG/Collector's Corner; 159b OPG/Saffron Walden Auctions; 160l OPG/B; 160t OPG/I.Booth; 160c OPG/Prime Cuts; 160b OPG/TR/Memory Lane; 161tl OPG/ST/Liberty/EMI; 161tr OPG/ST/United Artists/EMI Archives; 161c OPG/Beanos; 161b l OPG/ST/A&M/Beanos; 161b r OPG/Beanos; 162l OPG/Collector's Corner; 162t OPG/Collector's Corner; 162c Sotheby's Picture Library; 162b OPG/The Director's Cut; 163tl OPG/Cooper Owen; 163tr OPG/Cooper Owen; 163c OPG/Cooper Owen; 163bl CJ; 163br OPG/Ian Booth/So; 164l OPG/Vintage & Rare Guitars; 164r OPG/Beatcity; 164t OPG/Saffron Walden Auctions; 164b OPG/More than Music; 165l OPG/Collector's Corner; 165r OPG/Collector's Corner; 165t OPG/Ian Booth/C; 165bl OPG/Fleetwood Owen; 165br OPG/I.Booth/C; 166t OPG/ST/M.West; 166c B; 166bl OPG/TR/L.Brine; 166br OPG/TR/L.Bee; 167l B; 167r OPG/TR/Garady-Feuchtwanger; 167tl OPG/TR/L.Bee; 167tr OPG/TR/L.Bee; 167bl OPG; 167bcl OPG/TR/L.Brine; 168–170 Charles Tomlinson; 171r S; 171t OPG/C.Tomlinson; 171ct Charles Tomlinson; 171b Charles Tomlinson; 172 OPG/ST/E.Gaussen; 173tl OPG/Variety Box; 173tr OPG/ST/E.Gaussen; 173c OPG/ST/E.Gaussen; 173bl OPG/ST/E.Gaussen; 173br OPG/ST/E.Gaussen; 174l OPG/Dolphin Quay Antiques Co; 174r OPG/Books Afloat; 174t OPG/Medway Auctions; 174b OPG/DH; 175l OPG/Murrays Antiques & Collectables; 175r OPG/Cobwebs; 175tl OPG/DH; 175tr OPG/Cobwebs; 175b OPG/Cobwebs; 176t OPG/Murrays Antiques & Collectables; 176c OPG/Hall's Nostalgia; 176b OPG/DH; 177t OPG/Manfred Schotten; 177c OPG/B; 177bl OPG/Alan Pezaro; 177br OPG/So; 178tl OPG/So; 178tr OPG/So; 178c OPG/So; 178bl OPG/So; 178br OPG/Manfred Schotten; 179l OPG/Sworders; 179r OPG/Bob Gowland International Golf Auctions; 179t OPG/Manfred Schotten; 179c OPG/Lenson-Smith; 179b l OPG/Alan Pezaro; 180l OPG/Manfred Schotten; 180r OPG/Gorringes inc. Julian Dawson; 180t OPG/Dominic Winter Book Auctions; 180b OPG/Mullock & Madeley; 181tl OPG/Thomson, Roddick & Medcalf; 181tr OPG/Lenson-Smith; 181ctl OPG/Robert Toovey & Co. Ltd;

181bl OPG/Manfred Schotten; 181br OPG/B; 182l Dottie Ayers; 182t OPG/P.Anderson/Chuck & Cathy Steffes; 182b Christie's South Kensington; 182br C; 183tl Dottie Ayers; 183tr OPG/M.Pearson/J.Harrison; 183bl OPG/P.Anderson/Chuck & Cathy Steffes; 183c/Disney Characters (c)Disney Enterprises, Inc. Used by permission from Disney Enterprises, Inc; 184r OPG/M.Pearson/S.Pearson; 184tl OPG/M.Pearson/J.Harrison; 184tr OPG/M.Pearson/S.Pearson; 184c OPG/M.Pearson/S.Pearson; 184b OPG/M.Pearson/Banwell Castle; 185r OPG/M.Pearson/Banwell Castle; 185t OPG/M.Pearson/Banwell Castle; 185bl OPG/Unicorn Antiques Co; 185br OPG/Bears Galore; 186tl OPG/Dave Hardman Antiques; 186c OPG/J Cards/Childhood Memories; 186bl OPG/Dave Hardman Antiques; 186br OPG/The Old Telephone Company; 187tl OPG/Design Goes Pop; 187tr OPG/TR/Flying Duck Enterprises; 187cl OPG/ST/Flying Duck Enterprises; 187cr OPG/TR/Twenty Twenty One; 187b OPG/Dave Hardman Antiques; 188l OTA; 188r OTA; 188t OTA; 188bl OPG/Pro-Photo/B; 188br OPG/ST/P.Tozzo; 189tl OPG/Erna Hiscock & John Shepherd; 189cl OPG/W & H Peacock; 189cr OPG/Linen and Lace; 189b OPG/Echoes; 190t OPG/Echoes; 190tcr OPG/Linen & Lace; 190b OPG/Ann Lingard; 190bcl OPG/Linen & Lace; 191tl OPG/Cedar Antiques Ltd; 191tr OPG/Joanna Proops Antique Textiles and Lighting; 191bl OPG/Joanna Proops Antique Textiles and Lighting; 191br OPG/Hillhaven Antique Linen and Lace; 192tl OPG/photo TR/Flying Duck Enterprises; 192tr OPG/Linda Bee Art Deco; 192cr OPG/TR/Twenty Twenty One; 192bl OPG/Flying Duck; 192br OPG/High Street Antiques; 193 OPG/ST/J.Trevor Barton Collection; 194tl OPG/ST/J.Trevor Barton Collection; 194tr OPG/ST/Jacques Coles Collection; 194c OPG/RS/DH; 194b OPG/RS/DH; 195l OPG/ST/Richard Ball Collection; 195t OPG/RS/DH; 195c OPG/RS/DH; 195bl OPG/RS/DH; 195br OPG; 196 C; 197t C; 197bl C; 197br OPG/D.Agnew/Strutt; 198tl C; 198tr C; 198bl C; 198br OPG/D.Agnew/Strutt; 199–200 C; 201tl C; 201tr C; 201bl C; 201br OPG/Wheels of Steel; 202–203 C; 204l C; 204r OPG/RS/Off World; 204t C; 204b C; 205–206 C; 207l OPG/Collectors Corner; 207r OPG/D.Agnew/Strutt; 207t OPG/D.Agnew/Strutt; 207b C; 208l OPG/Houghton Antiques; 208r OPG/Variety Box; 208t OPG/Stephanie Davison Antiques; 208bl OPG/Humbleyard Fine Art; 208br OPG/Bread & Roses; 209l OPG/Gorringes inc. Julian Dawson; 209r OPG/Gorringes inc. Julian Dawson; 209t OPG/Gorringes inc. Julian Dawson; 209bl OPG/Michael German Antiques; 209br OPG/Geoffrey Breeze Antiques; 210 OPG/ST/Nick Wiseman, Harpers, York; 211 Kevin Monckton, Tickers, Southampton; 212t OPG/The Pen and Pencil Lady; 212cl OPG/TR; 212cr OPG/TR/Jim Marshall; 212b OPG/TR; 213tr OPG/TR; 213cl OPG/AJ PHotographics/ Andy Johnson; 213c OPG/TR; 213cr OPG/Beatcity; 213ctl OPG/TR/Jim Marshall; 213b OPG/TR